Introducing 3ds Max® 9

3D FOR BEGINNERS

DARIUSH DERAKHSHANI | RANDI MUNN

WITH JON McFARLAND

BICENTENNIAL
1807
WILEY
2007
BICENTENNIAL

WILEY PUBLISHING, INC.

Acquisitions Editor: Mariann Barsolo
Development Editor: Stephanie Barton
Technical Editor: Mark Gerhard
Production Editor: Rachel Meyers
Copy Editor: Kathy Carlyle
Production Manager: Tim Tate
Vice President and Executive Group Publisher: Richard Swadley
Vice President and Executive Publisher: Joseph B. Wikert
Vice President and Publisher: Neil Edde
Media Project Supervisor: Laura Atkinson
Media Development Specialist: Kate Jenkins
Media Quality Assurance: Kit Malone
Book Designer: Caryl Gorska
Compositor: Kate Kaminski, Happenstance Type-O-Rama
Proofreader: Nancy Riddiough
Indexer: Jack Lewis
Anniversary Logo Design: Richard Pacifico
Cover Designer: Ryan Sneed
Cover Images: Dariush Derakhshani and Jon McFarland; Dan Savage, Dan Figueroa, and "Crude Awakenings" from The Art Institute of California, Los Angeles. Used with permission

To Max Henry

Acknowledgments

We are thrilled to be bringing the successful *Introducing 3ds Max* format to the powerful Autodesk 3ds Max audience. Education is an all-important goal in life and should always be approached with eagerness and earnestness. We would like to thank our teachers who inspired us; you can always remember the teachers who touched your life, and to them we say thanks. We would also like to thank all of our students, who taught us a lot during the course of our many combined academic years. Equally, we would like to extend many thanks to the student artists who contributed to this book, many of whom are our own students from The Art Institute of California at Los Angeles. Thanks to the AI faculty for their help in gathering the inspiring work for the color insert and for their support in writing this book. ■ Having a good computer system is important with this type of work, so a special thank you goes to Dell, for keeping us on the cutting edge of workstation hardware. Special thanks go to Mariann Barsolo, Rachel Meyers, Stephanie Barton, and Kathy Carlyle, our editors at Wiley who have been professional, courteous, and ever patient. Our appreciation also goes to technical editor Mark Gerhard, who worked hard to make sure this book is of the utmost quality. ■ Tremendous gratitude goes to Jon McFarland for his fantastic contributions to the book; we would not have been able to finish the book without his help. Finally, thanks to our mother and brother for their love and support, not to mention the life-saving babysitting services.

About the Authors

Dariush Derakhshani is a Creative Director with Radium, a visual effects boutique, and a writer and educator in Los Angeles, California. Dariush used Autodesk's AutoCAD software in his architectural days and migrated to using 3D programs when his firm's principal architects needed to show their clients design work on the computer. Dariush started using Alias PowerAnimator version 6 when he enrolled in USC Film School's Animation program, and he has been using Alias animation software for the past 11 years. He received an M.F.A. in Film, Video, and Computer Animation from the USC Film School in 1997. He also holds a B.A. in Architecture and Theatre from Lehigh University in Pennsylvania. He worked at a New Jersey architectural firm before moving to Los Angeles for film school and he has worked on feature films, music videos, and countless commercials as a 3D animator, as a CG supervisor, and sometimes as a compositor. Dariush also serves as the editor in chief of *HDRI3d*, a professional computer graphics (CG) magazine from DMG Publishing.

Randi Lorene Munn is a staff instructor with The Art Institute of California at Los Angeles. She began working with computer graphics in 1992, and she was hired by her instructor to work at Sony Pictures Imageworks, where she developed her skills with 3ds Max and Shake, among many other programs. A teacher since 1999, Randi enjoys sharing her wisdom with young talent and watching them develop at The Art Institute, as well as at the UCLA extension. Currently, she teaches a wide range of classes from Autodesk 3ds Max to compositing with Apple Shake and Adobe After Effects. Juggling her teaching activities with caring for a little baby boy makes Randi a pretty busy lady.

Jon McFarland manages the CAD department for a national owner/developer/manager of retail, office, and residential mixed-use properties in Cleveland, Ohio. He creates and supervises the creation of architectural drawings, 3D mock-ups, and 3D animations using AutoCAD, 3ds Max, Photoshop, and an array of additional programs and applications. Jon also teaches computer animation and AutoCAD at the Virginia Marti College of Art and Design in Lakewood, Ohio. In addition to teaching, he has been an author or contributing author of several books, including *Master Visually 3ds Max 8* and *Mastering Autodesk VIZ 2007*. He has created instructor content and has been the technical editor for several titles.

CONTENTS AT A GLANCE

Contents

Introduction

Welcome to *Introducing 3ds Max 9: 3D for Beginners.* The world of Computer Generated Imagery (CGI) is fun and ever-changing. Whether you are new to CGI in general or a CGI veteran new to 3ds Max, you'll find this book the perfect primer. It introduces you to 3ds Max and shows how you can work with the program to create your art, whether it is animated or static in design.

This book exposes you to all facets of 3ds Max by introducing and plainly explaining its tools and functions to help you understand how the program operates—but it does not stop there. This book also explains the use of the tools and the ever-critical concepts behind the tools. You'll find hands-on examples and tutorials that give you firsthand experience with the toolsets. Working through these will develop your skills and the conceptual knowledge that will carry you to further study. These tutorials expose you to various ways to accomplish tasks with this intricate and comprehensive artistic tool.

Finally, this book explains the 3ds Max workflow. It explains how specific tasks are accomplished and why—that is, it explains how the tasks fit into the larger process of producing 3D animation. By doing that, these chapters should give you the confidence you need to venture deeper into 3ds Max's feature set, either on your own or by using any of 3ds Max's other learning tools and books as a guide.

Learning to use a powerful tool such as 3ds Max can be frustrating. You need to remember to pace yourself. The major complaints CG book readers have are that the pace is too fast and that the steps are too complicated or overwhelming. Addressing those complaints is a tough nut to crack, to be sure. No two readers are the same. However, this book offers the opportunity to run things at your own pace. The exercises and steps may seem confusing at times, but keep in mind that the more you try and the more you fail at some attempts, the more you will learn how to operate 3ds Max. Experience is king when learning the workflow necessary for *any* software program, and with experience comes failure and aggravation. But try and try again. You will find that further attempts will always be easier and more fruitful.

Above all, however, this book aims to inspire you to use 3ds Max as a creative tool to achieve and explore your own artistic vision.

What You Will Learn from This Book

You will learn how to work in CG with 3ds Max, but moreover, we hope that you will learn how CG works and that you will be able to apply the basic techniques and concepts to any software package to accomplish anything you need from modeling to animation. The important thing to keep in mind is that this book is merely the beginning of your CG education. With the confidence you will gain from the exercises in this book and the peace of mind you can have by using this book as a reference, you can go on to create your own increasingly complex CG projects.

Who Should Read This Book

Anyone who is interested in learning 3ds Max should start with this book. No other series of books provides a better, more solid foundation than the Introducing series. *Introducing 3ds Max* will give you more than just the basics of software operation; it will also explain how CG productions are accomplished.

If you are new to CG, or you are a veteran looking to pick up another program, *Introducing 3ds Max* will give you the core foundation you will need to progress further into Autodesk's 3ds Max software.

How to Use This Book

Introducing 3ds Max 9: 3D for Beginners approaches teaching CG by first giving you an informal look into the core concepts that make up this art form. The book aims to create a solid reference for you by showing you the commonly used toolsets and interfaces you will need to navigate to accomplish your goal. By following up the concepts and reference, *Introducing 3ds Max* gives you hands-on recitations in the form of exercises and tutorials, letting you flex your muscles and giving you a chance to try for yourself.

The process can be a bit daunting when you begin to learn a CG program. In that light, it's best to explore the material in this book at your own pace, and allow yourself to digest not just the nuts and bolts, but also the workflow and concepts behind how *and* why 3ds Max artists work the way they do.

Once you have a firm grasp of the concepts introduced in this book, you will be ready to tackle more advanced material in the form of an intermediate class or even another book. Learning CG is a tough hurdle to get over, and you can rest easy knowing that this book is targeted to give you the tools you need to begin a longer, deeper study of the craft.

How This Book Is Organized

Chapter 1, "Basic Concepts," begins with an introduction to the basic concepts of CG production as well as its terminology and general workflows and pipelines. This chapter gives you an overview of how CG is created and how 3ds Max relates to the overall process.

Chapter 2, "Your First Max Animation," creates a simple animation to introduce you to 3ds Max's workflow and give you a taste of how things work. By animating a simple mobile, you will learn the basic concepts of creating and animating in 3ds Max.

Chapter 3, "The 3ds Max Interface," presents you with the entire 3ds Max interface and shows you how to access all the tools you will need for a CG production. Beginning with a roadmap of the 3ds Max screen, this chapter gives you a rundown of the icons and explains their uses. You can use this chapter as a reference to which you can return for UI refreshers whenever they're needed.

Chapter 4, "Modeling in 3ds Max: Part I," is an introduction to modeling concepts and workflows in general. It shows you how to model using 3ds Max tools with polygonal meshes and modifiers to create various objects, including a human hand and a bedroom dresser.

Chapter 5, "Modeling in 3ds Max: Part II," takes your modeling lesson a step further by showing you how to model a complex object. You will use and add to the tools you learned in Chapter 4 to create a tank model. You will learn how to loft and lathe objects, as well as how to use Booleans.

Chapter 6, "Organic Poly Modeling," rounds out your modeling lessons by showing you how to use subdivision surfaces to create organic models such as an alien character.

Chapter 7, "Materials and Mapping," shows you how to assign textures and materials to your models. You will learn to texture various objects, such as a chess piece, as you learn the basics of working with 3ds Max's materials and UVW mapping.

Chapter 8, "Introduction to Animation," covers the basics of animating a bouncing ball using keyframes and moves on to creating more complex animation—throwing a knife at a target. You will also learn how use the Track Editor to time, edit, and finesse your animation.

Chapter 9, "3ds Max Animation II," expands on Chapter 8 to show you how to use Character Studio to create and edit a walk cycle. You will also learn how to use 3ds Max's IK system to rig the tank you created in Chapter 5.

Chapter 10, "3ds Max Lighting," begins by showing you how to light a 3D scene with the three-point lighting system, and then shows you how to use the tools to create and edit 3ds Max lights for illumination, shadows, and special lighting effects.

Chapter 11, "3ds Max Rendering," explains how to create image files from your 3ds Max scene and how to achieve the best look for your animation by using proper cameras and rendering settings. You'll also learn about different ways to implement ray-tracing, atmospheric effects, and motion blur.

Chapter 12, "Particles and Dynamics," introduces you to 3ds Max's particle systems and space warps, as well as the reactor physics simulation system. You will animate dynamic objects colliding with one another using rigid body dynamics, and you will learn how to use soft body dynamics.

Hardware and Software Considerations

Hardware changes constantly, and it evolves faster than publications can keep up. Having a good solid machine is important to a production, although simple home computers will be able to run 3ds Max quite well. Any laptop (with discrete graphics) or desktop PC running Windows 2000 Pro or XP Professional with at least 512MB of RAM and an Intel Pentium IV or AMD Athlon XP or higher processor will work. Of course, having a good video card will help; you can use any hardware-accelerated OpenGL or Direct3D video card. A computer system will have at least a 3GHz processor with 1GB of RAM, a few GBs of hard drive space available, and an Nvidia GeForceFX or ATI Radeon video card. Professionals may want to opt for workstation graphics cards such as the ATI FireGL or the Nvidia QuadroFX series of cards. The following systems would be good ones to use:

- Intel Pentium Core2Duo, 2GB RAM, nVidia Quadro FX1400, 400GB 7200 RPM hard disk
- AMD Opteron 2x, 2GB RAM, ATI FireGL V5000, 400GB hard disk

You can check the list of system requirements at Autodesk's website at `http://usa` `.autodesk.com/adsk/servlet/index?siteID=123112&id=5659453`.

The Book's CD

The companion CD in the back of this book provides all the sample images, movies, and files that you will need to work through the projects in *Introducing 3ds Max 9: 3D for Beginners*.

The CD is organized into project folders for each major tutorial in the book. It has a few chapter-specific folders for the shorter exercises. Each folder contains all the scene and support files for that project. The folders are arranged as 3ds Max 9 projects, so you can copy them to your hard drive and work directly from them.

You will also find a 30-day trial version of 3ds Max software on the CD.

Contact the Authors

You can contact the authors through Wiley or at `koosh3d.com`.

The Next Step

The next step is really up to you. *Introducing 3ds Max 9* is meant to give you a kick-start into learning CG. Your education beyond this primer can be from DVDs, classes, or more books—all bundled with a good amount of playing around and creating your own 3d productions. There is no better way to learn CG than to create something for yourself. Use these tools as a reference to help you get there.

CHAPTER 1

Basic Concepts

There are several ways to learn a program such as Autodesk 3ds Max 9, or any other computer graphics (CG) package. Ultimately, you'll get the best education through months or even years of working with the software in different capacities. Ask any successful student, and they will tell you one thing: there is no such thing as book smarts when it comes to good CG production—it all comes down to what you can achieve.

Achievement comes only from practice. You can't avoid the many pitfalls of production work without falling into and climbing out of them. Some readers may find this idea frustrating, but it is an intractable truth. The more you work with 3ds Max, the better you will become with it.

Topics in this chapter include:

- **How to Read This Book**
- **What Is CGI?**
- **Production Workflow**
- **Core Concepts for Animation**

How to Read This Book

First and foremost, you needn't read this book cover to cover and front to back to get the most from it. If you are the type who loves to jump right into the pool to learn to swim, then skip all this and jump into Chapter 2, "Your First Max Animation to start with the interface. If you already know how to get around 3ds Max, you can begin with any of the other chapters. You can leave this chapter for bathroom reading when you're bored or the cable goes out.

If you like dipping your toe in first, then by all means sit back, put on your bifocals, and have a long soak in this chapter. It will cover a lot of basic concepts and core topics that you may or may not be familiar with already. It serves as a gentle ease into the powerful program that is Autodesk 3ds Max 9.

No matter how you choose to read this book, it is crucial that you approach the lessons as a way to *begin* the learning process. This book aims to give you a solid foundation in many aspects of 3ds Max, so that you can take this beginning and move on to more study. In keeping with that ideal, you will need to understand that you will not necessarily become proficient in any one aspect of 3ds Max *just by reading* this book. Instead, you'll gain an understanding of how it works and how you can work with the program to create your animations and models.

Frequently, students are aggravated by tutorials that don't seem to lead them to perfection in the first go-around. This is the case for all tutorials and indeed all books teaching pretty much anything. The key is to use the lessons as a guideline not just once, but repeatedly. Doing a lesson multiple times will help you understand the concepts better and give you opportunities to try out a few different methods, stray a little from the dictated steps, and try your own ideas on for size. Ideally, you will obtain a stronger education, but doing so will perhaps be slower and require more patience from you the student. However, a good education must always be afforded this dedication.

What Is CGI?

CG is an acronym for *computer generated*. You may have heard the term *CGI* (Computer-Generated Imagery). They are indeed one and the same, and the terms refer to any image or images that are created with the aid of a computer. In this day and age, you'd be hard pressed to find anyone with any computer experience who hasn't messed around with computer images, from scanned pictures to digital photos. Learning a CG package such as 3ds Max is just an extension of that simple concept of playing around with a digital photo. The obvious differences are that 3ds Max adds the dimension of depth as well as control over time.

With the preponderance of cheap hardware and much easier-to-get software these days, CG is slowly becoming a more common toolset in the hands of the masses. Within the next decade or so, 3D should become as ubiquitous as *Photoshopping* a photo is today.

The following sections break down the common concepts behind CG.

3d Space

With *3d space*, the virtual canvas in which you create 3d objects, you have a simulation of space that is divided into three axes, *X, Y,* and *Z* representing (in loose terms) left-right, up-down, and in-out. Figure 1.1 shows 3d space in a Max window.

So what the heck do you with 3d space? In many ways, setting up a scene in CG is like setting up a photo shoot. With a photo shoot, you begin by gathering your subjects and posing them in your composition. You set up lights to illuminate however dramatically you need them to look and then take snapshots with your camera, framing the composition as needed. You then develop and fine tune your photos or adjust them with tools such as Photoshop before you print them. Finally comes the happy part of showing them off and sharing your work with others.

CG production has much the same workflow, although with CG you create everything from scratch (for the most part) in your 3d space. Instead of running out and hunting down the perfect models off the street and all the props and settings you need for a photo, you create them. You model everything in the beginning and then apply colors and texture to the surfaces you just created. Once you lay out your scene with all the settings and props you need, you set up your CG lights to illuminate the models. Lighting is perhaps the most important aspect of CG, as this stage in CG production really makes or breaks a scene.

Once your lighting is ready, you *render* the scene; this is akin to taking the photos and developing them. Knowing what the end result should be will dictate how you decide to render. You can choose several settings for quality and output, for example, so you can show off your scene to your friends—although hanging a QuickTime movie on the fridge is a bit hard to do.

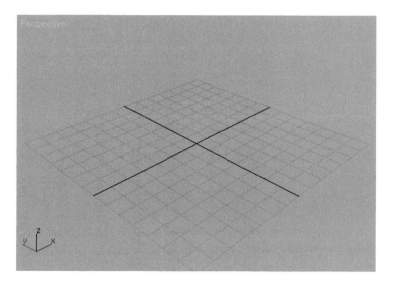

Figure 1.1

3d space never looked so good!

Of course, with CG you also have control over time; you can animate your scene. This workflow perhaps lends itself best to how films are produced. The next section briefly describes a film production workflow and how it applies to CG production.

Production Workflow

There are three major stages to producing films: preproduction, production, and postproduction. In preproduction, the script is written, storyboards are drawn up to outline the action, costumes and sets are designed and built, the actors are cast and prepared, and a production crew is put together. During the production phase, the scenes are set up and shot according to a production schedule that lays everything out in the most efficient manner possible. Finally, in postproduction, everything else happens. That means the film is printed and edited, a score and soundtrack are laid, any digital effects are added, and scenes are colored to match an overall aesthetic. Upon completion, the film is distributed for people to see.

Although the actual work is vastly different between CG and live action photography, the framework is useful to understand.

Preproduction

Preproduction for a CG workflow requires that the artist or artists gather together all the reference materials, motion tests, layout drawings, model sketches, and such to make the actual CG production as uncomplicated as they can.

Because everything is essentially made from scratch, the CG artist must formulate a strong plan of attack. You can't simply run out with some actors into the park and begin shooting. With CG, you have to make it all from nothing. (You could, of course, use model libraries to help you set up a scene; however, someone still had to create those from scratch.) The time spent in preproduction planning is vital to smooth production and postproduction, and it helps the overall outcome of the project. Never underestimate how much time and planning you should put into a CG project. You will seriously sandbag your project if you don't plan it effectively. This point can never be overstated, and although I'm sure you may get sick of hearing it, it will always be true.

For the exercises in this book, you will work with sketches and other files supplied on the accompanying CD as your preproduction. Additionally, you are more than encouraged to put together as much information as you possibly can about your intended project, no matter how short it may seem.

A poorly planned production will always fall short of its potential and give you many headaches throughout your project.

Writing a Script

Whether a CG project has a ton of dialogue or doesn't have a single spoken word, both the project and you will benefit from having a script. Even abstract animations can benefit from a highly detailed explanation of timings and colors laid out in a script, whether highly polished or scribbled on a roll of toilet paper in the back of a jail cell.

A script serves as your *intent*. Without having a clear intention stated in your production that defines what you wish to say with your film, your production time may as well be spent lying around with an ice tea in your hand; you will not get much done in either case.

Storyboards

A storyboard is an advanced definition of the script. It shows the timings and framing for the camera, as well as the action and dialogue—if any. To create an effective storyboard, you must first dissect your script into scenes, and then scenes into shots, with each shot being a distinct view from the camera or a distinct cut of action. A storyboard panel describes, shot-by-shot, what is happening in the script in a linear fashion to show you the overall action of the project and how it should come together in editing.

Even simple boards scribbled on napkins with stick figures are important to have in preproduction.

Concept Art

Conceptuals are the design elements that are needed for the CG production. If you don't have concept art, whether they're your own drawings or a smattering of photos or images grabbed from the Internet, you are seriously hosed. You must have an idea of how you want your CG to look; otherwise, you are just flapping your gums and not saying anything.

If you have CG characters, create *character sheets* for each character where characters are drawn into character sheets in three different neutral poses from the front, from the side, and from an angle called a 3⁄4 view. You can even sculpt reference characters in clay or Play-Doh if you need to have a better idea of how they should look in 3d space. In the following graphic, you can see a character sheet generated for a student produced short at The Art Institute of California at Los Angeles.

Sketch or download images of the props and sets you need in your scene. Essentially, map out the look for everything that you need to have in your scene. When you are working on your project, you won't be limited to the things you've already picked out; however, you will find that knowing how things should look will help enormously in getting you to your final product. The better your concept art and research, the smoother the production and the better your end result will be.

Production

Production is the meat of any project. Film production begins when you start filming your project. In the case of CG, production begins when you start creating assets for your projects, such as models or textures based on well-researched reference materials. The production phase lasts until the rendering phase, where you actualize your scene into image files.

Animation, texturing, and lighting are performed between the modeling and rendering phases. Later in this chapter, the CG production phase will be divided into more stages; however, most of the techniques you'll learn in this book are pretty much in the production phase.

Postproduction

Postproduction begins when your scene elements and animation are all set up and raring to be completed. Postproduction for a CG project is very similar to postproduction for a film. When you click the Render button, you'll end up with several image files or movie files that are then edited and essentially put together to make your project. You add sound, correct color, combine elements, and add any finishing touches in postproduction. Here is a quick rundown of the CG postproduction pipeline.

Rendering

All CG scenes need to be rendered to their final image or movie files. Again, this is the process by which the computer calculates how everything in the scene should look and displays it. Rendering places great processing demands on your computer. It usually requires the full attention of your PC, and it can take a lot of time. As you'll learn throughout this book, the decisions you make, such as how much detail you give the objects you create for a scene, can make a big difference in the rest of the process and can affect the rendering speed.

You can render one scene while another scene is in production, but working on a system that is rendering is not advisable unless you're using a dual-processor machine with plenty of memory. When everything is rendered properly, the final images are sorted and the CG project assembly begins. Rendering is the subject of Chapter 11, "3ds Max Rendering." Compositing, editing, and adding sound are advanced postproduction activities and beyond the scope of this book. However, you will find a multitude of books on these topics for further study.

Compositing

CG is often rendered in different layers where segments need to be put back together. For example, you could have multiple characters interacting in one scene and have each character rendered separately from the others and from the setting. *Compositing* is the process of bringing together rendered elements to form the final scene, usually using compositing software such as Adobe's After Effects or Apple's Shake.

Compositing programs allow you to compose CG elements together, but they also give you additional control over color, timing, and a host of other additions and alterations you can make to a scene. Compositing can greatly affect the look of a CG project; professionals consider it an integral part of CG creation.

> Students new to the CG process frequently assume that they need to generate a scene in one fell swoop. CG has an inherent component nature, and you can render items separately and composite them in the finishing stage and still make some changes in your project's show.

Editing

During the editing process, rendered and composited CG footage is collected and edited to fit the script and boards. This process is usually more straightforward for a CG film, as long as the preproduction has output good storyboards to follow when assembling the finished film.

When you are working with live-action, you shoot much more footage than necessary for the film. You do this to make sure you have enough material for all your scenes and to leave extra room for creative editing. If your preproduction was done well, it's just a matter of putting the shots together using an editing program such as Adobe's Premiere or even Apple's Final Cut Pro. With a live action film, you have the added exhaustion of running through all the footage and choosing takes to cut down to the final.

Because CG footage is much more time-consuming to generate than most live action, scenes and shots should be tightly arranged in preproduction boards. The entire production can be edited beforehand in storyboards, so the scenes that are built and animated can match the story, almost down to the frame.

Sound

Sound design can add an entirely new dimension of reality or mood to any CG. The audience needs to associate visuals with audio. Even a basic soundtrack adds a boost to a simple animation by helping provide realism, mood, narrative, and so on. A good music soundtrack and well-placed sound effects are very powerful.

Sounds effects, such as footsteps, can be added to match the action in the animation; this type of sound effect is also known in film as *foley sound*. Just as with any film, adding music to most animations can help with pacing as well as mood. In this case, music and live action sound design are pretty similar. Once you combine everything, you assess the sound needs. The one glaring difference is with dialogue.

When you shoot live action, you generally capture the sound and dialogue live as you shoot. With CG any dialogue needs to be recorded and edited *before* CG production begins. In CG, dialogue becomes a part of the preproduction and postproduction phases. In short, animators need to hear dialogue spoken so they can animate to match the lips of the characters speaking; this is known as *lip-sync*. Recording the dialogue with actors can also help you animate the CG characters; you can imitate the gestures and actions of the live actors to help make your animation more real.

CG Workflow

Due to how CG comes together, a typical production pipeline or workflow generally works best. You begin by modeling, texturing, animating, lighting, and then rendering. You can texture after you animate, of course; however, for the most part, this workflow works best. What is universally true, however, is that you will go back and forth between these stages several times throughout the process. You may have to change some textures once you see the lighting or change a model according to an unexpected animation need. CG becomes a collaborative effort where the stages of CG production work hand in hand to render your final images. The layout of this book and its exercises follow this overall workflow.

Modeling

Modeling is the topic of Chapters 4 through 6 of this book. Modeling is usually the first step in CG creation, and it can sometimes take the longest time. You probably already know that modeling and modeling tutorials are popular on the Internet, where you will find a generous amount of free and fee-based models. You might be able to find a lot of the props and characters you need for your scene online. Unless you enjoy modeling, take a look through Google and see what's already available.

When you do model, of course, you'll be faced with many choices about how to proceed. Most Max modeling is done using *polygons*; however, the specific tools you use will depend on how you like to work. The process of modeling can be easier when you have a good idea of your whole story via a storyboard and general reference. Identify your project needs as fully as you can first, and you'll be able to fulfill them more easily when you start modeling or gathering models.

With forethought, you will know how detailed your models need to be. If that park bench is shown in a wide shot from far away, there is no need for abundant detail or complicated surfacing. If you create a highly detailed model for that far-away shot, you will have wasted your time and increase your rendering times. In many cases, you can add detail to a model just through its textures.

However, when you have to show a park bench prominently in a close-up, it will need as much detail as possible. In such cases, viewers will see more of the bench and have more of an opportunity to question it. The more you use models in scenes, the better you will develop your eye for knowing how exactly much detail to give a specific model. As you begin with CG, however, it's better to give more attention to detail than needed. The detailing process will teach you a majority of what you learn of modeling. This in turn will benefit your overall speed and technique. With more experience, you will be able to discern the level of detail you really need.

Here is a quick rundown of some different kinds of modeling.

Character Modeling

Character modeling includes the modeling of any characters in your scene, from humanoids to animals to ordinary objects that are animated to life. Most characters are organic forms, such as animals, humans, aliens, and so on. However, a talking cheese sandwich is just as much a character as the person holding it. A good character modeler always keeps in mind the animation needs of a character when modeling. It's important to know what you need from your shot way ahead of time, so you can model appropriately.

Traditional characters, like people, need to appear seamless once they're modeled. Character animation usually requires the model to deform in some way—bending and warping at certain points such as at the elbows. The pieces that make up the model may tear apart if the character is not built to properly account for deformation and movement.

Similar to the park bench analogy, your character must also be built to the level of detail required by the scene. As a matter of fact, several models for a single character can be built to account for any differences. Using different versions of the same character can help keep the scene efficient and workable. A low-resolution (meaning it uses few polygonal faces) model of a character can easily be placed in wide shots, and a more-detailed higher resolution model can be used in close-ups.

Architectural and Environmental Modeling

3ds Max is a natural in this arena, where architectural and environmental modeling is used to previsualize during building design. This type of modeling includes the generation of backgrounds for sets and environments. For this, you model any buildings or interiors, as well as mountains and other required scenery, such as trees, roads, lamp posts, post office boxes, and so on.

Of course, you should keep in mind the level of detail you need to use. Do not create overly detailed environments when they are far off in the background. The biggest common mistake that new CG professionals make is over-creating detail. Doing this adds more geometry to a scene, creates inefficiency, and can crash a scene. The more geometry that is used in a scene, the slower the computer will run and the more time the scene will need to render.

You can create a good deal of the environment using clever textures on simple geometry. Detailed maps on bare surfaces are used frequently for game environments. The rule of thumb for all kinds of CG is "use whatever works."

Because your computer stores everything in a scene as vector math, the term *geometry* refers to all the surfaces and models in a scene.

Props Modeling

A *prop* is any object in a scene that is actively used by a character in his or her action. Any objects not used by the characters as props are called *scenics*, as they are often used to add realism to the set. Think about it. If your scene takes place in front of a desk, that desk will need scenics such as pens, notebooks, papers, etc. to make it look more realistic. Just showing an empty desk may not be enough to make the scene believable. You usually can find the props and scenics you need on the Internet, frequently in a format for 3ds Max.

Props, on the other hand, are useful in the narrative of the story. They help the characters' actions. A prop can be anything from a baseball bat that a character is swinging to a purse that another character is carrying.

Texturing

Texturing is typically applied immediately after modeling. Once you create a model, you'll want to finish its look. You can apply materials to its surface(s) to make it look right, whether it is supposed to look "real" or not. The process of texturing essentially applies colors and tactile feeling to models. 3ds Max automatically assigns simple colored materials to objects as you create them.

Of course, once you create materials for your scene, they may look different when you light and animate everything. You don't need to finalize every texture, as you'll be coming back and making adjustments all the time.

You'll learn more about texturing in Chapter 7, "Materials and Mapping."

Animation

Animation puts your scene into action and adds life to your characters. In essence, *animation* is *change over time*. Anything in a scene that needs to change from one second to another will need to be animated to do so.

Everyone, in their own way, has a reflexive sense of how things move. This knowledge is gleaned through years of perception and observation. Because of this, your audience can be more critical of a CG scene's motion than lighting or coloring or anything else. You know when something doesn't look right, and so will your audience.

Animation takes quite a lot of setup, sometimes beyond just modeling. For a character, you will need to create a *rig* (such as a Character Studio Biped) to attach to the model and then create controls to make animation easier to operate.

It's naturally very thrilling to see your hard work on a scene come to life with animation. On the flip side, it can also be extremely aggravating seeing your creation working improperly. This is how you learn things, and your frustrations will ease over time.

Chapter 8, "Animation Part I: Introduction to Animation," and Chapter 9 "Animation Part II: Character Studio and IK," cover animation techniques in 3ds Max.

Lighting

Lighting is often seen as the most important aspect of CG production. This area is where you get to see your models and textures, as well as set the mood of the project. During the lighting phase, you set up virtual lights in 3d space to illuminate the objects in your scene when it comes time to render. Lighting can drastically change how your scene looks. Using lighting wisely is a learned skill, and it takes tons of time to master. Not only are you dealing with the aesthetics of getting your shot to look great, but you are also dealing with rendering issues and bottlenecks that could make rendering your shot a nightmare. These issues come up with much larger scenes than what you will be using in the first years of your CG education; however, it's important to start learning how to use lighting efficiently as well as aesthetically.

Lighting can really make or break all your hard work. You can use lighting to affect the believability of your models and textures as well as to create the proper mood and tone.

In this stage of the pipeline, the lighting workflow begins in part when you are texturing your objects. You will need to very generally light your scene to evaluate how your textures are progressing. However, the final lighting and look really happen after everything else is done, and you are left to go back and forth with the render to check and recheck, fix and refix issues that come up in the rendered images. You may even find, for example, that a model you've built needs to be altered because a lighting scheme works for everything but that model. Therefore, a back and forth workflow with lighting does not just apply to texturing.

As a matter of fact, the more experience you gain with lighting, the more you will start to notice that lighting affects every stage of CG creation. Once you start mastering the subtleties of lighting and after years of modeling, you may change how you model to accommodate how you now light. Even your animation and texturing preferences may take a back seat to how a scene needs to be lighted.

In short, *CG is fundamentally all about light.* Manipulating how light is created and reflected is what you're doing with CG. Without light, we would not see anything, so it makes sense that simulating light is the most influential step in CG.

Luckily, in 3ds Max, lighting is set up to mimic the behavior of real lights used in live action (at least in principle), making the lighting process easier to use. You will learn how to light in 3ds Max in Chapter 10, "3ds Max Lighting."

Rendering

You've modeled it all, textured it, and lit your scene like a pro. Hundreds of hours and several cases of Red Bull later, you are ready to render. *Rendering* is the stage where your computer makes all the computations necessary to create images from your 3d objects. Depending on how much stuff is in your scene, rendering may be super quick or dog slow. The amount of geometry you used to model (the amount of polygons), the number and types of lights, the size of texture images, and the effects in your scene all affect render times. When time or resources are limited, you need to build your scene intelligently so that you don't spend hours rendering a single frame. The more efficient your scene is, the faster the rendering will go.

Having said that, there is really no magic formula to figure out how long is too long for a render. Some scenes require a magnificent amount of time to render, for whatever reason, and you are stuck with that—but most do not. Through time you'll be able to ascertain for yourself how long is too long for your renders.

A good gauge for render times is to identify what computers you have to render with and how much time you have before a project has to be completed. With a little simple math, you can determine an acceptable render time for your scenes and adjust your quality and output settings, as well as your lighting setup, to fit within your constraints.

> The general rule in production is: you're always out of time. Therefore, the most efficient pipeline will be your savior, because eventually your producer or boss will tire of hearing, "But I'm still rendering...."

For now, go ahead and use as much geometry and lighting as you think is necessary. With more experience, you'll start pruning your scenes and getting more efficient renders. Right now, knowing *how* a scene is put together is more important than knowing how efficient it needs to be.

CG Specialties

As in most professions, CG professionals specialize in specific areas. Those areas coincide with the stages of CG production preciously outlined.

Modelers create models for shows or projects. They need to have a keen eye for detail, as well as a sense of how objects come together. Environment modelers create settings, and character modelers specialize in creating organic surfaces for characters, such as people. In all cases, professional modelers need to understand form and function and be experienced in lighting, rendering, and texturing to effectively model professionally.

Animators are artists who work directly with the animation of a project. Character animators specialize in character movement, ranging from mimicking human movement to outlandish cartoon animation. There are also animators who specialize in mechanical objects. Frequently, good animators can span the divide between character animation and other types of animation because they inherently understand motion and timing.

In some cases, great animators are also great *riggers.* Studios sometimes hire character TDs (technical directors) who specialize in rigging characters for motion. This usually includes creating skeleton structures, such as Bipeds or Bones, for the character as well as skinning the model to such a system before handing it off to the animator(s). Character TDs can also work with motion-capture systems to transfer motion to a character. They use recorded data from a live action stage where actors are outfitted in special equipment that records their movements.

Effects TDs are specialists who generally animate special effects such as tornadoes, clouds, or explosions. These specialists generally rely on particles and dynamics, as well as textures, lights, and rendering tricks to perform their effects. This specialty requires a strong eye in all stages of CG production and a strong ability to troubleshoot and come up with solutions that are frequently not standard techniques in a program such as 3ds Max.

Lighters are used to light and render a scene once it is completed. Lighters specialize in being able to *final* a shot; in other words, to complete a shot for final approval and output. A good lighter needs to understand how models and textures behave in a scene and sometimes must remodel or retexture an object to make it work. More and more these days, good lighters are also being asked to be good compositors, because so much of CG can be broken into elements that later need to be put back together.

Compositing as a specialty requires much less knowledge of CG, although today's competitive compositors should know as much as they can cram in their brains about CG. Compositors not only have to assemble and *color time* (make final color decisions) CG shots, but they also have to work with live action footage that needs to be altered or affected. For example, a compositor will need to remove a green screen from behind an actor and effectively place that actor into a virtual rendered set. With color correction and other tools at their disposal, the compositors must make sure everything looks like it belongs in the shot. In many cases, the line between lighter and compositor is blurred, and the two specialties become one.

Generalists are CG artists who can do everything. This is not to say they are the be-all and end-all of all things CG. Many studios and boutiques have short term jobs that are small in scale (as compared to a production of the DreamWorks film *Madagascar,* for example). When a short turnaround is required, you need artists who can take a shot from beginning to end—to model, texture, light, animate, and render a scene. Commercials, for example, use generalists more than films.

Core Concepts

CG touches many disciplines, and you will come across many different concepts as you learn CG. There are issues to understand in physics, computer output, film, photography, sculpting, painting, and so on. This section introduces several key concepts that will make it easier for you to understand how CG is created. Again, if you've been around the block a few times, you can skip large parts of this chapter. However, you never know when you might come across a little tidbit that fills in an educational gap you never thought you had.

Computer Graphics Basics

Here are some general terminologies and methodologies used in computer graphics to help you understand how 3ds Max works. First on our plate is the critical distinction between *raster* (bitmap) and *vector* graphics and how this distinction affects you as a 3ds Max user.

Raster Images

Raster images (also known as bitmap images or bitmaps) make up the world of computer images today. Colored pixels are arranged to display a raster image on a screen; these pixels come together to form the image like a tapestry. The same is true of printouts, where dots of ink serve as pixels to form the printed image.

When you work in a program such as Photoshop, you are editing the pixels of an image directly by adjusting existing settings such as color, size, and position for all or part of an image. In this manner, you can bring a scanned photo or a digital picture of your house into Photoshop and paint one wall red, just to see how it would look before you shell out bucks for paint at the store.

Essentially, a raster or bitmap image is a mosaic of pixels, each pixel corresponding to a mosaic tile. The *resolution*—fineness of detail—of an image is defined by the number of pixels per inch (or other unit of measure) in the horizontal and vertical directions. Because raster images are based on a fixed grid, these images do not scale larger very well. The closer you zoom into a raster image (or the larger a raster image is scaled), the larger the pixels seem, which makes the zoomed or enlarged image blocky, or *pixilated*. To use larger raster images, you need to start with a higher resolution when the image is created. The higher the resolution, the larger the file size. Figure 1.2 shows what happens when you blow up a raster image.

So why are raster images even used if you can't scale them well? Most common displays and output methods such as television or computer screens, or even a printer, are actually raster displays. The term *raster* originally referred to the display area of a television or computer monitor. To form an image, the electronics in these devices essentially paint it as a grid of red, green, and blue pixels on a glowing screen. Every image generated by a computer, therefore, must either begin as a raster image or be *rasterized* as part of rendering for display.

Figure 1.2
A raster image does not scale up very well. Here is the front of a stereo receiver that is blown up by several hundred percent. The pixels look blocky.

Vector Images

So why does the interface for 3ds Max look so different from Photoshop's interface? Where is the original image to alter in 3ds Max? Autodesk 3ds Max and other 3d programs work with vectors. Vectors are created using mathematical algorithms and geometric functions. A vector program defines its images using coordinates and geometric formulas to plot points that define *areas, volumes,* and *shapes* instead of defining the color of each and every pixel in a grid of a raster image.

Popular vector-based image applications include Adobe Illustrator and Macromedia Flash, as well as practically all computer-aided design (CAD) programs such as AutoCAD and SolidWorks. These programs let you define shapes and volumes and add color and texture to them through their toolsets.

Vector files store the scene in 3d space using coordinates and equations of points in space and the color values assigned through materials. Therefore, when a vector image is scaled, the image does not suffer from the same blocky limitations as raster images. As you can see in Figure 1.3, vectors can be scaled with no loss of quality; they will never pixelate because they always redraw at the new scale.

Motion in a raster movie, such as a QuickTime movie, is stored in a long sequence of image files that, when played back, show animation or movement. On the other hand, motion in vector programs is stored in the changes in the coordinates of the geometry and in the math that defines the shapes and volumes.

When a Flash cartoon is played on a web page you are visiting, for example, the information for that cartoon is downloaded into your computer in vector form. The data contains the position, size, and shapes of all the elements of the animation. The vector information is then converted into raster images (called *rasterization*) so you can view the final image or animation. Your computer *renders* this information on-the-fly, in real time, into a raster display that you can enjoy on your screen.

This is roughly how things are done with 3d programs such as 3ds Max. You begin your work in Max's 3d space in vectors. When you are ready to render, Max renders the scene contents into raster images or movie files that you can display. You use the tools in

Figure 1.3

A vector image of a girl at its original size (left) and blown up to a few hundred percent (right) shows no loss in quality. The curves are not stepped or pixilated.

3ds Max to simply change the geometric information to change the scene, and then rerender to show the output. Changing a raster image, such as a digital photo, alters that original file (assuming you do not have a backup file) once you save your work because it directly affects the pixels of the image.

Image Output

When you're done with all your CG, you will probably want as many people to see your work as possible. As you well know, you will need to render the scene out to image files or a movie file. These files can be output and saved in many different ways. The kind of file output to use is determined by a combination of disk space, personal preference, project needs, and output requirements.

COLOR DEPTH

An image file stores the color of each pixel as three values, representing red, green, and blue. Image type depends on how much storage is allotted to each pixel (the *color depth*). These are the color depths common to image files in CG production:

Grayscale The image is black and white with varying degrees of gray in-between, typically 256. Grayscale images are good for rendering out black-and-white subjects; no extraneous color information is stored in the image file.

16-Bit Color Display or High Color 5-Bit Image File Each color channel (red, green, blue) gets 5 bits of space to store its value, resulting in an image that can display a maximum of 32,768 colors. Each color channel has a limited range of shades, but still gives a nice color image. You might notice the gradation in the different shades of each color that can result in *color banding* in the image.

8-Bit Image File This format is commonly referred to as 24-bit color display or True Color. Each color channel is given 8 bits for a range of 256 shades of each red, green, and blue channel for a total of 16 million colors in the image. This color depth gives the best color quality for an image and is widely used in most animation applications. The human eye cannot see quite as many shades of color as there are in a True Color image. Most of your renders from 3ds Max will probably be as 24-bit color files.

16-Bit Image File Used primarily in film work using such file types as TIFF16, this type of image file holds 16 bits of information for each color channel, resulting in an astounding number of color levels and range. Each file can exceed several megabytes even at low resolutions. These files are primarily used in the professional workplace and are standard for film work because outputting CG to film can require high levels of color and brightness range in the image.

Floating Point/32-Bit Image File Thirty-two–bit floating-point images are commonly used in film production to give the utmost attention to color depth. Your PC is capable of rendering a huge range in tone and color, and 32-bit floating-point images capture that range effectively. These files (such as EXR) are not easy to work with and require a lot of tweaking in compositing to output properly. HDR (High Dynamic Range) images are in 32-bit float format and are incredibly detailed in the range of contrast they store. You should not worry about high dynamic ranges such as this until you have gained a considerable amount of experience.

COLOR CHANNELS

As mentioned, each image file holds the color information in channels. All color images have a red, green, and blue color channel. Each channel is a measurement of the amount of red, green, or blue in areas of the image. A fourth channel, called the *alpha* channel, is used as a transparency channel. This channel, also know as the matte channel, defines which portions of the image are transparent or opaque. Not all image files have alpha channels.

FILE FORMATS

In addition to image types, several image file formats are available today. The most common perhaps is JPEG (Joint Photographic Experts Group), which is widely used on the Internet.

The main difference between file formats is how the image is stored. Some formats compress the file to reduce file size. However, the greater the compression, the poorer the image's color.

The popular formats to render into from 3ds Max are TIFF (Tagged Image File Format) and Targa (TGA). These file formats maintain a good 24-bit color depth using an 8-bit image file, are either uncompressed or hardly compressed (*lossless* compression), and are frequently used for broadcast or film work. These formats also have an alpha channel, giving you better control when you later composite images together.

To see an animation rendered in a file sequence of TIFFs, for example, you will need to play them back using a frame player, such as 3ds Max's RAM Player, or compile them into a movie file, such as a QuickTime file.

Your final image output format will depend on the project's needs. If, for example, you need to composite your CG together, you will need to output a format that can be used in your compositing or editing program. TIFF files are perhaps the best format to use as they are widely compatible, store uncompressed color, and have an alpha channel.

MOVIE FILES

Animations can also be output to movie files such as AVI or QuickTime. These usually large files are self-contained and hold all the images necessary for the animation that they play back as frames. Like image files, movie files can be compressed to keep their sizes to a minimum, but they suffer from quality loss as well.

3ds Max can render directly to an AVI or QuickTime movie file. This may seem like it saves you the hassle rendering out large sequences of TIFF files or such. In reality, you shouldn't render directly to a movie file at least for your final output. It is best to render a sequence of files in the end, because image sequences can easily be compiled into a movie file later using a program such as Autodesk Combustion, Adobe After Effects, Premiere, or even QuickTime Pro.

Rendering to images is less risky than rendering to a movie. In addition to having a sequence you can easily manipulate, you do not have to worry about crashing and losing rendering time. Sometimes, your render will crash or your machine will freeze. If you are rendering to a movie file when that happens, you'll need to restart rendering from the beginning, because you can't append to a half-rendered QuickTime. With a file sequence render, you can simply pick up the render from the last good frame, when your PC crashed.

With a sequence, you also have the option of reordering the frames or easily adjusting a few individual frames' properties, such as hue or saturation, without affecting the entire movie file.

Color

Color is how we perceive the differences in the frequency of light. The wide range of colors that we see (the visible spectrum) result when any of three *primary colors* of light—red, green, and blue—are "mixed" together. Color can be mixed in two ways, subtractive and additive. These color definitions are most often displayed in *color wheels*, which place primary colors equally spaced around a ring and place the resultant colors when the primaries are mixed in-between the appropriate primaries.

Understanding how color works will help you gain more from your CG's color scheme and help you design your shots with greater flexibility and better outcomes.

SUBTRACTIVE AND ADDITIVE COLOR

Subtractive color mixing is used when an image will be seen with an external light source. It's based on the way reflected light creates color. Light rays bounce off colored surfaces and are tinted by the different pigments on the surface. These pigments absorb and reflect only certain frequencies of the light hitting them, in essence *subtracting* certain colors from the light before it gets to your eyes. Pile up enough different colors of paint and you'll get black; all the color is absorbed by the pigment and only black is reflected.

With subtractive color mixing for painting, the traditional color wheel's primary colors are *red*, *blue*, and *yellow*. These three pigments can be mixed together to form any other color pigment. This is the basis for the color wheel most people are exposed to in art education. However, in the world of print production, a CMYK (Cyan, Magenta, Yellow, and blacK) color wheel is used, which places cyan, yellow, and magenta ink colors as the primary colors used to mix all the other ink colors for print work.

Projected light, however, is mixed as *additive color*. Each light's frequency adds upon another's to form color. The additive primary colors are *red*, *green*, and *blue*. These three colors, when mixed in certain ratios, form the entire range of color. When all are equally mixed together, they form a white light.

A computer monitor uses only additive color, mixing each color with amounts of red, green, and blue (RGB). Output for print is converted to a CMYK color model.

Warm colors are those in the magenta to red to yellow range, and *cool colors* are those in the green to cyan to blue range of the additive color wheel. Warm colors seem to advance from the frame, and cool colors seem to recede into the frame.

HOW A COMPUTER DEFINES COLOR

Computers represent all information, including color, as sets of numeric values made up of binary 0s and 1s (bits). In a 24-bit depth RGB color image, each pixel is represented by three 8-bit values corresponding to the red, green, and blue "channels" of the image. An 8-bit binary number can range from 0 to 255; therefore, you have 256 possible levels for each primary color. With three channels, you have 256 × 256 × 256 (16.7 million) possible combinations of each primary color mixed to form the final color.

Color value can also be set on the hue, saturation, and value (HSV) channels of a color. Again, each channel holds a value from 0 to 255 (in a 24-bit image) that defines the final color. The hue value defines the actual tint (from red to green to violet) of the color. The saturation defines *how much* of that tint is present in the color. The higher the saturation value, the deeper the color. Finally, value defines the brightness of the color, from black to white. The higher the value, the brighter the color.

HSV and RGB give you different methods to control color, allowing you to use the method you prefer. All the colors available in 3ds Max, from textures to lights, are defined as either RGB or HSV values for the best flexibility. You can switch from HSV to RGB definition in 3ds Max at any time.

CMYK COLOR SPACE

A CMYK color wheel is used for print work, and this is referred to as the four-color process. Color inkjet printers produce color printouts by mixing the appropriate levels of these inks onto the paper.

All output from a computer, which is RGB based, to a printer goes through a CMYK conversion as it's printed. For professional print work, specially calibrated monitors are used to better preview the CMYK color of an RGB image before it is printed. Fortunately, only the print professionals need to worry about this conversion process because most of it is handled by graphics software to a fairly accurate degree.

VIEWING COLOR

The broadcast standard for North America is called NTSC, as listed in the next section. Jokingly, industry folks sometimes refer to the acronym as Never The Same Color, calling attention to the fact that the color you see on one TV screen will inevitably differ on another TV. The same is true for computer monitors, especially flat panel displays. Unless made to do so, different screens are not calibrated to show the same color the same way, so what you see on one screen will display differently on another screen. If it is paramount that the color appear as you see it on a specific screen, it makes sense to finalize the work and show it on that screen. You can also download color bars from the Internet to display on monitors in an attempt to calibrate them to your eye. This is not the best way to go, but at least it will help a little, without exacting the costs and trouble of using color calibration equipment.

Resolution, Aspect Ratio, Frame Rate

Resolution denotes the size of an image in the number of horizontal and vertical pixels, usually given as # × #, such as 640 × 480. The higher the resolution, the finer the image detail.

You will adjust your final render size to suit the final medium for which you are creating the animation. The following are some standard resolutions:

VGA (Video Graphics Array)	640 × 480	Formerly, the standard computing resolution and still a popular television resolution for tape output.
NTSC D1 (National Television System Committee)	720 × 486	The standard resolution for broadcast television in North America.
NTSC DV	720 × 480	Close to the NTSC D1 resolution, this is the typical resolution of digital video cameras.
PAL (Phase Alternation Line)	720 × 586	The standard broadcast resolution for most European countries.
HDTV (High Definition TV)	1920 × 1080	The emerging television standard, sometimes also referred to as 1080i.
1K Academy (1K refers to 1000 pixels across)	1024 × 768	Typically, the lowest allowable resolution for film production at Academy ratio. Because film is an optical format (whereas TV is a raster format), there is no real set defined resolution for film. Suffice it to say, the higher the better.
2K Academy (2K refers to 2000 pixels across)	2048 × 1556	Most studios output CG for film at this resolution, which gives the best size-to-performance ratio.
4K Academy (4K is 4000 pixels across)	4094 × 3072	A high resolution for film, used for highly detailed shots.

Any discussion of resolution must include the matter of *aspect ratio*. Aspect ratio is the ratio of the screen's *width* to its *height*, and of course, there are standards:

Academy Standard	1.33:1 or 4:3	The most common aspect ratio. The width is 1.33 times the length of the height. This is the NTSC (National Television Standards Committee) television aspect ratio as well as the aspect ratio of 16mm films and some 35mm films, especially classics such as *Gone with the Wind*.
Widescreen (aka, Academy Flat)	1.85:1 or 16:9	The most often used 35mm film aspect today. When it's displayed on a television, horizontal black bars appear above and below the picture so that the edges are not cropped off (letterbox).
Anamorphic Ratio	2.35:1	Using a lens (called an anamorphic lens), the image captured to 35mm film is squeezed. When played back with a projector with an anamorphic lens, the image is projected with a width at 2.35 times its height. On a standard TV, the letterboxing would be more severe to avoid cropping the sides.

The number of frames that are played back per second determines the *frame rate* of an animation. This is denoted as *fps*, or frames per second. The following shows the three standard frame rates for media:

- NTSC: 30fps
- PAL: 25fps
- Film: 24fps

Knowing what your final output medium is going to be before you begin your project is pretty important. It is not crucial by any means, but knowing what the screen will look like (i.e., whether it is going to a small web window or a large television, for example) will help you better compose your scenes. You can always change your frame rate and render resolution at any time, but it is much simpler to begin with that already worked out.

Playing back a 24fps animation at 30fps will yield a slower-moving animation and will either require repeating some frames to fill in the gaps or ending the animation early. Conversely, playing a 30fps animation at 24fps will create a faster-moving animation that will either skip some frames or end later than it should.

Games, on the other hand, do not typically have a set playback rate for animation. When a scene is created for a game, the assets in the scene are rendered and played back on the user's computer system in real time; therefore, many factors contribute to the playback speed of scenes created for games.

Coordinate Systems

Coordinates are numerical representations of where an object is in 3d space. Every object in 3ds Max has a coordinate of where it exists. Without this coordinate, it would be gone— poof into thin air! Max's 3d space is organized with the Cartesian Coordinate System, which uses a three-pronged axis to define width, height, and depth as *X, Y,* and *Z,* respectively.

Figure 1.4

The Object space of the box aligns with the World Space.

The overall coordinate system in Max is called the World Coordinate System. It is an absolute coordinate that is fixed and unchangeable.

Objects in Max can have their own coordinate systems as well. When an object is created, it has its own width, height, and depth, again expressed as *X, Y,* and *Z.* Upon creation, the Local Coordinate System (belonging to the created object) and the World Coordinate System are aligned. However, when the object is rotated, its Local Coordinate System rotates with it. Because of this, an object created in a Front viewport (for instance) will have a different Local axis than if it were created in the Top viewport.

In Figure 1.4, you see a box. The *X-*, *Y-*, and *Z-*axes of the box are displayed in the center of the box and align with the axes of the home grid (which shows the World Space axes) displayed in the lower-left corner of the window.

However, when the box in the scene is rotated, instead of tossing out its own axes, Max retains them as Local space. The *X*-axis of the box does not change. Now the Local axis and the World Space axis are not aligned. This is not a bad thing, this is actually very good. It allows you to manipulate the box based on its original Local axes.

Basic Animation Concepts

A litany of information regarding animation concepts and techniques is available on the Internet. There are tons of books out there that also teach the basics of animation. In this very brief section, you will be exposed to a few important concepts behind animation. These concepts will help you better understand what you're doing in 3ds Max.

Frames, Keyframes, In-Betweens

Animation is based on change over time, so naturally you need a measurement of time. In animation, this is almost always expressed in *frames*. One frame is a single rendered image in an animation, or a single drawing in a traditional animation. Frame also refers to a single unit of time in your animation. The exact length of that time depends on the final frame rate with which the animation will be played back. For example, at film rate (24fps), a single frame will last 1/24 of a second. At NTSC video rate (30fps), that same frame will last 1/30 of a second.

Keyframes (or keys) are key frames at which the animator creates a pose for a character (or whatever is being animated). A keyframe in CG terms, is a frame in which a pose, a position, or some other parameter's value has been saved in time. Animation is when the object travels or changes between the keyframes. These frames, as the change is happening between *keys*, are called *in-between* frames. The computer extrapolates what needs to happen to get the object from its state in keyframe 1 to its state in keyframe 2. You will have plenty to keyframe in the coming chapters of this book.

In 3ds Max, a keyframe can be set on almost *any* parameter of an object—its color, position, size, and so on. In reality, you can set several keyframes on any one frame in CG animation. Figure 1.5 illustrates a keyframe sequence.

Weight

Weight is an implied facet of design and animation. Weight denotes the heaviness or presence of an element in a design. The more weight an element has, the more power it has in the composition. The weight of an object in a composition is affected by its color, the contrast, the background, position in the frame, and so on.

Figure 1.5

In the first frame of this sequence, a keyframe is set on the position, rotation, and scale of the cone. On frame 30, the same properties are again keyframed. The computer calculates all the movement in-between.

Keyframe at Frame 1

Frame 5

Frame 10

Figure 1.5

continued

Frame 15

Frame 20

Frame 25

Figure 1.5
continued

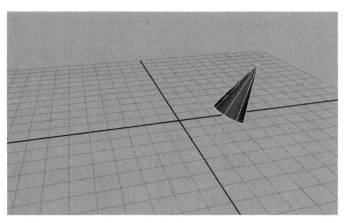

Keyframe at Frame 30

The weight of an object in animation roughly follows that idea, but more pragmatically denotes the actual weight of the object as it relates to its environment. Giving an object a good weight in animation is critical in the believability of the animation. You will have a chance to animate an object and edit the animation to give it weight in Chapter 8's Bouncing Ball and Knife exercises.

Weight in animation is a perception of mass. An object's movement and how it reacts in motion and to other objects need to be used to convey the feeling of weight. Otherwise, the animation will look bogus, or as they say, "cartoonish."

Over the years, animators have created a set of techniques they use to offer their subject weight in animation. Manipulating these concepts correctly in your work will greatly help your animations.

Squash and Stretch

Squash and Stretch is a cartoon concept that allows a character to physically squash down when he is landing from a jump, or stretch out thin while he is jumping up. The overall mass of an object should never really change. When you squash an object down, you should also reduce its height to make it seem as if it's squashing down. Similarly, when you stretch an object up, you should also thin it. This technique will make a character seem to respond to gravity. You will see how this applies in the Bouncing Ball exercise in Chapter 8.

Ease-In and Ease-Out

Things in the real world don't immediately come to an abrupt stop. There is always a slowing before a stoppage, no matter how fast the stop may be. This is called ease-out.

Just as objects don't suddenly stop, they don't immediately start moving either. Pretty much everything needs to gain speed, or accelerate, no matter how fast it begins moving. This is called ease-in. You will have a chance to animate a bouncing ball that will teach you the mechanics of ease-in and ease-out in Chapter 8.

Follow-Through and Anticipation

Exaggerating the weight of an object in animation is sometimes necessary. Objects ending an action usually have some type of *follow-through* motion. For example, a pony tail on a girl jumping down from a chair will continue to move about after she lands on the floor and stops moving herself. There is a slight resting follow-through to her action, such as bending slightly at the waist to center herself once she lands.

You can also create a small amount of movement before your action is in full swing. Before committing to an action, a character can wind up even if the wind-up is slight. Doing so will create a slight *anticipation* in the movement, like a hammer cocking back slightly before it strikes down or a spring that coils in before it springs out. These concepts are covered in Chapter 8.

Basic 3ds Max Terms and Concepts

Any 3d program has terms and concepts you need to nail down to become a good artist in that tool. Most of these terms are fairly transcendent in concept, meaning they apply to other packages in theory and general application as well—although you may find some of the names are slightly different. Here are several terms and concepts you will encounter in the world of CG as it relates to 3ds Max.

Object—Simply put, an element in your 3ds Max scene is called an object. An object may be converted to a more easily editable mesh at any time. You will learn about this concept in Chapter 4.

Primitives—Primitives are basic Max objects, such as spheres or boxes. Primitives can be shaped and altered to suit the needs of the model.

Sub-Object—Objects themselves are made up of components such as polygons, faces, vertices, etc. You can select and manipulate sub-objects in 3ds Max to alter the look or function of an object. Kinds of sub-objects include vertices, faces, polygons, edges, gizmos, centers, etc. The type of sub-object you are able to manipulate depends on the type of object you are manipulating. See Chapter 4 for more on sub-objects. Not all objects have sub-object components.

Normals—The face of a polygon has a direction in which it faces. A normal is a vector that defines which way a face points.

Spinners—Spinners are a function of the User Interface (UI) in Max. Spinners are the little arrows to the right of a value readout that allow you to adjust the value by clicking up or down on them. A spinner for a sphere's radius value is shown here.

Flyouts—Another UI term, a flyout is the name given an icon in 3ds Max that is actually several icons in one. If you press and hold a flyout icon, the other icons "fly out" and display themselves. Simply scroll to the icon you need and click to activate it. A flyout icon has a black triangle in its lower-right hand corner as shown here. These icons are further covered in Chapter 3, "The 3ds Max Interface."

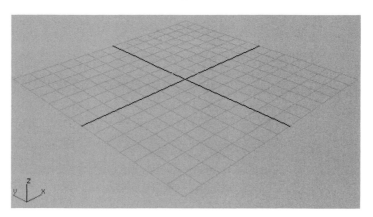

Home Grid—The Home Grid is a gray grid that displays the origin (0,0,0). It is useful for grounding yourself in the viewports, and it helps with proportion and direction as well. A Perspective viewport home grid is shown here.

Absolute/Relative—Absolute refers to an adjustment on an object that is based on a fixed reference, such as world space. An absolute scale of 2 will scale the object to a flat unit of 2. Relative refers to an adjustment made to an object that takes its current state into account. Scaling with a relative value of 2 will make that object twice its current size.

Track—A track is a term in 3ds Max used for an animated object. When an object has animation on several parameters, such as Translation X and Y, as well as Scale in X and Z, it is said to have four tracks. One track defines one animation on one parameter of that object on one axis.

SUGGESTED READING

The more you know about all the arts that are used in CG, the more confident you'll feel among your peers. To get started, check out the following excellent resources.

Art and Design

These books provide valuable insights into the mechanics and art of design. The more you understand design theory, the stronger your art will be.

Bowers, John. *Introduction to Two-Dimensional Design: Understanding Form and Function*. New York: John Wiley & Sons, 1999.

Itten, Johannes. *Design and Form: The Basic Course at the Bauhaus and Later*. New York: John Wiley & Sons, 1975.

Ocvirk, Otto G., and others. *Art Fundamentals: Theory and Practice*. New York: McGraw-Hill, 1997.

Wong, Wucius. *Principles of Form and Design*. New York: John Wiley & Sons, 1993.

CG

CG has an interesting history and is evolving at breakneck speeds. Acquiring a solid knowledge of this history and evolution is as important as keeping up with current trends.

Kerlow, Isaac Victor. *The Art of 3-D: Computer Animation and Imaging*. New York: John Wiley & Sons, 2000.

Dariush Derakhshani. *Introducing Maya 8: 3D for Beginners*. San Francisco: Sybex, 2006.

Kuperberg, Marcia. *Guide to Computer Animation*. Burlington: Focal Press, 2002.

Masson, Terrence. *CG 101: A Computer Graphics Industry Reference*. Indianapolis: New Riders Publishing, 1999.

Periodicals

Computer Graphics World (free subscription for those who qualify) `cgw.pennnet.com`

cinefex `www.cinefex.com`

HDRI3D `www.hdri3d.com`

3D World `www.3dworldmag.com`

Websites

`www.area.autodesk.com`

`www.animationartist.com`

`www.awn.com`

`www.highend3d.com`

`www.3dcafe.com`

Film

Block, Bruce. *The Visual Story: Seeing the Structure of Film, TV, and New Media*. Burlington: Focal Press, 2001.

Must Read

Myers, Dale K. *Computer Animation: Expert Advice on Breaking into the Business*. Milford: Oak Cliff Press, 1999.

Summary

In this chapter, you learned the basic concepts that drive the CG field. Starting with production workflow and moving into CG workflow, we discussed how productions are generally run. Then this chapter covered the different types of tasks used in CG production and the specialties that have risen from them in the professional field. Then you learned about core computer concepts, color space, and some output formats. Finally, you moved on to some important 3ds Max terms and concepts in which you will be immersed in the following chapters.

No matter how you take this chapter—or even if you skip it entirely to get right to the action—there is a lot of background information that can be useful in your overall knowledge of CG production. Although it takes some extra time to develop a base foundation, having one is always a good idea because a true understanding of a subject is fundamental to its mastery. Having said this, take the rest of the book as it comes, enjoy the challenges of the exercises, and remember that *some* frustration with an exercise will inevitably help you learn the concepts better, so keep at it.

CHAPTER 2

Your First Max Animation

This chapter gets your engine revving right away. It begins with an overview of the User Interface (UI) and starts you off with an exercise that will expose you to quite a few 3ds Max workflows and practices. The goal of the chapter is to put some concepts from the previous chapter into production so you can get your feet wet quickly.

Topics in this chapter include:

- Getting Around in 3ds Max
- Project and File Management Workflow
- The 3ds Max Interface
- Jumping Headlong into Animation
- Setting Up the Hierarchy
- Ready, Set, Animate

Getting Around in 3ds Max

At this point, it's important not to get caught up in the details of this great machine. Don't worry about the steps, buttons, menus, switches, and levers; just allow yourself to become comfortable with the tools that *you use* to create your artwork. Creating art is never about which button to press; it's about what to create. Always remember that, and your studies will be a great deal more successful.

Jumping straight into an exercise without knowing how to get around the interface might seem a little weird. However, you'll find everything you ever wanted to know, and then some, in Chapter 3, "The 3ds Max Interface." Learning is an experimental art, and there's no better way to learn than to start horsing around as soon as you can. The overall goal of this chapter is to expose you to the UI and show you how to get some things done in Max. Then you can proceed to the next chapter for a debriefing. You can, of course, skip ahead and get a rundown of the UI first and then come back to this chapter for your first experience.

Project and File Management Workflow

Autodesk 3ds Max 9 provides several subfolders automatically grouped into projects for you. Different kinds of files are saved in their own respective subfolders under the Project folder. For example, scene files are saved in a Scenes subfolder and rendered images are saved in a Render Output folder under the larger Project folder. The projects are set according to what you are working on, so everything is neat and organized from the get go.

The conventions followed in this book and on the accompanying CD will follow this project-based system so that you can grow accustomed to it and make it a part of your own workflow. Files organization is extremely important for professional work. If you do a lot of CG for fun or profit, it pays to be organized.

The exercises in this book are organized into specific projects, such as the one you will tackle in this chapter, *Mobile*. The Mobile project will be in a folder on your hard drive, and the subfolders for your scene files and rendered images will be in it. Once you copy the appropriate project folders to your hard drive, you can tell 3ds Max which project to work on by choosing File → Set Project Folder. This will set the current project to that project folder. For example, when you save your scene, Max will automatically take you to the Scenes subfolder of the current project.

Before we begin any project, we'll briefly explain the naming conventions and suggest a folder structure. Using these naming conventions and structures is a good habit to develop—it really is.

Naming Conventions

Every studio and professional production company worth its salt has an established *naming convention* for its files and folders. This is essentially a documented procedure that dictates how to name files and usually where to store them. Most organizations have different conventions, but the point is to have a convention and stick to it.

Students, in particular, tend to forgo any semblance of organization in their file-naming procedures. A common mistake is to save files to the local disk on the school computer, only to have the files erased by the support teams during the school's weekly purge. Designating a specific place on your PC or server for all your project files is important.

In addition to finding a suitable place to store your files, you need to name the files following some sort of convention. Your files will not only look neat when you're browsing, but they'll make sense months later when you try to figure out where that finished scene file is that you need. Typically, you should name a scene file with a project name or an abbreviation of such, then a brief description of what the file is, and a version number.

For example, if you are working on a project about a castle, begin by setting a new project called Castle. Choose File → Set Project Folder. On your hard drive, create a new folder by clicking the Make New Folder button to create a folder named Castle. 3ds Max will automatically create the project and its subfolders.

Once you save a scene, one of your scene filenames should look like this: `Castle_GateModel_v05.max`. This tells you right away it's a scene from your Castle project, and that it is a model of the gate. The version number tells you that it's the fifth iteration of the model and possibly the most recent version. Following a naming convention will save you oodles of time and aggravation.

Version Up!

The previous naming convention used a version number appended to the end of the filename. After you've spent a significant amount of time working on your scene, or after you've made a major change or big breakthrough in your work, you will want to "version up." This means you save your file using the same name, but you increase the version number by one to tell yourself, or your colleagues, that there was a big change since the last version. Version numbers are also useful for keeping track of your progress.

Version numbers can also save your hide. If you start down a path on your scene, but discover after hours of work (and saving your work as you go along, versioning up as you went) that this was indeed the wrong way to go, you can simply close the scene and open one of the previous versions before you started going in the wrong direction. This happens a lot more than you might think.

Disk space is cheap and scene files, even huge ones, aren't all that big in the face of the hundreds of gigabytes you can buy for less than $100. Keep a notebook and a pen next to your workstation so that you can take notes on your progress and record exactly what you did during your work sessions. Professionals do this regularly. They can't afford to waste time trying to figure out what file they should load to access a particular chunk of work.

Basic Project Structure Used in This Book

Each exercise will be its own 3ds Max project. Pick a place on your hard drive and start there. Create a folder called Max Projects on your C: drive (you can create one anywhere you want, including your My Documents folder). Place all of your projects in this folder. This will make it easy to find your files and back them up to CD or tape.

Let's create the first project we'll be working on, *Mobile*. Select File → Set Project Folder and navigate to your Max Projects folder (or My Documents folder), and then click Make New Folder. Name the folder **Mobile**. 3ds Max will create the subfolders for the project, as shown here.

That's pretty much it. Having a naming convention is easy; sticking to it is not, especially when you're first starting out. Make sure you stick to it.

Saving Your Scenes in Max

Save your scene frequently to protect yourself from mistakes and from losing your work. Choosing File → Save updates the current scene by overwriting the last save of the scene. If no scene was previously saved, this command opens the Save File As dialog box. Using it, you can select where to save the scene and enter your scene's name.

To "version up," you can save by using File → Save As and manually changing the version number appended to the end of the filename. Max, however, allows you to do this easily by using an increment feature in the Save As dialog box. Simply name your scene file and click the Increment button (the + icon) to the right of the filename text, as shown here.

Clicking the Increment button will append the filename with 01, then 02, then 03, and so on as you keep saving your work using Save As and the Increment button. In the previous example, the scene's base filename was SceneName_v. Clicking the Increment button added the two digit version number after the "_v." Adding the "_v" is a personal preference, of course, but it keeps with the naming convention set up in this book. It looks nicer, and you can easily determine the version number for your file by reading the number after the "_v."

The 3ds Max Interface

Here is a brief rundown of what you need to know about the UI and how to navigate in Max's 3d space. We will cover the interface in more detail in the next chapter, so feel free to jump back and forth if you need to know more about the UI.

The Menu Bar running across the top of the UI gives you access to a ton of commands—from basic file operations, such as Save, to advanced tools you may need for a scene. Immediately below the main Menu Bar is the main toolbar that contains several icons for functions such as Undo and the three transform tools (Move, Rotate, and Scale). You will use some of these icons for your exercise, and they are described in the next chapter.

The Undo and Redo icons are important, and you should be familiar with them. If you do something and then wish you hadn't, simply click the Undo icon (the icon on the left) or press Ctrl+Z. To redo a command or action that you just undid, click the Redo button (the icon on the right) or press Ctrl+Y.

The Command Panel

The Command panel is a vertical column or panel on the right side of the Max UI. It is segmented into tabs (as shown in Figure 2.1). Each tab displays the buttons and icons for a particular part of your workflow, such as creating objects, modifying objects, animating objects, etc. In each tab, the functions are grouped under headings that can be expanded or collapsed by clicking on the heading title. A plus next to the heading name means that you can expand the heading's view; a minus means that you can collapse the heading to save space.

If you move your mouse over the Command panel, the arrow pointer will change to a hand pointer, as shown in Figure 2.1, when it is not on a button or icon. While the pointer is a hand, you can click and drag to move the current panel up and down in the Command panel to see more functions in that space. You can also click on the far right side of the panel to scroll up and down if you don't want to use the hand.

As shown in the graphic to the left, the viewport controls with icons for various options for the 3d word windows (called *viewports*) are in the lower-right corner of the UI. These functions allow you to navigate the windows and their 3d space. However, you may find it easier to use hotkeys to invoke most of these viewport control functions to navigate 3d space. We will cover navigating 3d space and the appropriate hotkeys next.

Viewports

You'll be doing most of your work in the viewports. These windows represent 3d space using a system based on *Cartesian coordinates*. That is basically the smarty pants way of saying "space in *X*-, *Y*-, and *Z*-axes." You can visualize *X* as left-right, *Y* as up-down, and *Z*

Figure 2.1

The Command panel is segmented into headings called rollouts that group similar functions and icons.

as into and out of the screen. The coordinates are expressed as a set of three numbers such as (0, 3, –7). These coordinates represent a point that is at 0 in the X-axis, three units up in the Y-axis, and seven units back in the Z-axis. All CG programs, such as 3ds Max, are based on this coordinate system.

Four Viewport Layout

3ds Max's viewports are the windows into your scene (Figure 2.2). By default, there are four main views: Front, Top, Left, and Perspective. The first three: Front, Top, and Left are called Orthographic (2D) views. They are often referred to as *modeling* or *work windows*. These windows are best at expressing exact dimensions and size relationships. It's generally best to work in the orthographic windows when you are creating objects.

The Perspective viewport displays objects in 3D space using a simulation of perspective. Notice in Figure 2.2 how the distant cubes seem to get smaller in the Perspective view. In actuality, they are the same size—as you can see in the Orthographic views. The Perspective view gives you the best representation of what your output will be.

To select a viewport, just use the cursor and click in some blank viewport space (not on an object). If you do have something selected, it will be deselected when you click on the blank space. You can also just right-click anywhere in an inactive viewport to activate it. When active, the view will have a yellow highlight around it. If you right-click in an already active viewport, you will get a pop-up context menu called the *Quad menu*. You can use this shortcut menu to access some basic commands for a faster workflow. We will cover these menus in the next chapter, so don't fret just yet.

Figure 2.2

The 3ds Max viewports

Object and Axes Display in a Viewport

Viewports can display your scene objects in a few different ways. If you right-click on the viewport's name, you will see a context menu pop-up called the Right-Click Viewport menu, as shown in the following graphic. The most common view modes are Wireframe mode and Smooth + Highlights mode. Wireframe mode displays the outlines of the object, and it is the fastest because it requires less computation on your video card. The Smooth + Highlight mode is a shaded view where the objects in the scene appear solid. You will get the chance to experiment with the different display modes in the upcoming Mobile exercise.

Each viewport displays a ground plane grid (as shown in the Perspective viewport), called the *Home Grid*. This is the basic 3d space reference system defined by three fixed planes on the coordinate axes (*X,Y,Z*). The center of all three axes is called the *origin*, where the coordinates are (0,0,0). The Home Grid is visible by default when you start the software, but it can be turned off in the Right-Click Viewport menu. You can also toggle the grid by pressing G.

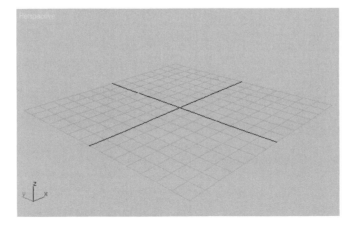

The Perspective viewport has a red, green, and blue axes marker, where the X-axis is red, the Y-axis is green, and the Z-axis is blue. Max uses this red, green, and blue color scheme to represent the X-, Y-, and Z-axes throughout the interface. As a matter of fact, most other 3d packages also use red, green, and blue to represent X, Y, and Z, respectively.

Selecting Objects in a Viewport

Selecting objects in a viewport is as easy as clicking on them. If the object is displayed in Wireframe mode, its wireframe will turn white while it is selected. If the object is displayed in a Shaded mode, a white bracket will appear around the object as shown here.

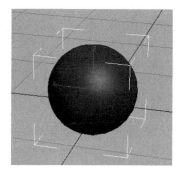

To select multiple objects, simply hold the Ctrl key as you click on the additional objects to add to your selection. If you Ctrl+click (i.e., press the Ctrl key and click) on an active object, you will deselect it. You can clear all of your active selection by clicking anywhere in the empty areas of the viewport.

Changing/Maximizing the Viewports

To change the view in any given viewport, say from a Perspective view to a Front view, right-click on the current viewport's name to bring up the Right-Click Viewport menu. From this menu, select View and then select the view you want to have in this viewport, as shown here.

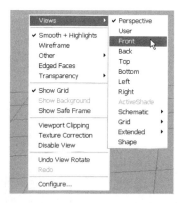

If you want to maximize the active viewport to a larger view from the default four-viewport layout, press the Maximize Viewport Toggle icon (⊡) in the lower-right corner of the Max window. You can also use the Alt+W keyboard shortcut to toggle between the maximized and four-viewport view.

Viewport Navigation

To work effectively, you will need to navigate in 3d space. Max allows you to move around its viewports by using either key/mouse combinations, which are highly preferred, or by using the viewport controls found in the lower-right corner of the Max UI. A full explanation of the viewport controls is in the next chapter. To navigate in the views, you should become familiar with the key/mouse combinations now.

Open a new, empty scene in Max. Experiment with the following controls to get a feel for moving around in 3d space. If you are new to 3d, this may seem odd at first, but it will become easier as you gain experience and should become second nature in no time. If you are coming to 3ds Max from another 3d package, such as Maya, you will notice several similarities that will definitely take a little getting used to. With time and practice, you should be able to hop back and forth between packages with little confusion.

- **Pan**—Panning a viewport will "slide" the view around the screen. Simply MM+ click in the viewport and drag the mouse to move the view.

- **Zoom**—Zooming will move your view in closer or farther away from your objects. To zoom, press Ctrl+Alt and MM+click in your viewport, and then drag the mouse up or down to zoom in or out, respectively. Zooming is sometimes called a *dolly* in other packages. It is more common to use the scroll wheel to zoom, however.

- **Arc Rotate**—Arc rotate will rotate your view around your objects. To arc rotate, press Alt and MM+click and drag in the viewport. By default, Max will rotate (or *tumble* as it's called in some other CG programs) about the center of the viewport to change your perspective.

The *arc rotate move* is used primarily in the Perspective views and not in the Orthographic views. If you accidentally arc rotate in one of the Orthographic views, you will be given a new User view. This view will be similar to a perspective; however, it will remain orthographic—meaning that there will be no vanishing point or perspective shift in the view; it is not a real camera view. You can reset the view back to your straight Orthogonal view by right-clicking on the User viewport's name and selecting your original view.

Jumping Headlong into Animation

Talk is cheap—unless you're calling long distance. Let's get busy and dive right into 3ds Max and create an animation. You may not understand the whats or whys for *all* the steps you're about to undergo, but you will get a quick trial by fire by getting into the program and following us as we guide you through some of the basic workflows for Max.

For your first experience, we will create a simple mobile. This example will teach you the basics of object creation, hierarchies, setting keyframes to create animation, and general workflow.

Plan of Attack for Making Objects

In production work, setting down a plan and having clear goals for your animation is very important. Without a good idea of where you need to go, you'll end up floundering and losing out on the whole experience. With that in mind, our goal in this chapter is to create a finished mobile, like the ones that hang over baby cribs. Because this is our first foray into Max, let's start with a simple object, so we won't be bogged down with the specifics of creating masterful models. Instead, we'll use simple objects easily created in Max.

Hierarchies

Once we model the mobile, we'll set up the pieces for animation. We will do this by creating proper hierarchies within the scene. The concept of *hierarchy* is a common feature in almost all CG packages. The hierarchy in a CG scene deals with how objects are arranged in a scene in relation to each other. *Parents* in a hierarchy lead *children*. Simply put, where a parent goes, the children follow. When you *translate* (move) or rotate or scale a parent object, its children will move, turn, or scale along with it.

However, children retain the ability to move themselves under their parent's supervision. The Mobile exercise is a perfect way to demonstrate the idea of hierarchies. Take a look at Figure 2.3, which displays the completed mobile. The top bar, from which the other bars hang, rotates and takes the lower bars with it. In this exercise, we will also animate the lower bars to rotate individually, just as a real mobile would.

Figure 2.3

The completed mobile object

Figure 2.4

The Create panel

The dangling shapes on the lower bars are the children of their respective bars. Those lower bars are children of the bars above them, and so on up to the top bar that controls the rotation of the entire mobile. Once you begin working on it, it will make more sense. As you can see now, hierarchy plays an important part in animation.

Don't get hung up on all the steps and what they mean. This is a quick dip in the pond to get your feet wet, and we will explain everything you do here in the next chapters. So why do you need to read about hierarchies now before you're finished with the model? It's always a good idea to go into something with a goal in mind. Knowing, even roughly, where you are headed will make things much easier. We'll go over this once we start to set up the mobile after it's been modeled.

Making the Mobile's Bars

To begin, we'll create the simple objects for the parts of the mobile. The mobile comprises horizontal bars and shapes that hang from the ends of each bar. We will forgo the strings used in an actual mobile and just make do with the bars and the shapes. To create the bars for the mobile, follow these steps:

1. In the Command panel, activate the Create panel (as shown in Figure 2.4) by clicking on the Create tab (   ). The Create panel is usually enabled by default. Click the Geometry button (   ) to display the Geometry Object Types; it is usually enabled by default. You will see a number of ways to create various objects. You will begin most, if not all, of your Max models in this panel.

2. With Standard Primitives selected in the pull-down menu, as shown in Figure 2.4, click the create Cylinder button. The Cylinder button will turn orange, and your cursor will turn from the obligatory arrow to a cross.

3. Go to the Perspective view. On the Home Grid, right-click and drag the mouse in any direction to begin the radius of the cylinder. Drag the mouse until it makes a circle, as shown in the top left graphic, and release the right mouse button. As soon as you release the button, you'll notice that as you move the mouse up or down, Max will pull the circle into a cylinder. Settle on a height for the cylinder and right-click to create the cylinder, as shown in the bottom left graphic. Don't worry about the size of the tube; we will modify it in the following steps to turn this cylinder into the top hanging bar for the mobile. Any size cylinder is fine for right now.

4. With the cylinder still selected in the Perspective panel, click the Modify tab (   ) in the Command panel to bring up all the nifty tools you can use to modify objects in Max. You will rename the cylinder and size it to be a bar for the mobile. At the top of the panel, you'll notice a text box with *Cylinder01* and a colored square next to it, as shown in Figure 2.5. The color swatch is the Object Color, and it helps you organize your elements in a scene. The color is easily changed by clicking on the swatch and simply choosing another color from the window that pops up (as seen in Figure 2.6).

This color is not necessarily the color your object will render in the final output of your animation (for more on rendering in Max, see Chapter 11, "3ds Max Rendering"). We're not too interested in the color of the bar right now, so you can leave the cylinder the way it is, or you can change it—whatever floats your boat.

Figure 2.5

The Modify panel allows you to change the name of the selected object and color it in the scene.

5. You do need to change the name of the cylinder, however. Click in the text box and change it from Cylinder01 to **Main Parent**. This name signifies that the cylinder will be the top bar of the mobile and the top parent to the rest of the objects in the scene. For more on hierarchies, see the "Hierarchies" section earlier in this chapter.

6. You need to size the cylinder (Main Parent) to make it a bar. Under the Parameters heading in the Modify panel, you'll notice a handful of parameters for Main Parent, as shown in Figure 2.7. If you don't see anything there, make sure the cylinder is selected. The Modify panel will display the parameters for the selected object only. To adjust the parameters for the bar, you can type values directly into the appropriate boxes. You can also use the Up and Down arrows on the right either by clicking on the arrows or by clicking and dragging up or down on the arrows. Change the Radius to 1 unit, Height to 100 units, and Height Segments to 1 (as shown in Figure 2.7). Your cylinder should look like a bar, as shown here. For a quick explanation of the other cylinder parameters, see the following note.

Figure 2.6

The Object Color helps you organize the scene by letting you assign colors to your objects.

Figure 2.7

The parameters of a selected object (in this case the Main Parent cylinder) can be changed to suit your needs.

NAMING OBJECTS AND KEEPING THE SCENE ORGANIZED

In 3ds Max, and in any CG package, it is incredibly important to keep things organized and as clean as possible. From personal experience, I hate to pick up a scene from a colleague and waste tons of time trying to figure out exactly what is in their scene. Many professional studios have strict naming procedures and conventions to minimize the confusion their artists may have when working in a *pipeline*—meaning that many artists will touch the same digital files and assets through a production. Even if you are the only person who will ever see the scene in Max, it is still an incredibly good idea to name and organize your objects. Get into the habit of naming your objects and keeping a clean scene. You will waste a lot of time if you don't—not to mention the dirty looks you'll get from other artists handling your cluttered scenes.

Every object in Max will have *parameters* that define it geometrically in the scene. The exact parameters that are available for editing depend on the object that is being edited. For this cylinder, for example, you've already seen what the Radius and Height parameters do. The Height Segments, Cap Segments, and Sides parameters basically determine how many polygons are used to define the shape, and hence how smooth it appears. Because the bar will not bend, you do not need extra polygons along the length. Therefore, the Height Segment is changed from the default of 5 to 1.

Positioning the Bar

Now you need to position the first bar, and then create copies for the other bars of the mobile, as shown in the following steps:

1. Click the Select and Rotate icon (⟳)—we'll call it the Rotate tool from now on—in the main toolbar running just below the Menu Bar. (You can also use the hotkey E to enable Select and Rotate.) Click on the Main Parent cylinder to select it and enable the Rotate tool. Notice the Rotate gizmo appears at the base of the cylinder.

2. You can click and drag on one of the axes to rotate the cylinder in that axis. For our needs, click on the *Y*-axis rotate *handle*, which is the green circle, and drag the mouse to rotate the cylinder to the right of the screen as shown in Figure 2.8. The green *Y*-axis handle turns yellow when you select it. The active axis handle on any given gizmo is yellow.

3. The bar needs to be rotated a perfect 90 degrees, and that is usually difficult to do by hand using the gizmo. Look at the bottom left of the Max UI, and you will see the orientation of the bar in three text boxes called the Transform Type-In boxes. You can enter a value of 90 in the *Y*-axis Transform Type-In box to set the bar to exactly 90 degrees, as shown in Figure 2.9.

Figure 2.8

The Rotate gizmo allows you to rotate the selected object.

Figure 2.9

Set the rotation to exactly 90 degrees in the *Y*-axis in the Transform Type-In box.

Copying the Bar

In the next steps, you will copy the bar to make the other bars. Because the bar is already the size and orientation we need, it'll be much faster to copy three more bars and place them. Copying objects in Max is actually quite easy; just follow these steps:

Figure 2.10

The Clone Options window asks you the type and number of copies to make.

1. Click the Select and Move Tool icon (⊕)—we'll call it the Move tool from now on—and select the bar. You can also invoke the Move tool with the hotkey W.

2. With the bar selected, hold down the Shift key and move the bar down in the *Z*-axis. A second copy of the bar will form: move it down in the *Z*-axis with your cursor. As soon as you release the mouse button, the Clone Options window will ask you what kind of copy you want to make (Figure 2.10). We will cover the different types of copies and what they mean in Chapter 4, "Modeling in 3ds Max: Part I." Can you feel the anticipation?

3. In the Clone Options window (Figure 2.10), keep the Copy button checked, enter **3** for the Number of Copies, and change the Name to **Parent01**. Click OK. Max will create three copies for you and position them down in the *Z*-axis the same amount you moved the original clone while you had the Shift key pressed. How's that for swanky?

4. We'll keep all the bars in the *Z*-axis for simplicity's sake. After all, this is your first Max animation; there's plenty of time for confusion later. You'll need to use the Move tool to position the lower bars as shown in Figure 2.11; just don't move the bars off the *Z*-axis by moving any of them in the *Y*-axis.

Try to position the bars so that the second bar's center lines up with the left end of the top bar. The third bar's center should be lined up with the top bar's right end. The fourth bar can line up with the top bar. Each level of the bars should be about five units down in the *Z*-axis from the last bar. Now you're ready to make the hanging objects.

Creating the Mobile's Objects

What kind of mobile has only four sticks hanging on a string? You'll have to make some objects to hang from the ends of the bars. These objects will be simple shapes you can create with the following steps:

1. Activate the Front viewport by clicking inside it. Maximize that viewport with the Maximize Viewport Toggle icon (⊞) in the bottom-right corner of the Max UI.

Figure 2.11

Position the bars for the mobile.

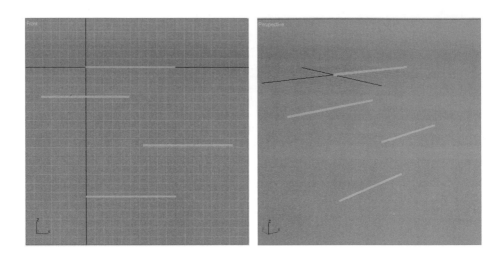

2. In the Command panel, click the Create tab and then click the Shapes button ( ) to display the creation options for various shapes. The Splines option should be shown in the Object Type pull-down menu, as shown in Figure 2.12.

3. Let's start with a circle. Click the Circle button. Your cursor will turn to a cross as it did when you created the cylinder. This time, expand the Keyboard Entry rollout. Enter a value of **20** for the Radius under the Keyboard Entry rollout in the Create panel, as you can see in Figure 2.13. Click the Create button and a circle with radius 20 will appear at the origin. This is a way to make objects with precise dimensions, as opposed to clicking and dragging as you did to create the cylinder.

VIEWPORT MODES

In Shaded mode, you see the objects in your scene as solid objects. This is the default mode for all the max Perspective viewports, but not for the Modeling viewports such as the Front view. To switch from one view mode to another, right-click on the viewport name in the upper-left corner of the viewport. A context menu appear will appear, as shown here.

You can select the view mode for that viewport by selecting it from the context menu. Other display modes, aside from Smooth + Highlights and Wireframe, are listed under the Other selection of the menu.

4. The circle is created with the name Circle01, which is fine, so there is no need to change its name. Use the Move tool to position it under the second bar, lining up its center with the left end of the second bar as shown in Figure 2.14. *Splines*, as with the circle you just created, are not renderable shapes by default. This means they will not render when you output your scene unless you specify otherwise. The circle will be displayed as a wireframe, even when the viewport is in Smooth + Highlights mode (aka Shaded mode; i.e., when objects are shown as solid in the viewport). For more on display modes in viewports, see Chapter 2 and the following brief sidebar.

Spline shapes, such as our lovely circle, are just curves that first need to be given a surface to be able to render as solid objects. To make the circle solid, you will *extrude* it:

1. Select the Circle01 object (the circle) and click the Modify tab (![icon]) in the Command panel. Under the Circle01 name text box, click on the Modifier List pull-down menu to access the tons of *modifiers* you can add to the circle (Figure 2.15). Under the Object-Space Modifiers heading, select Extrude.

2. In the box below the Modifier List pulldown menu, there is a new entry called Extrude that sits above the existing Circle entry for the selected Circle01 object. This box is called the *Modifier Stack* and is shown in Figure 2.16. The Modifier Stack displays all the modifiers that are contributing to the selected object, in this case the circle. The Circle modifier entry holds the original parameters of Circle01 while the new Extrude modifier entry holds the parameters for the extrusion you just applied to the circle. The circle now has a surface and is solid in the Perspective viewport (Figure 2.17).

Figure 2.12

Creating spline-based shapes

Figure 2.13

Under the Keyboard Entry heading, you can enter the exact radius to use for the circle.

Figure 2.14

Position the circle under the second bar.

> In 3ds Max 9, a flat object may display with one side black, whereas previous versions of 3ds Max displayed flat objects properly. This is due to *Backface Culling*, which is a display optimization toggle that is now turned off by default in 3ds Max 9. If you notice that one side of your flat object turns black, don't fret. Simply select the object and go to the Display tab of the Command panel (![icon]). Scroll down to the bottom of the panel under the Display Properties rollout and click to toggle on Backface Cull.

3. In the Modifier Stack, click the Extrude entry to bring up its parameters. Play with the Amount parameter to give the circle extrusion some depth and make a cylinder.

4. Let's go off topic just for a second to learn something a bit more general about Max. Go into Wireframe View mode in your Perspective window by right-clicking on the Perspective viewport name in the upper-left corner and selecting Wireframe from the context menu (you may also press F3). Make sure you right-click on the viewport name; right-clicking elsewhere in the viewport will bring up the Quad menu (which is explained in Chapter 3). Now that you see the wireframe of the extruded circle, change the Segments of the Extrude modifier to see what happens. Figure 2.18 shows the extruded circle with Segments of 1 on the left, and Segments of 4 on the right. You'll see that there are more geometry divisions (called *subdivisions*) which make the object smoother lengthwise. Because you don't need to bend this extruded cylinder, you do not need extra subdivisions along the length, so set the Segments back down to 1.

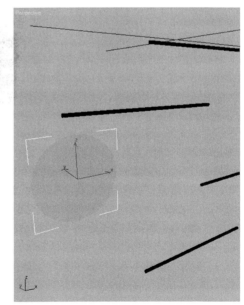

Figure 2.15

The Modifier List

Figure 2.16

The Modifier Stack shows off the Extrude modifier you just applied.

Figure 2.17

The circle is now a flat disc!

Figure 2.18

The extruded cylinder with a Segments value of 1 on the left, and a Segments of 4 on the right.

5. Back to the topic at hand, we need the circle to remain a flat disc, so set the Amount to **0.01** and keep the Segments at 1 as in the previous step.

6. Set the Perspective viewport back to Smooth + Highlights by right-clicking the viewport name, which is Perspective, and selecting Smooth + Highlights from the menu. You may also press F3 to toggle between the two display modes.

7. You should now see a flat solid disc as shown here.

8. Create a hexagon for the second shape. Go back to the Front viewport. In the Command panel, click the NGon button as shown here. In the Parameters heading, set the Sides to 6 for a hexagon. An *NGon* is a polygon with *N* number of sides. In this case, *N* is 6 to make a hexagon. In the Front viewport, click and drag to create the hexagon to a radius of about 20.

9. In the same way you created the disc using an Extrusion modifier on the circle, make a hexagon into a solid shape by adding an Extrusion modifier to it. Select the hexagon (named *NGon01*). In the Modifier panel, click the Modifier List pull-down menu and select Extrude (as seen in Figure 2.16). The NGon01 object will now have its own Extrude modifier in the Modifier Stack.

10. Use the Move tool (⊕) to place the NGon01 hexagon below and lined up with the other end of the second bar. Figure 2.19 shows the solid NGon01 surface in position.

11. Create four more shapes and place them to line up under the ends of the remaining bars as shown in Figure 2.20. You will need to create and extrude the remaining four shapes all at about the same size (radius of 20). The following table shows you the remaining shapes and what Object Type button to use to create them and what their names will be in the scene. It's important to keep the naming as printed here to avoid any confusion when we begin to set up the hierarchies for animation:

MOBILE OBJECT	CREATION TYPE	OBJECT NAME
Square	Use the Create Rectangle button	Rectangle01
Star	Use the Create Star button	Star01
Triangle	Use the Create NGon button with three sides	Ngon02
Donut	Use the Create Donut button	Donut01

Figure 2.19

The solid hexagon is in place.

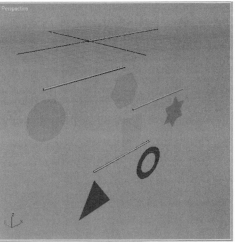

Figure 2.20
The shapes are now in position for the mobile.

You should already have created these first two shapes:

MOBILE OBJECT	CREATION TYPE	OBJECT NAME
Circle	Used the Create Circle button	Circle01
Hexagon	Used the Create NGon button with six sides	NGon01

If you are clicking and dragging to try to create a shape in the Perspective viewport and nothing happens, you will need to switch to one of the Orthographic views. In this Mobile example, make sure to create all the shapes in the Front viewport for simplicity's sake.

There you have it— a completed mobile model ready to set up and animate. The next sections of the chapter will take you through setting these objects up for animation in hierarchies so that when one bar rotates, its shapes and any bars beneath it also rotate with it. Go put your feet up and watch something dumb on TV for a little while; you've earned a break. It's actually important to take a break at this point, and make sure what you've gone through makes some sense. Feel free to go back and redo the exercise in part or in whole. In the next section, we will tackle hierarchies and setting up the mobile objects to animate properly.

Save your progress, making sure to version up so that you don't overwrite any previous scene files you might need later. You can check your work against the Mobile_v01.max scene file in the Mobile\Scenes folder on the CD.

Setting Up the Hierarchy

Before we continue with the next step in the Mobile exercise, let's take a look at hierarchies in action. Here is a quick introduction to how hierarchies work.

Parent and Child Objects

In the following steps, we will create a hierarchy of a few boxes to see how the relationship works when parents move, taking their children with them, and how children can move independently under their parents.

1. In a new scene, in the Create panel, click Box to create a new box. Click and drag in the Front viewport and draw out a box. Notice that when you drag the first time, a flat box is created. When you are happy with the size of the rectangle, click once and drag to "pull out" the third dimension of the box to give it depth. Click again when you are happy with the 3D box, and Max will create it. Your cursor will still be active in the Create Box tool. Click and drag to create two more boxes of approximately the same size to the right of the first box, as shown in Figure 2.21.

2. You need to set up a hierarchy so that the box on the right is a child of the box in the middle, which in turn is a child of the box on the left, like a row of ducks. In the main toolbar across the top of the UI, click the Select and Link tool (). The Select and Link tool works *upward*, meaning you select the bottom of the hierarchy and work your way up. In either the Front or Perspective viewports, click the box on the right

Figure 2.21

Create three lined-up boxes.

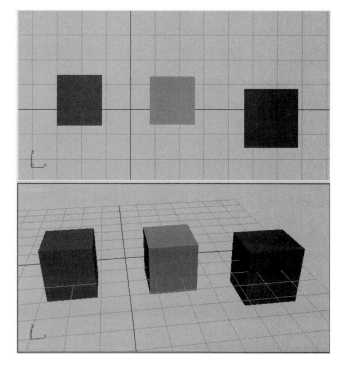

and drag the mouse over to the box in the middle. A dashed line and a cursor will change while you do this, as shown in the following graphic. When you release the mouse button, the two boxes will flash a white outline. This indicates that the link worked. The box on the right is now a child of the box in the middle.

3. Click on the Move tool () and select the middle box. Move it around in the viewport, and the box on the right (the child) will now follow as shown in the following graphic. Click on the child box on the right, and move it. Notice the child can move independently of its parent (the box in the middle).

4. Click the Select and Link tool () again. This time click on the box in the middle and drag to the box on the left. Select and move the box on the left, and all the boxes will follow. Now let's set a few keyframes on these boxes to get our juices flowing.

Setting Keyframe

The Time slider is at the bottom of the screen, as shown in Figure 2.22. The Time slider is used to change your position in time, counted in *frames*. As you read in the previous chapter, frames are the common increment for denoting time in an animation. You'll read more about the Time slider in the next chapter.

Figure 2.22

The Time slider allows you to change your position in time and scrub your animation.

You can click and drag the horizontal bar to change the frame in your animation on the fly. This is called *scrubbing* animation. The bar displays the current frame/end frame (it should read 0/100 before you click and drag it). Click and drag the slider to the left so your current frame is 0. Now, in the lower-right corner of the UI, click the Auto Key button, as shown in the following graphic. Both the Auto Key button and the Time slider will turn red. This means that any movement in the objects in your scene will be recorded as animation. How exciting!

Move the Time slider to the right to frame 20. Select the box on the left (the top parent) and move it across the Front viewport to the left along the *X*-axis. Next, click and move the middle box down in the *Y*-axis in the viewport, as shown here.

Now scrub the timeline between 0 and 20, and you will see your animation. Even though you did not set any keyframes on the box to the right, it follows along with both the left box and the middle box, doing a combination of their moves. The middle box goes with its parent, the left box, and its own animation, sliding down the viewport in the *Y*-axis. This is a simple hierarchy showing you how the relationships between objects build animation. You will use the same theory to build the animation for the Mobile exercise.

Hierarchies for the Mobile

Let's start with a simple hierarchy scheme much like the Boxes exercise. Start with your own Mobile scene, or load up the Mobile_v01.max scene file in the Mobile\Scenes folder on the CD. You will create the hierarchies for animation of the mobile using the following steps:

1. Remember, the Select and Link tool works from the children up the hierarchy to the top parent. You will link the shapes to their respective bars up the mobile. Click the Select and Link tool ( ) and then select the triangle. Drag the cursor to its bar, as shown here. The triangle is now linked to the bar above it.

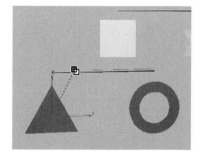

2. With the Select and Link tool still active, click and drag from the donut shape to the bar above it, as shown.

3. With the Select and Link tool, click and drag from the bottom bar that holds the triangle and donut to the square shape above it, as shown here. The bar is hanging from that square as if this were a real mobile, so you would link it as such. If you want to check your work, select and move the square and the bar. The shapes beneath it will move with the square. Just make sure to press Ctrl+Z to undo any moves you made to check the linking.

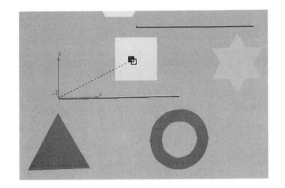

4. Now you just need to use the same steps to link the rest of the mobile:

   a. Click and drag with the Select and Link tool from the square to the bar above it.

   b. Link from the star to its bar.

   c. Link from the bar above the star and square to the top bar, as shown.

   d. Link from the hexagon to its bar.

   e. Link from the circle to its bar.

   f. Link from the bar above the circle and hexagon to the top bar, as shown.

You can refer to Figure 2.23 for a diagram of the linking order. It doesn't matter in what order you link the pieces, as long as you link from the bottom pieces up the chain.

Pivot Points

Now you've linked all the pieces of the mobile and created your first animation hierarchy. It's time to rotate parts of the mobile and test your handy work. This will be the last step before you animate the mobile. To test the mobile, select the bottom bar and rotate it on the Z-axis in either direction. Figure 2.24 shows the rotation of the bottom bar. Notice that the Rotate gizmo is at one end of the bar and not in the middle. You should also notice how the bar (along with the triangle and donut) is rotating around the end of the bar, although it should rotate in the middle, where the string would be hanging it from the square right above it.

Figure 2.23

The linking order determines the hierarchy of the mobile.

Figure 2.24

The bottom bar is rotating around one end instead of the middle.

Figure 2.25

The Hierarchy panel

Your results might be slightly different from what is shown here. Your bar might not rotate around the same end or it might rotate somewhere else along the cylinder. This is perfectly normal. The important thing is where the *pivot point* of the object is—and that pivot should be in the middle of the bar.

Simply put, the pivot point of an object in Max is the point about which it rotates. It is also the point on the object that defines the point in coordinate space where the object resides.

Because the pivot of the bottom bar is not in the middle of the bar, you will have to move the pivot to the middle. To do so, follow these steps:

1. Use Ctrl+Z to undo any rotations you have already put on the bottom bar. Click the Move tool (⊕) or press the hotkey W for the Move tool, and select the bottom bar if it is not currently selected. In the Command panel, switch to the Hierarchy panel, as shown in Figure 2.25, by pressing the Hierarchy Panel tab (⬗).

2. At the top of the Hierarchy panel, make sure the Pivot button is active and then click the Affect Pivot Only button to activate it (the button will turn purple). This will tell Max to move only the pivot point of the currently selected object and not to move the entire object. Your gizmo icon will change, as shown here.

3. Click on the *X*-axis Move handle (the small red arrow inside the larger outline of an arrow) and move the pivot along the length of the bar to the middle of the bar, as shown here.

4. In the Hierarchy panel, click the Affect Pivot Only button again to turn it off. Your cursor will return to the normal Move Tool gizmo. Select the Rotate tool from the main toolbar ( ) and rotate the bottom bar again. It will now rotate around the middle of the bar as it should, with the triangle and donut in tow, as shown in Figure 2.26.

5. To make sure the pivot points are all in the middle of the respective bars, check the other bars in the mobile. If not, use the previous steps to relocate the pivots to their proper places.

You can check your work against the Mobile_v03.max scene file in the Mobile\Scenes folder on the CD. Once the pivot points are all placed properly on the mobile's bars, you are ready to animate. Grab a juice box; you deserve it!

Figure 2.26

The bottom bar now rotates properly.

Ready, Set, Animate!

In this animation, we'll rotate *only the bars* of the mobile. Don't worry about rotating or animating the shapes for now. We will pick this exercise back up in Chapter 8, "Introduction to Animation," for further study.

You can use your own file, or you can load the Mobile_v03.max scene file in the Mobile\Scenes folder on the CD. In this file, the mobile is already linked properly for this animation and all the pivots are placed at the middle of each bar. To animate the mobile, follow these steps:

1. Scrub the Time slider to 0. Turn on the Auto Keyframe feature by clicking the Auto Key button, which is shown here. Both the Auto Key button and the Time slider will turn red.

2. Move the Time slider to frame 50. Click the Rotate tool (or press the hotkey E for the Rotate tool), and select and rotate the bottom bar (which will also rotate the triangle and donut shapes beneath it). You can rotate the bar in either direction on the *Z*-axis, as shown in Figure 2.27. Give it a few full rotations all the way around. Don't be shy.

3. You can scrub the animation to check it out. The bottom bar and its shapes should be spinning. Make sure you go back to frame 50 in the Time slider. With the Rotate tool still active, select the second bar from the bottom (the bar with the square and the star shapes), and rotate it in either direction in the *Z*-axis. Figure 2.28 shows how the bottom bar follows along.

Figure 2.27
Rotate the bottom bar with gusto!

Figure 2.28
Rotate the second bar and the bottom bar follows.

4. While still at frame 50, select the third bar from the bottom (the bar with the circle and the hexagon) and rotate it in either direction on the *Z*-axis. The circle and hexagon rotate with the bar, as shown here.

5. With the Rotate tool, select the top bar and rotate it in either direction on the *Z*-axis. The entire mobile will rotate along with it, because the top bar is the top parent of this hierarchy (Figure 2.29).

Scrub your animation, and you'll see that the mobile is in full swing! The bars rotate and carry with them the shapes and bars beneath them, according to the previously set hierarchy. If your shapes or child bars are not rotating with their parent bars, check your hierarchies or redo that portion of the exercise.

You may have noticed that this exercise asked you not to animate the rotation of the shapes linked under the bars. If you animate the shapes under the bars to rotate, you will probably get some strange results when you play back the animation. The shapes and some of the bars linked below the animated shapes will not rotate properly. To avoid overloading you with information, this stage of this exercise is specifically intended to animate only the bars. We will revisit this exercise to learn how to properly animate the shapes and the bars in Chapter 8.

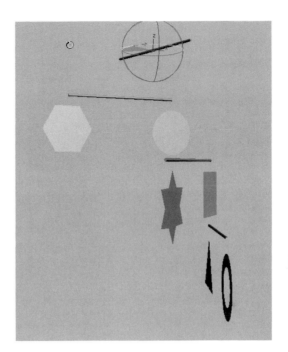

Figure 2.29

The whole mobile rotates with the top bar.

Summary

Understanding the underlying technique used here is important, so doing the exercise more than once is not a bad idea. These things can be frustrating, so take it easy and when you get confused or stuck, back up and try again.

In this chapter, you learned how project management and file workflow help you keep things organized. You learned how to navigate the User Interface to create and manipulate objects in the viewports. You learned about hierarchies and how to link objects together to create a hierarchy useful for our mobile animation. Finally, you learned how pivot points are used, and we also learned how to create animation using the Auto Key function.

CHAPTER 3

The 3ds Max Interface

This chapter explains the interface and the commonly used windows and panels. You already mucked about in the UI when you built your mobile in the previous chapter. This chapter will go into more depth regarding some of the tasks you performed, and it will give you a layout of where things are and what they do. Furthermore, we'll take a look at the commonly used windows and panels in Max and see how to operate them.

You can use this chapter as a reference as you work through the rest of this book. As you progress, you might want to check back here to bone up on some of the information. It's important to be in front of your computer when you check out this chapter, so you can try things out as we discuss them in the book.

Topics in this chapter include:

- **Screen Layout**

- **Command Panel**

- **Controls at the Bottom of the UI**

- **Navigation Controls**

- **Layer Editor**

- **Schematic View**

What Am I Looking At?

When you start up Max, you will be looking at a screen full of buttons, icons, menus, and panels. Although it may seem that there is no end to the switches and levers in Max, you'll be able to master the UI with experience. The more you use Max to create, the more comfortable you'll become with the UI and all of its nuances. Before you know it, the UI will be a nonissue for you—just give it time.

As with many other 3d applications, any command or tool can be accessed using several different ways. For example, you can access some tools through the Command panel, the Menu Bar, hotkeys, or context menus.

With so many different ways to perform any single function, how can you keep it all straight? Have a function or tool in several different places may seem like overload, but ultimately it gives users the most freedom to discover their preferred workflow. You may prefer to work mostly through the Command panel; others may find the Menu Bar easier to use. In either case, it's important to first experience the most common way to use Max, and then branch out and find your own. In this book, we will present the most obvious way to access a function first and give you alternative ways (such as hotkeys) later when you access that feature again and again.

Having said that, don't get too hung up on all the information you're about to be loaded with in this chapter. It's best to peruse this chapter at your own pace in front of your PC. Don't worry about memorizing all the information on all the buttons and panels. While you work on the exercises throughout this book, you'll find short descriptions of the UI elements you use when they first come up. You can always refer back to this chapter for a more thorough explanation or to brush up whenever you need.

Your first read through of this chapter should be to become familiar with and gain a *sense* of where everything is and how everything works. Experience and only experience will really show you how the tools work best; this chapter just shows you where they are.

If you skipped the previous chapter, make sure to go back to Chapter 2, "Your First 3ds Max Animation," and read the "The Max Interface" section for a run-through of how to work in Max's UI. In this chapter, you will find a fairly comprehensive explanation of Max's UI to build on what you already learned in the last chapter.

Screen Layout

Let's take a quick look at how the screen is laid out. Figure 3.1 shows the initial Max screen.

The Menu Bar is across the top of the Max UI, just as with many other applications. Here you can access tons of features to help you with your scene creation and manipulation. Right under the Menu Bar is the main toolbar, which contains the most often accessed tool icons. Everything from Undo to Render is in the main toolbar for easy access.

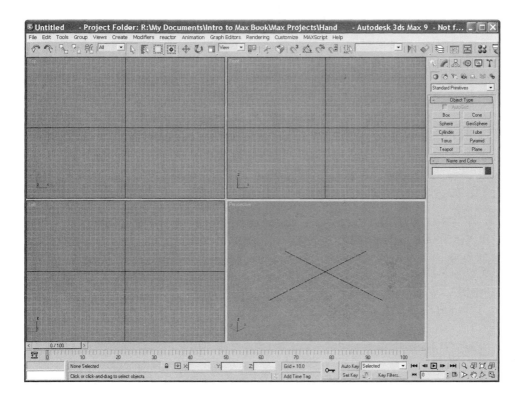

Figure 3.1

The default Max screen

Running down the right side of the Max UI is the Command panel. Object creation and manipulation tools are gathered here for your access. The Command panel, as you discovered in the previous chapter, is divided into tabs. Each tab has its own specific panel of tools, ranging from Create to Utilities.

The meat of the UI is in the viewports. These ports give you access to Max's 3d space through orthographic and perspective views. These viewports are where you do the bulk of your work, of course. By using mouse and key combinations, as you saw in the previous chapter, you can navigate through 3d space and around your scenes quite easily.

Running across the bottom of the UI are the tools for changing time values (such as the Time slider, which you experienced in the previous chapter), adjusting your panel views, and animating.

Each of these UI sections is explained in more detail in the following pages with a breakdown of the major components.

The Menu Bar

If you've ever played with a computer, you should be familiar with the layout of Menu Bars, so let's cut the chit chat. Here is a rundown of what to expect in each of the menus shown in Figure 3.2. Feel free to click along with the text to see for yourself what is in each menu.

Figure 3.2

The Menu Bar

File Menu—Here you will find the familiar commands for file management. Commands for creating, opening, and saving scenes; importing/exporting outside formats; setting project folders; viewing images; displaying/changing scene properties; and exiting.

Edit Menu—This contains the commands for editing and selecting objects in your scene. This is one of the areas where you will find the Undo/Redo functions, as well as easy selection methods (such as Select All). Under the Select By submenu heading in the Edit menu, you can select objects in the scene using a certain criteria, such as by their color or name.

Tools—This menu is where tools to manipulate your objects are located, such as Mirror or Align. Many of these tools and functions are found on the main toolbar and also found in the Command panels. You'll see how several of these tools operate in the coming chapters.

Group—Grouping lets you combine two or more objects into a single grouped object. Groups can be open/closed to access objects inside the group. You can also permanently break up the group by ungrouping or exploding (dissolves all nested groups).

Views—Options to set up and control viewports. From here, for example, you can disable the view of your gizmos in the viewports or toggle your home grids on and off.

Create—This menu gives tools for creating objects and is very extensive with many submenus. Everything that you would create for your 3d scene is found here. Some of the objects you created in the previous chapter for your mobile can be created through this menu as well as the Command panel's Create panel, which you used.

All the main menus are broken up into 15 categories. The main ones we will be using in this book are Standard Primitive, Extended Primitives, Shapes, Helpers, Lights, Camera and Particles.

Modifiers—A modifier is a type of Max object that controls and changes the basic structure of objects. Modifiers are used for modeling, animating, and adding special effects to objects. Through the Modifier menu you can apply modifiers to selected objects in the scene, though once applied, Modifiers are edited through the Modify panel.

Reactor—This is a plug-in for Max and allows you to create complex dynamics such as cloth and fluid simulation, and soft body dynamics. You will be introduced to reactor in Chapter 12, "Particles and Dynamics."

Animation—This menu has features for animation, constraints, controllers, and Inverse Kinematics (IK). IK is used for character animation.

Graph Editors—These are floating windows for managing a scene, hierarchy, and animation. Graph Editors give you access to scene components in graphical layout for easy use. Everything from nodes (a node represents an object in Max) to animation curves are displayed. Animation curves are animation expressed in mathematical graphs. It sounds harder than it is. You'll see plenty of curves later in the book.

Rendering—These commands are for scene rendering, setting up an environment and render effects, accessing video post for in-program compositing, and using a RAM player.

Customize—This menu is for all things relating to user interface customization. This book will, for the most part, use the default layout for the Max UI, as that is most universal for the readers. Once you get a feeling for Max and are more comfortable with it, you'll find yourself customizing the UI to your tastes.

MAXScript—These are commands for working with MaxScript, which is a scripting language for 3ds Max. MaxScript allows you to automate certain functions and program parts of your scene as needed. MaxScript will not be covered in this book as it is an advanced feature set.

Help—This provides access to online references, tutorials, and online support, and perhaps the most important menu in the program.

Main Toolbar

The main toolbar contains the tools most commonly used in Max conveniently located at the top of the interface. (Figure 3.3) The toolbar can be rearranged as a floating pallet or docked on the bottom, left, or right side of the interface. To do this, place your cursor to the far left side of the toolbar over the embossed vertical line. An icon of white boxes will appear next to your cursor. Simply click and drag to create a floating toolbar, or drag it to a side of the UI to dock it. You can also right-click on the embossed vertical line for a pop-up window, giving you options for docking and floating the toolbar, as seen in Figure 3.4. All palettes and bars in the Max interface can be rearranged like this.

Figure 3.3
The main toolbar

If your screen does not show all the icons you see in Figure 3.3, don't panic. Your display is probably set to a lower resolution than the width of the toolbar. In this case, you can drag the toolbar left and right to expose the missing end of the toolbar. Place your cursor over an empty part of the toolbar (not on an icon) and it will turn into a hand icon, as seen on the right of the graphic here. Click and drag the toolbar as needed.

The icons for the main toolbar are as shown in the following tables. You should use this as a reference while you use this book; you don't need to memorize everything here. For the most part, you will learn tools and functions in Max as you come across them in your work, so trying to memorize all the icons and their functions will just drive you nutty. Grab your mouse and click along with us to get a feel for the icons. Some icons, characterized by the small triangle in the lower-right corner have flyouts. *Flyouts* are additional options for the tool that appear as a context menu of new icons when you click and hold the icon, as shown here for the Scale tool.

Undo/Redo Icons

Undo and Redo are extremely useful in Max. You will find yourself painted into a corner many times—especially when you are first starting out—and Undo will let you back out of those corners. The icons are as follows:

ICON	NAME	FUNCTION
	Option+Undo	Reverses the effect of the last action. Right-clicking the Undo button shows a list of the previous actions. You must select a continuous selection; you cannot skip over any items in the list.
	Option+Redo	Cancels the last Undo. Right-clicking the Redo button shows a list of the previous actions. You must select a continuous selection; you cannot skip over any items in the list.

Figure 3.4

You can float Menu Bars easily in 3ds Max.

Linking and Hierarchy Icons

Linking and Hierarchy Tools are used to parent objects for animation, as you saw with the Mobile exercise in Chapter 2, "Your First 3ds Max Animation." The icons are listed here:

ICON	NAME	FUNCTION
	Select and Link	Allows you to create a hierarchical link of child and parent between objects.
	Select and UnLink	Allows you to remove the hierarchical link of child and parent between objects.
	Select and Bind to Space Warp	Allows you to bind an object to a space warp effect (like gravity, wind, or displace).

Selection Tools Icons

Selection tools allow you to select objects in a scene using different methods. The icons are listed here:

ICON	NAME	FUNCTION
	Selection Filter List	Allows you to screen out certain objects that can be selected. For example, if you choose geometry from the list, you will not be able to select anything other than geometry. This is particularly helpful when you have a very crowded scene. You can also create combination filters such as cameras and lights together.
	Select Object	Allows the selection of any objects in your 3d scene.
	Select By Name	Allows you to select an object from a list within the Select Objects dialog box, shown in Figure 3.5. The list contains objects currently in your scene and has filters for easy selection.
	Select Region flyout	Gives you different ways to select objects by defining a region by clicking and dragging in a viewport. The default is rectangle selection. There are five region selection methods Rectangle, Circular, Fence, Lasso, and Paint. These methods are similar to Photoshop's Marquee Selection tool and Lasso tool.
	Window/Crossing Selection toggle	This tool is probably one of the most overlooked and least used tools, but it's a very useful tool in the toolbar. It switches between window and crossing modes when you select by region. If you are in Window mode, it will select only objects that are entirely inside the windows region. In the default Crossing mode, you will also select objects that are touching the edge of the region. This tool will also work when you are selecting polygons in Sub-Object mode.

Transformation Tools Icons

As you saw in the previous chapter, transformation tools move, rotate, and scale your objects. The icons are listed here:

ICON	NAME	FUNCTION
	Select and Move	Selects and moves objects. For all the transform tools (Move, Rotate, and Scale), you can click-drag a region box around the object or objects to select them. You can also invoke this tool with the W hotkey.
	Select and Rotate	Selects and rotates objects. Click-drag a region box around the object or objects to select. You can also invoke this tool with the E hotkey.
	Select and Scale tool	This tool has a flyout with access to two other scale tools. The default Scale tool is the Uniform Scale tool (left icon), which allows you to scale along all three axes evenly. The middle icon in the flyout is the Non-uniform Scale tool, which allows you to scale along the axis you choose. The right icon is the Squash Scale tool, which is a type of scale used mainly for the "squash and stretch" style of animation found in cartoons. When you are scaling down in one axis, it scales up in the other two, and vice versa. You can also invoke this tool with the R hotkey.

Figure 3.5

The Select Objects by Name window

Coordinate Systems, Center Pivots, and Manipulator Icons

As you saw in the first chapter, coordinate systems define the axes that you use. The icons for this section of the main toolbar are listed here:

ICON	NAME	FUNCTION
	Reference Coordinate System	This list allows you to choose which coordinate system you want to use. Coordinate Systems are covered in depth at the end of Chapter 1, "Basic Concepts."
	Use Center flyout	These tools allow you to determine the pivot point of an object for its rotation and scale. By default, this is set to Use Pivot Point Center and is perfectly adequate the vast majority of the time, and it is used throughout this book as such. This icon has a fly-out to give you options to relocate the center point of your transformation tool. You can use it if you have multiple objects selected.
	Select and Manipulate	This tool allows you to edit the parameters of certain objects, modifiers, and controllers by dragging *manipulators* in viewports. Manipulators are similar to the gizmos you've already used. We will not cover manipulators in this book because they are an advanced way to edit and use objects in Max.

Snapping Icons

Snapping functions are for more accurate placement of objects in your scene. When you enable a Snap function while you move an object, for example, Max will "snap" the object to points on the home grid or to other geometry in the scene. Because you can snap to specific locations during creation and transformation of objects or sub-objects, Snaps give you control when you're creating, moving, rotating, and scaling objects.

There are several different types of Snaps; you can snap to a grid, pivot, or vertex. You can turn Snaps on and off by clicking their icons in the main toolbar or by pressing the S key while you are in the middle of a transform for an object. We will be using Snaps in the following chapters. Right-clicking on the Snap functions will open the Options window. In it, you can select exactly how you want to snap. Figure 3.6 shows the options for the Snaps toggle.

Figure 3.6

The options for the Snap functions allow you to set how you want to snap your objects.

Figure 3.7

Right-clicking the Angle Snap or Percent Snap tool will open the Snap's options.

ICON	NAME	FUNCTION
	2D, 2.5D, and 3D Snap toggle/flyout:	The 2D Snap (the default top Icon) allows you to snap to the home or construction grid or to any shapes or geometry on the grid.
		The 2.5D Snap (middle Icon) allows you to snap to only vertices or edges of an object.
		The 3D Snap (bottom Icon) will snap to any geometry in 3D space.
	Angle Snap toggle	Allows you to set the increment of rotation you want for rotating an object in a given axis.
	Percent Snap toggle	Allows you to define a set increment of scaling when you are scaling an object. To set the increment you want to snap to, right-click the icon to open the options, as shown in Figure 3.7.
	Spinner Snap toggle	Spinners are the number values you adjust with little arrows as seen in the icon itself. You will run into spinners constantly in Max. Use the Spinner Snap function to set the increment you want to increase or decrease.

Named Selection Sets Icons

Selection sets are a way to easily select several objects at once. To create a selection set, simply select the objects you want to select together during your workflow, and then type a name for the set in the Named Selection Sets field. That name will be added to the drop-down menu so you can select all those objects in the set by simply selecting the name. Later in this book, we will further explore selection sets.

ICON	NAME	FUNCTION
	Named Selection sets	To create a named selection set, select the objects for your selection set and enter a name for that set.
	Named Selection Sets dialog	This menu allows you to organize your selection sets and the objects that are members of those sets. Click the plus (+) or minus (–) to expand the object list for each set. The buttons along the top allow you to create or delete sets as well as add or remove objects. See Figure 3.8.

Figure 3.8

You can edit selection sets using this window.

Align and Mirror Icons

The Align and Mirror icons are next up in this main toolbar discussion. The Mirror function (Figure 3.9) allows you to mirror an object's orientation. Click this button to bring up the Mirror dialog box seen in Figure 3.9. In the dialog box, you can choose a mirror axis and offset the mirror amount. You can either mirror the object or create a clone that is mirrored by selecting the Copy option.

ICON	NAME	FUNCTION
	Mirror	Mirrors the selected object in the chosen axis. Can also copy a mirror of the object.
	Align	The Align flyout gives you access to all the Align functions discussed in the following table. This Align icon is displayed by default.

The Align flyout has several options. In essence, these Align tools allow you to line up your object as discussed in the following table. Simply select the object you want to align, click the appropriate Align Tool icon in the flyout, and then click the target object to which the object is to be aligned. You will have a chance to see the Align and Mirror functions in action in Chapter 4, "Modeling in 3ds Max: Part I," as well as throughout the book. Really, would we lie?

ICON	NAME	FUNCTION
	Align	Once you click on the target object to align to, Max will open the Align dialog box seen in Figure 3.10. From this window, you can choose which axis to align your selected object as position, rotation, or even scale.
	Quick Align	This function lets you instantly align the *position* of the current selection to that of a target object.
	Normal Align	Align two objects based on the direction of the normal of a face or selection on each object. A normal is an imaginary line that is perpendicular to the surface of a geometry.
	Place Highlight	Enables you to align a light or object to another object so that its highlight or reflection can be precisely positioned
	Align Camera	Lets you align a camera to a selected face normal. A normal is an imaginary line that is perpendicular to the surface of a geometry.
	Align to View	Lets you align an object with the current viewport.

Editing Window Icons

Layers, the Curve Editor, and the Schematic View are editing and organizational tools in Max. We will cover each of them later in this chapter. Their icons are explained in this table:

ICON	NAME	FUNCTION
	Layer Manager	Used to manage sets of objects in layers. Very useful for large scenes and complicated setups.
	Curve Editor	Allows for the editing of animation by manipulating mathematical curves.
	Schematic View	A node-based display of the objects in a scene allowing you to edit parameters as well as hierarchies.

Figure 3.9

The Mirror function

Figure 3.10

The Align options allow you to dictate how your objects are to be aligned.

The Material and Rendering Editors give you access to materials for shading and texturing, as well as the options for rendering out your scene. These windows will be covered later in this chapter, along with other commonly used windows and panels. Their icons are as follows:

ICON	NAME	FUNCTION
	Material Editor	Accesses materials to add to scene objects to give them their final look when rendered (also known as texturing or shading).
	Render Scene dialog box	Creates renderings and saves them to files. The Render Scene dialog box has multiple panels.
	Quick Render (Production)	Lets you render the scene using the current production render settings without displaying the Render Scene dialog box. This icon has a flyout icon as shown below.
	Quick Render (Active Shader)	Creates an ActiveShade rendering in a floating window. This icon is a flyout of the Quick Render (Production) icon above.

Whoa! Did Ya Get All That?

That was a lot to take in. You will be exposed to most of these tools in the next few chapters, and before long, using them will be second nature to you. There is, again, no need to memorize all this material; you will find the tool icons you need as you need them in this book's exercises. This part of the book is perfect as a reference guide, so bookmark these pages for easy access later.

The Command Panel

As you saw in the previous chapter, the Command panel is divided into tabs according to function. You easily access several commands and functions through the different panels that make a quick workflow in Max. Everything you need to create, manipulate, and animate objects can be found here.

You can easily scroll up and down a panel to access tools that are not visible on the screen because the panel is too long vertically. When you encounter a panel with more to show, Max will display a thin vertical scroll bar on the right side, as seen here. Your cursor will also turn into a hand cursor when you can click and drag the panel up and down. Try it. It's fun!

You will be exposed to more panels as you progress through this book. However, here is a rundown of the Command Panel panels and what they do.

The Command Panel tabs are the following:

ICON	NAME	FUNCTION
	Create panel	Create objects, lights, cameras, etc.
	Modify panel	Apply and edit modifiers to objects
	Hierarchy panel	Adjust hierarchy for objects, as well as adjust their pivots
	Motion panel	Access animation tools and functions
	Display panel	Access display options for scene objects
	Utilities panel	Access several functions of Max from motion capture utilities to the asset browser

The function or toolset you need to access will determine which panel you need to click. The division of panel tabs is very instinctive and easy to decipher.

Create Panel

The first panel, the Create panel, is used primarily for creating various objects for your scene. There are seven categories for the kinds of objects you can create. The panels under the Create panel are listed here:

ICON	NAME	FUNCTION
	Geometry	Create renderable objects, such as primitives or parametric objects
	Shapes	Create 2D lines or splines in various shapes
	Lights	Max lights simulate real-world lights to illuminate objects in the scene
	Camera	Create cameras to view and render your 3D scene
	Helpers	Helper objects are aids to constructing a scene
	Space Warp	Objects that deform the appearance of other objects
	Systems	The catch-all area where you will find functions, such as Bones and Biped Animation tools, as well as lighting systems to simulate sun and daylight

GEOMETRY

The Geometry category in the Create panel is responsible for renderable objects, also known as primitives or *parametric objects* (i.e., an object whose parameters may be changed at any time to adjust its original shape or appearance). The default is Standard Primitives. Click on the drop-down window to access more object types, such as extended primitives, compound objects, and particles.

When you created the mobile in the previous chapter, you made several shapes and modified them. You can access many of these creation objects through the Create menu as well (Figure 3.11).

Figure 3.11

The Create Geometry category for the Create panel

SHAPES

Shapes are 2D lines or splines that can be used as is. You can also create objects using modifiers, such as Extrude, as you saw in the Mobile exercise. You can use stock shapes, such as a circle or rectangle, or you can use the Line tool to create free-form shapes. Lines are used as components to create other objects. You can use splines to create motion paths, extrusions, lathes, lofts, and 3d objects. The drop-down menu will give you access to NURBS and extended splines. Figure 3.12 shows the Shapes Creation option.

LIGHTS

Lights in Max, just like lights in the real world, are used to illuminate objects. You can create lights that simulate indoor lights (such as incandescent or florescent lights), outdoor lights (such as the sun or street lights), or lights that don't simulate anything but the look you need for your scene. 3d lights are designed to simulate lights in the real world. Max provides two types of lights you can use: Standard and Photometric. The different light types are available in the drop-down menu. Standard lights simulate the basic light rigs used in film and stage, and Photometric lights are used to simulate *radiosity* (bounced light) within a 3d environment. You will use both kinds of lights later in this book when you learn how to light and render your scenes (Figure 3.13).

Figure 3.12

Creating shapes in the Create panel

CAMERA

Camera objects are designed to simulate real-world still and motion cameras. They are used to record the action you animate, and they output through rendering. Just as with real-world cameras, Max's camera objects allow you to use a variety of lens types. There is a standard camera and a camera that has a target to make it easier to follow an object or action. You'll get to use a camera a lot in Chapter 11, "3ds Max Rendering." You can see the Camera Creation category in Figure 3.14.

Figure 3.13

Creating lights

HELPERS

Helpers take care of the unglamorous and thankless jobs in Max. They help you construct scenes, but they aren't necessarily part of the scenes. Helpers help you position, measure, and animate a scene's renderable geometry. Figure 3.15 shows the various helpers you can create.

Figure 3.14

Camera Creation category in the Creation panel

Figure 3.15

Helpers help you create your scene.

SPACE WARP

Space warps are objects that deform or animate objects in your scene. They are known as *deformers* in other animation packages, such as Maya. You can create ripples, waves, and even blow up objects by applying Space Warp objects to them. In order for the space warp to work, it must be bound to the object using "bind to space warp." The drop-down menu shown in Figure 3.16 lists the different space warps available.

SYSTEMS

Systems category holds the typically advanced functions of Max. You can use them to set up Sun and Daylight lighting systems or Bones systems to animate a character or object rig. Figure 3.17 shows the various systems you can create.

Modify Panel

The Modify panel, as you saw with the Mobile project, houses all the modifiers you can apply to an object. It also houses a selected object's Modifier List (Modifier Stack). Using this list, you can reorder or remove the modifiers for an object, which can be invaluable in creating precisely the right object for your scene.

Figure 3.16

Creating space warps

This panel also allows you to change the parameters for existing objects, such as the radius or length of a cylinder, even after it has been created.

Modifiers are the bread and butter of editing objects in Max. This form of workflow is terrific because you can stack modifiers on top of each other when creating an object and you can go back and edit any of the modifiers in the stack (for the most part) to adjust the object at any point in its creation. This sort of workflow is akin to a *node-based* editing workflow, where any stage of the creation process can be adjusted at any time. Figure 3.18 shows the Modify panel for a selected Sphere object.

Almost all the parameters in the Modify panel can be animated. For example, you can create a sphere and animate its radius. Then you can add a taper modifier and animate the taper amount. You can also go into the sub-object level of a modifier, such as an FFD (free-form deformation), select the Control Points, and animate the points on the lattice. This can give you layer upon layer of animation. The downside of this is that editing the animation can be a nightmare. For instance, with the FFD, each control point has its own track in the Curve Editor. So, if you have a lattice with 4 × 4 × 4, you would have to edit 64 potential tracks. Yikes!

Figure 3.17

Systems creation

There are two types of modifiers. World Space modifiers attach to an object but use world space instead of local space. Object Space modifiers affect an object's geometry in local space. Figure 3.19 shows a Bend modifier applied to a box. The Bend modifier does what it says: it bends the geometry. It is an example of an Object Space modifier because it affects the entire object as one piece.

Hierarchy Panel

The Hierarchy panel is where you create and edit the hierarchies for your objects. As you saw in the Mobile project, creating parent-child relationships through linking allowed you to create complex animations—i.e., different rotations on different parts of the mobile. The children objects—or *nodes*—travel with their parents, but retain the ability to have their own motions once they inherit their parents' motion(s).

PIVOT

In the Hierarchy panel, you can also adjust the position of an object's pivot point. As you've already seen, the pivot point plays a critical role in how an object moves, rotates, and scales. Having control of the pivot is important to setting up the proper animation for any given object. All objects have a *pivot point*, a center for all transforms. A pivot also defines the transform relationship of a hierarchy, sets the center location of an added modifier, and defines IK (Inverse Kinematics) joint locations.

In the Pivot category of the Hierarchy panel, you can adjust the pivot by moving it, centering it, or aligning it to another object or the world space, as seen in Figure 3.20.

IK

Inverse Kinematics (IK) is a method often used in character animation; it provides an easier way to move the parts of a character's armature by using IK handles to place the limb's extremities, such as the feet. You simply animate the placement of the feet, and IK solves all the necessary rotations of the leg bones and animates the legs into the proper placement for the feet. The IK panel is shown in Figure 3.21. You will see how IK and bones work in Chapter 9, "Animation Part II: Character Studio and IK."

The IK category gives you all the tools you need for adjusting hierarchical linkage between objects.

Figure 3.18

The Modify panel for a sphere

Figure 3.20

The Hierarchy panel's Pivot category is a must for proper animation setup.

Figure 3.19

A Bend modifier is applied to a box through the Modify panel.

Figure 3.21

The IK section of the Hierarchy panel

LINK INFO

The Link Info section allows you to restrict the movement of objects in a hierarchy by limiting from which axes motion is inherited from parents.

Try this exercise:

1. In a new scene, create a box of any size and a Teapot object of similar size. You can find one in the Create panel's Geometry Standard Primitive category.

2. Link the teapot to the box so that the box is the parent of the teapot, as shown here:

3. Press the W hotkey for the Move tool. Select and move the teapot first in the X-axis, then in the Y-axis, and then in the Z-axis. The teapot freely moves with the box (assuming the link was created successfully).

4. Select and move the teapot in all three axes as you did the box. The teapot moves in all directions.

5. Select the teapot and click on the Hierarchy panel. In the panel, select the Link Info section. Under the Locks heading rollout, check the box in the Move section for the X-axis. In the Inherit heading rollout, uncheck the box for Move in the Y-axis, as seen here.

6. Select and move the teapot separately in the three axes. You'll see that the teapot has been locked in the X-axis and will not move at all in X. This is what a lock does to an object, no matter where it is in a hierarchy.

7. Select the box and move it separately in all three axes. You'll see that the teapot, except the Y-axis, moves along with the box as it should. The teapot is restricted from inheriting any motion in the Y-axis from the box parent. This what an inheritance lock does to a child under a moving parent.

Link Info is a great way to set limits for the motions of your objects.

Motion Panel

The Motion panel houses all the tools for controlling animated objects using keyframes editing and animation controllers. You will have a chance to dance with keyframes and controllers in Chapter 8, "Animation Part I: Introduction to Animation." The Parameters option allows you to edit keyframes without using the Curve Editor, which is usually the preferred and more powerful way to edit keyframes (Figure 3.22).

The Trajectories option in the Motion panel (Figure 3.23) allows you to display the path that an object travels in its animation. This way you can actually see the movement an object takes in its animation and adjust it visually to change its course.

Display Panel

The Display panel (Figure 3.24) allows you to choose how an object appears in your viewports. Use the Display panel to Hide/Unhide, Freeze/Unfreeze, and alter display characteristics of objects. This ability is extremely useful when you need to organize your scenes, no matter what their size.

The Hide by Category heading rollout allows you to turn off types of objects in 3ds Max to let you focus on certain objects. For example, if you have a scene replete with objects, but all you only need to adjust your lights, you can easily turn off your geometry and shapes to better see where your lights are in the scene.

Hiding objects is useful for getting parts of your scene out of the way temporarily. Hiding, as it implies, turns offs the display of the hidden object. Similarly, freezing objects allows you to still see frozen objects, but not select or transform them. This feature is useful when you still need to reference a model but don't want to move it accidentally. When you freeze an object, its display in the viewports turns dark gray.

The larger and more complicated your scenes become, the more you can rely on the Display panel to help you with your scene.

> You can also use the Layer toolbar, which is covered later in this chapter, to help you organize large scenes.

Utilities Panel

The Utilities panel (Figure 3.25) allows you to access different utility programs, or *plug-ins,* inside 3ds Max. Some plug-ins are already shipped with 3ds Max, and some are third party from different software makers. One such utility is Motion Capture, which allows you to import and work with animation data captured using external devices, such as a joystick or midi device configured to mimic puppetry animation. These utilities are all advanced and will not be covered in this book.

Figure 3.22

The Parameters in the Motion panel allow you to edit keyframes of an object's animation.

Figure 3.23

The Trajectories option in the Motion panel gives you a visual display of your animation's path.

Figure 3.24

The Display panel is important to keeping your scene organized.

Figure 3.25

The Utilities panel

Controls at the Bottom of the UI

Time controls, animation controls, playback controls, and viewport controls are aligned at the bottom edge of the Max UI. This section covers the icons and functions.

Time Slider and Track Bar

Running across the bottom of the Max UI is the Time slider and the Track Bar, as seen in Figure 3.26.

The Time slider allows you to move through any frame in your scene by *scrubbing* (moving the slider back and forth). By scrubbing, you can also view your animation playback in the viewports. You can move through your animation one frame at a time by clicking on the arrows on either side of the Time slider or by pressing the < and > keys.

You can also use the Time slider to animate objects by setting keyframes. A right-click on the Time slider brings up a Create Key dialog box, which allows you to create transform keyframes for the selected object. Figure 3.27 shows the Create Key window.

The Track Bar is directly below the Time slider. The Track Bar is the timeline that displays the timeline format for your scene. More often than not, this is displayed in frames, with each tick mark representing frames. On the Track Bar, you can move and edit your animation properties for the selected object. When a keyframe is present, right-click it to reveal individual transform values; these values can be edited within the dialog box. From this pop-up menu, you can delete keyframes and filter the Track Bar display. You will have a chance to explore using these tools in the chapters on animation in this book.

The icon to the left of the Track Bar is the Show Curves icon. This toggle displays a version of the Track View Curve Editor. The Curve Editor shows you your scene's animation as curves that you can edit.

The Status Bar

The Status Bar in 3ds Max gives you feedback and information as you work in your scene. The Status Bar runs across about two-thirds of the bottom of the screen as shown in Figure 3.28. Check it out, you'll love it.

Figure 3.26

The Time slider and Track Bar

Figure 3.27

The Create Key window lets you set a keyframe for a selected object by right-clicking the Time slider.

Figure 3.28

The Status Bar is chock full of useful information.

The elements on the Status Bar are the following:

MAXScript Mini Listener—This is a command prompt used for entering and seeing feedback for MAXScript. MAXScript is the scripting language used in 3ds Max to automate actions and customize functions. This line displays a single line of the actual MAXScript Listener window, which gives you easier access in a window to MAXScript.

Status Line—Displays the number and type of object selected in your scene.

Lock Selection—When your object is selected, use the selection lock to lock the object so you won't inadvertently deselect or select something else in your scene. The button turns yellow when turned on. The keyboard shortcut for this tool is the spacebar.

Relative/Absolute Transform Toggle—When you enter values in the Transform Type-In boxes (as you did with the Mobile exercise in the previous chapter), Max treats the values as *absolute*. If you set the toggle to *relative*, the values you enter will be used to offset the selected object from its current state.

Transform Type-Ins—You can enter values in these boxes (delineated as X, Y, and Z values as noted) to transform the selected object, whether it is moving, rotating, or scaling. Transform Type-In boxes allow you to make exact values for transforms instead of using the gizmo. When nothing is selected and you are moving the cursor around in a viewport, the Transform Type-In area displays the coordinates of your cursor.

Grid Settings—Shows the size of one grid square on the home grid in your viewport. To edit the size of your grid squares, go to the Grid and Snap Settings dialog box. This can be found by choosing Customize → Grid and Snap Settings (or by right-clicking the Snap Toggle tool) and clicking the Home Grid tab.

Prompt Line—This line in the Status Bar is similar to a guy standing behind you and tapping you on the shoulder to tell you what you need to do next. Here, Max displays instructions that prompt you for the next action in a function, such as "Click and drag to select and move objects" when the Move tool is active. The Prompt Line gives you ongoing feedback as you work with a tool. It can be a good place to look when you're unsure of what to do next. In addition, Tool Tips are displayed here when you mouse over icons and buttons. Mousing around and checking icon names is a good way to become more familiar with the interface.

Time Tag—Time Tag is an animation assistant that allows you to set up tags at a certain point in your animation that you can easily jump to by selecting the tag's name.

Animation Controls

The Animation controls are a selection of icons to the right of the Status Bar that are used in animation. Figure 3.29 shows the icons.

Figure 3.29

The Animation controls

The functions in the Animation controls are covered in Chapter 8. The rundown on the icons is as follows:

Set Key—Sets a keyframe for the selected object(s) at the current frame for all *tracks* of the object. A track is a specific translation type (move, rotate, and/or scale, or a parameter) on a specific axis. The keyboard hotkey for Set Key is K.

Auto Key Animation Mode—Toggles the Keyframing mode on/off. The button turns red when Auto Key Mode is on. Keyframes are automatically created when Auto Key button is on and objects are transformed. You don't need to set a key manually while in the Auto Key mode.

Set Key Animation Mode—You can create specific keyframes for a selected object by placing the object as you like and then setting a keyframe manually. This animation mode, along with the Key Filters (next), allows you to control exactly which tracks are keyed while you animate. With Set Key mode off, any keys you set will set for all tracks by default.

Figure 3.30

The Set Key Filters window allows you to select the keyframes for which you want tracks set.

Key Filters—Clicking this button will open the Set Key Filters window shown in Figure 3.30. This window is where you can pick the tracks and the desired axis or axes) you want to be keyframed as you animate. This keeps your scene free of extra keyframes you may not need.

Selection List—Gives quick access to named selection sets and track sets while working with Set Key. Lets you easily swap between different selection sets and track sets.

In/Out Tangent for New Keys—Shortcut for setting up tangent types for keys on curves for animation created with Set Key or Auto Key. This is only for new keyframes. Curves and keyframes are covered in detail in Chapter 8.

Animation Playback Controls

The Animation Playback controls (Figure 3.31) are similar to the ones you would find on a VCR (how old are you?) or DVD player.

Figure 3.31
The Animation Playback controls run your playback.

Go to Start—Moves the Time slider to the first frame in the active time segments.

Previous Frame/Key—Moves the Time slider back one frame or one key, depending on the Key Mode toggle.

Play/Stop—Plays your animation in the active viewport. The button is a flyout that lets you access another icon (an outline of a play arrow instead of the filled black arrow) to play only the animation of *selected* objects instead of the entire scene.

Go to End—Moves the Time slider to the last frame in the active time segments.

Current Frame—Also called **Go to Frame.** This field displays the current frame. It allows you to enter a frame number in the field to jump your Time slider to that frame. There is also a spinner that you can click/drag to change the frame number.

Key Mode—This tool allows you to jump from one keyframe to another. In order for it to work, you must turn on the button and then use the Previous and Next Key buttons to move from one frame to the next. When active, the Key Mode button turns cyan, and the Previous Key and Next Key buttons appear as shown in Figure 3.32.

Time Configuration—A dialog (Figure 3.33) that allows control over frame rates, time display, playback, and animation. You can use this to scale your animation length so it goes faster or slower, or to add more frames to the start or end of your animation. This is covered as well in Chapter 8.

Figure 3.32
Stepping keys instead of frames

Figure 3.33
The Time Configuration window

Figure 3.34

**The default View-
port Navigation
icons for a Perspec-
tive viewport**

Figure 3.35

**The default View-
port Navigation
icons for the Ortho-
graphic viewports**

Figure 3.36

**The default View-
port Navigation
icons for a light**

Figure 3.37

**The default View-
port Navigation
icons for a camera**

Viewport Navigation Controls

The tools for viewport navigation are extensive and many of the icons have flyouts with multiple tools nested therein. On top of that, the available tools change depending on the viewport you have selected—orthographic, user (a 3D view that is created when an orthographic view is rotated), perspective, camera, and light views. But don't let that freak you out; it will become second nature to you in no time.

When the navigation tools are selected, they turn yellow and stay selected until you choose another tool, right-click in a viewport, or press Esc.

Viewports are used for orthographic and perspective views, and also for views through cameras and lights. By setting a viewport to a view from a camera or light, you can easily position the camera or light exactly as you need it using the Viewport Navigation controls, interactively as you watch the result in that viewport. We will experiment with cameras and lights in later chapters in this book.

The Navigation controls, as they appear when the Perspective viewport is active, are as shown in Figure 3.34. They're shown as they appear while an Orthographic view is active in Figure 3.35.

In the following tables, *all* of the navigation icons are laid out and briefly explained. Don't stare at this list of icons and cry. The Max screen has a lot of icons, but experience will help you make sense of things very quickly. Take a look at these icons and click around to get a feel for how they work.

Create a few objects to have something to look at in your viewports, or even load up the Mobile exercise scene file. But definitely spend some time just ambling around the viewports looking at things. Use the Viewport Navigation controls and their key/mouse combinations to get used to navigating a bit more.

> The key to getting good at navigating Max, or any other 3d package, is to work on projects and get things done. You will gain the skills you need as you work toward a goal. As you will see, the exercises in the rest of this book will let you flex your muscles and give you a chance to become comfortable with Max.

As a reference for you, the individual icons are explained in the following tables. Match the individual icons with Figures 3.34 through 3.37 to see their relative locations.

TOOLS AVAILABLE IN ALL VIEWPORTS

These Icons are available in all of the viewports in Figures 3.34 through 3.37. Keep in mind that some of the following icons are nested icons beneath flyouts; to reveal them you will need to click and hold the flyout icon. An example of a flyout for the Navigation controls is shown here.

ICON	NAME	FUNCTION
	Zoom Extends All	Like the Zoom Extend tool, but it zooms in your scene in all four viewports. The keyboard shortcut for this tool is Z.
	Zoom Extends All Selected	Like Zoom Extends All, but for objects that are selected.
	Min/Max Viewport	Toggles between Normal viewport size to Full Screen viewport. The keyboard shortcut is Alt+W.
	Pan View	Will move the selected viewport up, down, and side to side. The shortcut is to click/drag the middle mouse button or Ctrl+P.

TOOLS AVAILABLE IN PERSPECTIVE AND ORTHOGRAPHIC VIEWPORTS

These Icons (Figures 3.34 and 3.35) are available in the Perspective and Orthographic viewports. Keep in mind that some of the following icons are nested beneath flyouts.

ICON	NAME	FUNCTION
	Zoom	Zoom magnifies the objects in your viewport from big to small by moving the view in and out of 3d space in the scene. Zoom works the same in both the Perspective and Orthographic viewports. The keyboard shortcut is Ctrl+Alt+middle mouse button. If you your mouse has a middle dial, you can use it as a Zoom tool by centering your cursor in the selected viewport and rolling the dial up to zoom in and down to zoom out.
	Zoom All	Same as Zoom except it zooms all four viewports at once.
	Zoom Extents	This flyout icon is nested with Zoom Extents Selected. You can call this the "Fit to Window" because Zoom Extents zooms all objects in your scene into the viewport. Works for only orthographic or perspective viewports.
	Zoom Extents Selected	This flyout icon is nested with Zoom Extents. Like the Zoom Extends tool but for selected objects.
	Field-of-View (FOV)	This Icon is a flyout icon nested with Zoom Region. This tool is available in the Perspective or Camera viewport when active. Field of View changes the amount of the scene that you can see in the viewport by adjusting the filed of view effectively zooming in and out just like a camera lens. This is not the same as Zoom, where the view is moved in and out of the scene.
	Zoom Region	This flyout icon is nested with Field of View (see following). Allows you to drag a rectangle marquee around a chosen area to zoom in on. This tool is available only in Orthographic/User and Perspective viewports.
	Walkthrough	This flyout icon is nested with Pan View (the hand icon). This very cool tool lets you move through a viewport by pressing the arrow keys. It is similar to the Pan tool, but you use the arrow key for navigation instead of the mouse. When you enter the Walkthrough Navigation mode, the cursor changes to a hollow circle that shows a directional arrow while you are pressing one of the arrow keys. Walkthrough is available only for Perspective and Camera viewports.
	Arc Rotate	This flyout Icon is nested with Arc Rotate Selected and Arc Rotate SubObject. Arc Rotate lets you rotate a viewport by clicking and dragging a series of handles on the gizmo (shown in Figure 3.38). Uses the viewport center as the center for its rotation. The shortcuts are Alt+MMB and Ctrl+R.

continued

continues

ICON	NAME	FUNCTION
	Arc Rotate Selected	This flyout Icon is nested with Arc Rotate and Arc Rotate SubObject. This icon has a white circle. Same as Arc Rotate but uses the selected object as the center for rotation. The object remains in the same position as the viewport rotates around the object.
	Arc Rotate SubObject	This flyout Icon is nested with Arc Rotate and Arc Rotate Selected. This icon has a yellow circle. Similar to the Arc Rotate Selected, but it rotates about SubObject selection. This will be discussed in more detail in the chapter on modeling in 3D.

CAMERA VIEWPORT CONTROLS

A camera view shows your scene through the lens of a virtual camera. These tools give viewport control of your camera. Tools will change depending on whether you are using a Free or Target camera. Cameras will be covered in Chapter 11.

Again, use this section as a reference, and click along with the descriptions. You don't need to memorize it all or understand everything at once. You can come back to this chapter when you need to look up something.

To be able to access these navigation tools, you will need to create a camera and switch a viewport to its view. To create a camera, follow these steps in a new scene or a current scene:

1. Choose Create → Cameras → Free Camera, and click in one of your viewports to place the camera. You may also click in the Create panel under the Cameras category and click the Free icon. Figure 3.38 shows a camera placed in the scene.

Figure 3.38

A camera

2. Right-click a viewport name in the upper-left corner of the viewport, and select Views → Camera01, as seen in Figure 3.39. This will change the viewport to the camera's view. You will now be able to access the Camera Viewport navigation tools shown in the following table.

Figure 3.39

Set your viewport to the new camera.

Once you have created a Free Camera in your scene, as per the previous steps, click the following icons as you explore to see how they'll help you navigate in a Camera viewport. Some of these navigation icons apply to a Target Camera only, and several of these icons are flyouts nested with other icons:

ICON	NAME	FUNCTION
	Dolly Camera	Moves the camera object to and from the object at which it is pointing.
	Dolly Target	Moves the camera's target to and from the object. This may not show any changes unless you use other camera tools, such as Orbit.
	Dolly Camera + Target	Moves the camera and target to and from the object at which it is pointing. This is available only if the camera has a target.
	Perspective	Adjusts Field Of View (FOV) and Dolly. Acts like a zoom camera lens.
	Roll	Rolls the camera around the line of sight for a Target Camera or if it is a Free Camera around the local *Z*-axis
	Truck	Moves the camera from side to side, parallel to your scene.
	Orbit	Rotates the camera around the target object selected in the scene. This is a flyout with the Pan Camera icon.
	Pan Camera	Rotates the target around the camera. This is a flyout with the Orbit icon.

LIGHT VIEWPORT CONTROLS

This set of tools shows your scene through the perspective of a light. This seems a bit unusual, but it can be very useful for exact positioning of your lights. Some tools for the light objects have the same name and are used the same as the Camera (Dolly, Roll, Truck, Orbit and Pan) navigation tools. Therefore, their icons are not repeated. However, the Light Viewport controls that are specific to lights are listed.

You will need to create a light in your scene just as you did for a previous camera in order to access these icons in the Viewport Controls section of the UI. To make a light in the scene, follow these steps:

1. Choose Create → Lights → Standard Lights → Free Spotlight, and click in one of your viewports to place the camera. You may also click the Create panel under the Lights category, and click the Free Spot icon. Figure 3.40 shows a light placed in the scene.

2. Right-click a viewport name in the upper-left corner of the viewport, and select Views → Fspot01, as shown in Figure 3.41. This will change the viewport to the light's view. You will now be able top access the Camera Viewport navigation tools shown in the following table.

ICON	NAME	FUNCTION
◎	Light Hotspot	This tool allows you to adjust the angle of the light's hotspot, which is the brightest part of the circle of light.
◉	Light Falloff	This tool allows you to adjust the angle of the light's falloff, which is the light fading to the back of the circle of light.

Light Viewport controls help you place your lights just the way you want them. You'll have plenty of hands-on experience with lights in Chapter 10, "3ds Max Lighting."

Tired of icons yet? Ninety-five percent of your viewport navigation will be performed using the keyboard shortcuts and the mouse buttons. This rich set of navigation tools gives you many options in how to move around in 3d space, but you needn't really worry about any of them until you are comfortable just getting around—and by now this should be coming easier to you.

Figure 3.40

A Free Spotlight

Navigating Viewports

The easiest way to navigate the viewports is to use the keyboard/mouse button combinations you used in the previous chapter while working on the Mobile exercise. Here again is a rundown on these keyboard/mouse actions:

Figure 3.41

Set your viewport to the new camera.

> **Pan**—Panning a viewport will "slide" the view around the screen. Simply **MM** click in the viewport and drag the mouse to move the view.

> **Zoom**—Zooming will move your view in closer or farther away from your objects. To zoom, use the middle wheel, or press Ctrl+Alt and **MM** click in your viewport, then drag the mouse up or down to zoom in or out, respectively. Zooming is sometimes called a *dolly* in other packages, while their version of a *zoom* deals with the virtual camera's lens itself.

> **Arc Rotate and Arc Rotate Selected**—Arc Rotate and Arc Rotate Selected will rotate your view around your objects. To use either of the two Arc Rotate tools, press Alt and **MM** click and drag in the viewport. By default, Max will rotate (or *tumble* as it's called in some other CG programs) about the center of the viewport to change your perspective. However, if an object is selected, 3ds Max will revert to Arc Rotate Selected, which will rotate about the center of the selected object instead of the center of the viewport. This way the object remains in the same position as the viewport rotates around the object.

The Viewports

Finally! We get to the hot action of the viewports. This is where 3d space is simulated. Viewports in 3ds Max are always set up in with four equally sized views when you first start with a Top, Front, Left, and Perspective viewport. When you are looking at your four views, you will notice one has a yellow highlighted border. This means that viewport is the selected view. You can activate a view by working in it, or you can just right-click your cursor in a view. Be careful about just clicking because if something is selected, it will be deselected.

You can also resize your viewports. Just center your cursor over the splitter bars that separate the views. Your cursor will change to a four-sided arrow, and you can click/drag to the size desired. To switch the viewport layout back to the default, right-click over the center splitter bars. A pop-up tag with "Reset Layout" will allow you to go back to the default. Let's not forget the Min/Max Viewport tool in the navigation area (or just press Alt+W). This will change the equally sized views into one full-screen view of the active viewport.

One way to change the default look of your viewports is to use the Viewport Configuration/Layout dialog box. You can find it by choosing Customize → Viewport Configuration and clicking the desired layout, as seen in Figure 3.42.

In each of the viewports, the axes are displayed in the lower-left corner of the World Space tripod. The axes are always displayed in red, green, and blue format to represent the *X*-, *Y*-, and *Z*-axes respectively, as seen in the Perspective viewport. You have seen this familiar color scheme at work in the gizmos as well.

You've undoubtedly noticed the Home Grid in your views by now. This grid is a ground plane that centers around the Origin (0,0,0). The Home Grid is a helper for construction of objects. When you create a new object, it is placed on the grid. The Home Grid's defaults can be edited for more effective scene creation, and they can be turned on and off easily by right-clicking the viewport name to access the pop-up menu. In that menu, you will see Show Grid. Click the grid to toggle it on and off. To use the keyboard shortcut to toggle the grid, press G.

The grid displays the units of your scene. The default is set up as Max Units where 1 unit equals 1 inch. Each grid division is 10 units. The best approach is to choose a grid

spacing that matches your unit of measurement. For example, if you are using centimeters make 1 grid square equal 1 centimeter. To access the Grid dialog box, choose Customize → Grid and Snap settings, and click the Home Grid tab as shown here. With the Home Grid tab, you can set the spacing of your home grid.

Changing Viewport Views

As you saw earlier, the viewports are flexible and can be changed to different displays by right-clicking on the viewport name and choosing the new viewport from the menu (Figure 3.43).

This way you can change which view you have in a viewport. You can also use keyboard shortcuts to access any of the viewports. In an active viewport, simply press the hotkey for the view desired view, as indicated in the following table:

HOTKEY	VIEW
T	Top
B	Bottom
F	Front
L	Left
C	Camera
P	Perspective
U	User or Axonometric—a 3D view without perspective

Figure 3.43

Changing viewports is easy.

These keys are extremely helpful when one viewport is maximized and you need to access different views quickly. For scenes that have more than one camera, press the C key to bring up a pop-up menu from which you can select the camera. With so many ways to change viewport views, you'll be able to find the way that works best for your workflow.

> Because the R shortcut enables the Select and Scale tool there is no keyboard shortcut for the Right viewport.

Viewport Rendering Levels

In a viewport, you have the ability to view your scene in a few different ways. For example, in the Mobile exercise you saw how you can switch between Wireframe and Smooth Shaded views. How you view objects in a viewport is referred to as *viewport rendering*. Again, you can access the different viewport rendering methods by right-clicking the viewport's name, as shown in Figure 3.44. Depending on the size of your scene, your viewport may be more responsive and have a less-taxing rendering display level.

Figure 3.44

Selecting the viewport's rendering level

The viewport rendering levels are explained in the following list:

Smooth+Highlights—Displays scene objects with smooth shading and specular highlights from the scene lights. This gives the best feedback for your objects.

Smooth—Displays objects with no highlights and only smooth shading.

Facets+Highlights: Displays scene objects with flat shading and displays specular highlights. This is a fast way to see your solid objects with highlights when Smooth+ Highlights is too taxing with heavy scenes.

Facets—Displays polygons as flat surfaces that are shaded, but includes no smoothing or scene highlights.

Flat—Displays each polygon in its raw diffuse color, disregarding any scene lighting or light sources. This viewing method is useful when you need to see every polygon rather than to see them shaded.

Hidden Line—A Wireframe mode that allows you to use the Wireframe mode without seeing through every object. In this display mode only, the wireframe color is determined by choosing Customize → Customize User Interface in the Colors tab under Elements → Viewports and selecting Hidden Line Unselected color, not the object or material color.

Lit Wireframes—Displays objects as their wireframes with a flat shading for a sense of lighting.

Wireframe—Draws objects as wireframes only. This is the fastest viewing method that still let's you see an object's shape.

Bounding Box—Displays objects as *bounding boxes*. Bounding boxes are approximations of the amount of volume a shape occupies. No shading is applied.

3ds Max will automatically display objects as bounding boxes when the geometry in a complex scene is too much for the display to handle when the viewport is being moved. You probably will not encounter this feature, called *adaptive degradation*, until you begin dealing with very large scenes. You can disable Adaptive Degradation by pressing the keyboard shortcut O.

Edged Faces—Edged Faces draws the wireframe of an object back onto its shape when it is displayed in one of the shaded modes: Smooth, Smooth+Highlights, Facets+Highlights, or Facets. This way you can see the wireframe lines and faces of an object for easier editing, while still seeing it shaded.

Setting the viewport rendering levels will help you with larger scenes. More often than not, you will be able to view your scenes with the Smooth+Highlights mode, giving you the best feedback. You consider changing the rendering level a notch or two lower to improve your system's responsiveness *only* when you notice that navigating inside a viewport is becoming slow.

Gizmos

As you saw in the Mobile exercise in the previous chapter, gizmos are ways of manipulating objects in your viewports interactively to transform them—i.e., translate (move), rotate, and/or scale. The gizmos appear in the viewport on the selected object at their pivot point as soon as you invoke one of the transformation tools.

When you invoke the Move tool by pressing W (or you access it through the toolbar), your gizmo looks like this:

The *XYZ*-axis gives you handles to move an object on one specific axis. You can also click on the box between two axes as shown to move the object in that plane, which is shown here as YZ:

Invoke the Rotate tool by pressing E. Your gizmo will turn into three circles as shown. You can click on one of the circles to rotate the object on the axis only, or you can click anywhere between the circles to freely rotate the selected object in all three axes.

Invoke the Scale tool by pressing the R key, and your gizmo will turn into a triangle, as shown here:

Clicking and dragging anywhere inside the yellow triangle will scale the object uniformly in all three axes. By selecting the red, green, or blue handles for the appropriate axis, you can scale along one axis only. You can also scale an object in a plane between two axes by selecting the side of the yellow triangle between two axes as shown here (along the *Y*- and *Z*-axes):

Keep in mind that the gizmos appear at an object's pivot point; therefore, if you have an object where you have relocated the pivot point away from the object itself, the gizmo will appear there and not on the object itself, as shown here where the rectangle's pivot is to the right of the object.

Using gizmos is a fast and effective way to transform your objects with interactive feedback. The Transforms Type-In boxes at the bottom of the screen display coordinate or angular or percentage information on the position/rotation/scale of your object as you transform it.

In the following graphic, a cube is being transformed in the *Y*-axis. The Transforms Type-In box indicates how much it is being moved.

Managing Scene Objects

Max has a few ways to organize and manage your scene elements to make working with things easier. These tools include the Layer Manager, the Schematic View, the Material Editor, and the Curve Editor/Dope Sheet. The Layer Editor works with objects to organize them in layers. The Schematic View allows you to view, manage, and edit your scene's hierarchies. The Layer Editor and Schematic View windows are outlined for you here, and they are used extensively throughout this book.

The Material Editor allows you to manage your scene's materials and textures. The Material Editor is covered in Chapter 7, "Materials and Mapping." The Curve Editor manages the animation in your scene by giving you access to animation curves. The Dope Sheet manages the animation in your scene by giving you access to animation ranges or sets of keys. The Curve Editor is covered in Chapter 8, and the Dope Sheet is covered in Chapter 9.

Layer Editor

The Layout Editor can be accessed through the main menu: Tools → Layer Manager or through the Main Toolbar icon 📚 (Figure 3.45).

Layers can be used to group and organize scene objects. 3ds Max layers are organized similarly to Photoshop layers; you can organize different elements of an image in separate layers. Layers are mainly used for object visibility, default color control, and freezing and hiding control. All of these functions help you organize your scene and make object management easier. You will use the Layer Manager in future exercises in this book. The icons across the top of the Layer Manager are explained here:

Create New Layer—Creates a new layer when you have objects selected in your scene.

Delete Highlighted Empty Layers—Deletes selected layers if they are empty.

Figure 3.45
The Layer Manager

Add Selected Objects to Highlighted Layer—Moves currently selected objects into the selected layer.

Select Highlighted Objects and Layers—Selects all of highlighted objects, as well as all objects contained in any highlighted layers.

Highlight Selected Objects' Layers—Highlights layers containing the currently selected objects and automatically scrolls so that highlighted layers are visible in the layer manager.

Hide/Unhide All Layers—Toggles the display of all layers.

Freeze/Unfreeze All Layers—Toggles the frozen state of all layers.

The columns in the window are the following:

Layers—Displays the names of the layers/objects. To select or rename a layer, just click on the name. To display object or layer properties, click the object icon to open the Object Properties dialog box for all highlighted objects.

Current Layer Toggle—The unlabeled column to the right of the layer name indicates the current layer. It lets you make a different layer current. The check mark next to a layer means it is selected and current.

Hide—Hides and unhides layers. When a layer is hidden, it's invisible.

Freeze—Freezes layers. Frozen layers can not be selected.

Render—When on, objects appear in the rendered scene. Nonrendering objects don't cast shadows or affect the visual component of the rendered scene.

Color—Changes the default color on highlighted objects.

Radiosity—When on, objects are included in the radiosity solution.

Using the Layer Editor

Let's take a quick look at how the Layer Manager can help you with a scene. Just follow these steps:

1. Open a new scene and create four new objects: a box, a sphere, a cone, and a torus as shown here.

2. Open the Layer Manager by choosing Tools → Layer Manager or by clicking the Layer Manager icon ⧉ in the main toolbar. Click the Create New Layer icon ⧉ to create two new layers.

> To select more than one object in a viewport, press the Ctrl key as you click on additional objects to add to your selection. Many applications use the Shift key to add to a selection; however, Max uses Ctrl.

3. In the viewport, select the box and the sphere and assign them to Layer01 by selecting Layer01 and clicking the Add Selected Objects to Highlighted Layer icon ⊕ in the Layer Manager, as shown here.

4. As you did in Step 3, assign the cone to Layer02. Select Layer01 and turn on Freeze. The sphere and box will turn gray in the viewport and will no longer be able to be selected. Click Hide, and the box and sphere will disappear from the viewports.

Experiment with toggling Hide and Freeze for the objects or the layers so that you can see how your scene reacts when they are on and off. You will quickly see how useful the Layer Manager can be for organizing and managing your scene objects. You will use the Layer Manager throughout the rest of this book.

Schematic View

The Schematic View is another way to organize and manage your scene, particularly object hierarchies. This window displays the objects in your scene in a flowchart scheme, allowing you to see how objects are linked or grouped together. Parents connect down the flowchart to their children. This method of viewing hierarchies is powerful, because you get an immediate visualization of how the objects in your scene work and relate to each other.

While we're talking about hierarchies, let's return to the Mobile exercise from the previous chapter and see how the Schematic View depicts the scene. Figure 3.46 shows the Mobile scene in the Schematic View.

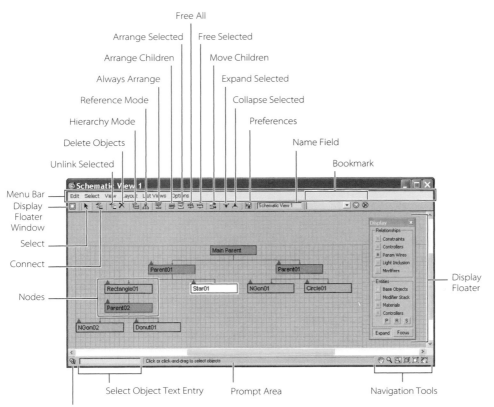

Figure 3.46
The Mobile scene displayed in the Schematic View immediately tells you how the objects are organized.

The Schematic View makes editing character rigs easier, allowing you to view, create, and edit links between objects. A scene can become so complicated that trying to select one object is impossible. The Schematic View can help you simplify the selection process. It displays every object in the scene clearly as a box with the object's name displayed in it. You can use the MM button to pan around in the Schematic View, or you can use any of the familiar navigation icons found in the lower right-hand corner of the window, as seen in Figure 3.46.

When you select any object in the schematic, its parameter automatically appears in the Modify panel for easy editing. Because objects can have different states of being, different conventions are used to indicate an object's current state in the scene, with the more important states listed here:

Red Border—The object is animated.

White Fill—The object is currently selected in the Schematic View window.

White Border—The object is currently selected in a viewport.

Up Arrow—To simplify a view, pressing the Up arrow collapses that node and its dependent child nodes up to the next highest parent, collapsing them into one node for simpler display. This is useful for large characters and long hierarchy chains, so you don't have to see all the child nodes in a large scene. This does not remove the hierarchy, it only affects the display of them.

Down Arrow—Conversely, to gain more information from a group of objects, clicking the down arrow expands the next child down from that node to show you its immediate child node(s).

In the Mobile scene, you can see how the Main Parent node runs the show. This is the top bar of the Mobile, and the second row of bars hangs from it as its children. The shapes on the Mobile are below them.

The toolbar across the top of the Schematic View is used for editing hierarchies in your scene. We will experiment with reordering the Mobile hierarchy in the Schematic View in just a moment. First, here are the tools as called out in Figure 3.46:

Display Floater—This toggles the Display Floater window, which gives you access to display toggles for certain object types in the Schematic View.

Select—This allows you to select objects in the Schematic View. When you select an object in a viewport, its node in the Schematic View will be outlined in white. However, it will not necessarily be selected in the Schematic View as well. If you want to be able to select an object in either window just once and have it selected in both the Schematic View and the viewports, choose Select → Sync Selection in the Schematic View window.

Connect—Just as you created links between objects in the Mobile project, you can create links in the Schematic View. Simply click on the child object and drag it to the desired parent.

Unlink Selected—To break links between objects, simply click the child to unlink and click this icon.

Delete Objects—Deletes the selected object(s) from the scene. If you make a mistake, you can press the Undo icon in the main toolbar or press Ctrl+Z to get the object(s) back.

Hierarchy Mode—Lays out the Schematic View as an outline view, as seen here.

References Mode—Lays out the view in the Schematic View, as shown here. This view is good for viewing object relationships and materials.

Always Arrange—The Schematic View will keep the node display rigid. As you see in the Reference Mode graphic, you will not be able to freely move nodes around. Turning this Always Arrange mode off allows you to arrange the nodes any way you want, as shown here.

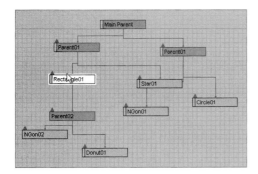

The next group of icons—Arrange Children, Arrange Selected, Free All, and Free Selected—all have to do with automatically arranging nodes when you turn off Always Arrange.

Move Children—When you click and drag a node, all of its child nodes will follow it when this icon is toggled on.

Expand and **Collapse Selected**—This icon is used to reveals or hide the child nodes of the node selected.

Preferences—This icon is used to toggle the Preferences window for the Schematic View. You can filter certain object types (such as lights, cameras, objects, etc.) from displaying in the schematic.

Schematic View Name Field—One very useful feature of the Schematic View is that you can save certain views to recall later for easy access. When you have a heavy scene, with tons of nodes to view, getting to the right place in a complicated hierarchy can take some time. You can simply type a name for your current view into this text box

Figure 3.47

Accessing a saved Schematic View

and 3ds Max will save the view for you. To access that particular view again, in the main Menu Bar, select Graph Editors → Saved Schematic Views → Schematic View Name. See Figure 3.47.

Bookmark Name Field—In this field, you can define a selection of nodes in the Schematic View as a bookmark that you can later return to them easily.

Using the Schematic View with the Mobile

Let's take a look at the Schematic View in action, and have another whack at the Mobile scene's hierarchy.

You can start with your own Mobile scene file, or load the scene `Mobile_v04.max` from the scenes folder in the Mobile project on the companion CD. Just follow these steps:

1. With your Mobile scene loaded, open the Schematic View by choosing Graph Editors → New Schematic View or by clicking Schematic View (Open) icon in the main toolbar, as shown in Figure 3.48.

2. Unlink the Star object from the Mobile and relink it to the Circle object. To do this, click the Connect button and then select the Star01 node and drag it to the Circle01 node, as shown in Figure 3.49.

3. When you release the mouse button, notice that the Star01 node is linked under the Circle01 node, as shown in Figure 3.50. The Star was automatically unlinked from its old parent.

Figure 3.48

The Schematic View for the Mobile scene

Figure 3.49

Reconnecting the Star to the Circle

Figure 3.50

The Star is linked under the Circle.

You can see how easy it is to restructure your scene hierarchies using the Schematic View. All the controls for viewing and arranging nodes might be a bit much for one window. You probably won't need half those icons, but knowing how to use the Schematic View is important. It is an important tool in organizing and setting up your scenes for animation. You will continue to use the Schematic View throughout this book.

Summary

Wow! That was a lot of information. Reference this chapter as you work with Max on the tutorials in this book and any other Max work you have. This chapter was less about absorbing all that information than about giving you a single reference to use to look up UI issues.

Nevertheless, you learned how to navigate the menus, toolbars, icons, panels, and windows in 3ds Max. This chapter outlined the icons and buttons you will come across most often, and it attempted to show you everything on the main Max UI screen and briefly describe what it does.

Complete understanding of how to use Max comes with time and experience. To develop that understanding, you need to work on projects that further challenge you and get you moving around inside the UI. This book begins that ride and tries to give you a good push in the right direction. Take everything in this chapter with a grain of salt, and head into the coming chapters.

CHAPTER 4

Modeling in 3ds Max: Part I

Modeling in 3d programs is akin to sculpting or carpentry; you essentially create objects out of shapes and forms. No matter how you look at it, even a complex model is just an amalgam of simpler parts. The successful modeler can dissect a form down to its components and translate them into surfaces and meshes.

3ds Max's modeling tools are incredibly strong for polygonal modeling. The focus of this book will be on polygonal modeling because the majority of 3ds Max models are created with polygons. In addition, you will model organics here. You will get to model an alien creature and use that model to animate a character, using SubDivision surfaces.

In this chapter, you will learn modeling concepts and how to use 3ds Max modeling toolsets. You will also tackle two different models.

Topics in this chapter include:

- **Planning Your Model**
- **Modeling Concepts**
- **Modifiers and the Modifier Stack**
- **Modeling a Chest of Drawers**
- **Modeling a Hand**

Planning Your Model

The most important thing to know before you begin to model is exactly *what* you are going to model. That seems rather stupid to say, but it's true. You need to think about your model and gather as many references as you can. The best training you can hope to gain is simply by observing the core elements and forms that make up objects in everyday life. Learn how to dissect things around you into component shapes that you can picture in a 3d window. When you look at a barbell, for example, you should see several cylinders connected to each other. When you see an office chair, you should see a few boxes and cylinders arranged and rounded at the edges. When you begin to see objects in this manner, the idea of modeling them may not seem quite as daunting.

"Yeah, but all my friends can sit down and model anything they want." Be that as it may, if you are a novice to 3d, surround yourself with references. Even if you are not new to 3d or to modeling, you should surround yourself with as many references as you can. Not having a clear picture in your head of where you need to go for your model will just aggravate the process and give you a slack result.

Take pictures all around the proposed object. Get the dimensions, sizes, angles, and slopes of the surfaces of your subject. You could even try to first re-create the object in a different medium. Try sketching the subject, or grab some children's Play-Doh or a plate of mashed potatoes and make a rough sculpture. It may seem like a lot of effort to build something trivial, but it will pay off in the long run.

But enough of that old lecture.

Your first question should be, "How detailed should I make the model?" As you may have read in the first chapter, it's always a good idea to match the level of detail for a model to what is needed in the shot. If you are featuring the object up close and personal, then you should take care to build it with extra detail, adding as many polygons as it takes to make it look good and still render. If, however, the object is far away and half obscured, detailing the heck out of it would be a waste of time. In Figure 4.1 on the left, you can see a park bench in a far shot compared to a view of the bench up close on the right. It would be a waste of effort and time to detail the bench to exacting levels when the bench will be seen *only* in a far shot.

You should ask yourself what the model will be used for when you are deciding how best to detail it. If you are not sure of how the model will be used in the end, it's generally best to create as much detail as you think necessary. You can always prune down the details later if, for example, your scene ends up very large and will not render.

Here's another thing to confuse you: you can always add detail to a model with texturing. Textures, when applied well, can really turn an otherwise ho-hum model into a spectacular object when rendered. Such details as grooves, dents, and engravings can easily be

Figure 4.1
The level of detail in a model depends on how much of the model is seen.

added with certain texture maps called *bump maps* or *displacement maps*. You will learn about them in Chapter 7, "Materials and Mapping." Don't worry about it, though. Most people begin by modeling all the details they can into their model, and as they gain more experience, they start to realize that some of the modeling work can be handed off to the texturing phase.

Modeling Concepts

To get a foothold in modeling, you will need to understand a number of things. If you are not new to CG, feel free to skip ahead and get your hands dirty modeling. However, you still might want to peruse this section for some concepts and terms that may make things easier for you in the coming exercises.

Polygons

A *polygon* is a surface created by connecting three or more points in 3d space. This flat surface connects to other polygons to form more intricate surfaces. In Figure 4.2, you see a sphere. The facets of the sphere are polygons, all connected at common *edges* at the correct angles and in the proper arrangement to make a sphere.

The points that generate a polygon are called *vertices*. The lines that connect the points are called *edges*. If the polygon has three vertices, its surface is called a *face*. Polygons are made up of triangular faces by design. In the example of the sphere in Figure 4.2, the polygon facets all have four vertices. As you can see in the following graphic, the same sphere is seen, although now a face is selected. See how the face is half of the polygon, using three of its vertices.

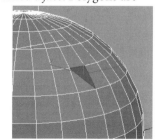

Figure 4.2

A sphere is made up of polygons.

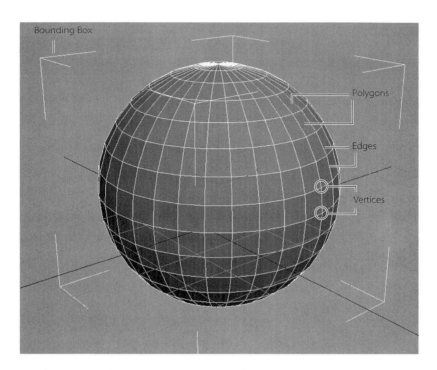

The more polygons you have in a model, the more detailed it becomes. However, greater numbers of polygons tax your system and take longer to render. This is where the term *low-poly modeling* originates. In computer or console games, the machine renders the scene on the fly, so its computation requirements are strict. The fewer the polygons in the scene, the faster the game can play back. Games frequently use low-poly models to maximize the effect in their game without sacrificing precious computational cycles.

Higher resolution models are typically used in television and film, because the scenes are all rendered beforehand and then laid off to video tape or output to film. A computational ceiling is still dictated by the machines that are used in creating the TV or film animations, however, so it is always a good idea to be smart when creating models.

Primitives

Primitives are the basic 3D geometric shapes that are automatically generated by 3D modeling applications. As such, they do not need to be constructed from scratch. A considerable amount of modeling (perhaps most) begins with primitives, which are then edited and used with other primitives to create more complex objects. Use primitives as the core of your object. For example, to sculpt an apple, you might start out with a sphere primitive.

As you can see in Figure 4.3, 3ds Max affords you plenty of primitives to choose from for your original form. All of these primitives have their own parameters for customizing the form to your liking. You have already seen how to create some of these objects in Chapter 2's Mobile exercise.

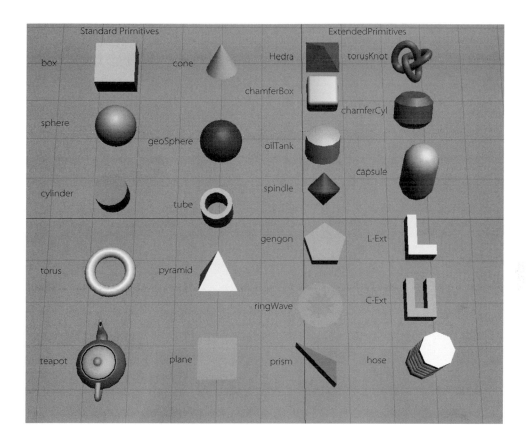

Figure 4.3

3ds Max standard and extended primitives

Objects such as the primitives would be useless in Max if you could not edit them to suit your needs. For example, you could sculpt a sphere into the shape of an apple. To sculpt a surface, you will need to convert your object (such as the sphere for the apple) into an editable object, frequently called a *mesh*, to get to the object's component level where you can move points and reshape faces that make up the object or primitive. We will look at that in the next section.

Meshes and Sub-Objects

Once you have chosen a primitive that will best work for your intended model, you begin the modeling process by *changing the primitive into a mesh object* to access the components of the object with which you will edit the model (such as vertices, faces, etc.).

In 3ds Max, *mesh* objects are defined by smaller component pieces that form the object as a whole. The smaller components (called *sub-objects*) can be manipulated to adjust the shape of the object or to form more complex models. Once you convert your object in 3ds Max to an editable object such as a mesh, you can edit using the sub-objects available for that object.

For instance, mesh models break down your object into a number of individual flat surfaces—polygons and faces. With meshes, you can select any of the sub-objects at different component levels such as the polygons, vertices, or faces of the mesh to make adjustments while sculpting your model.

In 3ds Max, there are two ways to create a mesh object: by applying a *modifier* to the base object or primitive, or by *converting* the primitive to a mesh. Both methods give you access to the sub-object level for editing. The one big difference, however, can be critical if you need to edit the base object—for example, if you want to change the radius of a primitive sphere *after* you start editing it as a mesh. Instead of converting, you are better off using the modifier method because it preserves the original primitive object intact and allows you to modify the object's *original* parameters (such as radius for a sphere) even after you begin to edit the mesh.

In this exercise, you will create an object and turn it into a mesh in the following steps:

1. Create a sphere in a new scene using the Create panel. You will turn this object into a mesh to check out the sub-objects at your disposal.

2. With the sphere selected, switch to the Modify panel. Figure 4.4 shows the newly created sphere. Notice the Sphere heading in the Modifier List on the right.

Figure 4.4

The newly created sphere awaits your command.

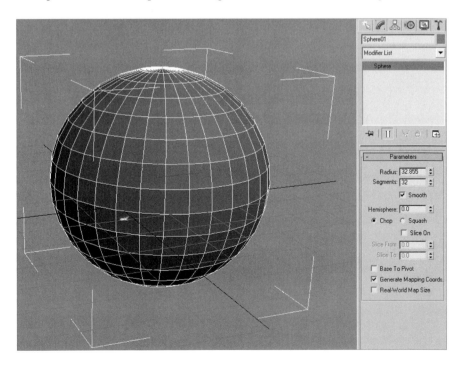

3. With the sphere selected, choose Modifiers → Mesh Editing → Edit Mesh. This will apply an Edit Mesh modifier to the sphere, giving you access to the sub-objects that a mesh affords you.

4. The Modifier Stack will display a heading called Edit Mesh. Highlight Edit Mesh in the Modifier Stack to see what is shown in Figure 4.5.

5. Under the Selection heading in the Modify panel, select the type of sub-object you would like to begin editing. Choose the first icon ·.· for Vertex.

6. As you can see in Figure 4.6, small dots appear on the sphere. They are the vertices you can now select. Choose the Move tool and select one of the vertices on the sphere. Click and drag to move the vertex anywhere to sculpt the surface of the sphere, as shown in Figure 4.6.

7. Change your sub-object selection to polygons by choosing the Polygon icon ■ in the Modify panel. The vertices will disappear from the viewport. Change to Edged Faces display mode in the viewport either by right-clicking the viewport name or by pressing the F4 shortcut.

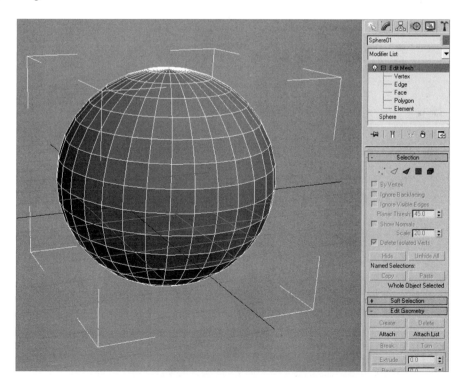

Figure 4.5

You now have access to the Edit Mesh's sub-objects.

8. Click on a polygon to select it. Notice the polygon turns red in the viewport. Move the selected polygon around to see how the surface of the sphere mesh changes (Figure 4.7).

9. Try selecting the other sub-object types and changing the shape of the sphere.

10. In the Modifier Stack, click on the original sphere entry. You will still have access to changing the radius and other parameters of the original primitive. Changing any of these parameters does not negate the Edit Mesh modifier.

Figure 4.6

Adjusting sub-objects such as vertices allows you to sculpt your model.

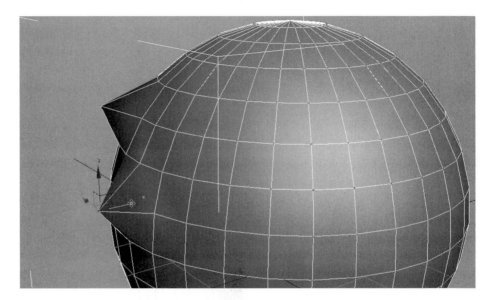

Figure 4.7

Selecting and playing around with a polygon sub-object on the sphere mesh

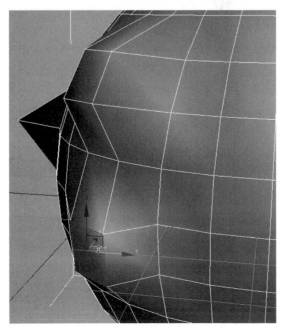

As you can see, you have greater control over the shape of your model once you access the sub-object levels of an Edit mesh. You'll see quite a bit of mesh editing in the exercises throughout this book. One exercise you can do now quickly is to try to sculpt a simple cartoon head using nothing but sub-object manipulation on a base sphere.

In some 3d packages, you have inherent access to a model's components (such as a vertex or face). However, with Max you will need to either convert created objects into meshes or add the appropriate modifier to create a mesh, as you did in the previous exercise, to manipulate the sub-objects. You will be modeling with meshes later in this chapter, and you will learn other ways to access sub-objects on a model.

Modifiers

Modifiers, as you have already seen, are a way to edit your objects in 3ds Max. In almost all cases, you can apply several modifiers to an object to get the desired result. In the Modify panel's Modifier Stack, you can access any of those modifiers to change any of its parameters at any time in your modeling. This is perhaps one of the strongest aspects of modeling in 3ds Max.

Max has tons of modifiers that accomplish any number of tasks. These tasks need not be limited to editing models, though; many modifiers work well in animation and dynamics chores as well. In this section, we will cover a few modeling-specific modifiers and more importantly, we will see how the Modifier Stack operates.

Figure 4.8

The Twist modifier is now applied to the box. You can still access the original parameters of the box.

Applying Modifiers

Let's take a quick look at how modifiers work on editing objects. In the following steps, you will apply a few modifiers to an object.

1. In a new scene, create a tall box in the Perspective viewport, as shown here.

2. With the box selected, choose Modifiers → Parametric Deformers → Twist. The box gains an orange outline and Twist shows up in the Modifier Stack. Go to the Modify panel to see the Modifier Stack, as shown in Figure 4.8. Click Twist in the Modifier Stack to access its parameters.

3. Click the Angle spinner and drag the mouse to increase the Angle to 240 or so. As you can see in Figure 4.9, the box gets completely strange. You can see the box twist pretty nicely at first, but the higher the Angle on the Twist, the more shearing the box will undergo, to the point where it no longer resembles what a twisted box should look like.

4. The box is suffering from a case of low definition, meaning the box does not have enough *segments* to handle the twist deformation without turning inside out. You will need to add more segments to the box for a smoother twist effect. In the Modifier Stack, click the Box entry to access the parameters for the box, before the Twist modifier.

5. To see the effect of adding more segments to the box better, enable Edged Faces in the viewport (right-click Perspective, the viewport name) and select Edged Faces from the context menu.

6. Click the Length Segs parameter spinner and increase the value to 4. Increase the Width Segs to 4 and the Height Segs to 16. As you increase the segments in the original box, the Twist Modifier takes on a much nicer shape. Figure 4.10 shows the box with more segments.

7. You can increase the segments as much you prefer; however, it's best to use the least number of segments in an object that will give you the desired result. Increasing the segments essentially increases the polygons in the surface.

Figure 4.9

The box is twisted out of shape.

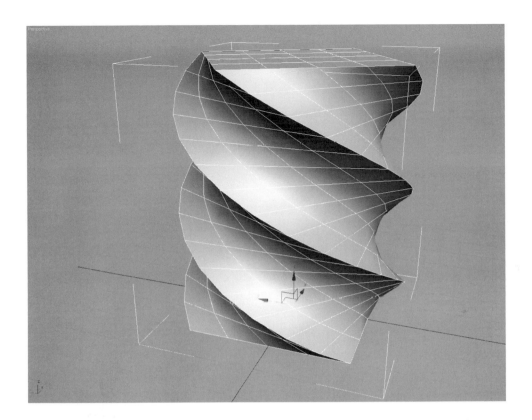

Figure 4.10

Adding more segments to the box makes the deformation from the Twist modifier smoother.

8. Now add another modifier to the box. Select the box and highlight the box entry in the Modifier Stack. Choose Modifier → Parametric Deformers → Spherify. Your box should look like a ball (Figure 4.11). Neat!

9. Play with the Spherify modifier's only parameter (Percentage) to see how the twisted box can turn into a sphere. Although this is kind of a neat trick, you don't really need this modifier, so go ahead and remove it from the stack. In the Modifier Stack, click the Spherify entry and click the Trash Can icon ☋ at the bottom of the Modifier List, as shown here. This will remove the Spherify modifier without harming anything else, and it will return the box to its twisted state.

Modifiers are powerful editing and animation tools. Take some time to play around in a scene such as the one from this previous exercise, and apply different deformers to objects and see what they do. It's really best to learn by experience sometimes. The Parametric Deformer modifiers are especially fun to play with, as you can see. You have not seen the last of modifiers in this book; they are an integral part of the 3ds Max workflow and will be used all throughout this book. We will take a look at the Modifier Stack in the next section, now that you have had some exposure to it already.

Figure 4.11
Spherify the box.

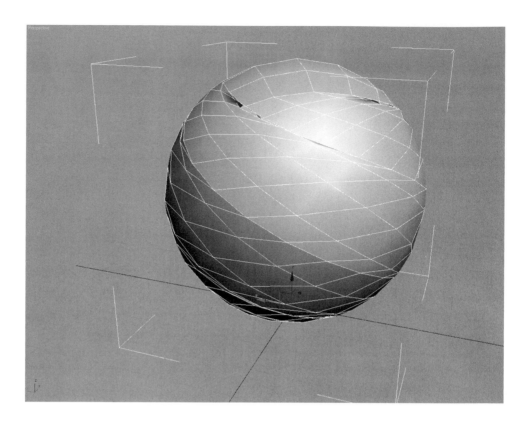

Modifier Stack with a Side of Maple Syrup

The Modifier Stack displays the modifiers added to any objects. It gives you access to any of the parameters for the modifiers applied to the object, as well as the original parameters of the object itself. When working with the Modifier Stack, you have several options you can in access through the icons below the stack itself, as shown in Figure 4.12.

Pin Stack If you want to freeze the display on the Modify panel controls on the currently selected object, click this icon. Pin Stack locks the stack and all the controls in the panel so that you can see that object's stack even while you have other objects selected in the scene.

Show End Result When on, it shows the effect of the entire stack on the selected object. When off, it shows the effect of the stack only up to the currently highlighted modifier.

Make Unique With a certain type of object duplication (instancing), making any adjustments to the instanced copy also reflects in the original object. Make Unique separates the objects and disallows a shared adjustment, so if you apply a modifier to an instanced copy, it will not reflect in the original object when Make Unique is applied.

Figure 4.12

**The Modifier Stack's
controls**

Remove Modifier This deletes the current modifier from the stack, eliminating all changes caused by that modifier.

Configure Modifier Sets This displays a menu that allows you to configure the display of the Modify panel and choose which modifiers will be available to you directly from the Modify panel, without having to access the drop-down list.

Sub-Object Icon The plus or minus icon to the right of the Modifier name signifies that you have access to the sub-object (or sub-modifier) levels.

Light Bulb Icon This turns the effect of the modifier on and off. This is very useful for troubleshooting and verifying the effect of a particular modifier in a stack.

Order in the Stack

Unless changed, the Modifier Stack contains a history of an object's modifiers in the order they were applied. The Stack is read and applied to the object from the bottom going up, with the original object's entry at the very bottom. As you can imagine, the order in which you stack your modifiers is very important. You can get very different results from the same objects with the same modifiers in a different order.

Fortunately, changing the order of modifiers in the stack is very easy. In the Modifier Stack, simply click the modifier you want to move and drag it to its new position in the stack. Once you release the mouse button, a blue line will demarcate where in the stack the modifier will be placed.

For example, you can start with a cylinder and apply the Bend modifier (Modifiers → Parametric Deformers → Bend) to the cylinder first, as seen in Figure 4.13.

Figure 4.13

A cylinder with the Bend modifier applied

Now if you want to pinch in, or taper the bent side of the cylinder, you can add a Taper modifier (Modifiers → Parametric Deformers → Taper) to the stack. The results won't look the way you would expect, as you can see in Figure 4.14.

Figure 4.14

Trying to taper the bent side of the cylinder does not work with the Taper modifier—yet.

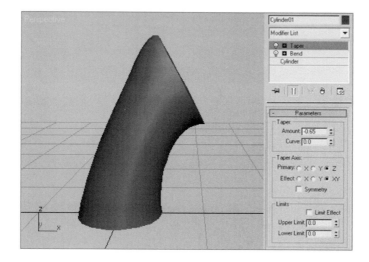

Now go to the Modifier Stack, click and drag the Taper modifier, and move it below the Bend modifier (Figure 4.15). These are the results you want to see. You want to "Bend the Taper" not "Taper the Bend."

Figure 4.15

This is the way it's supposed to look.

Look at the Mesh You Got Us Into!

As you saw earlier in this chapter, to access the sub-object level of objects, you will need to turn them into a mesh. You've seen how you can add an Edit Mesh modifier to an object so you can begin to sculpt the surface using vertices and faces. What if you were told there are tons of editing tools that come with meshes? Yeah, it's like that.

When you create a mesh from an object, you not only have access to the sub-objects of that object but also a host of tools to allow you to edit the surface. How do you get to a mesh? There are at least four different ways to get a mesh.

Convert Versus Modifier

You can *add* the Edit Mesh or Edit Poly modifiers to an object, or you can *convert* to an Editable Mesh or Editable Poly. Converting to an Editable Mesh or adding an Edit Mesh modifier is roughly the same; they both host the same toolset and allow you the same sub-object levels for the mesh. However, adding a modifier allows you to edit the parameters of the original object, as you may have seen earlier in the chapter.

To experiment with the modifiers, try this exercise:

1. Create two spheres in a new scene, and place them side by side, as seen here in Figure 4.16.

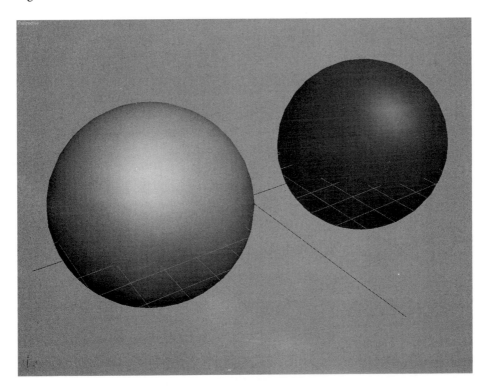

Figure 4.16

Two spheres side by side

2. Select the sphere on the left and apply an Edit Mesh modifier to it (choose Modifiers → Mesh Editing → Edit Mesh).

3. Select the sphere on the right and convert it to an Editable Mesh by first right-clicking on the sphere's entry in the Modifier Stack. From the context menu that appears when you right-click, choose Editable Mesh under the Convert To: heading, as seen here.

4. Take turns clicking back and forth between the two spheres. You should notice very little difference in the toolsets in the Modify panel. Figure 4.17 shows the Modify panel for the sphere with the Edit Mesh modifier, and Figure 4.18 shows the Modify panel for the Editable Mesh sphere.

5. Notice, however, that the Editable Mesh sphere no longer has the same Modifier Stack entries. This sphere now simply displays as Editable Mesh in the Modifier Stack. You should also note that the Editable Mesh sphere also has a rollout at the bottom of the Modifier panel called Surface Properties. Aside from those two issues, the modifier and the conversion are exactly the same.

The Convert method has its own advantages, however. Converting to an Editable Mesh, as opposed to applying the Edit Mesh modifier, saves memory and is more efficient because it doesn't have to save the base object's parameter information. However, using the modifier gives you the little bit of comfort because you can always go back to the original object and remove the Edit Mesh modifier at any time. You cannot reconvert an Editable Mesh back to its original object.

Mesh Versus Poly

What about Edit Mesh versus Edit Poly modifier and Editable Mesh versus Editable Poly? Which is better to use? Well, so far you have seen the Edit Mesh modifier and the Editable Mesh. A more up-to-date toolset for sub-object tools is obtained through the Edit Poly modifier or Editable Poly, and it is the preferred way to go for many 3ds Max artists. Then why show the Edit Mesh modifier and Editable Mesh? They are all good to know, and you should understand how they function relatively.

Having said that, we'll concentrate on the Edit Poly modifier and Editable Poly for this chapter's exercises—so let's take a look!

Edit Poly Modifier/Editable Poly

The Edit Poly modifier gives you plenty of controls to edit an object, just like the Edit Mesh modifier does. Figure 4.19 shows the Modify panel entries for the Edit Poly modifier on a sphere.

Figure 4.17

The sphere with the Edit Mesh modifier

Figure 4.18

The sphere converted to an editable mesh has basically the same toolset.

Figure 4.19

Edit Poly modifier applied to a sphere

Figure 4.20

Polygon faces on this box have three edges or sides, making them triangular. A Polygon on this box has four edges, or sides, making it a square.

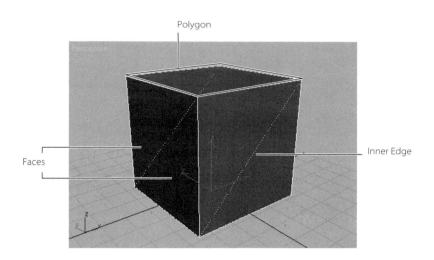

The differences between Mesh and Poly are few. Editable Mesh gives you a sub-object level called *faces* that are polygons with just three edges (they have three vertices). Figure 4.20 shows you faces on a box object.

When modeling with an Editable Mesh (or through the Edit Mesh modifier), having faces gives you an inner edge where the faces meet along the center of the polygon. The inner edge can cause all kinds of problems even when you are working in Poly mode. An Editable Poly is similar to an Editable Mesh, but it gives you access to four-sided polygons instead of faces. It also hosts a slew of other, more refined tools and selection options.

In addition, the toolsets found in the Edit Poly/Editable Poly are more fleshed out than Edit Mesh/Editable Mesh and have been updated more, so they will give you slightly more options. The major difference between the toolsets in the Editable Poly and the Edit Poly modifier is that you have inherent access to SubDivision modeling on the Editable Poly.

In the next section, you will find the Edit Poly modifier and the Editable Poly.

Edit Poly/Editable Poly Tools

In this section, you will explore the actual toolsets in the Edit Poly/Editable Poly world. Most of these toolsets will also apply to the toolsets you will find in the Edit Mesh/Editable Mesh world as well, although some may be used slightly differently. In either case, using an Edit Poly modifier or an Editable Poly is preferred.

Similarly, the toolset in an Editable Poly is very similar to those found with the Edit Poly modifier, so here is a rundown on the rollouts and toolsets you will find for the Editable Poly (and many cross over for the Edit Poly as well).

When you convert a primitive to an Editable Poly, in the Modify panel interface, you can see the controls for manipulating an object at sub-object levels. They are very similar to the sub-objects you learned about earlier in the book with the Edit Mesh modifier. In all, there are six rollouts (as shown here). The main ones are Selection, Edit Geometry, and Subdivision Surface.

Selection Rollout

The Selection rollout contains tools used to access different levels of the object's sub-objects and their display in the viewport. You can also find information about the selected components in this rollout, as shown in Figure 4.21.

When you first create an Editable Poly and access the Modifier panel, you are in the Object level, meaning you will select the object. By clicking the different sub-object level icons at the top of this rollout (see Figure 4.22), you can access the different selection levels as well as their relevant tools. Clicking the icon off will return you to the Object selection level again.

You can also select the desired sub-object level by clicking the plus sign (+) next to the Editable Poly entry in the Modifier Stack and selecting one of the entries, as shown here.

Here are the different sub-object levels for an Editable Poly:

Vertex Vertices define the structure of other sub-objects that make up the poly. They are simply points in space. However, when a vertex is moved, the geometry that they form is changed accordingly. While your Editable Poly is selected, you can use keyboard shortcut 1 to select the Vertex level.

Edge The line connecting two vertices together is an *edge* and, therefore, creates the side of a polygon. Edges can be shared by only two polygons. You can use keyboard shortcut 2 to enter Edge level selection.

Figure 4.21

The Selection rollout for an Editable Poly

Border A *border* is the edge of a hole. A surface's edge contains polygons that are not flanked by other polygons; in essence, they are on the edge of the surface. The row of edges on the perimeter of that surface is the border. You may invoke Border-level selection by pressing 3.

Polygon A *polygon* is a flat shape created by connecting three or more vertices, forming a closed shape. Polygons are what actually render when you output your scene in rendering. Press the 4 key to enter the Polygon level.

Figure 4.22

The sub-object icons for an Editable Poly

Element   An Element allows you to select all the polygons in an object. Press the 5 key to enter the Element level.

Also, the Selection modifier has a few selection options that will help you quickly alter your selection to suit your needs better. The following covers a few of the important selection options:

By Vertex   When you click the check box, you can select sub-objects by selecting the vertex they are near. This feature is grayed out when you are in Vertex mode.

Ignore Backfacing   When you click the check box you can select only the sub-objects that are facing you. With the default, which is *off,* you can select any sub-object(s) whether they are facing you or even visible. Think of it like selecting a dot on an orange. With Ignore Backfacing turned on, you can select a dot only on the side of the orange you can see. With Ignore Backfacing off, you can select any dot—even if it is on the side of the orange that's away from you.

By Angle   When you select a polygon with By Angle enabled, 3ds Max will also select the neighboring polygons based on the value given for the angle in the text box next to this check box. This value determines the maximum angle between neighboring polygons that may be selected.

Shrink   When you have made a sub-object selection, but you feel the selection is too wide, use Shrink. Shrink will deselect the outermost sub-objects to shrink your selection.

Grow   Conversely, you can make a small selection of sub-objects and use Grow to increase the selection area outward in all available directions.

Loop   Once you select an edge, you can propagate that selection to all the edges continuously around the mesh object by clicking the Loop icon. In the image on the left, a single edge is selected. The entire loop of edges is selected in the image on the right.

Ring Similar to the Loop function, Ring propagates an edge selection to the ring of edges perpendicular to the edge selected. In the following image on the left, there is a single edge selection. In the image on the right, the edges are selected with the Ring function.

Soft Selection Rollout

As you already know, a regular selection simply selects what you pick in the viewport for editing. You can, however, create a *soft selection* (shown in Figure 4.23), where a falloff effect emanates from your selection area toward the unselected sub-objects. In this case, the unselected sub-objects gain a partial selection value that is displayed in the viewports as a color gradient on the vertices or faces. When you apply a transformation—for example, if you move the soft selection—the actual selection will transform at a 1:1 ratio, while the falloff area of the "partial" selection will react at a lesser ratio according to the gradient falloff. This is similar to picking up a tablecloth with two fingers. The cloth between the two fingers is the full selection, while the cloth around the fingers falls off and does not lift up off the table as high as your fingers.

You can adjust the amount of falloff using the Falloff, Pinch, and Bubble parameters. In Figure 4.24, a sphere's vertices are being pulled outward with a soft selection. The area in the falloff, as you can see, is smoothly holding back as the main selection vertices are

Figure 4.23

The Soft Selection rollout

pulling out. The sphere in the back of the viewport in Figure 4.24 has a vertex pulled out without the benefit of a soft selection.

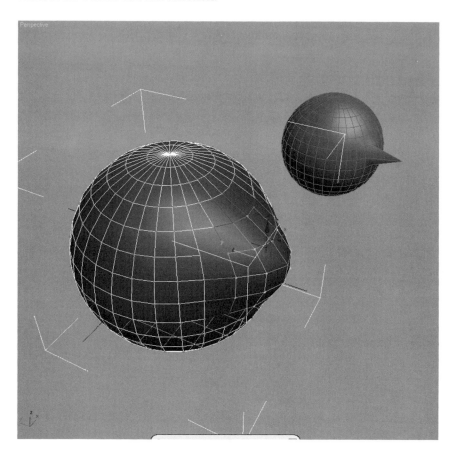

Edit (Sub-Object) Rollout

These rollouts provide specific tools for editing the sub-object of your poly object. There are tools that are specific to the sub-object and ones that are the same for all sub-objects. The rollout heading name changes to reflect the sub-object level you are currently in and shows you the tools available for just that sub-object.

Try this exercise:

1. In a new scene, create a sphere. Convert the sphere to an Editable Poly.

2. Select the poly sub-object level and select a single poly on the sphere, as shown here. Make sure Soft Selection is not enabled.

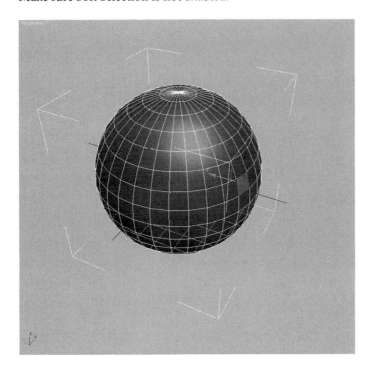

3. In the Edit Polygons rollout, choose Extrude, as shown here.

4. Your cursor in the viewport will change. Click on the polygon you already have selected, and drag the mouse up to extrude the polygon out from the sphere. If you drag the mouse down, the polygon will extrude into the sphere, creating a square tunnel. Pull the polygon out as shown and release the mouse button.

5. Select another polygon and extrude the face inward by dragging down on the cursor, as shown here.

6. Select a third polygon on the sphere, and this time select the Bevel tool in the Modifier panel. Similar to an Extrude, Bevel allows you to taper the extruded polygon. Click on the polygon, and drag the mouse to pull the polygon out. When you release the mouse button, 3ds Max allows you to select the taper amount by simply moving the mouse up or down. When you have the desired taper, as shown here, click once to exit the tool and set the bevel as you see it.

Figure 4.25

The Edit Geometry rollout

Essentially, the Edit rollout tools give you access to functions such as Extrude and Bevel to help you shape your model. The next section, "Editable Poly Tools," will give you some more experience with these toolsets. You will also use many of these tools in the Chest of Drawers exercise in this chapter.

Edit Geometry Rollout

This rollout (Figure 4.25) is the same for all the sub-objects. These tools allow you to edit your object. You will be using many of these tools in the upcoming Chest of Drawers and Hand exercises in this chapter.

Subdivision Surface Rollout

You have probably heard of Subdivision surfaces and SubD modeling, as they're called. A SubD surface is a surface that has been divided to have more faces. However, the SubD surface retains the original object's general shape, which is sometimes called a *cage*. You subdivide to add more detail to a model, but you can still edit the original cage of the model to alter its overall shape and form.

The Subdivision Surface rollout lets you access tools specific to modeling with a subdivision surface, as seen in Figure 4.26.

You will be modeling with subdivision surfaces a little bit later in the Hand exercise in this chapter and then again in Chapter 6, "Surface Tools and Modeling."

Figure 4.26

The Subdivision Surface rollout

Editable Poly Tools

Let's experiment with some of the other Editable Poly tools. Roll up your sleeves and dive right into the following exercises.

Extrude

When you *extrude* a vertex, 3ds Max moves it along a *normal*—that is, a line that is perpendicular to the surface in most cases. The extrusion creates new polygons that form the sides of the extrusion that also connect the vertex to the object.

We will start by extruding a vertex on a sphere:

1. Create a sphere by going to the Create panel and selecting Sphere. Create the sphere with about 20 units radius. Convert the sphere to an Editable Poly by right-clicking on the sphere and choosing Editable Poly under the Convert To heading in the right-click menu. Go to Vertex mode, or press 1 on your keyboard. The vertices will appear as blue dots on your model.

2. Select a vertex on your sphere, and the vertex will turn red. Go to the Edit Vertices rollout in the Modify panel, and press the Settings button next to Extrude to bring up the dialog box in Figure 4.27. Set an exact extrusion height and base width, and click Apply to create the extrusion. You can also click and drag to interactively pull out the vertex. Figure 4.28 shows a single extruded vertex.

Extrude acts the same in any of the sub-object modes—Vertex, Edge, or Poly. Figure 4.29 shows an extruded edge, and you saw what an extruded polygon looks like earlier in the chapter.

You will be able to work with more extrude options in the Creating the Fingers exercise later in this chapter.

Figure 4:27

The Extrude Vertices dialog box

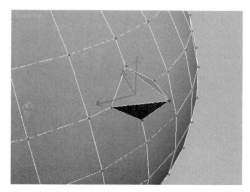

Figure 4.28

A single extruded vertex

Figure 4.29

A single extruded edge

Chamfer

In the following steps, you will use a different tool, called Chamfer, to create extra detail on an Editable Poly:

1. Undo the vertex extrusion with Ctrl+Z, or start with a fresh sphere and select a vertex. Hold down the Ctrl key and select two more vertices on either side of the one already selected. Click the Chamfer Settings button in the Modify panel to open the Chamfer Settings dialog box, shown here.

2. The new vertices are created around the ones you selected. You can dial in the exact value for your chamfer in the Options window and click Apply or OK. You can also simply click the Chamfer button (and not the Settings button), and click and drag in the viewport to interactively set your chamfer distance.

When you chamfer a sub-object, 3ds Max creates new faces around the area you have selected, complete with connecting edges, as you can see in Figure 4.30. Having been offset from the original vertex location, the three vertices are split into four new vertices each and arranged in a diamond formation. Chamfering, in this case, is good for creating some extra area of detail in your mesh or poly.

You can also use Chamfer to cut a hole in your surface. If you click the Open option box in the Chamfer Settings window, 3ds Max will cut a hole where the Chamfer exists, as seen in Figure 4.31.

Figure 4.30
_____

Chamfer three vertices right next to each other.

Figure 4.31
_____

The Open option in the Chamfer Settings window will cut holes in your model.

When you are in the Edge sub-object level, you can chamfer edges. In this case, the chamfer splits an edge into more edges and offsets them from their original location. In Figure 4.32, the corner edge of a box (shown on the right) is selected and chamfered (shown on the left).

Use Chamfer with some caution, because you can create overlapping geometry without realizing it.

Figure 4.32
_____

Chamfering an Edge

Weld

Welding vertices helps you combine vertices on a poly or mesh that should occupy the same space. It helps simplify the model by taking out extra vertices that need not be there. Welding also can help shape your model. The following steps show you how to weld vertices together:

1. Start with a new Editable Poly sphere, in a new scene if you wish. Remember, to get an Editable Poly sphere, create a sphere and convert it to an Editable Poly by right-clicking on the Sphere entry in the Modifier Stack and selecting Editable Poly.

2. Select two vertices next to each other on the sphere. Select the Weld Settings button to open the window seen here.

3. Use the Weld Threshold spinner in the Weld Settings window to weld the two vertices together, as seen in Figure 4.33. The Weld tool combines selected vertices that are within the threshold you set.

Weld is used a lot when detail is added to a model, such as with a chamfer, and some of the points need to be pulled together and combined into a single point.

Bevel

As you saw earlier in the chapter, a Bevel command creates a rounded edge for an extrusion. First, select the polygon, and then click Bevel in the Modify panel under the Edit Polygon rollout to create a bevel like the one shown in Figure 4.34. You can also click the Settings button next to Bevel to open the Bevel Settings window shown here.

Figure 4.33

Welding two vertices together

Figure 4.34

A pair of beveled polygons

Outline

The Outline function allows you to resize a polygon cleanly. Follow these steps to outline a polygon:

1. With a new Editable Poly sphere, go into Polygon level and select a polygon on the face of the sphere.

2. Select the Outline Settings button and set a desired Outline Amount value in the Settings window, as shown here. Then click OK or Apply. The polygon will change size, and the edges of the polygons around it will shift to accommodate the newly outlined polygon, as seen in Figure 4.35.

Outline lets you increase or decrease the size of the edges of a polygon. Using Outline is similar to selecting the polygon and scaling it with the Scale tool, but Outline is cleaner and easier to control.

> Clicking OK and clicking Apply in a dialog window are not the same. Clicking OK will perform the respective function and close the Settings window. Clicking Apply will perform the action but keep the window open.

Inset

Similar to the Outline function for a polygon, the Inset function creates a tapered version of the original polygon that is inset from its original location. An inset is similar to a bevel, but it doesn't add any height to the polygon. Simply select a polygon on your Editable Poly, and select Inset from the Modify panel's Edit Polygons rollout. You can click and drag in the viewport to set the Inset size, or click the Settings button next to the Inset button to open the Inset Settings window, as seen here. Figure 4.36 shows an Inset polygon on a sphere.

Figure 4.35
An Outlined Polygon on the sphere

Figure 4.36
An Inset is similar to a beveled polygon, but without any height added to it.

Hinge from Edge

Now let's see some of the more involved tools in the Editable Poly toolset. The Hinge from Edge tool creates a series of new polygons that rotate along an edge on the surface of an existing poly, connecting it to the original object. You can think of it as an extrusion with a rotation.

Follow these steps to see Hinge from Edge in action:

1. Create a new sphere in a new scene, and convert it to an Editable Poly. Enter into Polygon-level selection.

2. Select a polygon and click the Hinge from Edge button, as shown here, to open the Hinge Polygons from Edge Settings window in Figure 4.37.

3. Select the edge that will be the hinge, or the edge about which the polygons will extrude and rotate. To select the hinge edge, click the Pick Hinge button in the dialog box next to the Current Hinge parameter. Then, in the viewport, go to the selected polygon and choose which edge you want to use.

4. Once you select the hinge, the polygon will hinge out, rotating about that selected edge however many degrees are cited in the Angle parameter. You can use the spinner to select or you can enter the desired angle value for the hinge. The model will interactively hinge the polygon as you set the Angle value. Figure 4.38 shows a small hinge. Notice the hinge is flat, as it only has a Segments value of 1.

5. In the Settings window, change the Angle value to 90, and the Segments value to 5. Press OK to complete the function. Figure 4.39 shows the results.

The Hinge from Edge tool is an interesting way to extrude, and it can be handy in many instances, such as when you're creating an awning or a curved overhang. Remember, the smoother you need the hinge to be, the more segments you will need to add.

Figure 4.37

The Hinge Polygons from Edge Settings window

Figure 4.38

A hinged polygon on the sphere, but with only one segment

Figure 4.39

A smoother hinge is created when you increase the segments parameter.

Cap

The Cap function creates a new polygon to fill a hole on a surface. For this function, you'll need to be in the Border-level selection. To see a cap in action, follow these steps:

1. Create a new sphere and convert it to an Editable Poly.

2. Select a few polys that are next to each other, side by side, and delete them by pressing the Delete key. You should now have holes in your sphere, as shown.

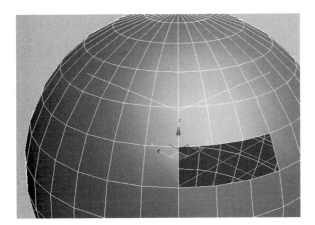

3. You may be wondering why you did that. You need to have a hole in the polygon surface for a Cap function and to check out the Border sub-object. As you may recall, a Border-level selection is the row of edges around a hole in a surface or on the edge of a surface, where only one side of the edge has a polygon. In the case of this sphere, the border is the line of edges surrounding the hole.

4. Now you need to cap the hole. Enter the Border level selection by pressing the Border icon or pressing 3. Under the Edit Borders rollout, select Cap. The hole should be filled with a single polygon, as shown in Figure 4.40.

Figure 4.40

The Cap function fills in a hole with a single polygon.

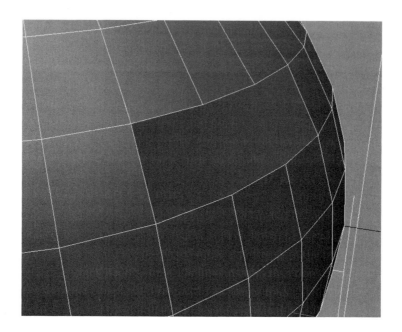

This tool can be very convenient. If you have done something to a polygon but don't like it, you can delete that poly and use the Cap tool to create a new one. Keep in mind, however, that cap will use a flat polygon to fill the hole, so a complex surface hole will not be patched with the same surface contours as the original.

Extrude Along a Spline

The Extrude Along a Spline function works just as it sounds. It will extrude a polygon sub-object along a spline path—that is a curve drawn in 3ds Max. Splines will be introduced later in this chapter and covered more extensively in the following chapters.

To see the Extrude Along a Spline function in action, open the `Path Extrude.max` file found in the Chapter 4 directory in its Scenes folder. This file has a sphere that has already been converted to an Editable Poly and a spline that will act as the path of extrusion. To continue, follow these steps:

1. Select the sphere and go into Poly mode (use shortcut 4, or select the Poly icon in the Modify panel's Selection rollout). Select a polygon; it doesn't matter which one.

2. Click the Settings button next to Extrude Along Spline to open the Settings window for the tool, as seen here.

3. Click the Pick Spline button and click the spline next to the sphere.

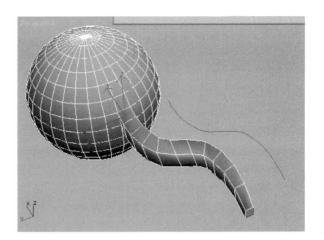

Figure 4.41

A polygon on this sphere is extruded along a spline path.

4. Immediately, you will see an extruded element coming from the sphere. It probably doesn't look very good because you still need to work with the parameters.

5. Start by adding more segments; 15 to 20 should give you a good looking extrusion. The extrusion in Figure 4.41 is the result of 11 Segments, –0.5 Taper Amount, and 2.0 Taper Curve.

Play around with some of the settings to get a good feel for what this tool can do. As a matter of fact, it's a really good idea to play around with all of the tool settings you have seen here, and some of the ones you haven't. This is a good way, if not somewhat frustrating, to learn 3ds Max—or any 3d program for that matter. Use this sphere, or another Editable Poly you create, to experiment with the different tools available in this rollout for all the sub-object levels to get a basic idea of how things work. You can rely on the text in this book, as well as *3ds Max's User Guide*, to help you along the way.

Modeling a Chest of Drawers

Let's finally put some of your newfound knowledge into practice. If you skipped to this section from the beginning of the chapter, or even from the beginning of the book, look at the previous sections in this chapter after you finish this model. Doing so will help fill some of the educational gaps and better explain *how* or *why* you've accomplished some of this exercise's topics.

In this section, you will model a chest of drawers (or dresser) to develop your Editable Poly muscles. Why buy a chest of drawers when you can just make one in 3ds Max? Make sure you make it large enough for all your socks.

Ready, Set, Reference!

You're so close to modeling something! You'll want to get some sort of reference for what you're modeling. Study the photo in Figure 4.42 for a look at the desired result.

Figure 4.42

**Modeling this chest
of drawers**

There are plenty of reference photos, and you will access them throughout this exercise to help build different parts of the chest. You may want to flip through the following pages to see the various photos to get a better idea what you will be modeling.

Of course, if this were your chest of drawers, you could have captured tons of pictures already, right?

Ready, Set, Model!

Create a Project called Dresser, or copy the Dresser project from the companion CD directly to your hard drive. It's never a good idea to work from a CD. To learn how to create a new project, see Chapter 2, "Your First 3ds Max Animation."

Top of the Dresser

To begin the chest of drawers model, follow these steps:

1. Begin with a new scene (choose File → New, and click New All in the pop-up window). Select the Perspective viewport and enable Edged Faces mode in the view (right-click the viewport name and toggle on Edged Faces from the menu). Go to the Create panel. In the Geometry heading, click Box. You are going to create a box using the Keyboard Entry rollout seen here.

2. Using the Keyboard Entry rollouts allows you to specify the exact size and location to create an object in your scene. Leave the X, Y, and Z values at 0, but enter these values: Length of **15**, Width of **30**, and Height of **40**. Click Create to create a box aligned in the center of the scene with the specified dimensions.

3. With the box still selected, go to the Modify panel. You can see the box's parameters here. You will need to add more height segments, so change the Height Segs parameter to 6. Your box should look like the box in Figure 4.43.

4. Convert the box to an Editable Poly by selecting the box and choosing Modifiers → Mesh Editing → Edit Poly. As seen in Figure 4.44, you can always go through the Modifier Stack to convert the box to the Editable Poly instead of using the menus.

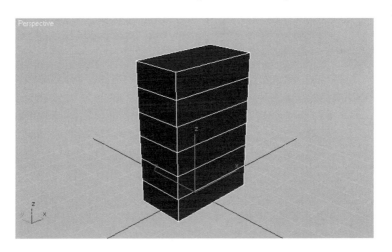

Figure 4.43

The box from which a beautiful chest of drawers will emerge.

Figure 4.44

The lip of the dresser

5. Press 4 on your keyboard to take you to the Polygon sub-object mode. Now select the polygon on the top of the box. As you can see in the viewport, the polygon is shaded red when it's selected.

6. Now go to the Edit Polygons rollout in the Modify Panel and select the Settings button next to Bevel. We are going to bevel several times to create the lip on the crown of the dresser seen in Figure 4.45.

7. Enter the following parameters: Height: **0.5** and Outline Amount: **1.3**. Keep the Bevel Type set to Group as shown. Bevel Type will be explained in the Hand Modeling exercise in the next section. For now, just know that when you bevel only one poly, the Bevel Type is irrelevant; it is only for multiple polygons. Click the Apply button (*not* the OK button), and Max will apply the specified settings without closing the window to give you results that should be similar to Figure 4.46.

8. After the first Bevel is applied, add more bevels to round out the crown. In the still open Bevel Polygons window, input these parameters: Height: **0.1** and Outline Amount: **0.06**. Click Apply (you want to keep the Bevel window open because you'll need to bevel several times). This will bevel a very slight bit up, as seen in Figure 4.47.

9. For the third bevel, input the following values: Height: **0.1** and Outline Amount: **0.03**. Click Apply. Next, input these values: Height: **0.1** and Outline Amount: **0**. Click Apply. This creates a slight curve in the crown. Again enter new values: Height: **0.3** and Outline Amount: **0**. Click Apply. For the sixth bevel, change the values: Height: **0.1** and Outline Amount: **–0.06**. Click Apply. Finally, enter these values: Height: **0.1** and Outline Amount: **–0.08**. Click OK. Your dresser's top should resemble Figure 4.48 and Figure 4.49.

Figure 4.45

The lip of the dresser

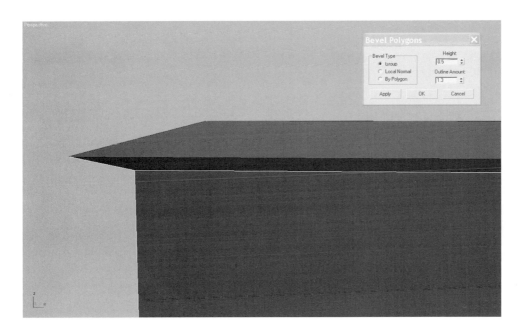

Figure 4.46

The first bevel for the crown of the dresser

Figure 4.47

The second bevel is hardly noticeable.

Figure 4.48

**The crown lip of the
dresser's top**

Figure 4.49

**The dresser top is
ready.**

These bevel amounts are not necessarily set in stone. You can play around with the settings to get as close to the image as you can or to add your own design flair. You can load the Dresser01.max scene file from the Scenes folder in the Dresser project on the companion CD.

Bottom of the Dresser

Now it is time for the bottom of the dresser. This dresser doesn't have legs, but it has a nice detail at the bottom nonetheless, as you can see in Figures 4.50 and 4.51. To create this detail, you need to extrude a segment.

1. You should already be in Poly Sub-Object mode if you are continuing with your own file, so select the poly on the bottom of the dresser as seen here.

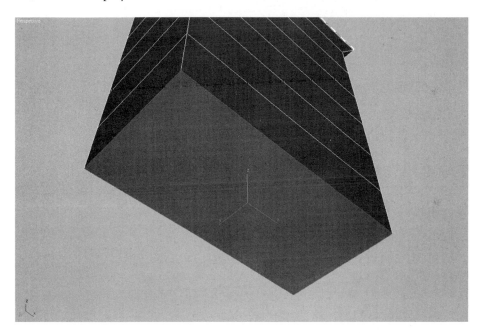

2. Go to the Edit Poly rollout, select the Extrude Settings button, change the Extrusion Height to 2.5, and click OK. This will extrude a polygon out from the bottom of the dresser, essentially adding a segment to the box as seen in Figure 4.52.

Figure 4.50

An angle view of the dresser's bottom corner

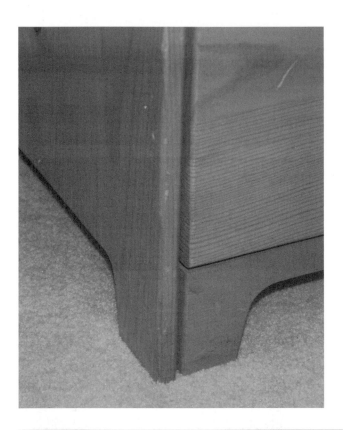

Figure 4.51

A straight view of the dresser's bottom corner

Figure 4.52

Extrude the bottom of the dresser.

3. The polygon will still be selected, so select the Inset button, change the Inset Amount to 0.6, and click OK. This creates an inset poly, as seen here.

4. The poly is still selected, so select the Extrude Settings button, enter an Extrusion Height of **–2.0**, and click OK. Figure 4.53 shows how the bottom of the dresser has moved up into itself slightly.

Figure 4.53

The dresser's
bottom lip

Figure 4.54

A mock-up of how
the bottom lip needs
to be cut

To create the detail to the bottom, you need to add more segments in the newly extruded polygons. Figure 4.54 shows a mock-up of how the bottom lip should be cut. To do this, you will use the Slice tool. The Slice tool works only when the polygons are selected. You will start by slicing into the extruded polygons on the front and back of the bottom lip.

1. Select *all* the polygons that make up the front and back lip of the bottom. *Make sure you select the front, back, and bottom of the front and back lip as shown in the following graphic.* The selections are marked darker in the graphic. It is also a good idea to lock your selection. The Lock icon 🔒 appears at the bottom of the interface. When that icon is highlighted yellow, whatever you have selected will be locked and will not be deselected until you disable the Selection Lock.

> The keyboard shortcut for the Selection Lock toggle is the spacebar.

2. When all the necessary polygons are selected, go to the Edit Geometry rollout and click the Slice Plane tool. When you select the Slice Plane tool, a yellow wire box will surround the selected polygons; this is the Slice Plane gizmo. Position/rotate the gizmo where you want to slice your polygon, as shown in Figure 4.55.

3. Until now, when you selected a polygon, it turned solid red in the viewport. You can change it to display as outline when a polygon is selected, and not as solid red. You will need to do this so you can see the new edges you are creating. To turn off Shaded Edge mode, press F2. Your selected polygons will now show red only around the edges.

4. With the Slice Plane tool still active, right-click in the viewport to bring up the Quad menu. Go to the Transform menu and select Rotate. Figure 4.56 shows this shortcut for the Transform tools.

Figure 4.55

The Slice Plane gizmo

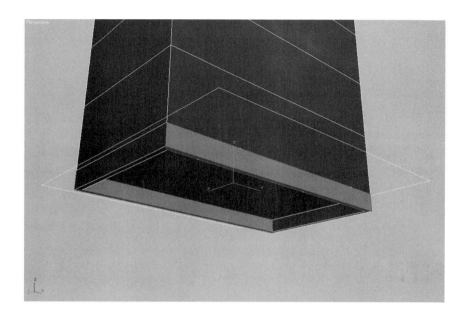

Figure 4.56

Rotate the Slice Plane gizmo

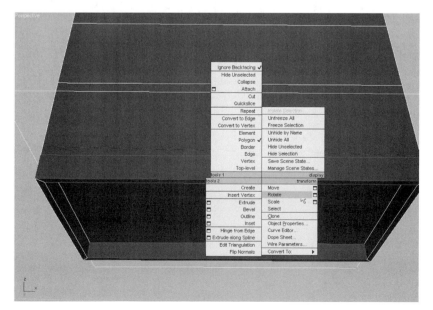

5. You need to rotate the Slice Plane gizmo 90-degrees along the *Y*-axis. Center the cursor over the Transform gizmo's *Y*-axis (green wire), and click/drag until the Transform Type-in box at the bottom of the interface reads 90 in the *Y*-box, or you can enter the rotation amount for *Y* and press Enter. As you rotate, you will see the slice interactively displayed as a red line on the selected polygons.

6. Use the Move tool (W) to position the Slice Plane gizmo, where you want the first slice. The movement will be along the *X*-axis or horizontal along the box. When the Slice Plane gizmo is positioned as shown in Figure 4.57, go to the Edit Geometry rollout and click Slice. Don't click Slice Plane because that will deactivate only the Slice Plane tool. You must click the Slice button because it is like clicking an Apply button for the Slice Plane tool. Once you click Slice, the polygon will have a new segment at that location. The Slice Plane tool should still be active.

7. You need four slices at each end of the dresser bottom, as shown in Figure 4.58. Keep in mind that the polygons are selected on the front and back so that the Slice Plane tool will slice only polygons that are selected within the gizmo. Click the Slice Plane button to deactivate the tool when you have placed four vertical slices in all four corners of the front and back bottom lips of the dresser, as shown in Figure 4.58.

Figure 4.57

Place a slice in the corner for the foot of the dresser.

Figure 4.58

Place four vertical slices at each corner.

8. Press the spacebar to unlock your selection. You are going to use a combination of moving edges and polygons to create the detail on the bottom of the dresser. Simply select the relevant polygons, and use the Move tool to place them as shown in Figure 4.59.

Don't worry if your adjustments don't have a perfectly smooth curve. Unless the camera is right on top of the detail, it will look good from a distance. A perfect curve is not necessary, especially for our purposes.

You can use the same techniques in the Steps 1 through 8 to create detail in the side bottom lip of the dresser, as shown in Figure 4.60. Make sure you save your work.

Figure 4.59

Move polygons to create detail in the dresser feet.

Figure 4.60

Use the same steps to create the details on the sides of the bottom.

Making the Drawers

In the beginning of this exercise, you created a box with six segments on its height. You can use those segments to create the drawers. This is an example of thinking ahead and planning your model before you start an object. This was by far the easiest way to go; using the Slice Plane tool to add segments for the drawers after the box was made would have been more laborious.

For simplicity's sake, you will not create drawers that can open and shut in this exercise. If this dresser were to be used in an animation in which the drawers would be opened, you would make them differently.

First, take a look at the drawers and see where you have to go. Figure 4.61 shows the drawers and an important detail we need to consider. Luckily, you needn't worry about the junk on top of the dresser.

Figure 4.61

Checking out the real dresser drawers

Gap Between Drawers and Dresser

To model the drawers, begin with these steps:

1. Create a small gap around the edge of the box. This gap will represent the space between the drawer and the main body of the dresser (Figure 4.61). Go to Polygon mode (press 4), and select the six polygons on the front of the box that represent the drawers. Remember to hold the Ctrl key while selecting the additional polygons; this will allow you to make multiple polygon selections.

2. Go to the Edit Polygons rollout in the Modify panel, and click the Inset Settings button. Set the Inset Amount to 0.6 and keep the Inset Type to Group, as shown here. Click OK. Figure 4.62 shows the result of the Inset operation.

You can load the Dresser02.max scene file from the Scenes folder in the Dresser project on the companion CD to check your work or to begin the next series of steps.

Figure 4.62

The Inset creates the detail needed to make the drawers.

3. Keep those newly inset polygons selected, and go back to the Edit Polygons rollout to select the Extrude Settings button. Change the Extrusion Height to –0.5, keep Extrusion Type set to Group, and press OK. The faces will now extrude inward a little bit, as shown here.

4. In the original reference picture (Figure 4.42), the top drawer of the dresser is split into two, so you need to slice that top drawer polygon vertically to create two drawers. Make sure the selected polygons are displayed with the red outlines instead of the solid red color (toggle with F2). Switch your viewport to a Front view.

5. Select the polygon that represents the top drawer, as shown in Figure 4.63. Select the Slice Plane button in the Edit Geometry rollout. Rotate and move the Slice Plane gizmo so that it is vertical and centered on the polygon as shown here, and click Slice. Click the Slice Plane button to release the tool.

6. The polygons are still selected after the Slice operation, so go back to the Edit Polygons rollout and click the Inset Settings button. Set the Inset Amount to 0.25. This time we are going to change the Inset Type from Group to By Polygon, as shown below. This setting insets each polygon individually, instead of it taking place across multiple, contiguous polygons as does the Group option. Click OK to run the Inset operation. Your polygons should resemble the ones in Figure 4.64.

Figure 4.63

Select the top drawer polygon.

Figure 4.64

The drawers are inset separately.

7. Perform the same inset operation on the remaining drawer polygons on the front of the box (as shown): Set the Inset Amount to .25, set the Inset Type to By Polygon. This will inset the five lower wide drawers.

8. Select all of the "drawer" polygons. Go to the Edit Polygons rollout and click the Extrude Settings button. Set the Extrude Amount to 0.7. You don't need it to extrude very much; you just want the drawers to extrude a bit more than the body of the dresser.

Go grab yourself a frosty beverage! The dresser is finished. Go ahead and name the dresser. You can even change the color of the dresser if you'd like. Go to the Name and Color Type-In (shown in Figure 4.65), and change the name of the object to **Dresser** and pick a nice light color.

Object Name Type-In   Object Default Color

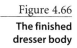

Figure 4.65

Name the dresser and pick a nice color.

The finished dresser body should look like the dresser in Figure 4.66. Remember to save this version of your file. You can also load the Dresser03.max scene file from the Scenes folder in the Dresser project on the companion CD to check your work or to skip to this part in the exercise.

Creating the Knobs

Now that the body of the dresser is done, it's time to add the final bit of detail to make the dresser complete: knobs. We will use Splines and a few surface creation tools new to your workflow. Goose bumps, anyone? Take a look at the reference for the knobs in Figure 4.67. You are going to create a profile of the knob and then rotate the profile around its axis to form a surface. This technique is known as *Lathe*, not to be mistaken for *latte*, which is a whole different deal and not really covered in this book.

Here's a quick rundown of what a spline is: a spline is a group of vertices and connecting segments that form a line or curve. To create the knob profile, we are going to use the Line Spline, shaped in the outline of—you guessed it—a knob. The Line tool allows you to create a free-form spline.

Figure 4.66

The finished dresser body

Figure 4.67

Knobs

Figure 4.68

The intended profile curve for the knob

You can use your last file from the Dresser exercise, or you can load `Dresser03.max` from the Scenes folder of the Dresser project on the companion CD. To build the knobs, follow these steps:

1. Make sure you are in the Left viewport, so you can see which side of the dresser the drawers are on. You are going to create a profile of half the knob, as shown in Figure 4.68. Don't worry about creating all the detail in the knob because detail won't be seen; a simple outline will be fine.

2. Go to the Create panel and choose Shapes . Click the Line button. Use the current default values in the Creation Method rollout, as shown here.

3. In the Left viewport, click once to lay down a vertex for this line, starting at the bottom of the intended profile for the knob. This is the starting point for the curve. When you are creating a line, every click lays down the next vertex for the line. In essence, the vertex controls the position of a point of the line. If you want to create a curve in the line, click once and drag the mouse in any direction to give the vertex a curvature of sorts. This curve vertex creates a curve in that part of the line. You will need to follow the rough outline of a knob, so click and drag where there is curvature in the line. Once you have laid down your first vertex, continue to click and drag more vertices for the line clockwise until you create the half-profile knob shape shown in Figure 4.68. Figure 4.69 shows the profile line with the vertices numbered according to their creation order.

> To create a straight line segment between two vertices, press and hold Shift to keep the next vertex to be laid down orthogonal to the last vertex, either horizontally or vertically.

4. Once you lay down your last vertex at the top, finish the spline by either right-clicking to release the Line tool or clicking on the first vertex you created to close the spline. For this example, it really doesn't matter which method you choose. Either an open or closed spline will work: however, a closed spline is shown in Figure 4.69. Drawing splines entails a bit of a learning curve, so it might be helpful to delete the one you did first and try again for the practice. Once you get something resembling the spline in Figure 4.69, you can edit it. Don't drive yourself crazy; just get the spline as close as you can.

> When you are creating a line, click once to create a corner vertex for the line, but click and drag to create a Bezier vertex to put a curve into the line.

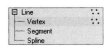

5. With the spline selected, go to the Modify panel. In the Modifier Stack window, you will see the entry Line with a plus sign in a black box next to it denoting that it has Sub-Object modes. Click the plus to expand the list of sub-objects, as shown here.

Figure 4.69

The knob's profile line's vertices are numbered according to the order in which they were created.

A LINE'S VERTEX TYPE

When you center your cursor over a line's vertex and right-click to bring up the shortcut menu, you will have access to several vertex controls. In that shortcut menu, under the menu heading Tools1, you can choose a vertex type.

The vertex types are the following:

Smooth: A Smooth vertex creates a smooth continuous curve. The actual curvature at a smooth vertex depends on the spacing of the adjacent vertices. This is a nonadjustable vertex, meaning it has no handles with which you can control the curvature directly.

Corner: A Corner vertex is nonadjustable and that creates sharp corners.

Bezier: A Bezier vertex is a vertex that has locked continuous handles that create a smooth curve. You can directly adjust the curvature at a Bezier vertex by manipulating its handles. Adjusting a handle on one side of the vertex will also adjust the other side's handle, as they are continuous.

Bezier Corner: A Bezier Corner vertex creates a sharp corner like the Corner vertex, but it has discontinuous tangent handles with which you can control the curvature of the line at that vertex. The handle on one side of the vertex will not affect the handle on the other side.

In some ways, Line's sub-objects are similar to the Editable Poly Sub-Object modes. However, when you are working with a spline, you are working with a 2D nonrendering object. A spline is made up of three sub-objects: a vertex, a segment, and a spline. As you know, a *vertex* is a point in space. A *segment* is the line that connects two vertices. The Spline mode allows you to select and/or transform a single or multiple splines within a spline object. To continue with the project, follow with these steps:

6. Choose the vertex sub-object for the line. Make sure you are still working in the Left viewport. When you're working with 2D splines, it is always best to work in Orthographic view. Use the Move tool to click on one of the vertices. The vertex has a Transform gizmo just like an object. Use the Move tool to edit the shape to better fit the outline of the knob. Be sure to read the sidebar in this section titled "A Line's Vertex Type" to learn more about the types of vertices a line can have, and how it can change the curvature of a line. If needed, you can change the vertex type of your line's vertices to control the curvature.

Figure 4.70

Eeek! That isn't a knob at all.

To catch up to this point, you can load the `Dresser04.max` file from the Scenes folder of the Dresser project on the companion CD.

7. The profile line is ready to turn into a 3D object. This is where the modifiers are used. Get out of Sub-Object mode for your line. Choose Modifiers → Patch/Spline Editing → Lathe (you could also go to the Modifier List and choose Lathe from the alphabetical list of modifiers). When you first put the Lathe modifier on your spline, it won't look anything like the knob (see Figure 4.70)—but don't panic! You need to futz with the parameters to get it right (Figure 4.71). Basically, the object is turned inside out.

8. Go to Parameters rollout and under the Align Heading, click the Max button. It's a knob! Now, that is more like it. You just had to change the alignment of the axis so the lathe revolution would be correct.

> If Step 8 does not work properly for you, try clicking the Min button instead of Max under the Align heading. When you are creating a line, where you begin to create that line and in what order you place the vertices, clockwise or counter-clockwise, are both important. This example drew the knob's profile line in a clockwise direction.

Figure 4.71

The titillating parameters for the Lathe

9. Rotate the Perspective view so you can see the top of the knob. You should notice a strange artifact. To correct this, check the Weld Core box under the Parameters rollout for the lathe.

That's it! Check out Figure 4.72 for a look at the lathed knob. By using Splines and Lathe, you can create all sorts of surfaces for your models. In the next section, you will resize the knob, position it, and copy it to fit on the drawers.

Copying the Knob

Now that you have a knob, you may need to adjust it and make it the right size. If you still want to futz with the knob, go back down the stack to the line to edit your spline. For example, you may want to scale the knob a bit to better fit the drawer (refer to the reference photo in Figure 4.67). Select the Scale tool, and click and drag until the original line is about 40 percent smaller. The Lathe modifier will re-create the surface to fit the new size. You can also delete the knob and restart with another line for more practice. In the following steps, you will copy and position the knob for the drawers.

Figure 4.72

The lathe completes the knob.

1. Position and rotate the knob to fit on to the front of a top drawer. Change its default color (if you want) and change its name to **Knob**.

2. You'll need a few copies of the original knob, one for each drawer. Choose Edit → Clone (Figure 4.73). You are going to use the Instance command. An *instance* is a copy, but an instance is still connected to the original. If you edit the original or an instance, all of the instances change. Click OK to create an instance.

3. Simply position the instanced knob in the middle of the other top drawer.

4. Using more instances of the original knob, place knobs in the middle of all the remaining drawers of your dresser, as seen in Figure 4.74.

Figure 4.73

Using an instance to copy the knob

As you saw with this exercise, there are plenty of tools for the Editable Poly object. Your model doesn't have to be all of the same type of modeling either. In this example, we created the dresser using *box modeling* techniques, where you begin with a single box and extrude your way into a model, and with surface creation techniques using splines.

You can compare your work to the scene file `Dresser05.max` from the Scenes folder of the Dresser project on the companion CD.

Figure 4.74

The dresser, knobs, and all

Modeling a Hand

Now that you've had some experience modeling in 3ds Max, you can tackle modeling a simple hand. The goal is to acquire experience with some other tools Max has to offer. Before you begin modeling, look at a reference. Luckily, you probably have one or two hands at the ends of your arms.

Starting the Palm

There are several ways to model a hand, but you'll start with the same modeling techniques you started with in the Dresser exercise. To begin box modeling the hand, follow these steps:

1. Start a new 3ds Max file in a new project called Hand, or copy the Hand project from the companion CD to your hard drive.

2. Make sure the Perspective viewport is active. Create a box on the home grid in the Perspective viewport. You are going to use Keyboard Entry to create the box to certain specifications. In the Keyboard Entry rollout in the Create panel's parameters for the box, enter the following parameters: Length of **90**, Width of **150**, and Height of **30**, as shown in the following graphic. The X-, Y-, and Z-parameters in the Keyboard Entry rollout are used to place the object in your scene by using the coordinate you specify. Keep those values at 0 to create the box in the center of your scene. Choose the Create button at the bottom of the rollout to create the box as defined.

3. Go to the Modify panel, and you will see the parameters for the box. You need to subdivide the box so it has more polygons. Press F4 to toggle on Edged Face mode in your viewport. In the Modify panel's Parameters rollout, set the box Length Segs to 4, Width Segs to 3, and Height Segs to 1, as you see here.

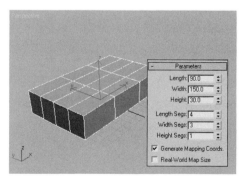

4. Look at the box and imagine that it is the palm of the hand. The polygons facing you in Figure 4.75 are going to be the fingers. The poly farthest from you will be the pinky finger, and the one nearest will be the index. This should help you get oriented.

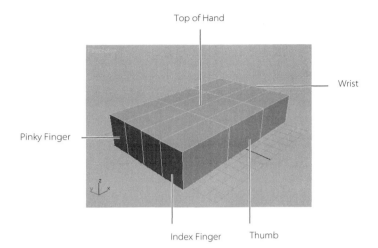

Figure 4.75

The box will be the palm of the hand, and the fingers will be extruded from the polygons facing you.

5. Convert the box into an Editable Polygon. You can reference the Dresser exercise in this chapter if you have skipped to this section.

6. The fingers polygons will need to be slightly splayed out, so they will not all stick together when you extrude them. Use the Edge Sub-Object mode to do this. In the Modifier Stack, click the plus sign to reveal the sub-objects for the box.

7. Use the keyboard shortcut 2 to choose the Edge Sub-Object level. Select the edge closest to you (which will be the outer edge of the index finger), as seen in Figure 4.76.

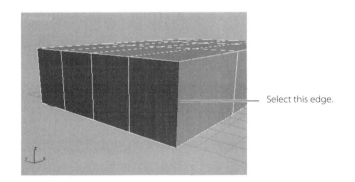

Figure 4.76

Select the edge of the index finger.

8. Click the Lock Selection icon or press the spacebar to lock this selection so you don't lose the selected edge. The Lock button will turn yellow, indicating it is in use.

9. Use the keyboard shortcut W to enable the Move tool. Move the edge along the *X*-axis. You might find it easier to use the Top viewport for the move. Use the Transform gizmo—center the cursor so that the *X* and the tail of the *X*-axis arrow are yellow.

Yellow indicates that the axis is locked. This will confine the movement to the *X*-axis and no other, as shown here.

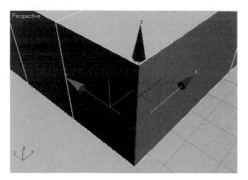

10. Switch to the Top viewport and move the Edge, as shown here. Press the spacebar to release the selection Lock.

11. Move the other Edges to create a slight arch where the top of the palm will be, as shown in the following graphic. This will ensure that when you extrude the polygons for the fingers, there will be space for the webbing in-between. If you don't want the fingers spread apart this much, make the arc less curved. This repositions the polygon to a different angle so it won't extrude out straight.

Figure 4.77
Save!

Incremental Save

Now is a good time to save with File → Save As. Make sure you use the plus sign (+) instead of pressing the Save button, as this will add a number increment to the end of your filename (for instance: *hand01.max*) as shown in Figure 4.77. To catch up to this point or to check your own work, load the scene file Hand01.max from the Hand project on the companion CD.

Creating the Fingers

Now it is time to extrude out the fingers.

1. With the box selected, select the Polygon Sub-Object mode or press 4 on your keyboard. Go to the Perspective view, Click on the polygon that represents the index finger (closest to you), as you see here.

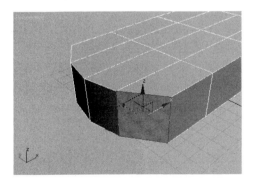

2. Go to the Modify panel under the Edit Polygons rollout. Click the Extrude Settings button ▢ (the Settings button is directly to the right of the extrude button) to bring up the Extrude Settings dialog box. See the sidebar titled "Extrusion Options" for more about the parameters and options for the Extrude function.

EXTRUDE OPTIONS

Using the palm model of the hand for reference, the options for an extrude operation will behave as indicated here. All of the polygons on the front of the box are selected:

Group—The polygons are extruded out along their averaged normals, effectively extending the palm out, as seen here.

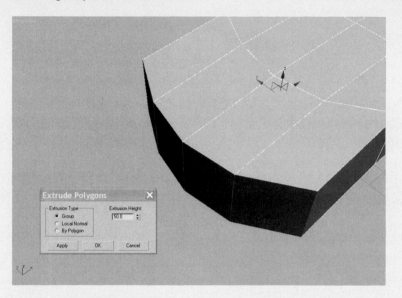

Local Normal—The polygons are extruded straight out along their normal (usually perpendicular to the polygon's face), creating a flare at the end of the palm.

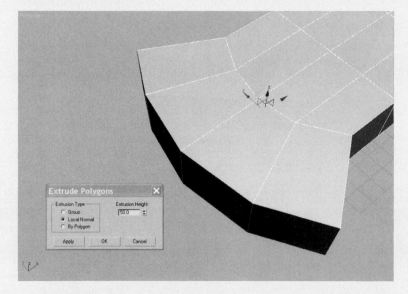

EXTRUDE OPTIONS

By Polygon—Each polygon is extruded individually along its own normal.

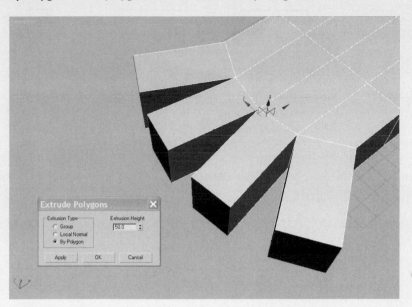

Extrusion Height—Specifies how much to extrude in scene units. As you've already seen, positive values extrude out away from the object, and negative values extrude into the object.

3. We are going to extrude the first finger so that it has three sections, so instead of doing one extrude, we are going to do three back to back. This will give the finger more segments with which to work. If you look at your own finger, you will notice the lower joint is the biggest joint, getting smaller toward the tip of the finger. In the Settings dialog box, set the first Amount to 60 units. The Setting dialog box allows you to interactively perform the functions, so you can see the extrude before you apply it. The 60 unit extrude looks good, so click Apply. This keeps the Settings window open. Go to the Extrusion Amount and enter **50**; this will change the extruded segment to 50 units. Click Apply again for the second extrusion. Change the Extrude Amount to 40, and press OK for the last extrusion of the index finger. Figure 4.78 shows the first finger.

Figure 4.78

The index finger is extruded into place.

Figure 4.79

Fingers!

4. Using the same techniques and the following settings for the Extrusion Amounts, extrude the rest of the fingers.

FINGER	FIRST EXTRUDE	SECOND EXTRUDE	THIRD EXTRUDE
Middle Finger	70	60	50
Ring Finger	60	50	40
Pinky	50	40	30

Figure 4.79 shows all the fingers extruded. You can use other values as long as you have three segments in each finger. Use your own hand as a guide.

This is a good time to do another Save As; make sure you use the plus sign (+) instead of pressing the Save button. To catch up to this point or to check your own work, load the scene file Hand02.max from the Hand project on the companion CD.

Creating the Thumb

Now you will create the thumb, also using extrusions. Follow these steps:

1. Select the polygon in the middle of the side of the hand, as shown here. As with the fingers, the thumb will have three segments. Select the Extrude Settings button and enter an Extrude Amount of **30** units. Click Apply twice for two 30 unit extrusions, and then click once more with an Extrude Amount of **20**. Click OK.

Figure 4.80

Extruding the thumb

Figure 4.81

Notice how the thumb extends from a hand.

2. To shape the thumb, you will use a combination of adjusting edge and poly locations. Figure 4.81 shows a picture of a hand; notice how the thumb extrudes from the bottom of the hand. Using Edge mode, rearrange the edges in the extruded thumb to create a shape as shown in Figure 4.82.

Save an iteration of your scene. Now you should have the general shape for the hand. It is still very rough, with no detail. To catch up to this point or to check your own work, load the scene file Hand03.max from the Hand project on the companion CD.

Subdivision Surfaces

You may be wondering how to take this boxy thing and turn it into something more organic and realistic. By using Subdivision Surfaces, or SubDs, you can take a relatively simple object with very few segments and subdivide the polygons. SubD makes a flat surface appear smoother.

Follow these steps to use Subdivision Surfaces for your hand:

1. To apply the SubD, with the hand selected, check the Use NURMS Subdivision box in the Subdivision Surface rollout in the Modify panel. Figure 4.83 shows the hand before and after you apply the NURMS Subdivision.

Figure 4.82

Shape your thumb to match by moving and adjusting edges and polygons.

Figure 4.83

Using NURMS subdivision to smooth out the hand

2. Once the smoothing is applied, you will see an orange cage surrounding the hand if you are in any Sub-Object mode. This allows you to work with this low-res cage while the smoother version is updating at the same time.

3. You can control how much smoothing applies to the hand using the Iterations parameter, which is by default set to 1. Be very careful how many Iterations you add. The higher the number, the harder the computer has to work to process the information. You can leave Iterations set to 1 for the hand.

4. Uncheck Isoline Display in the Subdivision Surface rollout. When Isoline Display is off, Max displays all the faces added by the smoothing, as shown on the right in Figure 4.84. The default of *on* shows only the objects original edges, as shown on the left in Figure 4.84.

Figure 4.84

When Isoline Display is turned off, all of the faces added by the smoothing operation are shown.

5. Make sure you are in Polygon Sub-Object mode. Press F2 to toggle the Shaded Face mode, so that when you select a poly, it will be shaded in red and easier to see. Now, select a polygon on the hand and right-click to access the shortcuts menu. Select Transform → Move. Move the polygon in any direction. The polygon will pull the surrounding polygons with it, but the selection is softer (Figure 4.85). This makes it possible to model in a push and pull fashion, just as if molding clay.

You don't want to save what you have done with the SubDs, so either undo all the smoothing changes or reopen the last saved file. It is actually easier to work with the boxy hand before the NURMS smoothing. You can also just uncheck the Use NURMS Subdivision. You will come back to this later.

Figure 4.85

You can mold the hand by moving polygons.

Adding Detail to the Hand

You are going to begin adding some simple detail to the hand. One of the easiest ways to do this is using the Cut tool, which is a part of the Cut and Slice Group. You will find the Cut tool in the Edit Geometry rollout, which is shown here.

The Cut tool allows you to divide an edge at any point. You then divide a second edge at any point, and the tool will create a new edge between the two points. To create more edges for detail on the hand, follow these steps:

1. With the hand selected, click on the Cut Tool button. Now click on the first edge (use Figure 4.86 as a reference) at the first knuckle on the index finger. A new vertex is created where you clicked. A dotted line will track along with your cursor until you click a second edge. Click on the opposite edge from your initial one to add a new edge next to the first segment on the index finger. Right-click to exit the tool. Similarly, add new edges to the knuckle areas shown in Figure 4.86. You may want to add the new edges in a Nonperspective viewport. Working with the Cut tool in a Perspective view may be a bit difficult; the newly created edges may appear to jump around the hand or won't place correctly. In the Orthogonal views, it is simpler to read where the Cut tool is placing edges. In addition, while working with the Cut tool, turn on Ignore Backfacing in the Selection rollout to avoid selecting edges on the back of the hand by accident.

With the Cut tool, you can cut across any number of faces. Also, if you simply double-click on the first edge, 3ds Max will divide that edge at the point where you clicked by adding a vertex there. You need not click on a second edge if you double-click. Right-click to exit the tool.

Figure 4.86

Add new edges where shown to add detail to the knuckles.

2. With all the new edges, use the Move tool to move those edges to create the knuckles and the fleshy area on the bottom of the fingers. You can also rearrange the edges at the tip of the finger to give the fingers a more tapered look. Click on Use NURMS Subdivision to see how the knuckles and fingers look with smoothing, as seen in Figure 4.87. You can see how the NURMS SubDs really smooth out the detail, so don't be afraid to exaggerate the detail so that it looks better when smoothed, as you can see in Figure 4.87. Click off Use NURMS Subdivision to return to the boxy hand.

Figure 4.87

See how the smoothing will affect the detail you are adding to the fingers.

3. Let's add some knuckles at the end of the fingers. You are going to use a tool for adding detail that is another way of subdividing a polygon. Tessellate doesn't give you the control options the Cut tool does, but it can be more precise. The Tessellate button is under the Edit Geometry rollout in the Modify panel. Two Tessellate methods are available: Edge and Face (Figure 4.88).

Figure 4.88

The Tessellate Selection window

See the sidebar in this section titled "Tessellate Options" for more on Tessellate before you use it in action in the following steps.

TESSELLATE OPTIONS

Edge—Vertices are inserted in the middle of each edge of the selected polygon, and a line is drawn connecting the new vertices to form new edges inside that polygon. The number of new polygons will be equal to the number of sides on the original polygon.

Face—A vertex is inserted into the middle of the selected polygon, and edges are drawn from the original vertices of the polygon to the new vertex. Again, the number of new polygons will be equal to the number of sides on the original polygon.

Tension—This parameter controls the Edge tension value, which essentially pulls vertices inward or outward from the plane, creating a concave or rounding effect, respectively. You can see how the edge is concave in this graphic.

Continue with these steps to add detail with the Tessellate function:

1. Before you Tessellate any of the polygons on the hand, edit the poly size. The polygons are too long and they should be squarer. Just select the lower edge of the polygons and move them closer to the base of the fingers, as you can see in Figure 4.89.

Figure 4.89

Move the edges to make the knuckle polygons squarer.

2. Select the polygons at the base of the fingers and hold the Ctrl key to allow you to select all four polygons, as seen in Figure 4.90. Select the Tessellate Settings button under the Edit Geometry rollout. You are going to use the Edge option with Tension set to 0. Click OK, and your hand should tessellate as in Figure 4.91.

Figure 4.90

Select all four polygons where the fingers meet the hand.

3. Switch to Vertex mode and select the vertices in the center of the subdivided polys. Right-click to access the shortcut menu and choose Move. Move the vertices up away from the hand along the Z-axis, as shown in Figure 4.92. Check the Use NURMS Subdivision box to see the smoothing of the hand with the raised knuckles (as shown in Figure 4.93). You may want to go back to Vertex mode while in NURMS to use the SubDs cage to refine the changes. Continue to edit until you are satisfied with the look. Don't forget to save another iteration.

Now that you have created the basic shape for the hand, you should use the NURMS cage to refine and edit the look. Remember you have to be in a Sub-Object mode for the cage to appear.

To check your work, load the scene file Hand04.max from the Hand project on the companion CD.

Don't bog yourself down trying to model small details such as knuckle wrinkles or lines on the palm. Those details can be added using materials in texturing.

Summary

In this chapter, you learned how to model with 3ds Max. Through exploring the modeling toolsets to creating a dresser and a hand, you saw firsthand how the primary modeling tools in Max operate.

You began by first examining how to best plan a model. Then you learned some modeling concepts and how to use modifiers and the Modifier Stack effectively. You moved on to learning the differences between objects and meshes, and how to use sub-objects to edit your surfaces before you began a series of short exercises describing some of the poly editing tools. With that under your belt, you learned how to put these tools to use by making a dresser and finally modeling a hand.

Modeling is an artful craft. It is best to know where you are trying to go in your mind's eye, so you can effectively get there with your models. Becoming a good modeler takes time and patience, so stick with it.

Figure 4.91

The polygons are tessellated to give you more detail.

Figure 4.92

Raise the knuckles.

Figure 4.93

Check the smoothing to make sure the knuckles look good.

CHAPTER 5

Modeling in 3ds Max: Part II

Building models in any 3D package comes down to creating and arranging vertices so that the appropriate polygonal shapes and organization of faces are sent to the renderer. The difference between a mesh shaped like a box and one shaped like a drum is how the vertices arc organized. In recent releases of 3ds Max, the functionality and stability of the Polygon Modeling tools have been some of the most addressed areas. When using the Editable Poly toolset, or the Edit Poly modifier, the sub-objects of a mesh can be finely controlled to create almost any mesh object conceivable.

In 3ds Max, you can directly affect geometry objects and you can transform two-dimensional objects into three-dimensional geometry. Extruding, beveling, lofting, and lathing are just some of the ways to create geometry from splines. In this chapter, the Editable Poly toolset, the Lathe and Bevel modifiers, and the Loft compound object are covered while creating a low-polygon tank. We will also examine the ShapeMerge compound object, the Snapshot tool for creating copies of animated objects, and the Boolean Subtraction tool.

Topics in this chapter include:

- Setting Up the Scene

- The Editable Poly Tools

- Lofting the Barrel

- Lathing the Wheels

- Using Snapshot to Create the Tracks

Setting Up the Scene

Using reference materials will help you efficiently create your 3D model and achieve a good likeness in your end result. The temptation to just "wing it" and start building the objects is often strong, especially when time is short. This temptation should always be suppressed in deference to a well thought-out approach to the task. Sketches, photographs, and drawings can all be used as resources for the modeling process; you can place them in a scene as backdrop images and model over them. Existing, similar models and even video clips or screen captures can be added to a scene as background images.

Creating Planes and Adding Materials

There are two common approaches for adding backdrop images for modeling: using the viewport's Background Image feature and placing the reference images on crossing plane objects or thin boxes. In this exercise, the crossing boxes technique is used as the starting point to build a low-polygon tank.

1. Open or reset 3ds Max.

2. In the Top viewport create a tall, wide box running along the X-axis.

3. In the Parameters rollout of the Command panel, set the Length to 0.1, Width to 400, and Height to 100.

4. With the box still selected, click the Move tool (⬦) in the Main toolbar. Using the Transform type-ins at the bottom of the user interface, move the box to the origin by entering **0** in all three axis fields.

◈ X: 0.0	◆ Y: 0.0	◆ Z: 0.0 ◆

Right-clicking on the spinner arrows to the right of an entry field immediately sets that field to its lowest possible, non-negative value.

The box will move to the origin.

Figure 5.1

The crossing boxes setup

5. Create another box in the Top viewport. This one should run primarily along the *Y*-axis.

6. Set the Length to 150, Width to 0.1, and Height to 100.

7. Move this box to the origin as well. The Perspective viewport should look similar to Figure 5.1.

Adding Materials

Materials are covered in more depth in Chapter 7, "Materials and Mapping." For this exercise, you only need to know enough about the Material Editor to get the reference images to appear on the faces of the boxes. For now, the image maps must be in the same folder as the project file. Chapter 7 will show you how to assign paths where 3ds Max can look for the required support files.

1. Click the Material Editor button (⊞) in the Main toolbar to open the Material Editor.

WHY CHOOSE BOXES INSTEAD OF PLANES?

In this exercise, boxes are used instead of planes simply because the scene can be set up slightly faster using boxes. The pivot point of a plane is at its center, and the pivot point of a box is at the center of its base. Using the Transform Type-Ins, the boxes can quickly be centered at the origin.

The top-left sample sphere has a white border. This is the sample slot where you will make the first material. Your Material Editor might display fewer sample slots.

2. Expand the Maps rollout and click the Diffuse Color button currently labeled *None*.

3. Double-click Bitmap at the top of the Material/Map Browser that opens.

4. In the Select Bitmap Image File dialog box that opens, navigate to the location of the Chapter 5 files from the companion CD and select the Tank Front.jpg file. A thumbnail image of the file will display in the Preview window. Click the Open button to add the first tank image to the material.

5. In the Material Editor's horizontal toolbar, click the Show Map in Viewport button. This causes the image map to be displayed in all viewports using the Smooth + Highlights display.

6. With the shorter box selected, click the Assign Material to Selection button in the Material Editor toolbar. The tank front image will display on the face of of the box.

FREEZING AN OBJECT WITH REFERENCE IMAGES

When objects are used to hold reference images in a scene, you often will want to make sure they do not move. Freezing the objects, so that they cannot be selected, is one solution. When objects are frozen, the default setting has them displayed in gray and the background image is no longer visible. To maintain the visibility, but lose the visual cue that an object is frozen, right-click on the object and choose Object Properties from the Quad menu to open the Object Properties dialog box. In the Object Properties section, in the lower-left corner of the dialog box, uncheck Show Frozen in Gray. When the selected object is in a frozen state, it will continue to display the reference image. Be aware though, that the object must be unfrozen to be hidden or moved in the scene. Because background Image objects are often hidden or moved, the exercises in this section do not freeze them.

7. In the sample slot area, select the sample slot to the right of the current slot. Its boundary turns white to indicate that it is the current material.

8. Repeat Steps 2 through 5, this time choosing the Tank Side.jpg file in the Select Bitmap Image File dialog box.

9. Select the longer box, and then click the Assign Material to Selection button. Your Perspective viewport should look like Figure 5.2. If the images do not appear in the viewport, right-click on the viewport's title and choose Smooth + Highlights from the pop-up menu to change the viewport rendering mode.

10. Close the Material Editor.

Figure 5.2

The scene with the reference images applied to the boxes

The Editable Poly Tools

The Editable Poly toolset available in 3ds Max 9 is very comprehensive and offers almost limitless potential for creating models. Using the proper tools and techniques, both low-polygon models, suitable for games or background objects, and smooth organic-looking objects are well within the capabilities of a skilled artist or modeler. In addition to moving and rotating the editable poly sub-objects, you will often use the following tools in polygonal modeling; you also had the chance to experiment with these tools in Chapter 4.

Weld Vertices Two adjacent polygons can share a vertex or each have its own collocated vertices. Welding combines any selected vertices, within the threshold distance apart, as a single vertex.

Chamfer Edges or Vertices This creates a new surface between two or more adjacent polygons. The angle of the new polygon is one-half the angle between the original polys. This creates a smoother transition between the adjoining surfaces.

Bridge Borders This builds polygons that span the distance between two borders on the same editable poly object.

Cap Borders This closes the selected border by creating new polygons.

Extrude Polygons Polygons are moved along the axis of their *normal,* creating additional vertices, edges, and polygons to connect them back to previously adjacent polys.

Bevel Polygons This is similar to Extrude, with the additional option to scale the relocated poly.

Inset Polygons This creates a new polygon by creating a new set of edges inset from the current polygon's perimeter.

Hinge from Edge This pivots the selected polygons about a user chosen edge. New polygons are created to span the gap.

Attach This attaches two or more editable polys to each other. The result is a single editable poly consisting of multiple, noncontiguous elements.

Cut This creates a new edge on the surface of a polygon.

Connect Edges This connects the selected edges by subdividing them the inserting edges at the newly created endpoints.

This chapter focuses on low-polygon modeling, and Chapter 6, "Organic Poly Modeling," addresses the tools and techniques used in organic modeling. In this exercise, the Vertex and Polygon sub-object levels are mainly used to form the tank's body and turret. In the later exercises in this chapter, lofting, the Lathe modifier, and the Snapshot tools are used to complete the tank.

Building the Tank Body

To begin creating the body of the tank, follow these steps:

1. Continue with the previous exercise or open the Tank1.max file from the companion CD.

2. Right-click on the title of the Front viewport and change its Rendering mode to Smooth + Highlights. Right-click on it again and choose Edged Faces to display the scene objects' edges as well as their surfaces. Do the same to the Left viewport and turn on Edged Faces in the Perspective viewport; only the Top viewport should display the scene in wireframe.

   To construct the tank, you need to build the tank's body by making a box, converting it to an editable poly and then editing its sub-objects.

3. Create the box in the Top viewport to represent the volume of the tank's body between the treads. The Length, Width, and Height values should be approximately 76, 310, and 33, respectively.

4. Change the number of Length Segments to 3, Width Segments to 5, and Height Segments to 2. You want enough segmentation to account for the major changes in the body's structure, but not so much that manipulating the model becomes unwieldy.

5. Move the box into the proper location, as shown in Figure 5.3. Make any necessary changes to the box's parameters so that it matches the volume of the tank body.

One situation that must be addressed is the fact that the box obscures the view of the background images. This is resolved by changing the box's properties so that it is displayed in See-Through mode.

6. With the box selected, right-click in the viewport and choose Object Properties from the Quad menu.

In the Object Properties dialog box that opens, check the See-Through option in the Display Properties section and then click the OK button. The box becomes transparent in the viewports, and the edges remain visible, as shown in Figure 5.4. The keyboard shortcut for this feature is Alt+X.

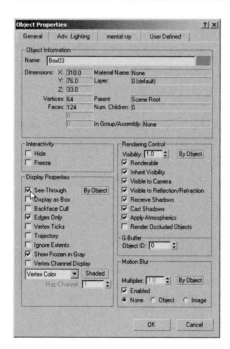

7. Right-click again and choose Convert To → Convert to Editable Poly. The box is no longer a parametric object. It is now a collection of vertices, edges, and polygons, and the Command panel automatically switches to the Modify tab.

8. In the Command panel, change the name of the box to **Tank Body**.

Figure 5.3

The box moved into the proper location

EDITABLE POLY OR EDIT POLY MODIFIER?

In addition to the editable poly object, 3ds Max has the Edit Poly modifier. The Edit Poly modifier has the same toolset as the editable poly object, but it is applied through the Modifier Stack. The Edit Poly modifier has the advantage of allowing you to experiment with the sub-objects and their configurations. If the modifications are acceptable, the Modifier Stack is collapsed to an editable poly object. If the modifications are not acceptable, the modifier is deleted from the stack and the object reverts to its original configuration.

Converting an object directly to an editable poly or collapsing the Modifier Stack requires fewer system resources than maintaining the Modifier Stack intact.

Making changes to the object at a level below the Edit Poly modifier usually adversely affects the model when they are transferred up the stack to the modifier. This is why a warning appears whenever an entry in the Modifier Stack below an Edit Poly modifier is selected.

Forming the Body

1. Maximize the Front viewport and zoom in to the front half of the tank.

2. In the Selection rollout, click the Vertex button ( ) to access the Vertex sub-object level.

3. Drag a selection region around the vertices. Instead of clicking directly on a vertex, use a selection region because doing so will select all the vertices within the region and not only the vertex that is clicked on directly.

4. Move the selected vertices until they are at the top of the leading edge of the tank.

5. Select and move the two rows, one row at a time, to match the perimeter of the front of the tank.

6. Continue forming the tank body by moving the vertices along the top of the tank. In Figure 5.5 the box's See-Through mode is turned off for clarity.

Figure 5.5

The vertices of the front and top of the tank have been moved.

7. Move the middle, horizontal row of vertices to follow the line at the top of the skirt that covers the top of the track. Move the bottom row of vertices to follow the bottom of the skirt. The vertical edges, when possible, should match the edges of the skirt panels.

Creating the Skirts and Refining the Model

The basic shape of the body has been roughed in. The next step is to extend the body to encompass the track skirts. The polygons along the side of the model need to be extended and the sloped top surface need to be created.

1. Continue from the previous exercise or open the Tank2.max file from the companion CD.

2. Select the tank body object if necessary and click the Polygon button (■) in the Modify panel.

3. In the Perspective viewport, select all of the polygons on the right side of the tank.

Several of the Editable Poly tools have two methods of implementing them: direct manipulation and a dialog box. Clicking on most tool buttons allows the user to click and drag on the selected sub-objects in order to manipulate them manually. Clicking the box-shaped Settings button ( ) next to a tool button, when available, opens an associated dialog box where the tool's parameters can be set and previewed.

Clicking the Apply button in a Settings dialog box applies the dialog's current values to the selected sub-objects and then previews the same parameters applied to the newly created and selected sub-objects. Clicking the OK button in a Settings dialog box applies the dialog's current values to the selected sub-objects and then exits the dialog box.

4. In the Edit Polygons rollout, click the Settings button next to the Extrude button to open the Extrude Polygons dialog box.

5. Extend the Extrusion Height value until the polygons reach the inside edge of the skirt shown in the tank's front reference image, and then click the OK button. (See graphic on bottom left.)

6. Deselect the top row of polygons, and then click the Extrude Settings button again. The selected polygons initially extrude to the same amount as the previous extrusion. Reduce the Extrusion Height value until the polygons extend to the outside of the skirt. (See graphic on bottom right.)

7. Render the scene, and you will see the shelf you just created that runs the length of the tank as shown in Figure 5.6. This is the top of the skirt. The small vertical surface above it needs to be collapsed to form the slope at the edges of the tank body's top surface. Vertical edges and their corresponding vertices must be added to the polygons to achieve an acceptable result.

Figure 5.6

The second extru-
sion has created a
shelf along the
tank's top surface.

You may find yourself turning See-Through mode on and off or hiding/unhiding the background images throughout the modeling process. Alt+X is the shortcut to toggle the See-
Through mode.

8. Zoom in to the front-left edge of the model.

9. In the Edit Geometry rollout, click the Cut button.

The Cut tool places vertices on a model and creates the required edges to sub-divide
the polygons. You need to be aware of the Cut tool's cursor appearance. A cursor that
looks like a square over a cross indicates that the vertex will be placed on the surface
of a polygon. A large cross indicates that it will be placed along an edge. A smaller
cross uses an existing vertex as the end point for the new edges.

10. Place the cursor at a vertex on the top or bottom of the shelf where there is no corresponding vertex on the opposite edge, as shown in the left image in Figure 5.7.

11. Click and then move the cursor away from the vertex, and you will see the new edges
forming as shown in the middle image in Figure 5.7.

12. Place the cursor over the edge in the middle of the shelf, as shown in the right image
in Figure 5.7, then click to create the new vertex and edges.

Figure 5.7

Creating the vertical edges needed to slope the top surface.

13. Continue moving back along the tank's left side. Create vertical edges and corresponding vertices wherever the top surface of the tank changes shape, usually to accommodate the tapered edges of the vehicle where the top meets the side.

14. Switch back to the Vertex sub-object level and zoom into the front-left section of the tank again.

15. In the Edit Vertices rollout, click the Target Weld button. Using Target Weld, a selected vertex is moved and then welded to another specific vertex on the object.

16. Select a vertex along the top edge of the tank body. A rubber banding line connects the vertex to the cursor.

17. Move the cursor over the vertex directly below the currently selected vertex and click to complete the weld.

18. Continue welding the vertices of the vertical edges down the length of the tank.

Creating the Track Well and Making the Model Symmetrical

The left side of the tank body is nearly finished. In this section, the bottom of the tank is opened—using Booleans—so that the tracks and the model can be made symmetrical.

1. Continue with the previous exercise or open Tank3.max from the companion CD.

2. Exit any sub-object mode if necessary.

3. Arc Rotate the Perspective viewport so that you can see the bottom of the tank.

4. In the Command panel, click Geometry → Box and check the AutoGrid option at the top of the Object Type rollout.

5. Make sure the 3D Snap Toggle ( ) is active and that only the Vertex snap is selected. Snapping to a vertex is used so that long, thin faces are not created by subtracting a box that does not lie directly along one of the tank's edges.

6. Click the vertex where the skirt meets the first flat poly at the bottom of the tank, and then click again on the vertex at the opposite corner of the last flat poly on the left at the rear of the tank. Drag and click to give the box some height. The box should project downward, from the bottom of the tank, equal to about half the tank body's height. Your scene should look similar to Figure 5.8.

Figure 5.8

Make a box that will be used to delete part of the model using the Boolean functions.

7. Using the S shortcut key, turn off the 3D Snap Toggle. Then move and adjust the box to completely envelop the volume that will be the track well, as shown here.

8. Select the tank body, and then choose Create → Geometry → Compound Objects → ProBoolean, as shown here.

9. Select Subtraction in the Parameters rollout, and then click the Start Picking button in the Pick Boolean rollout.

10. Click the box object in the viewport. The box will be deleted, taking the shared volume of the tank with it. Click the Start Picking button to turn it off.

11. The object is now a Boolean. Convert it back to an editable poly using the Quad menu; there is no need to maintain the data required to edit the object at the Boolean sub-object level.

12. Select and extrude and move the vertices of the polygons on the underside of the tank to match the front reference image.

13. Exit any sub-object mode.

The tank is a symmetrical object; however, rather than repeat the modeling process on the opposite side of the object, we will instead apply the Symmetry modifier. The Symmetry modifier maintains a symmetrical balance between both sides of an object.

14. With the tank body object selected, choose Symmetry from the Modifier List drop-down list.

15. In the Symmetry modifier's Parameters rollout, choose the mirror axis that the object should mirror about. 3ds Max will choose the side of the object that is mirrored about the Mirror axis. If it chooses the wrong side, check the Flip option. Uncheck Slice Along Mirror; this will create a row of edges that aren't needed for this project. Your model should look similar to Figure 5.9. In the figure, the backdrop images have been hidden for clarity.

Making the Exhaust Vents

The last feature to add to the tank body is a series of exhaust vents at the rear of the vehicle. A simple box is created and then the Editable Poly tools are used to inset and isolate the polygons that are then hinged from one edge.

1. Continue from the previous exercise or open the Tank4.max file from the companion CD.

2. Zoom in to the back of the tank.

3. Select Create → Geometry → Standard Primitives → Box, and check the AutoGrid option if necessary.

4. Create a box centered on the rear faces of the tank with a Length, Width, and Height of approximately **18**, **70**, and **7**. Give the box **3** length segments, **4** width segments, and **1** height segment.

5. Convert the box into an editable poly.

Figure 5.9

Apply the Symmetry modifier to model the right side of the tank.

6. Enter the Polygon sub-object level to select all twelve polygons on the rear surface of the box.

7. Click the Settings button next to the Inset button in the Edit Polygons rollout.

8. Set the Inset Amount to 0.85, choose By Polygon in the Inset Type area, and then click the OK button. By Polygon insets each polygon separately, rather than the entire selection as a single object.

9. The exhaust vents need to pivot away from the tank as if they are hinged from the top edge. Select the top row of inset polygons and then click the Settings button next to the Hinge From Edge button in the Edit Polygons rollout.

10. Enter an Angle value of **30**. Click the Pick Hinge button in the Hinge Polygons From Edge dialog box and then click any of the top edges of a selected polygon. All the selected polygons are pivoted about the same axis as the edge you select.

11. Click the Apply button. Apply pivots the selected polygons about the chosen hinge edge and leaves the dialog box open. However, the previous polygons are still selected and have been hinged again.

12. Select all of the polygons in the next row. The previous polygons revert to their hinged state before the Apply button was clicked while the newly selected polygons hinge at too great an angle. They also hinge from the same edge as the previous hinge operation.

13. Click the Current Hinge button, and then select an edge at the back of the middle selected row of polygons.

14. Repeat Steps 11 through 13 on the remaining row of polygons. Click the OK button to close the dialog box and then exit the Polygon sub-object level.

    The exhaust vent is currently a separate object and should be just another part of the tank. The two objects are combined using the Attach feature of the Editable Poly tools. Attach adds the components of one object to another, leaving a single object with the combined features of both. Each object becomes an Element sub-object of the newly formed entity. Exit the sub-object selection level by clicking at the top of the Modifier Stack or using the 6 shortcut key.

15. Select the tank body object. In the Modifier Stack, click on the Editable Poly entry. Changes made to the object below the Symmetry modifier are then passed up to the modifier, maintaining the symmetrical balance of the model.

16. In the Edit Geometry rollout, click the Attach button.

> If more than one object must be attached, or if the objects to attach are difficult to select in the viewports, click the Settings button next to the Attach button. This opens the Attach List dialog box where the objects to attach are selected by name.

17. Click on the exhaust vent. The vent will become part of the tank body object.

18. Click the Attach button again to turn it off. Click Symmetry in the Modifier Stack to leave the Editable Poly level.

Modeling the Turret

The turret must be able to rotate independently of the body, so it needs to be modeled as a separate object. We will start the modeling with a two-dimensional spline, convert it into an editable poly, and then use the Editable Poly tools to form the turret.

1. Continue with the previous exercise or open the Tank5.max file from the companion CD.

2. In the Command panel, select Create → Shapes → Splines → NGon and then drag in the Top viewport to create the shape.

3. Set the Radius value to 35 and the number of Sides to 5.

4. Rotate the ngon so that the point faces forward and the flat edge is parallel to the rear of the tank.

5. Move the shape up to the top of the tank body object and rename it to **Tank Turret**.

6. Convert the shape into an editable poly and then access the Polygon sub-object level.

7. In the Edit Polygons rollout, click the Settings button next to the Bevel button. Bevel is similar to Extrude, but it has the additional capability to scale the selected polygon.

8. Set the Height to 2 and the Outline Amount to 21 to create the initial extrusion and bevel, and then click the Apply button.

9. A second application of the same Bevel settings is applied to the new, currently selected polygon. Set the Height to 18 and the Outline Amount to –10 to create the next level of the turret's height. Click the OK button to apply the bevel and close the dialog box.

9. The rear of the turret needs to be extended and raised so that it does not impact the rear of the tank body when it rotates.

10. Select the polygon at the rear of the turret. Using the Move Transform gizmo, move the polygon toward the rear of the tank and raise it slightly using the background images as references. The edges of the adjacent polygons extend to maintain contact with the poly being moved.

The current sub-object level, or the top level, of an editable poly can quickly be accessed from the tools 1 quadrant of the Quad menu or by using the number keys along the top row of the keyboard as shortcut keys (not the keys in the numeric keypad). The shortcuts are 1 = Vertex, 2 = Edge, 3 = Border, 4 = Polygon, 5 = Element, and 6 = Top Level.

11. Exit the Polygon sub-object level and use the Cut tool to add a horizontal edge dividing the rear polygon. Right-click to discontinue creating edges and then click the Cut button to turn it off.

12. Switch to the Vertex sub-object level. In the Front viewport, use a selection region to select each group of vertices at the rear of the turret and move them into place.

13. Switch to the Left viewport and then select the vertex at the leading point of the turret.

14. In the Edit Vertices rollout, click the Chamfer button.

15. Click and drag in the Left viewport to chamfer the selected vertex and create an additional polygon.

16. Use the Move tool to relocate the new vertices appropriately.

17. Exit the Vertex sub-object level.

Creating the Access Hatch

The tank's crew needs to enter the tank from an access hatch on the top surface. This is also where the vehicle commander will sit to examine the battlefield. To create this feature, the ShapeMerge compound object is used to project the edges of a two-dimensional shape onto a three-dimensional surface, creating new edges and polygons on the 3D surface.

1. In the Top viewport, drag out a donut shape. Set the Radius 1 value to 10 and the radius 2 value to 15.

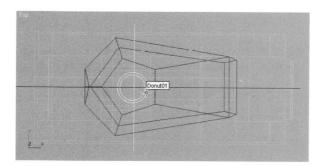

2. Move the donut in the *Z*-axis above the turret, so that the shape's edges will be projected onto the top of the turret.

3. Select the tank turret object, and then select Create → Geometry → Compound Objects → ShapeMerge.

4. In the Pick Operand rollout, click the Pick Shape button and select the donut in the viewport.

5. New edges appear on the top surface of the turret in the shape of the donut. Click the Pick Shape button to turn it off and then convert the turret back into an editable poly.

6. Select the donut shape and then delete it.

7. Select the outer ring of polygons and extrude them 1.5 units. Select the inner circle of polygons and extrude them 0.75 units. Exit the sub-object level when you are done. Save your work.

The main form of the low-poly tank model is now complete. The body has a sloped top and exhaust vent, and the turret has the crew's access hatch. In the next exercise, the Loft compound object is used to model the tank's barrel.

Lofting the Barrel

You can make a simple three-dimensional object by extruding a single two-dimensional shape perpendicular to the shape's orientation using the Extrude modifier. You can quickly complete building boxes, tubes, and even simple 3D text can quickly using the Extrude modifier. In contrast, the Loft compound object also builds 3D models by extruding one 2D spline along a second 2D spline. The first spline, called the *shape object,* becomes the cross section of the new 3D as it follows the second, *path object.* Tunnels, roller coaster tracks, fancy 3D text, and any object that needs to maintain a shape along a path are excellent opportunities to use the Loft compound object.

The Loft compound object has many features and only a few restrictions. The shape object can be complex, consisting of several noncontiguous splines and even nested splines. A new shape object can be selected at any point along the path, and the cross section automatically transitions from one shape to the next. Any 2D shape can be used as the shape object, but only shapes consisting of a single spline can be used as the path object.

Creating the Barrel Shapes and Path

To begin this exercise, several shapes are made to represent the different cross sections found along the length of the barrel.

1. Continue with the previous exercise or open the Tank6.max file from the companion CD.

2. Hide all of the objects in the scene.

3. In the Top viewport, create three circles, each with a radius of 2.75. Create three more circles, one with a radius of 3.75, one with 4.0, and one with 4.5.

4. From smallest to largest, rename the last three circles created to **Barrel**, **Barrel Aim**, and **Barrel Evacuator**.

5. Align each of the smaller circles with one of the larger circles using the Align command. The X, Y, and Z Position check boxes should be checked, as well as the Center option for both the current and target objects.

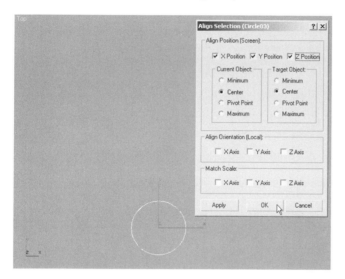

6. Select one of the larger circles, right-click and convert it to an editable spline from the Quad menu.

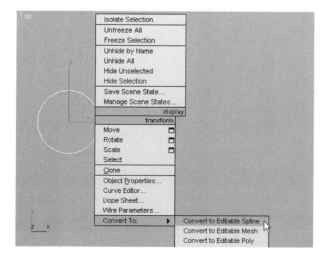

7. In the Geometry rollout, click the Attach button and select the corresponding inner circle. The inner circle will be made a spline component of a two-spline, noncontiguous shape. Click the Attach button to turn it off.

8. Repeat Steps 6 and 7 for the remaining two pairs of circles.

9. Create an ellipse object overlapping the outer circle of the barrel aim object and then attach this ellipse to the barrel aim object. Turn off the Attach tool when you are done.

10. Access the editable spline's Spline sub-object level, and then select the outer circle.

10 Similar to the Boolean operation used earlier in this chapter, spline Booleans can attach, subtract, or display the area of overlapping splines. With meshes, two separate objects are combined to form a single compound object. When using shapes, two separate spline sub-objects of the same shape are combined.

11. In the Geometry rollout, make sure the Union button is selected before clicking the Boolean button.

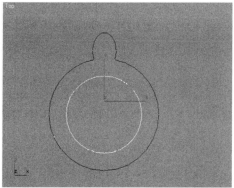

Figure 5.10

Combine the two splines using the Spline Boolean tools.

12. Click the ellipse-shaped spline as shown in the left image in Figure 5.10. The two splines are combined as a single spline as shown in the right image in Figure 5.10.

13. Exit the Spline sub-object level.

14. Unhide the box that shows the side view of the tank.

15. Click the Line tool in the Create ➜ Shapes panel and turn on AutoGrid mode at the top of the Object Type rollout.

16. Click just inside the turret to place one end of the line.

17. Click again at the opposite side of the barrel and right-click to terminate the Line tool.

Lofting the Barrel

The shape or the path objects can be selected when the Loft tool is initiated. When the shape is selected, an instance of the path is moved to the shape; when the path is selected, an instance of the shape is moved to the path. The path is already located properly, so this object is used as the base for the barrel loft operation.

1. With the line already selected, select Create ➜ Geometry ➜ Compound Objects ➜ Loft.

2. In the Creation Method rollout, click the Get Shape button.

3. Place the cursor over the Barrel object—it changes when it is over a valid shape object—and then click.

The shape is lofted along the path.

4. The Loft object is too dense for our needs; the barrel is not going to be bent or twisted, so the number of segments is higher than necessary. Expand the Skin Parameters rollout. Decrease the Shape Steps value to 2 and the Path Steps value to 0. Shape Steps defines the number of subdivisions between each vertex of the shape object, and Path Steps defines the number of subdivisions between each vertex of the path.

Turn on See-Through mode for the barrel. Look closely to the right end of the path in the Front viewport. You should see a yellow cross at the end of the line. The cross indicates the location along the path at which the shape object is placed. The Path field in the Path Parameters rollout sets the percentage or distance along the line where the cross is located. Any shape object placed at the current location of the cross extends to the end of the path unless another shape is placed farther along the path. Only one shape can be placed at any one location along the path.

5. Increase the Path value, in the Path Parameters rollout, until the yellow cross is even with the first, wide portion of the barrel.

6. Click the Get Shape button and then click the Barrel Evacuator shape. The new shape is applied to the path at the current location of the yellow cross, but the cross section transitions from the start of the barrel rather than the immediate transition shown in the reference image.

7. Change the Path value to 0.01 units lower than its current value. The Get Shape button should still be active; if it is not, click it and then click the Barrel shape again. There is a 0.01 transition distance between the cross section shapes, but this will not be noticeable.

The Get Shape button stays active while the Path value is changed. You do not need to turn it on and off while changing the cross sections of a loft.

8. Increase the Path value to the end of the wider section of the barrel, as shown in the following image, and then click on the Barrel Evacuator object.

9. Increase the Path value a small amount, and click the Barrel shape again. The evacuator cross section ends after only a short span, and the barrel's standard diameter begins again.

10. Increase the Path value until the yellow cross is near the end of the barrel, where the aiming point is located. Click the Barrel shape.

11. Increase the Path value a small amount, and then click the barrel aim shape. The Aim Point section of the barrel will appear, but it will be rotated improperly and there the barrel will be twisted as shown in Figure 5.11. These will be fixed shortly.

Figure 5.11

The Barrel Aim cross section is rotated improperly.

12. Increase the Path value until is approximately 98 percent along the path, and then click the barrel aim object again.

13. Increase the Path value a little more, and then click the Barrel shape again. The barrel will extend to the end of the path. Click the Get Shape button to turn it off.

Fixing the Rotation of the Shapes

Each spline has one vertex designated as the first vertex, which defines the direction of the spline. Open splines can have the first vertex at either end point, but not in the middle. Closed splines can have the first vertex at any vertex. Shapes that consist of several spline sub-objects have a first vertex for each spline.

Each cross section of the barrel cleanly transitions to the next, except for the transitions that include the barrel aim shape. To make the transitions, the designated first vertex is matched on each spline used as a shape object in the Loft. This is done so that when the circles are used exclusively, the first vertices will match well because all of the circles will have four vertices and each of their first vertices will be in the same relative location. When the Boolean operations were executed on the Barrel Aim object, the first vertex was relocated so that it no longer aligns with the other shapes.

The Shape and the Path components maintain a relationship with the Loft compound objects. This ensures that any changes made to either are reflected in the Loft. In this section, you will refine the spline shapes so that their vertices match up better.

1. Select the Barrel Aim shape, and then access the Vertex sub-object level. The first vertices are shown in yellow, and all others are shown in white.

If you do not see the vertices, choose Customize → Preferences → Viewports and uncheck Show Vertices as Dots

2. Select the vertex at the top of the ellipse—it turns red to indicate that it is selected—and then click the Make First button in the Geometry rollout. Deselect any vertices, and the top vertex will turn yellow, indicating that it is the new first vertex.

3. Exit the Vertex sub-object level, and then select the Barrel object and access its Vertex sub-object level.

   In addition to designating the top vertex as the first vertex, you will also add additional vertices to match the number found in the barrel aim object. Although this step isn't absolutely necessary when lofting, it adds to the result in this case.

4. Select the top vertex of the outer ring and make it the first vertex.

5. In the Geometry rollout, click the Refine button and click in two places—once on each side of the first vertex to correspond to the extra vertices created when the ellipse was added to the Barrel Aim outer circle. Turn off the Refine button and exit the Vertex sub-object mode.

6. Select the barrel evacuator object and make the top vertex of its outer ring the first vertex, similar to Steps 1 and 2.

7. Select the barrel loft object and rotate it 90 degrees counterclockwise, so the aim point is at the top of the barrel.

8. Rename the Loft01 object to **Barrel Loft**.

Lathing the Wheels

In the previous chapter, you used the Lathe modifier to create knobs for a chest of drawers. Here, you will use the Lathe modifier to create the wheels for the tank.

1. Continue with the previous exercise or open the Tank7.max file from the companion CD. Unhide all hidden objects.

2. In the Front viewport, create a box primitive with a Length and Width of 22 and a Height of 17. Increase the Length and Height Segments to 2. In the Left viewport, move the box over the track area of the background image. This is a temporary stand-in object that is the approximate size of the tank's lower wheels.

3. Click the Line tool in the Create panel, and turn on the AutoGrid option. Draw a line and then modify the vertices until the shape is similar to the line shown in Figure 5.12. The shape should be open on the bottom.

4. Delete the reference box.

5. Select the spline and apply the Lathe modifier.

6. Choose X in the Direction section and Min in the Align section. These parameters cause the line to be revolved around its X-axis and place the pivot point near the bottom of the shape.

7. If necessary, check the Flip Normal option to expose the opposite side of the object's faces.

Figure 5.12

Draw the line to be lathed to create the wheel.

8. Expand the Lathe modifier in the Modifier Stack and choose the Axis sub-object level.

9. In the Left viewport, drag the *Y*-axis handle of the Move Transform gizmo downward to reposition the Lathe axis and expand the radius of the wheel. Be sure not to leave a noticeable hole at the center of the wheel.

10. Exit the Axis sub-object level and rename the object to **Wheel Lower**.

11. Move the wheel to the front of the track. Make seven instanced clones of the wheel and place them over the existing wheels in the background image.

The rear drive sprocket has a different design than the other wheels. Feel free to lathe a different shape to create that object.

12. Select all of the wheels and click the Mirror tool ( ) in the Main toolbar.

13. In the Mirror dialog box, choose Instance in the Clone Selection area. Decrease the Offset amount until the instanced wheels reach the tracks on the opposite side of the tank. Click the OK button to close the dialog box.

Using Snapshot to Create the Tracks

The *tracks* are a series of identical tread objects that are linked together to form a continuous belt. To quickly make all of the track treads, a single tread is made and then it is animated following the path that defines the path for all of the treads. The Snapshot tool is then used to create instanced clones of the tread at a user-specified increment of time. You don't need to know the proper time increment; the value can be "walked-in" by undoing and reapplying the Snapshot tool until the clones are made properly.

Creating the Tread and Path

In this section you will create a single tank tread, using splines and the editable poly's Extrude function. The tread is then copied many times to form a continuous belt of treads.

1. Continue with the previous exercise or open the Tank8.max file from the companion CD.

2. Hide all of the tank objects in the scene. Leave the background panels in place.

3. Zoom into one of the tracks in the Left viewport.

4. Use the Rectangle tool to make a rectangle that roughly follows the perimeter of one of the treads. Use the Line tool to draw a spline that follows the perimeter of the tread shoe. Make sure that the second spline is closed. You may need to move

the Tank Front Reference image box back, behind the construction plane, to see your new objects.

5. Convert one of the objects into an editable poly and then attach the other object to it.

6. Rename this object **Tread**.

7. Select both polygons and bevel them with a Height of 0.7 and an Outline Amount of –0.4. Click OK to apply the bevel and close the dialog box.

8. Select the inner polygon and bevel it with the same settings as the previous bevel. Exit the Polygon sub-object level.

9. Mirror the tread to the other side of the track, choosing Copy in the Clone Selection area. Attach the new editable poly to the tread object.

10. In the Front viewport, draw a line that represents the path that the treads follow. Be sure to close the spline by placing the last vertex point over the first one and clicking the Yes button in the Close Spline dialog box that opens. Edit the path as necessary.

11. Rename the line to **Tread Path**.

Animating the Tread

The Tread must be animated following the path that you just drew. To do this, the Path Constraint is applied to the tread and the path is assigned as the object to follow.

1. Select the Tread object.

2. Click the Motion tab (⚙) of the Command panel.

3. Expand the Assign Controller rollout and select the Position entry in the Controller window.

4. Click the Assign Controller button (). The Assign Position Controller dialog box opens and displays a list of all the possible controllers that can dictate how and object is positioned or moved in the scene.

5. Select Path Constraint from the list and click the OK button. The dialog box will close, and the Path Constraint parameters will appear in the Motion panel.

6. In the Path Parameters rollout, click the Add Path button and then select the tread path object in the viewport.

7. The path name will appear in the Target window. Check the Follow and Allow Upside Down options in the Path Options section. The Follow option causes the animated object to change its orientation to match the angle of the path segment at its current location. The Allow Upside Down option prevents the tread from flipping to maintain an upward orientation when the path returns the treads to the starting point.

You can no longer move the Tread object using the Move Transform gizmo. The position of the tread is now constrained to the location of the path.

8. Move the path to the right until the tread is centered on the treads in the background image.

9. The tread is now animated so that it follows the path over the available length of animation. Drag the Time Slider, which runs along the bottom of the viewports, to the

right until the tread is visible along the top section of the path. As you can see, the tread is oriented improperly; it is rotated vertically instead of horizontally.

10. Select the tread and rotate it exactly 90 degrees to lay it flat along the path.

11. Drag the Time Slider back and forth and watch the tread object in the viewports; it maintains a constant orientation match to the path as it follows it from start to finish.

Creating Tread Clones with Snapshot

The Snapshot tool creates clones of selected objects at any designate interval of frames. This section uses Snapshot to create many identical treads.

1. The Snapshot tool is located on the Extras toolbar. Right-click on a blank area between any tools on a toolbar, and then click Extras on the context menu that appears.

2. With Tread selected, click and hold on the Array tool to display the flyout buttons. Release the mouse over the Snapshot tool to open the Snapshot dialog box.

3. In the Snapshot section, choose Range and make sure the From and To values are 0 and 100, respectively. Set Copies to 80, and choose Instance in the Clone Method section. These settings mean that over the course of the 100 frame animation, instance clones of the tread are created every 1.25 frames for a total of 80 clones (100/80=1.25). Click OK.

4. The clones will be created and then the dialog box will close.

5. If the gap between the Tread clones is incorrect, Undo the Snapshot command and then initiate it again. The last settings used in the Snapshot dialog box are retained and just need to be tweaked.

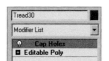

6. Apply a Cap Holes modifier to any of the Tread clones. Cap Holes creates a surface at the back of the tread objects. Without Cap Holes, the treads would not appear in a rendered scene as they pass under the tank wheels. This is because, with no surface on the under side of the treads, the normals of the visible faces would face the wrong directions and would not be rendered.

7. Hide the tread and tread path objects, as well as the background image boxes; they are no longer needed.

8. Unhide the tank body, tank turret, barrel loft, and wheel.

9. Copy the Tread clones, as instances, to the opposite side of the tank.

10. This completed low-poly tank project, with lights and a camera, can be opened as Tank Complete.max from the companion CD.

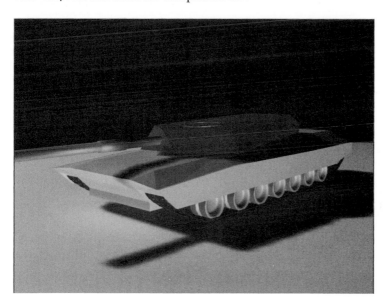

Summary

This chapter explored many of the tools used to create models with lower polygon counts. After setting up the scene with background images, some of the tools within the Editable Poly toolset were used extensively. The Extrude and Bevel tools were used to add or change the topology of polygons, and the Cut tool was used to add edges to surfaces. Booleans for mesh objects and splines were both briefly used to display just a bit of their capabilities, and the Symmetry modifier was used to maintain the model's symmetrical form. The Loft compound object displayed its abilities to extrude one shape along another's and change the cross section entirely at any point. Finally, the Snapshot tool was used to create many instanced copies of a single animated object.

In the next chapter, we will continue exploring the Editable Poly tools while creating a smooth, more organic model.

CHAPTER 6

Organic Poly Modeling

Poly modeling generally takes one of two forms: low polygon-count modeling and high polygon-count, or *organic,* modeling. Because they require less memory, can be easier to animate, and can render quickly, low polygon-count models are useful in games. They can contribute to more realistic scenes by filling in background areas with less-detailed objects. An organic model's elements flow together seamlessly. Take the human head as an example; there may be no clear distinction between where the lower lip stops and the jaw starts or where the top of the nose ends and the forehead begins. A basic knowledge of anatomy and an understanding of balance and proportion are important when you're designing a character that is appealing and believable.

Realistic computer-generated (CG) characters are becoming very common in television and films; they appear as stunt doubles, masses of individuals, and even main characters. Using CG characters can often be safer and cheaper than using an actual actor or a stunt person and, at one time or another, most 3D artists strive to create a character they can call their own. This chapter focuses on using the Editable Poly toolset to create an organic alien model suitable for character animation. With the exception of the alien's eyes, the model is a single object created from a very basic form.

Topics in this chapter include:

- **Setting Up the Scene**

- **Creating the Basic Form**

- **Adding Detail**

- **Final Touches**

Setting Up the Scene

As mentioned in the previous chapter, acquiring and utilizing good reference material is essential for creating an adequate character in 3ds Max. At the minimum, sketches of the character's front and side features are necessary to use as background images. Additional perspective sketches from several points of view and sketches of specific features, such as headgear, weapons, or other devices should be near at hand during the modeling process for quick reference.

Creating Planes and Adding Materials

Like the Tank exercise in Chapter 5, "Modeling in 3ds Max: Part II," this exercise begins by creating crossed boxes and applying the reference images to them.

1. Open or Reset 3ds Max.

2. In the Top viewport, create a tall, wide box running along the *X*-axis.

3. In the Parameters rollout of the Command panel, set the Length to 0.01, Width to 66, and Height to 56.

4. Rename this box **Alien Front Image**.

5. With the box still selected, click the Move tool (⊕) in the Main toolbar. In the Transform Type-Ins at the bottom of the user interface, move it to the origin by entering **0** in all three axis fields.

   The box will move to the origin.

6. Create another box in the Top viewport. This one should run primarily along the *Y*-axis.

7. Set the Length to 20, Width to 0.01, and Height to 56 and then rename the box **Alien Side Image**.

8. Move this box to the origin as well. The Perspective viewport should look similar to Figure 6.1.

Adding the Materials

The reference materials must be added to the boxes to provide a visual cue during the modeling process. It's important to ensure that the significant features of the character, which appear in both reference images, are at the same height. For instance, the top of the head and the shoulders should be at the same scene elevation to make the modeling process easier, eliminating as much guess work as possible.

Figure 6.1

The crossing boxes setup

1. Click the Material Editor button ( ) in the Main toolbar to open the Material Editor.

2. Select the top-left sample sphere by clicking in it. This is the sample slot where you will make the front material.

3. Expand the Maps rollout, and click the Diffuse Color button currently labeled *None*.

4. Double-click the Bitmap entry at the top of the Material/Map Browser that opens.

5. In the Select Bitmap Image File dialog box that opens, navigate to the Chapter 6 files on the companion CD and select the `Alien Front Sketch.jpg` file. Click the Open button to add the first alien image to the material.

SETTING UP THE SCENE ■ 229

6. In the Material Editor's horizontal toolbar, click the Show Map in Viewport button. This causes the image map to be displayed in all viewports using the Smooth + Highlights display after the material has been assigned to the scene objects.

7. With the Alien Front Image box selected, click the Assign Material to Selection button in the Material Editor toolbar. The alien's front reference image will be displayed on the face of the box.

Reference images should not be drawn on white paper before they are scanned to a digital file. By default, white is the color of selected objects in 3ds Max. They can be visually lost on a white background. If the drawings are on white background, use Photoshop, or another image-editing package, to process the images so the background is gray.

8. In the sample slot area, select the sample slot to the right of the current slot. Its boundary will turn white to indicate that it is the current material.

SEEING QUALITY BITMAPS IN THE VIEWPORTS

The Show Map in Viewport toggle ( ) in the Material
Editor determines whether the maps in a material are
displayed in all viewports set to the Smooth + Highlights display mode. In many cases, the quality of the
images displayed is high enough to align bitmap features to model features but not high enough to effectively use the images as reference elements. The quality
of the bitmap display is set in the Preference Settings
dialog box. The following steps and images explain the
method for changing the bitmap viewport quality
when using the DirectX video driver. The steps to follow when using the OpenGL or Software drivers are
similar.

1. From the Main menu, select Customize →
   Preferences.

2. Click on the Viewports tab, and then click on the Configure Driver button
   in the Display Drivers section.

3. In the Configure Direct3D dialog box that appears, select a resolution
   in the Download Texture Size section or select the Match Bitmap
   Size as Closely as Possible option to increase the displayed resolution
   of any maps shown in the viewports. This does not affect the actual
   size of the images used in the scene, only how they are shown in the
   viewports.

4. If necessary, repeat Step 3 to increase the resolution of the background
   image in the Background Texture Size section.

5. Click OK in both dialog boxes to accept the changes. You must close and
   then reopen 3ds Max for the changes to take affect.

Be aware that increasing the displayed resolution can decrease viewport
performance and increase the system resources required to manage the
scene.

Figure 6.2

The scene with the reference images applied to the boxes

9. Repeat Steps 2 through 5, this time choosing the Alien Sketch Side.jpg file in the Select Bitmap Image File dialog box.

10. Select the narrower box and click the Assign Material to Selection button. Your Perspective viewport should look like Figure 6.2. If the images do not appear in the viewport, right-click on the viewport's title and choose Smooth + Highlights from the pop-up menu to change the viewport rendering mode.

11. Close the Material Editor.

Creating the Basic Form

The alien character's form is pretty common: one head, one neck, two arms, a torso, and two legs. This is a frequently seen standard for bipedal, humanoid 3D characters. This form can be further refined by adding facial features and modeling the arms and legs into upper and lower segments with clearly defined fingers and toes, similar to the exercises in Chapter 4, "Modeling in 3ds Max: Part I."

When you create an organic character, you might be tempted to try to model one piece of the final product, such as the head or hands, to completion before you begin modeling another piece. This is rarely a good method because the scale and balance of the components must be built precisely from the beginning. A better practice is to block out the basic form and focus on the size and crucial shapes of major elements and then add detail for the finer features. The following exercises describe the steps required to block out the alien's major features.

Blocking the Torso

The basic structure for the torso will begin with a simple box primitive. After converting the box into an editable spline, you will add the Symmetry modifier to the object so that any manipulations performed on one side are instantly performed on the other.

1. Continue with the previous exercise or open the Alien1.max file on the companion CD.

2. Right-click on the name of each Smooth + Highlights–rendered viewport and choose Edged Faces to display the rendered surfaces and the edges of each face.

3. In the Top viewport, create a box with two Length, Width, and Height segments. Rename the box to **Alien** and change its color, if necessary, to a hue that contrasts with the boxes that display the reference images.

4. Move the box upward until it is centered on the torso in the reference images and modify its parameters to fit. It's better if the box is slightly smaller than the sketch so that the image is visible beyond the box similar to the box shown in Figure 6.3.

5. Convert the box into an editable poly object.

Figure 6.3

Move and adjust the box to match the reference images.

6. Access the Vertex sub-object level, and delete the left half of the box by dragging a selection region around the left-most vertices and then pressing the Delete key.

7. Exit the Vertex sub-object level. It's important that the next step occur at the object level.

8. Switch to the Modify tab of the Command panels and apply the Symmetry modifier to the box. The Symmetry modifier allows you to model only one side of the character while it automatically models the reciprocal side.

The box currently obscures the reference images and can make modeling more difficult. Turning on the See-Through mode in the object's properties will reduce this problem.

9. With the Alien object selected, right-click in the viewport and choose Object Properties from the Quad menu.

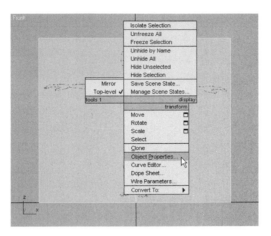

10. In the Object Properties dialog box that opens, check the See-Through option in the Display Properties section and then click the OK button. The object will become transparent in the viewports and the edges will remain visible.

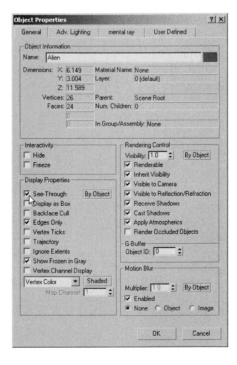

Forming the Torso

You will begin forming the basic shape of the torso my moving the editable poly's vertices and extruding its polygons.

1. In the Modify panel, select the Editable Poly level of the Modifier Stack. The left side of the object will disappear. This will allow you to select vertices, with a selection region, in the Right viewport without selecting the vertices on the opposite side.

2. Access the Vertex sub-object level and start to form the torso by moving the vertices in the Front viewport to match the background image, as shown in Figure 6.4. Use a selection region to select both the front vertices and the vertices directly behind them.

3. Switch to the Right viewport and move the vertices to match the other reference image.

Figure 6.4

Adjust the editable poly's vertices to match the background image.

The alien's back has two curves; a concave curve at the lower part of the spine and a convex curve at his rear. The alien's front has a similar, more subtle compound curve. The editable poly object, however, does not have enough vertices to match the complexity of the image. The Chamfer tool is generally used to refine or soften an edge by subdividing it into two colinear edges, with new polygons located between them. The angle between the new polys and the old polys is one-half the previous value. When the polys on both sides of the edges are coplanar, no new angle is introduced to the model, but a gap is created between two new edges.

4. In the Selection rollout, click the Edge button (⟨) to switch to the Edge sub-object level.

5. Select the four edges that horizontally bisect the object. Switch viewports as necessary to select them all.

6. In the Edit Edges rollout, click the Chamfer button.

7. Click and drag on any of the selected edges to chamfer all of them.

8. Release the mouse button. Click and drag again to add two more rings of edges and further refine the mesh. Make sure that you do not drag so far that the new edges overlap.

9. Switch back to the Vertex sub-object level and continue to move the vertices to match both the front and side reference images.

10. Switch to the Perspective viewport. Zoom and arc-rotate the view to see the top polygon in the model.

11. In the Polygon sub-object level, select the top polygons in the model and click on the Extrude tool in the Edit Polygons rollout. Be sure to select both the front polygon and the rear polygon hidden behind the box holding the front reference image.

12. Click and drag the top polygons to extrude them approximately one-third the distance to the alien's armpit. Release the mouse button and repeat the process two more times until the top polygon is even with the top of the alien's armpit.

13. Switch back to the Vertex sub-object level and move the new vertices to match the reference images. The inner pair of vertices should be higher than the other pair, causing the top edges to no longer be parallel to the others.

Cleaning Up the Geometry

When you create models with the editable poly toolset, you will often generate unnecessary or unwanted polygons. In this section, you will eliminate some internal polygons that the model doesn't need.

1. Continue from the previous exercise. Select all of the polygons in the model, right-click in the viewport, and choose Isolate Selection from the Quad menu. The two boxes will disappear and the torso will remain.

2. Arc-rotate the viewport to look at the inner surfaces between the two halves of the model. You will be able to see the six internal polygons created with the Extrude tool, as shown in Figure 6.5. You might need to turn off the See-Through mode to see these polygons clearly. These, and the six additional polygons created by the Symmetry modifier, are undesirable because they make the model unnecessarily complex and can affect later results when you use several of the Polygon Editing tools.

3. Select and delete the six internal polygons.

4. In Edge sub-object mode, select all the edges, front and back, from the alien's shoulder to its hip and then chamfer these edges. The new polygons created by the Chamfer tool will become the curvature around the sides of the alien.

Figure 6.5

The internal polygons created with the Extrude tool

5. Exit the Edge sub-object level. Click the Symmetry entry in the Modifier Stack to see the model of the torso thus far.

6. Exit Isolation mode.

Adding the Arms

The next step in roughing out the basic form is to add the alien's shoulders, arms, and hands. The arms will be partitioned into a shoulder/clavicle element and an upper and lower arm. Modeling a character's hands was covered in Chapter 4, so we will only skim over it here.

1. Continue with the previous exercise or open the Alien2.max file on the companion CD.

2. Select the Alien object, click the Editable Poly entry in the Modifier Stack, and access the Polygon sub-object level.

3. Select the four top polygons at the alien's shoulder area, including the chamfered polys.

4. In the Edit Polygons rollout, click the Settings button next to the Hinge From Edge button to open the Hinge Polygons From Edge dialog box.

5. Click the Pick Hinge button and select either of the straight, horizontal edges near the armpit. The selected polygons will be previewed in the target orientation in the viewports.

6. Set the Angle value to about 17 and click the Apply button. The previewed orientation will take affect. The selected polys will be previewed rotating another 17 degrees about the selected edge. Click the OK button to accept the second hinge action and exit the tool. Your model should look similar to Figure 6.6.

7. Switch to the Vertex sub-object level and adjust the vertices to define the clavicle and shoulder area.

Throughout the modeling process, you may find yourself turning the See-Through mode on and off to hide and unhide the background images and to isolate the model. The images in this chapter switch between these modes and practices as required. Press Alt+X to toggle See-Through on and off easily. Alt+Q will get you into (but not out of) Isolation Mode.

The Chamfer tool in the Edit Vertices rollout is similar to the same tool in the Edit Edges rollout. Rather than subdividing an edge into two colinear edges, it creates a new polygon by creating new vertices, projecting into all the polygons that share each selected vertex. If the arm were extruded now, it would be very boxy and would require the edges to be chamfered. By first chamfering the vertices, the resultant extrusion is more acceptable.

Figure 6.6

Hinge the shoulder area twice.

8. Zoom into the shoulder and select the four vertices at the corners of its perimeter. Click the Settings button (▢), next to the Chamfer button in the Edit Vertices rollout.

9. In the Chamfer Vertices dialog box that opens, increase the Chamfer Amount to divide the angle between the perpendicular edges. Click the OK button when you are done.

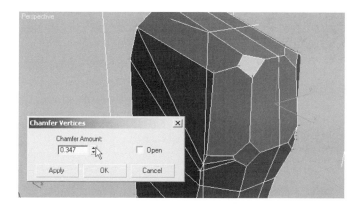

There is a vertical edge that bisects the polygons that will be extruded to make the arm. If this remains, it will create undesired internal polygons. Selecting and deleting the offending edge would also delete the polygons that it contributes to the perimeter, and it would leave a hole in the model. The Remove tool, however, deletes the edge and combines the adjacent polygons into a single polygon.

10. In Edge sub-object mode, select the edge and click the Remove button in the Edit Edges rollout. The edge will be deleted and the perimeter will remain intact.

11. Select the polygon where the arm will be, and extrude it to about half the length of the upper arm.

12. Move the vertices to straighten the arm, and then select and scale all end vertices down slightly.

13. Repeat Steps 11 and 12 two more times, scaling the vertices up at the elbow and then down at the wrist.

14. Similar to the modeling procedure described in Chapter 4 and here in Chapter 6, block out the basic form for the alien's hand. When completed, the hand and fingers should look similar to those shown in Figure 6.7.

Adding the Legs

To create the legs and feet, you'll use methods similar to the ones you used to create the arms and hands. Extrusions of polygons, chamfering of vertices and edges, and scaling vertices and polygons are all mainstays of polygonal modeling. In this section, you will also use the QuickSlice tool to add edges to polygons where additional detail is necessary.

Figure 6.7

The modeled hand and fingers

1. Continue with the previous exercise or open the Alien3.max file from the companion CD.

2 Hide the Alien Front Image object or move it behind the model so that it doesn't obstruct the view in the Perspective viewport.

3. Arc-rotate and zoom into the polygon that will be extruded to create the leg at the bottom of the model.

4. Select the edge that bisects the bottom polygons. Use the Remove tool to delete the edge.

5. Select the bottom polygon. In the Edit Geometry rollout, click the QuickSlice button. The cursor will turn into an arrow.

6. The intent here is to add an additional polygon near the centerline of the model to accommodate the detail around the crotch. Click on the edge in the front of the model that runs from the center to the side, near the symmetry plane that divides the model in half.

7. Move the cursor. A thin line that projects from the initial point through the tip of the cursor to the edge of the selected polygon will be selected.

8. Click in a similar location on the opposite edge at the back of the model. A new edge will appear, and the single selected polygon will be divided into two coplanar polygons.

9. Click the QuickSlice button to turn it off.

10. Select the larger polygon and extrude it about half the distance to the knee.

11. Select and then move and scale the vertices at the end of the leg to match the reference images.

12. Repeat the leg extrusions at the alien's knee, mid-calf, and ankle. Adjust the vertices at each location.

13. Arc-rotate so that you can see the inner portion of the leg. These edges are not chamfered like the edges on the outside of the leg. Select one inside-vertical edge at the front of the model and another at the back of the model.

14. In the Selection rollout, click the Loop button. Loop expands the selection to include all edges that meet, end to end, that are aligned with the selected edges.

Instead of expanding the selection, you can use the spinner arrows, next to the Loop button, to shift the edge selection to the next aligned edges. The Loop tools at the other sub-object levels work in a similar fashion.

15. All of the inside edges, from the ankle to the crotch are selected. Use the Chamfer tool or the Chamfer Settings tool to subdivide the edges.

Adding the Feet

Now that the alien has a leg to stand on, you need to give him a foot. You'll continue using the Extrude and Chamfer tools along with the Hinge Polygons From Edge dialog box, as you did with the hand.

1. Continue from the previous exercise. Extrude the polygon at the base of the leg, until it extends to the bottom of the foot.

2. Select the polygon at the back of the foot and use the Hinge Polygons From Edge dialog box to create the polygons that make up the heel portion of the foot. Pick the edge at the top of the heel as the hinge. Click OK to close the dialog box.

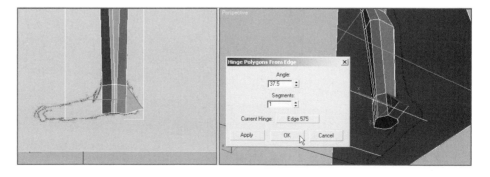

3. Chamfer the edges of the polygons created with the Hinge From Edge tool, and then adjust the vertices as required.

4. Extrude the polygon, at the front of the ankle, twice to create the foot. The first extrusion is used to make the transition from the ankle to the foot and the second extends the foot to the beginning of the toes.

5. If the foot is pivoted incorrectly, select all of the vertices from the ankle down and rotate them until the foot points forward or slightly outward.

6. Continue to edit the vertices and edges of the feet to block out their basic forms.

7. Use the QuickSlice and Extrude tools, along with the transforms, to create the alien's toes and complete the leg.

Modeling the Head

The last major component to add to the model is the alien's head. In addition to the tools that have already been covered, the Cut tool, the Soft Selection method, and the Shaded Face Toggle option are added to your 3ds Max modeling toolset options.

1. Continue with the previous exercise or open the Alien4.max file from the companion CD.

2. Zoom into the top of the model, where the neck will be. Select the vertices at the base of the neck, along the symmetry plane, and move them vertically as shown here.

3. Select the two polygons at the top of the neck and click the Z button, next to the Make Planar button in the Edit Geometry rollout. This will rotate all of the selected polygons until they are flush with the Z plane.

4. Select the edge that divides the top polygons and delete it with the Remove tool.

5. You will want to refine the edges of the neck that will be extruded to create the neck in the next step. The objective here is to reduce the angle of the intersecting edges at the corners of the top polygon by adding additional edges. Instead of chamfering the edges or vertices, click the Cut tool in the Edit Geometry rollout. Create a new edge by clicking at each point where you want the new vertices to be. Right-click to begin a new cut line. Click the Cut button when you are done.

6. Extrude the neck polygon and adjust its vertices to match both of the reference images. The alien's chin will drop well below the top of the neck in the side image.

7. Using the Extrude tool, move the vertices as required to form the front and sides of the head so it will be similar to the model shown in Figure 6.8.

8. Extrude the polygons at the back of the head about half the remaining distance to the back of the head in the reference image, and then scale the vertices down a bit.

When sub-objects are moved, rotated, or scaled, the effect is applied explicitly and fully only to the selected sub-objects. This can result in a blocky, uniform appearance that is unappealing in an organic model. Soft selection lessens that effect by applying the transforms fully to the selected sub-objects and then, to a lesser degree, to the sub-objects that are in close proximity to the selection. The sub-objects that are closer to selection are more affected by the transform, and those that are farther away are less effective. When soft selection is used, 3ds Max color codes the selected sub-objects to provide a visual cue regarding how much of an affect the transforms will have. The colors range from red to orange to yellow to green to blue, with red sub-objects being fully affected and blue being unaffected.

Figure 6.8

The modeled head after the front and sides are blocked out

9. In the Soft Selection rollout, check the Use Soft Selection option and click the Shaded Face Toggle button.

10. Increase or decrease the Falloff value until the non-blue colors extend to polygons at the side of the head.

11. Move and scale the end polygons to match the reference image.

Refining the Head

You can see that the head needs additional segmentation to match the reference image. We'll use the Connect tool to add that segmentation. The Connect tool adds edges to a model by subdividing pairs of selected edges.

1. Continue from the previous exercise. Turn off Use Soft Selection and switch to the Edge sub-object level.

2. Select any of the nearby horizontal edges on the side of the head that need to be subdivided.

3. In the Selection rollout, click the Ring button. Similar to the Loop tool, the Ring tool selects all edges that are nearly parallel to the selected edge and lie along the same plane. All the horizontal edges that need to be subdivided are selected, as shown in Figure 6.9.

4. To open the Connect Edges dialog box, click the Settings button next to the Connect button in the edit Edges rollout. Set the Segments value to 2 and click the OK button. All of the selected edged are subdivided into three edges each.

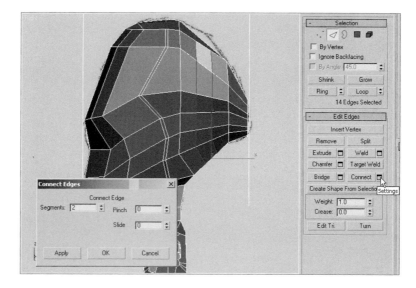

Figure 6.9

The modeled head after the front and sides are blocked out

5. Turn Use Soft Selection back on and reduce the Falloff value until only two rings of polygons, outside of the selected edges, show any colors other than blue.

6. Move the selected edges upward to match the reference image.

7. Continue shaping the head using the Connect option, Remove option, Soft Selection option, and some transforms to block it as desired.

8. Many polygons were created on what will become the internal area of the head. They must be removed.

9. Access the Polygon sub-object level. In the Front viewport, use a window selection to select all the unwanted polygons and then delete them.

The basic form of the alien model is complete. Anyone looking at it can clearly see a humanoid character with a large head that slopes down in front and tapers in the back. In the next section, we'll cover adding details to the model, including a more-defined musculature, eyes, and a mouth.

Adding Detail

With the basic form blocked out, the alien needs to have detail added to define its appearance and make it unique among its peers. You'll start by adding the TurboSmooth modifier to subdivide and smooth the mesh, and then you'll continue the modeling process by working on the legs, arms, torso, and finally the head. TurboSmooth creates a nonrendering framework around the mesh, with its own vertices that can be weighted to control the localized deformation of the mesh.

The TurboSmooth modifier has two iteration options: Iterations and Render Iterations. The Iterations option determines the amount of smoothing the model has in the viewports. If Render Iterations is unchecked, Iterations also determines the amount of smoothing in renderings. When Render Iterations is checked, the amount of smoothing in renderings can be different, usually higher, than the smoothing shown in the viewports. This allows very dense models to be rendered, while less dense models are worked on in the viewports.

The TurboSmooth Modifier

In this section, you'll apply the TurboSmooth modifier to the alien model to smooth its surfaces.

1. Continue with the previous exercise or open the Alien5.max file on the companion CD.

2. Exit any sub-object level, if necessary, and then select the Symmetry modifier in the Modifier Stack.

3. Expand the Modifier List and click the TurboSmooth modifier. The modifier appears at the top of the Modifier Stack.

> To quickly locate a modifier in the Modifier List, repeatedly press the letter key that corresponds to the first letter in the modifier's name. 3ds Max will select the first modifier that starts with that letter and then cycle through the list, selecting the next modifier that starts with that letter each time the key is pressed.

4. Set Iterations to 1 and make sure that Isoline Display is unchecked in the Main section of the TurboSmooth rollout. Isoline Display causes only the model's original edges to display, rather than all the edges in the newly subdivided mesh. When Iterations is set to a high value, this may be beneficial by reducing the complexity on the model in the viewport.

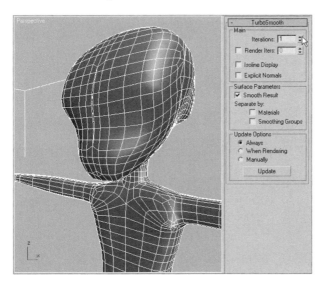

> Use caution when increasing the Iterations value. Dragging the Iterations spinner upward quickly, or entering a high value in the Iterations field, can cause Max to generate an enormous number of polygons that may exceed the memory capacity of your system, resulting in a crash. It is best to increase the Iterations value in increments of 1 until the minimum acceptable level of smoothing is obtained.

While remaining in the Editable Poly level of the Modifier Stack, you will need to see the smoothed result of your character throughout the modeling process. This is quickly accomplished by clicking the Show End Result On/Off Toggle button (▯ / ▯) just below the Modifier Stack.

Adding Detail to the Legs

The legs need more detail, especially around the knee, to allow them to deform properly when they are animated.

1. Unhide any reference images and zoom into the area around the alien's leg.

   The knee is one area that needs additional detail to accommodate any deformations caused by animating with bones or Character Studio.

2. Select all of the polygons directly above and below the knee, and then use the Quick-Slice tool twice, once above and once below the knee, to add additional segmentation. The angle of the slice plane should match the angle of the edges above or below the new edges.

3. In Vertex sub-object level, select the vertices at the front of the knee. Turn on Use Soft Selection, and then reduce the Falloff value until only the vertices near the front of the knee are fully or partially selected.

4. Move the vertices forward to create the bulge of the knee cap.

5. Turn off Use Soft Selection and then use the Connect tool to further subdivide the edges in the calf area. Move the new edges so they are concentrated around the mid-calf area.

6. At the Vertex sub-object level, move and scale the vertices to sculpt the calf.

7. Do the same for the thigh area, making sure the vertices near the center do not cross the centerline of the model.

8. Use the tools discussed in this section to finish modeling the legs the way you want them. Using the Cut tool and then using the Bevel Polygons tool is an excellent method for modeling the calcaneus, the bone that protrudes from the side of the ankle. To make sure the edits are effective and generating the correct result, toggle the Show End Result button and render the scene frequently.

9. Zoom out and render the legs.

Adding Detail to the Arms

To allow proper deformation, additional detail must be added to the elbow area, in a manner similar to the way you detailed the legs. Additional musculature is also required in the arms and at the shoulders. Be sure to toggle the Show End Result button back and forth to see how the low-polygon modeling affects the final, smooth object.

1. Select the vertical edges in the arm, from the bicep to the wrist, and use the Connect tool to add additional vertical edges to the arm, as shown here.

2. Move the new edges near the elbow, leaving one vertical loop of edges at the bicep and the forearm.

3. With Use Soft Selection turned on, move and scale the elbow until it is slightly larger than the arm.

4. Select the edge that defines the bulge of the bicep. With the character's hands oriented with the palms face down, the bicep should bulge forward and not upward.

The character has long slender fingers that tend to look like tubes or tentacles when the diameter of each segment is similar in size. To help define the individual finger bones, you need to increase the size of the knuckles.

5. Select all of the edges located at the alien's knuckles, including the thumb, and chamfer them twice. The second chamfer should concentrate two sets of edges closer to the centerline of the knuckles.

6. Select the inner pair of edges at each knuckle and scale the edges to increase their diameter.

7. If the knuckles appear to change the fingers' diameters too abruptly, turn on Use Soft Selection and scale them again along the X-axis only.

8. The hand tapers too smoothly from the wrist to the fingers, and there is no clear line of delineation between the forearm and the fingers. Use the QuickSlice tool to add an additional edge across the hand, and then move and scale it to define the hand better.

9. The thumb is tucked under the hand in an unnatural position. Select and move the vertices of the thumb and the inside heel of the palm forward and out from underneath the index finger.

10. Make any additional changes to the hand that you like. For instance, if the finger tips are too boxy in a smooth rendered image, move the vertices, near the end of the fingers, back a bit, or select and bevel the end polygons.

TARGET WELDING VERTICES

Having multiple vertices in close proximity can result in long thin faces that are difficult to deform, unacceptable folds or creases in the surfaces, and undesirable results when using the Bevel or Inset tools. These modeling problems are all common. They can be reduced or eliminated by welding the vertices. *Standard welding,* which is covered later in this chapter, replaces two or more selected vertices, within a specified distance from each other, with a single vertex located at the averaged location of the original vertex selection.

Target welding works somewhat differently. With the Target Weld button activated in the Edit Vertices rollout, you click the vertex to be eliminated and then click the target vertex. The original vertex moves to the target vertex, adjusts its associated edges and polygons, and is welded to it. The original vertex and target vertex must be separated by only a single edge.

Refining the Shoulder

The shoulder is currently flat from the end of the arm to the neck. In this section you will add the detail required to place a bulge at the top of the shoulder that tapers into the clavicle.

1. Continue from the previous exercise. Select and chamfer the loop of edges that runs over the shoulder and under the arm pit.

2. Select the three edges that run along the clavicle and use the Connect tool to add two more sets of perpendicular edges.

   When Editable Poly sub-objects are moved in a viewport, they adhere to the same transform coordinate system restrictions as any other object in a scene. Similar to using the Local transform coordinate system, the Constraints option in the Edit Geometry rollout, allows you to limit the movement of the sub-objects to be parallel to the associated edges or polygons. This diminishes any unnecessary deformations caused by moving a sub-object away from a surface of the model.

3. With the four new edges selected, expand the Constraints drop-down list in the Edit Geometry rollout and choose Edge.

4. Move the edges closer to the shoulder. Note that they do not leave the plane in which they lie.

5. Change the Constraints option back to None.

6. Select the vertex at the top of the shoulder. Using Soft Selection, move it upward to create the shoulder bulge.

7. Zoom out and render the modeled arm; it should look similar to Figure 6.10.

Figure 6.10

The model after adding detail to the arm, hand, and shoulder

Adding Detail to the Torso

The shape of the alien's torso is fairly plain, and decidedly not anatomically correct, so the detail added will be subtle. You will need to add some bulges for the wider hips and a belly button.

1. Continue from the previous exercise or open the Alien6.max file from the companion CD.

2. Zoom into the alien's hips, and select the three bands of horizontal edges that circle the alien at the waistline.

3. Chamfer the new edges. Using Edge Constraints, concentrate the edges around the hip area.

4. Turn the Constraints off and turn Use Soft Selection on. Then move the hip vertices into place.

5. Use the Cut tool to create the perimeter of the belly button and remove any internal edges that may occur.

6. Select the edges that encircle the belly button, omitting the edges along the center line of the model, and chamfer them. The chamfer prevents the next step from affecting the polygons and edges that are relatively distant from this small detail.

7. Select the polygon at the center of the belly button and move it into the alien's abdomen.

Adding Detail to the Head

Besides the overall shape of the head, the two main features that must be considered are the eyes and the mouth. Without lips, a tongue, or teeth to consider, the mouth is the simpler of the two features to model; it consists of a mouth-shaped hole in the head. Rather than deleting faces, the mouth will be extruded into the head to prevent the appearance of a hollow skull.

The areas surrounding the eyes are modeled using the Cut tool to define the shape and then Chamfer and Extrude to create the raised perimeter. The eyes themselves are spheres that are altered using the Hemisphere parameter.

Creating the Mouth

The mouth is going to be a simple extruded polygon, with the extrusion projecting into the alien's head. You'll create the perimeter of the mouth using the Cut tool.

1. Zoom into the mouth area.

2. Use the Cut tool to draw the edges around the perimeter of the mouth.

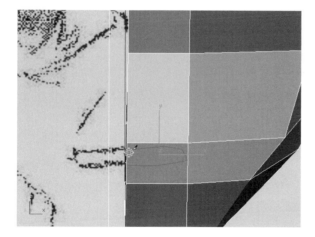

3. Use the Bevel Polygons dialog box to extrude and scale the polygon into the alien's head. A negative Height value causes the bevel to recess the polygon, rather than extrude it farther into the scene.

4. Select the edge at the center line of the mouth and delete, rather than remove, it to open that side of the mouth and eliminate any internal faces.

5. Start modeling the eye area by moving the vertices to cause the vertices to flow around the edges of the raised eye ridge.

6. To subdivide an edge at a particular location, switch to the Edge sub-object level. Click the Insert Vertex button in the Edit Edges rollout. Click on any edge to place a new vertex.

7. Continue to manipulate the vertices and edges until the eye area is a single, flat polygon. Select the eye polygon and use the Inset Polygons dialog box to create the ring of faces that surrounds the eye.

8. Delete the central eye polygon and then select all of the polygons that surround the new hole.

9. Bevel the selected polygons to create the eye ridge.

Creating the Eyes

Rather than creating the eyes as components of the alien model, you will make them as separate objects that can be linked to the model. This method allows for greater flexibility when apply materials to, or animating, the eyes.

1. Exit any sub-object level. Create a sphere with a Radius of approximately 3 in the Front viewport.

2. Decrease the Hemisphere value until the visible boundary of the sphere is slightly larger than the eye hole.

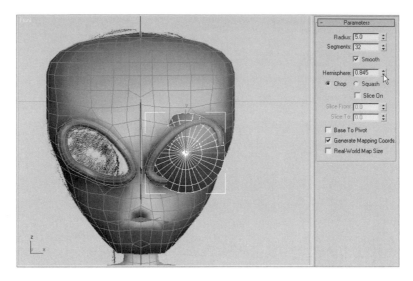

3. Convert the eye to an editable poly. Rotate and move it to position it correctly in the eye socket.

4. Make any necessary edits to the vertices or edges to hide any portions of the sphere that protrude through the surface of the alien.

5. Exit any sub-object level. Rename the object **Eye Left**.

6. Click the Mirror tool (▶◀) in the Main toolbar to open the Mirror dialog box. Set the axis to X and set Clone Selection to Copy. Increase the Offset amount until the new eye appears correctly in the other eye socket.

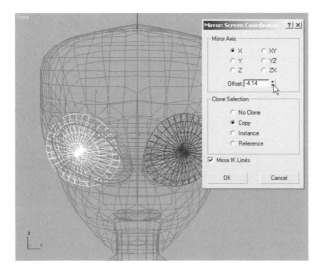

7. Rename the new object to **Eye Right** and make any changes required to make the eye fit in the socket.

8. Select both eye objects and link them to the Alien object to cause them to follow the alien's transforms.

Final Touches

The major portion of the modeling is complete. The only remaining tasks are to weld the seams, clean up any remaining areas with unwanted sharp corners, and add a few asymmetrical features so that the model does not look quite so computer generated.

1. Continue with the previous exercise or open the `Alien7.max` file from the companion CD.

2. Hide the reference images if necessary.

> Before you proceed with the next step, you should always save a copy of the model or the entire scene, in case you need to edit it at the Symmetry or TurboSmooth level.

3. Select the alien and convert it to an editable poly.

4. Select all of the vertices that share the center line of the model or border an opening at the center generated during the modeling process. Make sure you don't select any of the vertices from the eye ridges that are close to the center line.

5. Click the Settings button, next to the Weld button in the Edit Vertices rollout, to open the Weld Vertices dialog box.

6. The Weld Threshold is the maximum distance that selected vertices can be apart before they are welded. Slowly increase the Weld Threshold value until the visible gaps are closed.

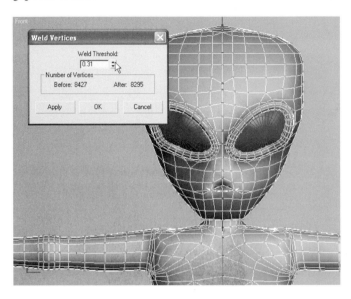

7. Examine the model closely, especially around the mouth and eyes. Make any corrections you like.

   3ds Max uses a paintbrush analogy to reduce the sharpness, or tension, between adjacent polygons. Adjust the size of the virtual brush and click and drag over the areas to be smoothed.

8. In the Paint Deformation rollout, click the Relax button.

9. The brush will appear in the viewports as a circle with a line projecting from its center. The circle always remains parallel to the surface of the model. Reduce the Brush Size value to about 1.0.

Beginners' Gallery

On the following pages, you will find several examples of what student artists can do with Autodesk 3ds Max and some hard work.

Some of these artists have been using 3ds Max for only a short period of time, and already they've been able to use the tools and techniques they've learned to channel their artistic eye and creativity into some beautiful and interesting imagery.

These images are from "Crude Awakenings," a student-produced short created at The Art Institute of California, Los Angeles. The Shooting Stars Production team used 3ds Max to create the title character Al, a homeless man who dreams of the good life. The entire production had a core of 15 dedicated students at the heart of the 35 or so students who worked on the project that spanned several semesters.

Beginners' Gallery

On the following pages, you will find several examples of what student artists can do with Autodesk 3ds Max and some hard work.

Some of these artists have been using 3ds Max for only a short period of time, and already they've been able to use the tools and techniques they've learned to channel their artistic eye and creativity into some beautiful and interesting imagery.

ABOVE: This image was created by Dan Savage to replicate his kitchen. This exercise focused primarily on texturing. The use of real-world texture samples taken from photographs enhanced the look of the image.
BELOW: Javier Araiza modeled and rendered this house in 3ds Max for a modeling class at The Art Institute. It was rendered with a radiosity lighting to generate soft shadows. Javier modeled some details, such as the cornices and window panes, into the house. An eye for detail is a big plus in modeling.

AR-15

Jordan Walker

Ferrari 360 Spider   **3ds Max Patch Modeling**

ABOVE: Jordan Walker of Piedmont Community College textured this AR-15 rifle model. His goal was to create a very-low-polygon-count model and use textures to create detail in the rifle. The ability to work with low poly counts and the aptitude to create well-done textures are great skills for game artists to have. **BELOW:** Jordan Walker created this Ferrari model using surface patches. Patches allow for smooth curved surfaces, which are perfect for car chassis such as this. Jordan's work in models and textures earned him his first job with a game company.

ABOVE: Khalil Harper-Bowers created the model of this castle for her class at The Art Institute. Here you can see how simple shapes can be used to create a complex model. Khalil's use of secondary models, such as the catapults, adds a lot of ambience to the setting. BELOW: Dan Figueroa (of The Art Institute) modeled this train and rendered it without textures to show off his modeling. Notice the detail put into the cables and pipes that run the length of the train engine. Details such as these go a long way in making a solid model.

When he was a graduating senior at The Art Institute, Miguel Guerrero created these alien head models using 3ds Max and Zbrush. He started with a cube and then modeled them into basic head shapes, between 500 and 800 polys. Once the basic model was done, he exported an Obj into ZBrush and began sculpting using the "Simple Brush," pushing and pulling the mesh to manipulate the desired proportions. He continued to refine the mesh using a higher subdivision level and added the fine detail with Projection Master along with "Alpha Brushes." He then exported the displacement map to 3ds Max and applied it to the low-res mesh. After some tweaking, he created color, bump, and specular maps in Photoshop and Zbrush. He rendered in Max using mental ray.

ABOVE: Ramiro Trevino's The Art Institute class was asked to replicate a picture of a room in their houses. Ramiro used the corner of his bathroom to model, texture, and light. Ramiro used textures from the actual bathroom products to help create the scene for this introductory lighting and texturing class. **BELOW:** Dan Figueroa used detailed textures to make this simple window model look photo-realistic. Notice the use of weathered wood grain images for the color as well as bump maps. Also note the added layer of dirt on the window frame.

ABOVE: This living room model was created by Denise Abtey for a lighting and texturing class at The Art Institute. The volumetric light rays coming from the skylights add atmosphere to her image, and the background image places the living room in a viable setting. **BELOW:** Mike Pugh created this house model for a beginner class in 3ds Max at The Art Institute. The plants and stonework in the garden add a nice touch to the house, helping make an interesting image.

10. To reduce the angle between the adjacent polygons, click and drag the brush over the areas to be smoothed.

   Humans, animals, and many other living real-world creatures are basically, but not perfectly, symmetrical. The asymmetrical imperfections are natural and should be reflected in your models. The vertices around the eyes, the brow, and the mouth are areas to consider altering. The changes should be subtle and should not call attention to the varied area, unless that feature is significant to the character's makeup.

Summary

This chapter explored and explained several tools used to create organic models. From a simple box, a torso was formed to match the general shapes shown in the reference images. The Symmetry modifier required you to model only half of the character while it generated the reciprocal half. The legs, arms, and a head followed, all remaining in a simple boxy configuration. The TurboSmooth modifier was added to the top of the Modifier Stack to subdivide and smooth the polygons. Additional detail was added and then the model was collapsed and fine-tuned.

   Although we used an alien character here, this toolset can be utilized for any type of organic model.

CHAPTER 7

Materials and Mapping

Applying materials is the phrase used in 3ds Max to describe applying colors and textures. *Mapping* is the term used to describe applying textures to materials (for example, adding wood grain to a wooden object). After you create your objects, 3ds Max assigns a simple color to them, as you've already seen. This allows them to render and display properly in your viewports.

To put it simply, a material defines an object's look—its color, tactile texture, transparency, luminescence, glow, and so on.

You define a material in 3ds Max by setting values for its parameters or by applying textures or maps. These parameters define the way an object will look when rendered. As you can imagine, much of an object's appearance when rendered also depends on the lighting. Applying materials and lighting go hand in hand. In this chapter and in Chapter 10, "3ds Max Lighting," you will discover that materials and lights work closely together.

In essence, how you see an object in real life depends on how that object transmits and/or reflects light back to you. Materials in 3ds Max simulate the natural physics of how we see things by how objects reflect and or transmit light.

Topics in this chapter include:

- **Materials**
- **The Material Editor**
- **Mapping a Pool Ball**
- **Maps**
- **Mapping Coordinates**

The first half of the chapter shows you the parameters and functions of the materials and the Material Editor window. If you want to skip ahead to work on a mapping exercise, go to the "Mapping a Pool Ball" section later in the chapter. Make sure you come back to skim over the hows and whys in the first half of the chapter.

Materials

Materials are useful for making your objects appear more lifelike. If you model a table and want it to look like polished wood, you can define a shiny material in 3ds Max and apply a wooden texture, such as an image file of wood, to the color of that material.

Materials also come in handy when you want to add the appearance of detail to an object, but without actually modeling it. For instance, if you want a brick wall to look like real brick, but you don't want to model the bricks in the wall, you could use a brick texture. Using a texture would be a time-saving alternative. You can plainly see a brick wall in Figure 7.1. However, in Figure 7.2, the wall shows the appearance of detail in each line of bricks using a texture map (called *bump mapping*). This texture map renders the appearance of dimension for each brick and the inset grooves between each of them, without the hassle of actually modeling the surface of the wall with that level of precision.

This shortcut is an easy trap to fall into. Using texture maps to accommodate too much detail can make your scene look fake and primitive. Don't depend on textures to do the work for you. A model that is not detailed enough for a close-up shot more than likely will not be saved by a detailed texture map. In the end, the level of detail that is needed boils down to trial and error. You have to see how much texture trickery you can use to keep a model's detailing at bay before the model no longer works in the shot. In the beginning, it's safe to assume you should model and texture as much detail as you can. You can work toward efficiency as you learn more about 3ds Max and CG.

Figure 7.1

A brick wall

Just as a model needs to be as detailed as the scene calls for, the same applies to texture maps. You will want to gauge the detail of your texturing based on the use of the object in the scene. A far away object won't need to have a massive texture map applied to its material. Textures mapped onto a material often add the final element of realism to a scene, and it takes a lot of experience to determine how detailed to make any textures for mapping. So let's start gaining some of that experience now.

Material Basics

What makes a material look the way it does? The primary force in a material is its color. However, there are several ways to describe the color of a material. In 3ds Max, three main parameters control the color of a material: *ambient* color, *diffuse* color, and *specular* color.

Ambient color is the color of a material when it is exposed to ambient light. This essentially means that an object will appear this color in indirect light or in shadow. Ambient gives you the very base color of the object, upon which you add the diffuse and specular colors.

Diffuse color is the color of a material when the object is exposed to direct light. Typically, the ambient and the diffuse colors are not too far apart.

Specular color is the color of a shiny object's highlight. The specular highlight on an object may be controlled by more than just its color—for example, its size and shape. The color, however, sets the tone of the object and, in some cases, the degree and look of its shine.

For example, in a new scene, open the Material Editor by choosing Rendering → Material Editor (Figure 7.3). The spheres you see in the Material Editor represent the materials in the scene. Each tile, or slot, represents one material that may be assigned to one or more objects in the scene. As you click on each slot, the material's parameters are displayed below. You edit the material through the settings you see in the Material Editor.

Select one of the material slots, and click it. Let's change the color of the material. Under the Blinn Basic parameters, click on the gray color swatch next to the Diffuse parameter. This opens the Color Selector window, as shown here.

Figure 7.2

The same brick wall from an angle. The detail in the texture mapping of the wall was created with texture mapping.

Using the sliders on the right, you can set the Red, Green, and Blue values for the color, or you can control the color using the Hue, Sat (Saturation), and Value levels. For more on color and RGB/HSV values, see Chapter 1, "Basic Concepts."

You can also very easily select the desired color from the gradient on the left by dragging your mouse over the colors until you find one you prefer. It's best to pick the general color you need from the swatch on the left and then tweak the exact color by using either the RGB or the HSV controls on the right. The Hue of a color represents the actual color itself. The Saturation defines how saturated that color is. The Value sets how bright the color will be.

Once you have a color you like, you simply close the Color Selector. If you want to restart the color, press Reset to *zero out* any changes. You'll notice that the ambient color changed as well as the diffuse color. You will see why in the next section on the Material Editor itself.

In addition, you can map textures to almost any of the parameters for a material. Notice the blank square icon next to the Diffuse color swatch. Click on that icon, and you will get the Material/Map Browser window, as shown here. The Material/Map browser is used throughout the chapter.

The Material Editor

The Material Editor is the central place in 3ds Max where you do all of your material creation and editing. You create materials to assign to any single or group of objects in the scene. You can also have different materials assigned to different parts of the same object. In a full scene, it's customary to have several different materials

It is wise to get to know how the Material Editor works first, and then get to know the types of materials and shaders in 3ds Max. Open the Material Editor by choosing Rendering → Material Editor or by pressing the keyboard shortcut M. Figure 7.3 shows the Material Editor and its major parts.

The following list describes the functions of the Material Editor:

Sample Window The sample window provides you with a quick preview of your material. Each material is displayed on a sphere in one of the tiles (or slots) you see in the Material Editor window. Right-clicking on any of the materials will give you a few more options, including the ability to change how many sample tiles you can see in the Material Editor (as shown here). The fewer samples, the quicker the Material Editor will load.

Get Material This button brings up the Material Library browser. The Material Library stores a collection of saved materials that you can bring into the current scene. You can use 3ds Max's default materials or create your own and store them in your own custom library.

Figure 7.3

The Material Editor

Assign Material to Selection You can use this button to assign the material to the selected object(s) in the scene. You can also apply materials by clicking and dragging the preview from the Material Editor directly onto the object in the viewport; however, this can be less accurate, especially if you have a lot of objects.

Reset Map/Mtl to Default Settings This function resets the values for the map or material in the active sample slot.

Put to Library You can save your material to a library using this function. Building up a library of useful materials can save time, especially when you're trying to re-create complex materials. Once you've gotten a material just right, there's no reason you shouldn't save it to your library by using this button.

Material Effects Channel Here you can assign an effect ID to the material. Effects are used in the video post or Combustion for things such as glow, highlights, and so on. Some of these effects will be covered in Chapter 11, "3ds Max Rendering."

Show Map in Viewport This will display your material in the viewport. This means that you won't have to render every time you want to see how your material appears on a 3D object. However, displaying your map in a viewport has limitations. The limitations are basically those of your graphics card and your chosen method of displaying 3D in the viewport (Open GL, Direct 3D, or Software). The difference between viewing the map in the viewport and in its final rendered state may be quite different. However, seeing a map in the viewport is useful on many levels.

Go to Parent Just as you created objects that related to each other, materials in 3ds Max may have several components to them (such as texture maps) that work in a hierarchy, where information from one node is fed upstream into the parameter for the material. When you are working with submaps, this option will take you back to the base material. This makes it easier to navigate in the Material Editor when you are editing your materials.

Go Forward to Sibling This function is the reverse of Go to Parent. This option will take you into the submaps levels.

Preview Type Sometimes the default sphere won't give you an adequate preview of the material. You can change the preview to a cube or a cylinder.

Pick Material from Object When you need to edit a material on an object, you can use this button to select the material from an object in the scene. The material is placed in the active sample slot.

Material Name This is a unique name for the material. 3ds Max will not allow any identically named materials, so make sure you provide a good descriptive name here.

Material Type Different materials have different uses. When called on to create a more complex material, for example, you can change the material type to Blend. A Blend material will mix the results from two different materials together for a compound effect. The default material type is Standard. Material types are explained in the next section.

Shader Type Shading types describe how the surface responds to light. How an object looks depends on how its surface reacts to light, so the Shader type for a material is very important. Shaders provide different options for specific materials. The default shader is Blinn. Shader types are covered later in this chapter.

Miscellaneous Settings These are fairly basic settings to change the appearance of the material. Here are the two more important settings:

> **Wire** When you turn Wire on, the object attached to this material will render as a Wireframe object. This simple setting is very powerful; it's used when you need to render line art or Wireframe views.

2-Sided This setting enables you to render both sides of a single surface. By default, only one side of a surface will render, and that is typically all you need. Sometimes, however, when you penetrate through a surface, you will have to see the other side. In this example, a hemisphere is rendered without 2-Sided turned on, in the image on the left, and with 2-Sided enabled in the image on the right. Notice the inside of the hemisphere.

Locks Here you can lock the Ambient parameter to the Diffuse parameter and lock the Diffuse to the Specular. Any changes made to one while the locks are enabled affect both.

Ambient, Diffuse and Specular Color Changing the ambient color will affect the way the material appears for ambient light. Changing the diffuse color affects the overall color of the material. Specular color changes the color of the highlighted light. You change the color by clicking on the color swatch next to the parameter.

Diffuse and Specular Maps These buttons provide shortcuts to the maps for Diffuse and Specular. A map applied in Diffuse (for example: bitmap; i.e., an image file) will affect the base appearance of the material. A map applied to Specular will use the mapped image to define the color of the shine. Mapping is covered in the Pool Ball exercise later in this chapter.

Specular Level This setting determines how shiny the material appears. For something such as a metallic surface, the setting will be up around 180 to 220. You can also map a grayscale texture to determine which areas will appear as shiny and which will appear as dull.

Glossiness This setting determines the spread of the specular shine. A higher value means that it will look more plastic (high gloss across the surface of the model).

Self Illumination This slot defines how the material is affected by light. The more self illumination it is given, the less the material is affected by lighting, but the more flat it will become.

Opacity A material's opacity determines how transparent it appears. If it is set to 100 (the default), then the material is 100 percent opaque—that is, it's solid. If it is set to 0, then it is completely invisible. You can apply a grayscale texture map here to use a bitmap (or other map) to define which portions of the material are transparent. Areas of white on the map will be opaque, whereas the black areas will render transparent; the intermediate values of gray will have different levels of transparency.

Maps Maps allow you to apply bitmap textures, which are maps that help define the material beyond simple color and opacity settings. Common maps include bump maps (use grayscale values to simulate bumps and dents), displacement maps (use grayscale maps to mathematically calculate depth and height and redefine the mesh accordingly), reflections, glossiness, and so on, as shown in Figure 7.4.

Material Types

Different materials have different uses. The Standard material is fine for most uses. However, when you require a more complex material, you can change the material type to one that will fit your needs. To change a material type, click the Material Type button called out in Figure 7.3. By default, it displays Standard in the button. Once you click the button, the Material/Map Browser window opens (as shown here) from which you can choose the material type.

Standard

Standard material is the default type for the materials in the Material Editor. This material has values for ambient, diffuse, and specular components. With it, you can imitate just about any surface type you can imagine. The more advanced surface types (see the following discussions) combine elements of different shaders for more complex effects.

Blend

Just as it sounds, this material type blends two materials together. Figure 7.5 shows the parameters for a Blend material type. Notice the controls for mixing two different materials. You assign the materials through the Material 1 and Material 2 parameters.

Composite

Similar to the Blend, a Composite material combines up to 10 materials, using additive colors, subtractive colors, or opacity mixing (Figure 7.6).

Figure 7.5

The Blend material type allows you to mix two different materials together.

Figure 7.6

The Composite material type allows you to blend up to 10 materials.

Double Sided

The Double Sided material type simply divides the material into two submaterials, one for the outward face and one for the inner face. Figure 7.7 shows the parameters for the material. To set the Facing Material, you can click on the bar to create and edit a new material, or you can click and drag an existing material from the Material Editor onto the Facing Material bar. You set up the Back material in exactly the same way.

In the following graphic, you can see how you can assign one material to the outer face of an object and another one to the back of the surface. Here, a bowl has a solid blue material mapped to the outside, and the inside face is a checkerboard pattern map.

Neither the facing nor the back material need to have 2-Sided enabled for the Double Sided material to render both sides of the surface.

Ink 'n Paint

Ink 'n Paint is a powerful "Cartoon" material that creates outlines and flat cartoon shading for 3D objects based on Falloff parameters. Figure 7.8 shows the parameters for an Ink 'n Paint material. Figure 7.9 shows you a sample render with the Cartoon shading material applied to a bowl and a cone.

Matte/Shadow

Use Matte/Shadow material when you want to isolate the shadow. The material will receive shadows, but remain transparent for everything else. It is useful for rendering objects onto a photo or video background because it creates a separate shadow that you can composite on top of the background. Rendering in separate passes, such as a separate shadow, is very useful because you can have total control of the image by compositing just the right amount of any particular pass.

Multi/Sub-Object

Use this material when you need to apply different materials to portions of a 3D object that have different material IDs. You can then assign different surface treatments to a single object. This keeps modeling simpler because you do not have to make separate objects for everything that needs a different material.

Figure 7.7

A Double Sided material allows you to assign two materials to either side of a surface.

Figure 7.8

The Ink 'n Paint material's parameters

Figure 7.9

A Cartoon-shaded render using the Ink 'n Paint material

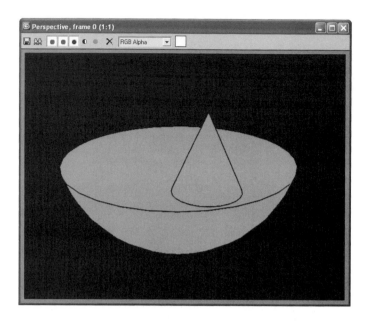

Raytrace

The Raytrace material is a powerful material that expands the available parameters to give you more control over photo-real renderings. The material uses more system resources than the Standard material at render time, but it can produce more accurate renders—especially when true reflections and refractions are concerned. You will use this material in Chapter 11.

Shellac

The Shellac material superimposes one material on another using additive composition. This allows you to create a material that is highly glossy, such as a finely varnished wood surface (Figure 7.10).

Top/Bottom

Top/Bottom divides the material into a top material and bottom material with an adjustable position (Figure 7.11). The material is in the first slot in the Material Editor in the figure. This material is useful for creating an object that has two different materials on either side, such as a cookie with chocolate on the top. Mmmm, cookie.

Most of your work will probably be with the Standard material type, unless you are working with architectural files. You will need to change the material type only for special needs. However, you will need to change the Shader type more often to achieve certain surface qualities. You will explore Shader types next.

Shader Types

The way light reflects from a surface defines that surface to your eye. In 3ds Max, you can control what kind of surface you work with by changing the Shader type for a material. This option will let you mimic different types of surfaces such as dull wood or shiny paint or metal. The following descriptions outline the differences in how the Shader types react to light.

Anisotropic

The Anisotropic shader (shown in the following graphic) is good for surfaces that are deformed, such as foil wrappers or hair. *Anisotropic* is defined as having properties that differ according to direction. This creates a specular highlight that is uneven across the

Figure 7.10

The Shellac material allows you to superimpose a shiny layer on top of another material

Figure 7.11

The Top/Bottom material type

surface, changing according to the direction you specify on the surface. The other surface types, as you will see in this section, typically create rounded specular highlights that spread evenly across a surface. Figure 7.12 shows the Material Editor for an Anisotropic material. Notice the extra controls for the specular highlights. These allow you to control how the specular will fall across the surface.

Blinn

This is the default material in 3ds Max because it is a general-purpose, flexible shader. The Blinn shader (shown here) creates a smooth surface with some shininess. If you set the specular color to black, however, this shader will not display a specular and will lose its shininess, making it perfect for regular dull surfaces, such as paper or an indoor wall. Figure 7.13 shows the Blinn shader controls in the Material Editor.

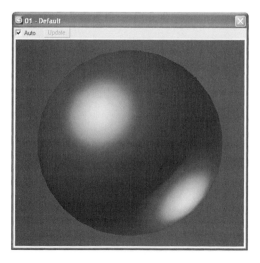

Because this is the most-often used shader, let's take a look at its Material Editor controls. The ambient, color, and specular colors all work as you've seen earlier in this chapter. You simply set the color you want by clicking the color swatch, or you can map a texture map to any of these parameters by clicking the Map button and choosing the desired map from the Material/Map Browser window.

SPECULAR HIGHLIGHT CONTROLS

The parameters in the Specular Highlights section of the Blinn Basic Parameters rollout are interesting for this shader. The specular color, which defaults to white, controls the color of the highlight. Decreasing the brightness of that specular color, whatever the color may be, will decrease the brightness of the specular highlight on the object, making it seem less shiny. Changing the specular color to black will negate any surface shine.

Figure 7.12

Material Editor for the Anisotropic material

Figure 7.12

Material Editor for the Anisotropic material

The surface shine is also regulated by the Specular Level parameter. The higher the value, the hotter the specular highlight will render on the object. Figure 7.14 shows a sphere with a Blinn with a Specular Level of 0 on the left, a Specular Level of 35 in the middle, and a Specular Level of 100 on the right.

The Glossiness parameter controls the width of the specular highlight. With the same sphere with a Specular Level of 35, Figure 7.15 shows you a Glossiness of 0 on the left (which creates a broad specular), a Glossiness of 35 in the middle (which creates a fairly tight, shiny specular highlight), and a Glossiness of 75 on the right (which creates a high gloss pin point specular highlight). The higher the value, the glossier the surface will appear.

Finally, the Soften parameter controls the softness of the specular highlight. Figure 7.16 shows a sphere with a Blinn material assigned with a Specular Level of 55, a Glossiness of 10, and with a Soften value of 0 on the left and a Soften value of 1 (the max) on the right.

Figure 7.14
The Specular Level of a Blinn controls the amount of highlight on the surface.

Figure 7.15
The Glossiness parameter controls the width of the specular highlight.

Soften controls the specular breadth on specular highlights that are already broad—that is, they have lower Glossiness values. You may want to look at these parameters at work in a Max scene, as your monitor will display the specular highlights better than a printed page.

You've probably noticed the graph (shown here) in the Material Editor when you work with the Specular Level, Glossiness, and Soften parameters. This graph shows you the falloff of the specular you are editing for the material. The shorter the graph, the lower the level of specular highlight. The rounder the graph, the broader and softer the specular highlight.

For shiny objects, you will need to use a fairly sharp specular. For extremely shiny objects, such as polished metals, a pinpoint specular is best. Plastic objects will work best with a broad, diminished specular. Matte objects, such as paper or cloth, work great without a specular highlight, or at least a very darkly colored one.

SELF-ILLUMINATION AND OPACITY

The Self-Illumination parameter adds incandescence to the material, as if the object is giving off its own light. The higher this value, the flatter the object will appear, because Self-Illumination will essentially negate any shadowing or ambient falloff on the material. The specular highlights on the material will still show up on a material with Self-Illumination turned all the way up to 1.0. You can also change the color of the Self-Illumination by clicking the Color check box and choosing a color in the swatch that appears when Color is enabled. This allows you to have a different incandescence color than the color of the material itself. Figure 7.17 shows a Self-Illumination value of 0 on the left and a Self-Illumination value of 1.0 on the right. Notice how the sphere flattens out as Self-Illumination helps keep the shadow areas as bright as the diffuse.

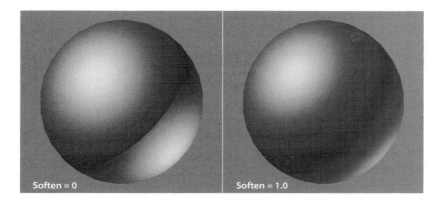

Soften = 0   Soften = 1.0

Figure 7.16

The Soften parameter helps reign in broad specular highlights by softening their edges.

Figure 7.17

**The Self-Illumina-
tion value sets the
incandescence of a
material.**

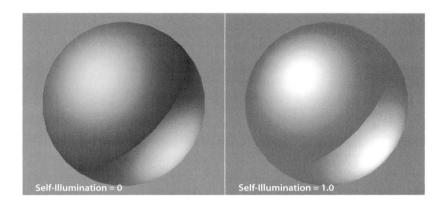

Self-Illumination = 0   Self-Illumination = 1.0

A Self-Illumination value does not emit a light in the default scanline renderer—that is, the object will not illuminate other objects in the scene. For such an effect, you will need to use more advanced rendering techniques with mental ray, for example.

Finally, the Opacity setting sets the transparency of an object, as you may have read earlier in the chapter. The higher the Opacity value, the more solid it renders. The lower the Opacity value, the more see-through the object will render.

Metal

The Metal shader is not too different from the Blinn shader. Metal creates a lustrous metallic effect, with much the same controls as a Blinn shader, but without the effect of any specular highlights. When you are first starting, it's best to create most of your material looks with the Blinn shader, until you're at a point where Blinn simply cannot do what you need. The following graphic displays a sphere with a Metal shader with a Specular Level of 120 and a Glossiness of 60.

The black areas of the shader may throw you off at first, but keep in mind that a metallic surface is ideally black when it has nothing to reflect. Metals are best seen when they reflect the environment. As such, this shader requires a lot of reflection work to make the metal look just right.

Multi-Layer

With some surfaces, you need complex highlights. In some cases, while an Anisotropic might be useful, you may need further control in the complexity of your specular shape and falloff. A Multi-Layer shader will stack two Anisotropic highlights together to give you increased control over the highlights you can create.

Here you can see a Multi-Layer material assigned to a sphere. The two layered specular highlights are created in such a way, as seen in Figure 7.18, to create an "X" formation for the highlight.

Oren-Nayar-Blinn

The Oren-Nayar-Blinn shader (shown here) generally creates good matte surfaces such as cloth or clay. The shader has specular highlight controls very similar to those of the Blinn shader.

Phong

By all accounts, the Phong shader (shown here) looks very similar to the Blinn shader, and it has the same controls. Phong creates smooth surfaces with some amount of shininess, just as Blinn does. However, Phong does not handle highlights as well as Blinn. This is especially true for glancing highlights, where the edge of a surface catches the light. Phong is good for creating plastic objects, as well as many other surfaces.

Figure 7.18

The Multi-Layer shader lets you create complex highlights.

Figure 7.19

A Translucent shading material allows light to scatter through the object.

Phong is a legacy shader that was created before the introduction of the Blinn shading model.

Strauss

The Strauss material (shown here) can create metallic and nonmetallic surfaces. Its main controls are Color, Glossiness, Metalness, and Opacity. The specular highlights, for the most part, are governed by the Glossiness of the material. The higher the Metalness value, the darker the unlit portions of the surface become, again relying on reflections for the metallic look.

Translucent

The Translucent shader (shown here) is very similar to the Blinn; however, this shader adds a touch of translucency to the material. *Translucence* is where light is scattered as it passes through the material—for example, a flashlight shining behind a parchment. You can also simulate frosted and etched glass by using translucency. Figure 7.19 shows the Material Editor for a Translucent shader material.

Mapping a Pool Ball

Let's put some of that hard-earned knowledge to work and map an object. You will be creating and texturing a pool ball. Although this may not seem the most exotic thing to texture, you can learn a lot about surfaces, shading, and mapping techniques by texturing it. You'll be able to flex your mapping muscles even more in exercises later in the chapter.

If you have skipped to this section from the beginning of the chapter, have a run through and get a good taste of texturing in 3ds Max. Feel free to reference the earlier parts of the chapter to explain some of the hows and whys of what you will accomplish in the next exercise. Otherwise, roll up your sleeves and follow along with these steps to texture a pool ball.

Starting the Pool Ball

You can begin with your own project, or you can copy the PoolBall project found on the companion CD to your hard drive. It contains a texture image file you'll need for this exercise.

1. In a new scene, create a sphere. The size doesn't matter here. How's that for fast modeling?

2. Open the Material Editor by pressing the keyboard shortcut M or clicking the Material Editor icon () in the main toolbar.

3. In the Material Editor, select one of the sample slots. Go to the Blinn Basic Parameters rollout.

4. The most logical thing to start with is the color. The base color of an object is defined by the Diffuse parameter—although Ambient is also locked to Diffuse, which is fine. The Diffuse parameter is shown here.

5. Click on the color swatch to the right of the Diffuse parameter to open the Color Picker window. Pick any color at this point. Once you have chosen your color, click the Close button, and you will see that the sphere in the sample slot has changed to your color.

Choosing a Surface Type

The next step is to decide what the surface of your object is going to be. Will it be shiny or matte? You will need a shiny surface, because real pool balls are glossy. We will have to adjust the specular highlights using the Blinn's controls.

1. Go to Specular Highlights under Blinn Basic Parameters. Set the Specular Level to 98 and the Glossiness to 85. Keep Soften at the default. The specular graph here is quite sharp.

2. That is it for the basic material. Now apply it to the object by dragging the material from the sample slot to your sphere in the viewport and release the mouse button. The sphere will change to the color you chose for the diffuse, and in the sample slots the corners will become outlined with white triangles as shown here.

The corner triangles on a sample slot in the Material Editor mean the material is "hot" or applied. Before you apply the material, it is "cool" and there are no corners. This is the default. When the corner triangles are solid white, the material is "hot" and the object it is applied to is currently selected.

The material is now linked to the material on the object. If you were to change any of the parameters of the material, it would be instantly updated on the object. For the most part, once a material is applied it cannot be deleted—it can only be replaced with another material. You cannot go back to the default color of the original object.

Figure 7.20 shows you what the pool ball should look like, most noticeably its specular highlight. However, viewing in the viewport isn't the same as a rendered image. The viewport gives the lowest level of quality, and it should not be used to make final decisions on the look of your material. Instead, it should be used as a point of reference. Figure 7.21 shows this pool ball rendered. Rendering combines the materials, lights, shadows, and environments within a scene to create the final look. Rendering will be covered in detail in Chapter 11. Notice how much more detailed the specular highlight is in the render. To check your render, simply click the Quick Render icon ( ) in the main toolbar.

Figure 7.20

The pool ball in a viewport

Figure 7.21

The pool ball rendered

Mapping the Pool Ball

This simple material is only part of the story. You still need to add the markings of a real pool ball, not just a solid color. Just creating a sphere and making it shiny and green doesn't make a realistic ball. Figure 7.22 shows some real pool table balls. Pool balls have a graphic strip or number in a circle. You can't create this detail using the basic parameters of the Standard material. What you need is a bitmap.

A bitmap replaces the diffuse color with an image. The image you use can be hand drawn and scanned, created in a program such as Adobe Photoshop, or taken with your digital camera. The image we are going to use was created in Photoshop (Figure 7.23). A white circle with a "2" is in the middle and then one that is cut in half is on either side. This has to do with texture placement. As you gain more experience, you'll learn how to prepare your texture images for your models.

Figure 7.22
Pool balls

Figure 7.23

**The proposed
bitmap texture for
the ball**

The theory behind this image is quite simple. Pool balls have the number on opposite sides of the ball. In your texture map, you'll need to make two 2s in the blue backdrop. The two halves of the white circle and the 2 will simply tile together when the texture image wraps around the sphere, much the way a wrapper wraps around a candy. Mmm…Candy. This way you have two 2s on the ball, easy as pie. To apply this bitmap as a texture, follow along here:

1. Go to the Material Editor and select the sample slot that is applied to the sphere. Go to the Maps rollout and click on the bar to the right of Diffuse Color, which is currently marked *None*. The Material/Map browser will appear.

2. Make sure the Browse From group is set to New. Select Bitmap and click OK, as shown here. An Explore window (Figure 7.24) will appear. Navigate to the map `Pool-BallColorTexture.tif` file in the Sceneassets\Images folder in the PoolBall project on the CD (or the one copied to your hard drive).

3. The Material Editor has changed, and you are in a separate module from the Material parameters. You are in the Bitmap parameter. There are several rollouts that we are going to ignore for now. The most important rollouts in the Bitmap section are Bitmap Parameter and Coordinates. The Bitmap Parameter rollout deals with the actual bitmap image; the Coordinate rollout controls how the bitmap image moves relative to the surface of the object. Leave all the settings at their default.

Figure 7.24

Selecting a bitmap image for the material

Figure 7.25

The Material Editor shows the parameters for your bitmap image.

If you ever need to change a bitmap image in a texture already applied, simply go to the bitmap's Material Editor and under the Bitmap Parameter rollout, click on the bar with the filename to the right of the Bitmap parameter. The file browser will reopen. Choose another image file, and it will replace the current bitmap file.

4. You will be able to see the bitmap in the sample slot, but not in the viewport. To fix this, click the Show Map in Viewport button (⊕) on the Material Editor's toolbar (just below the sample slots).

Think of the Material Editor as a literary outline. The heading of the outline is the full material, and its parameters when they are mapped (like Diffuse or the entries in the Maps rollout) are like an outline's subheadings that all fall under the main material.

5. Right now you can see only the Bitmap parameters. What if you want to go back and adjust the specular on the material itself? The Go To Parent button (↰) is on the Material Editor's toolbar. The parent is the material. Clicking this icon will take you back to the material's own parameters, where you will find the Blinn Basic Parameters again. Any map that is added to a material is known as a *child* to that material, much the same way as the hierarchy worked in the Mobile project in Chapter 2, "Your First 3ds Max Animation."

As a matter of fact, you can have an outline view of your materials. Open the Material/Map Navigator (Figure 7.26) with the Material/Map Navigator button (▣) located on the Material Editor's toolbar.

Figure 7.26

The Material/Map Navigator window displays your materials in an outline format.

The Material/Map Navigator is a floating palette; you can use it to navigate through your material and maps. This is very useful for complex materials that use a lot of maps. It is a very simple dialog: the blue sphere represents the material and its main parameters and the parallelogram is for the bitmap. The parallelogram is green by default and red when the Show Map in Viewport has been activated. Just click on the entry you need to show in the Material Editor to edit its contents.

6. Now render the ball to check the map's appearance. With your Perspective viewport active, click the Quick Render icon (the teapot). Figure 7.27 shows the pool ball with the mapping.

Figure 7.27

The ball with the mapped image

MAPPING COORDINATES

When you put a 2D image onto a 3D object, think of it as being "projected" onto the surface, as if you had a white object and a slide projector were projecting a picture onto the white. Mapping coordinates describe how the image is projected or wrapped around the surface. Coordinates are spelled out in terms of U, V, and W. U is the horizontal dimension, V is the vertical dimension, and W is the optional depth. All primitives have mapping coordinates, including our sphere. That doesn't necessarily mean the image will wrap itself correctly, although it works fine for our pool ball exercise (imagine that!). Merely having the mapping coordinates only means the map will show up. In order to edit the mapping coordinates, you need to use the Coordinate rollout. You will learn more about mapping coordinates later in the chapter.

Adding a Finishing Touch—Reflection Mapping

With the image applied, the pool ball looks pretty good at this point (Figure 7.27)—but it's not perfect. The small nuances are what really make a render look good. One thing this pool ball is missing is a reflection of its environment. Now, short of creating and texturing a pool table and several other pool balls, we need to make a cheat.

There are two ways to create reflections: the "cheat" method by mapping and using raytrace. Both methods require us to go to the Maps rollout in the Material Editor. We are going to add a bitmap into the Reflections Map slot. We are going to use the "fake it" method.

Raytrace is a rendering methodology that traces rays between all the lights in the scene with all the objects and the camera. It can provide true reflections of objects in the scene. Chapter 11 covers raytracing in more in depth.

To fake the reflection, you'll need an image that looks like the "room" around the ball. We are going to use a photograph taken for this occasion and saved as the image file ReflectionMap.tif in the Sceneassets\Images folder of the PoolBall project on the companion CD (Figure 7.28).

This image has all the elements that you might see around a pool ball—specifically, more pool balls! To add this image as a reflection for the ball, follow these steps:

1. Go to the Material Editor and make sure you are at the material's parameters; use the navigator or Go to Parent button if you are still in the diffuse bitmap area where you applied the image file.

Figure 7.28
The reflection map used to "cheat" the reflections on the pool ball

Figure 7.29
The reflections are a bit heavy. If you could reduce the amount of reflection, they'd be better.

2. Go to the Maps rollout and click on the bar currently marked *None* next to the Reflections parameter. Select Bitmap from the Material/Maps window, and then navigate to ReflectionMap.tif in the Sceneassets\Images folder of the PoolBall project on the CD, or on your hard drive if you've already copied it.

3. Do a quick test render with the Quick Render icon (the teapot). The reflections are pretty strong (Figure 7.29).

4. You need to adjust how much reflection is on the ball. Click the Go to Parent button, and go to the Maps rollout. The type-in area next to the names lets you specify the amount of map applied to the material. Change the value next to Reflections from 100 to 10. Test render the pool ball again. You should notice a much nicer level of reflection (Figure 7.30). Voilà!

Figure 7.30
The reflections look much better and add a certain realism to the pool ball.

If you have lost the view of your pool ball somehow, or if you simply want to center it in the Perspective viewport (or any other viewport), simply press the Z shortcut to focus the viewport on all the objects in the scene. In this case, it will center the pool ball.

Background Color

You may notice that the background in the renders in Figures 7.29 and 7.30 are white, whereas your renders' backgrounds are probably black. A simple setting change and there are many reasons why you would want to control this option. You may want a specific color to offset your scene (for example, blue to represent the sky) or you may want a picture in your background.

To change the background of your renders, go to the main menu and choose Rendering → Environment (shown here). The Background parameter is at the top of the dialog box. Click on the color swatch and choose your color. That's it!

To add an image to the background, click on the bar marked *None* to add a bitmap, just as you did with the bitmaps on the pool ball. Once you do, the image will render in the background with your scene. To change the image, click on that bar, which at that point should list the path and filename of the current image, to take you to the Material/Map browser where you can select a new bitmap and image.

Mapping, Just a Little Bit More

Now that you know how to add maps to a material, removing them is very simple. In the Material Editor for the parent material's parameters (not the map's parameters), you can right-click on the map name, as seen in Figure 7.31, to select Clear from the context menu.

If you don't want to clear the map entirely, but just need to turn it off for a little while, you can just uncheck the box to the left of the parameter name, as shown in Figure 7.32. Check it back on to use that map again.

Figure 7.31

Removing a map from a parameter

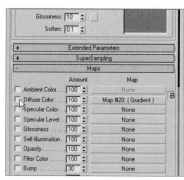

Figure 7.32

Unchecking this box will temporarily remove the map from the parameter.

Seeing More Sample Slots

If you have a scene with several materials, and you need to see more sample slots than the default in the Material Editor, simply right-click on any slot and select either 5 × 3 Sample Windows or 6 × 4 Sample Windows from the context menu. This will help you navigate a heavy scene that has tons of materials that you need to modify. In the following graphics, you can see the sample slots multiply!

5×3 Sample Windows

6×4 Sample Windows

As you've seen, the sample slots for any given material in the Material Editor constantly update to show you any changes you've made to that material. However, if you want a larger image than the relatively small sample slot, right-click on the slot and select Magnify from the context menu, as shown in Figure 7.33. 3ds Max will open a larger window (Figure 7.34), which is resized by dragging the corners of the window, with a sample of that material. It will by default update automatically as you make changes to the material.

Figure 7.33

Magnify gives you a larger view of your material.

You've already noticed that there are only 24 sample slots in the Material Editor. This does not limit the number of materials you can use to 24. You should consider the Material Editor as a scratchpad of sorts. You can create as many materials as you'd like in a 3ds Max scene; however, at any one time, only 24 can be loaded in the Material Editor window at the same time.

If you click the Get Material button in the Material Editor, you can list all the materials that are used in the scene. When the Material/Map browser is open, click the Scene radial button for the Browse From parameter, and all of the materials assigned in the scene will be listed. When an object's material is not shown in a sample slot, it does not mean it has been deleted. You can load it back into any sample slot for editing at any time.

Figure 7.34

A larger view of your material sample

Assigning Materials to Sub-Objects

You've seen several times how to assign a material to an object. You can, for instance, drag the material from the Material Editor to the object in a viewport. You can also select an object in the viewport, and then select a Sample Slot material and click the Assign Material to Selection button () in the Material Editor.

However, you may want to assign materials to sub-object polygons as well as whole objects. One approach is to use the Multi/Sub-Object material type briefly discussed earlier in the chapter (the Multi/Sub-Object material will not be covered in this book, as it is beyond the beginner scope).

There is a much easier way to assign materials to sub-objects, however. Just select the appropriate polygons on the surface (the object must be an editable mesh or poly, or have an Edit Mesh/Edit Poly modifier applied), and assign the material as you regularly would (with the Assign Material to Selection button or drag the material to the selected polygons in the viewport). A sphere with several polygons assigned to different materials is shown in Figure 7.35.

Once you apply a material to a sub-object, a new Multi/Sub-Object material is created in the scene automatically. You can load the new Multi/Sub-Object material by using the eyedropper to click on the object in the viewport to load the material into a sample slot.

Figure 7.35

Applying materials to a mesh's Sub-Object polygons is easy.

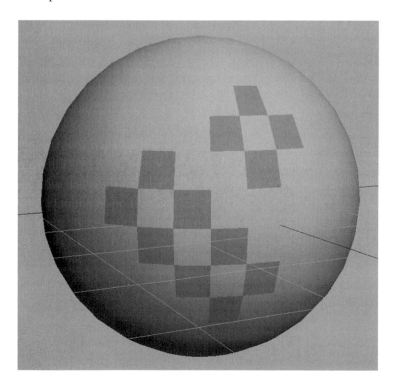

Maps

By now you've noticed that the Material/Map browser has different maps you can access. These maps are divided into categories.

Open the Material/Map browser. The categories are listed on the left. By default, All is selected as shown here. You've already used the bitmap map a few times. Let's take a look at the rest of the maps by category.

The categories and their more important maps are explained in the following sections.

2D Maps

2D maps are two-dimensional images that are typically mapped onto the surface of geometric objects or used as environment maps to create a background for the scene. The simplest 2D maps are bitmaps; other kinds of 2D maps are generated procedurally.

Procedural maps are generated entirely within 3ds Max and rely on a set of parameters you set for their look. Images brought in the way the pool ball's color and reflection maps were brought in are not *procedural*. They are *bitmaps*—that is, raster image files. For more on raster image files, see Chapter 1.

Click on the 2D Maps category in the Material/Map browser to see the available 2D maps.

Bitmap

As you've already seen, a *bitmap* is an image file that you load into 3ds Max. It can be a photo, a scan, or any image that is readable by 3ds Max.

Checker

A procedural map, the checker map is a checkerboard pattern that is generated in 3ds Max. Its parameters in the Material Editor, which are shown here, control the look of the checkerboard. A sphere is also shown with a checker applied to its color.

The Tiling values under the Coordinates rollout determine the number of checkers. The higher the number, the more checkers. Color #1 and Color #2, of course, control the two colors of the checkerboard; black and white are defaults. Click on the color swatch to change the color, or you can click the Maps bars next to each color (labeled *None* until you assign a map). Also, the Blur parameter allows you to blur the edges of the checkers, and the Soften parameter under the Checker Parameters rollout blurs the checkers together.

Gradient

A *gradient is* a procedural map (the parameters are shown here) that grades from one color to a second color that grades to a third color. Here, a cylinder is shown grading from black (top) to white (bottom).

In the Coordinates rollout, the parameters are much the same as they are for the Checker map. These coordinates are pretty much the same for all procedural maps, as they allow you to position the map as you need on the object by setting the options such as Tiling and Offset.

The colors for the gradient are set by Color #1, Color #2, and Color #3. You can also map these colors. The Color 2 Position parameter sets the *relative* location of the middle color to the upper and lower colors—i.e., 0.5 is the middle because the other colors are at 0 and 1.0.

Gradient Ramp

Similar to the Gradient map, but much more powerful, the Gradient Ramp is a procedural map that allows you to grade from and to any number of grayscale shades. Here, a gradient is shown in the Material Editor that is applied to a cube.

Use the sliders along the ramp in the Material Editor to set the position of the gray value. Click in the ramp to create a new slider at that grayscale value. The Black and White sliders at the very ends do not move. To delete a slider, right-click on it, and choose Delete from the context menu that appears. Notice the value and position readout above the ramp.

Gradient Ramps are perfect for creating maps that fall off (for example, for opacity affects where the opacity fades away).

3D Maps

Similar to 2D maps that are generated in two dimensions, 3D maps are patterns generated procedurally in all three dimensions. For example, Marble has a grain that goes through the assigned geometry in *X, Y,* and *Z.* If you cut away part of an object with Marble assigned as its texture, the grain in the cutaway portion matches the grain on the object's exterior.

When you create a 3D map, notice that the Coordinates rollout has Tiling and Offset parameters in three axes, whereas the 2D maps only have *X* and *Y.*

Try using some of the 3D maps (such as Marble, Wave, Stucco, and Wood) to see how they work on a simple object in your scene. They all have basically the same Coordinates rollout; however, each has its own Parameters rollout to control the color and other settings.

Marble

A Marble map creates veins of colors that run through an object. The 3D aspect of the map allows it to spread across all three dimensions, creating a more realistic texture. Color #1 and Color #2 control the two colors of a Marble map, while the third color is a grainy blend of the two together.

The Marble map's parameters are shown applied to a cube, which is also shown here.

Noise

Noise is a great way to easily add some randomness to a parameter or to add a bit of randomness to a surface's color or specular highlight, for example. Its parameters and a sample cylinder are shown here.

Used sparingly, noise can add great detail to highlights for any shiny object when mapped to the specular color. In this case, just make sure the colors in the noise do not contrast too much against each other, which would make the map faint.

Wood

Wood is a quick way to add wood grain to a material. Its parameters and a sample cylinder are shown here.

Just like the Marble map, you can set the color of the wood grain with Color #1 and Color #2. Adding Radial Noise and Axial Noise will make the wood appear to have more burls.

Compositor and Color Modifier Maps

Compositors are meant specifically for compositing colors or maps together for some advanced effects. In image processing, *compositing images* refers to superimposing two or more images to combine them in a variety of ways.

Color Modifier maps alter the color of pixels in a material for some advanced effects. Color modifiers and Compositor maps will not be covered in this book.

More Mapping Exercises

In a previous exercise, you turned a boring old sphere into a pool ball using Diffuse and Reflection maps. Now let's look at two important mapping techniques with the Material Editor.

Making a Chess Piece

To begin, you will create a chess piece (Figure 7.36) to learn about *bump mapping* and using reflections to create the illusion of shine and dents on the surface of the object. Just follow these steps:

1. Open the Chess Piece.max file in the Texture Scene Files folder on the companion CD.

2. In the Material Editor, create a Standard Blinn material that has a red Diffuse Color with the these approximate values in the Color Picker window: Red: 200, Green: 15, and Blue: 0.

Figure 7.36

Hey, it's a chess piece!

3. Even though the Chess Piece model in the scene may look red in the file you loaded from the CD, it does not have a material applied. That color is simply the color of the object set through the Name and Color text box at the top of the Modify panel. So, apply your Red material to the chess piece model. Click the Quick Render button, and you'll be able to see that this doesn't look anything close to a real chess piece (Figure 7.37).

Figure 7.37

That's not a chess piece yet!

For an added treat, why don't you try to model the pawn chess piece itself for this example. You could also try to model different chess pieces, such as a rook or a knight.

Adding Shine

The next step to making this piece more realistic is to add shininess, which you will accomplish in two actions.

1. Go back to the Material Editor. In the Material, change the Specular Level to 95 and Glossiness to 90. Your sample material should have a nice specular, as shown here.

2. The second part to making the piece shinier is to add a touch of reflection. Go to the Maps rollout and select the bar next to Reflection. You are going to add a bitmap to fake a reflection, as you did with the pool ball earlier in the chapter. In the Material/Map browser, select Bitmap.

3. In the File browser for the bitmap, navigate to the Texture Scene Files folder on the CD and choose `Reflect Map.tif`, as shown in Figure 7.38.

Figure 7.38
This bitmap will serve as a reflection for the chess piece.

4. Choose the `Reflect Map.tif` image. When you map a reflection, it is important to find an image that will be believable in your scene. Ideally, it should be the room around the object. In this case, you just want a little something to reflect faintly in the chess piece.

5. Select the Go to Parent button (![icon]). Go to the Maps rollout and change the Amount of the Reflection from 100 to 15. Test render the chess piece (Figure 7.39). It still doesn't look very realistic, but don't worry. We are going to fix it with a bump map.

Figure 7.39

The chess piece with a slight reflection map

Applying a Bump

Bump mapping is very common in CG. It adds a level of detail to an object fairly easily by creating bumps and grooves in the surface and giving the object a tactile feel in its appearance.

Bump mapping takes the intensity values of an image or procedural map to simulate bumpiness on the surface of the model, without changing the actual topology of the model itself. You can create some surface tactile texture with a bump map; however, you will not be able to create extreme depth in the model. For that, you may want to model the surface depth manually or use displacement mapping. Displacement maps are not covered in this book because they are a more advanced mapping technique.

> Displacement mapping is used to change the topology of the model, whereas bump mapping uses light and dark in the colors of the render to trick the eye into seeing surface detail.

To apply a bump map to the chess piece, follow these steps:

1. While still in the Maps rollout for your chess piece material, click on the bar labeled *None* next to the Bump. We are going to use another Dent map. Select Dent from the Material/Map browser. Change the Size to 400 and change the Strength to 2.0. *Do not*

change the colors because you want the map to be black and white. Bumps work best when you are using high-contrast maps. Leave all the other parameters at their defaults. Quick render your scene and your chess piece should look like Figure 7.40. You can play around with the Size and Strength and Iterations to achieve different looks.

2. Click the Go to Parent icon to get back to the Material parameters and go to the Maps rollout. You can play around with the Bump amount until you have an acceptable result. Also, remember that the amount of bump you use will also depend on how close the object is to camera. The farther away an object is, the less visible the bump will be.

To check your work, you can open the Chess Piece01.max file in the Texture Scene Files folder on the CD. Because there is a lot of wiggle room in the values, you may achieve a better material with slightly different numbers. Use the numbers given in this exercise as a guideline at best. Always build your scene to your own liking. You will also discover that the difference between a plastic chess piece, such as the one you worked on here, and a richly painted and lacquered wooden piece is just a matter of settings for your material. The artistry takes off in the little numbers.

Let's try a slightly different look now using the following steps:

1. Go to the Material Editor. Select the red plastic material you created in the previous exercise.

2. Click the Go to Parent button to get back to the Material parameters and go to the Maps rollout.

3. Select the bar labeled *None* next to the Diffuse Color. Navigate to where the maps are and select Wood1.jpg from the Texture Scene Files folder on the CD. This bitmap image will replace the red diffuse color. You won't see the change in the viewport until you select the Show Map in Viewport icon ( )

4. Render and you will see that the wood image has wrapped itself around the chess piece. You can edit the image through the Coordinate rollout (shown here) in the Bitmap parameters. Offset U will move the image horizontally. Offset V will adjust it vertically. Tiling scales the image, and Angle will rotate it across the surface.

Figure 7.40

Adding a bump helps the chess piece look more realistic. You can add a lot of character to an object through its bump mapping.

Later in the chapter, you will learn a more efficient way to edit the image on the object, known as *UVW mapping*.

Opacity Maps

Figure 7.41

The chain link texture

Opacity mapping allows you to cut out parts of an object by making those parts invisible. You can also create wonderful fading effects using Opacity maps. With opacity mapping, you don't have to model certain details, which can be a real time saver. In this example, you will create a chain link fence. However, you will not model a fence. You will create it entirely from mapping. To make a chain link fence, follow these steps:

1. Open the `Chain Link Opacity Map.max` file in the Texture Scene Files folder on the companion CD. Open the Material Editor and select a sample slot. First, you are going to add a bitmap to the diffuse color, so go to the Maps rollout. Select the bar next to Diffuse Color. Pick Bitmap from the Material/Map browser and navigate to the Texture Scene Files folder on the CD. Choose `Chain Link.tif` (shown in Figure 7.41).

2. Go to the Coordinates rollout and change both the U and V Tiling parameters to 3.0. This will scale down the image because the image repeats three times.

3. Apply the Material to the Plane geometry in the scene. Click the Show Map in Viewport button. Render and you will see something similar to Figure 7.42. As you can see, the Chain Link image appears on the plane, but you can't see the objects on the other side.

Figure 7.42

The chain link fence is rendered.

4. Go to the Material Editor. Click the Go to Parent button to get to the Maps rollout for the parent material. Click on the bar next to Opacity and select Bitmap from the Material/Map browser. In the Explore window, navigate to the Texture Scene Files folder on the CD and select Chain Link OP.tif (shown here).

5. The tiling values for the Opacity map must be the same as the diffuse map; otherwise the transparency of the fence will not line up with the links of the fence. Go to the Coordinates rollout, and change both the U and V Tiling to 3.0. Render to see the results shown here.

You can see immediately how useful opacity mapping can be. 3ds Max uses the white portions of the image map to display full opacity, whereas the black areas become transparent. If you did not have an opacity file such as the one in this exercise, you could easily create one by painting a black-and-white matte of the color image that you are using for the material.

Mapping Coordinates

An *image map* is a two-dimensional entity that has length and width but no depth, while geometry in 3ds Max extends in all three axes. How is a material, which contains 2D image maps, applied properly to a scene object? Are the maps projected in a single direction onto the object's surfaces or do they envelop the object cylindrically or spherically? The answer depends on the type of *mapping coordinates* applied to the object. Mapping coordinates define how and where image maps are projected onto an object's surfaces and whether the maps are repeated across those surfaces.

Mapping coordinates are applied to objects in several ways. When primitive objects are created and the Generate Mapping Coords option is checked, at the bottom of the Parameters rollout, the appropriate mapping coordinates are created automatically. The Generate Mapping Coords option is on by default.

Loft objects, which are covered in Chapter 5, control mapping in the Mapping section of the Surface Parameters rollout. The Length Repeat value determines how many times the material's maps are repeated along the length of the Path object, and the Width Repeat value determines how many times the maps are repeated around the shape object. The configuration of the shape or path object is irrelevant to the application of the mapping coordinates; the loft object can create mapping coordinates for any loft object. Figure 7.43 shows a loft object with a simple checker pattern repeated five times along the object's length and three times around the perimeter of the shape.

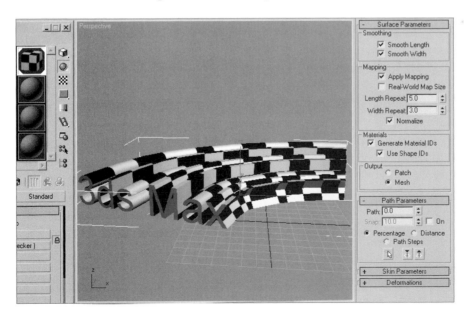

Figure 7.43

A loft object controlling a checker map's repetition in the Surface Parameters rollout

> Objects that have been collapsed or converted to editable polys, editable meshes, or editable patches do not have inherent mapping coordinates. They must have the UVW Map modifier applied to utilize mapped materials.

The UVW Map modifier is a common method for applying and controlling mapping coordinates. You select the type of mapping projection, regardless of the shape of the object, and then set the amount of tiling in the modifier's parameters. The mapping coordinates applied through the UVW Map modifier override any other mapping coordinates applied to an object, and the Tiling values set for the modifier are multiplied by the Tiling value set in the assigned material.

Assign the UVW Map Modifier

Now let's take a look at how to apply a UVW Map Modifier in a scene. The following exercise examines the use of the UVW Map modifier:

1. Open the UVW.max file in the Texture Scene Files folder on the companion CD. This scene consists of a wall object with a linked window and two significantly different boxes.

MAPPING COORDINATES AND BOOLEANS

Boolean compound objects handle mapping in their own unique ways. When only Operand *A* has a mapped material, that material and its mapping coordinates are inherited by the resultant Boolean object. When only Operand *B* has a mapped material, the option of applying that material and mapping appears in the form of a dialog box. When both operands have mapped materials, the Material Attach Options dialog box presents several options to use or discard the materials and mapping.

2. Open the Material Editor and then assign the Brick Wall material to the wall object. The material appears on the object in the Camera01 viewport.

The problem is that the long wall is approximately 17 feet long and the short wall is approximately 7 feet long, and the Brick map used in the material is only eight bricks wide. The default mapping coordinates for a wall object applies the entire map to any vertical surface of the wall, regardless of how long that wall is. The long wall has eight bricks stretched along its length, just as the shorter wall does.

3. Select the wall. In the Modify panel, expand the Modifier List and then select the UVW Map modifier.

The mapping changes and now appears to streak vertically, as shown in Figure 7.44. This is because the default Planar mapping type projects the map onto the object parallel to the plane-shaped gizmo. The vertical lines that appear are the same color as the brick image's pixels where the surface of the object intersects the gizmo. To fix the issue, continue with the following steps:

UNDERSTANDING UVW MAPPING

The UVW Map modifier consists primarily of a yellow gizmo that determines how the image maps are projected onto the surfaces of an object. The images are projected outward or inward from the gizmo and extend through the assigned objects to all surfaces. The size and orientation of the gizmos affect how the maps are projected onto the relevant objects. The properties of the different mapping types are listed here:

- **Planar**—Projects the image maps perpendicular to the perimeter of the rectangular gizmo.

- **Cylindrical**— Projects the maps outward from the center of a cylindrical gizmo as if the map were wrapped around the object in two axes.

    - **Cap**—Projects the maps to the end caps of the cylindrical gizmo in a planar fashion.

- **Spherical**—Projects the maps outward from the center of a spherical gizmo as if the map were completely enveloping the object. The top and bottom of the image maps are gathered at the poles of the gizmo and may cause some distortion.

- **Shrink Wrap**—Similar to the Spherical method, except that the four corners of the image map are gathered at a single location.

- **Box**—Projects the image in six perpendicular planes from the center of the gizmo.

- **Face**—Applies the image maps to each face of an object regardless of their size or orientation.

- **XYZ to UVW**—Used with procedural maps, such as Noise or Smoke, to control the maps when the object changes size.

Figure 7.43

The rectangular Planar mapping gizmo causes the map to streak vertically.

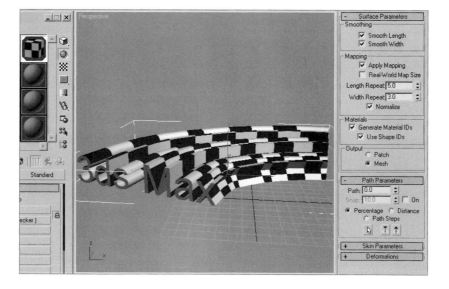

4. In the UVW Map modifier's Parameters rollout, select the Box option. The mapping changes to the same state that it was prior to applying the modifier in the first place, indicating that the Box mapping method is the default type for wall objects.

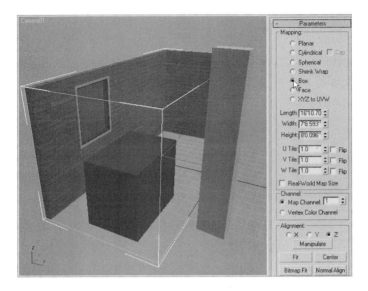

5. In the Parameters rollout, increase the Width value until it is equal to the Length value. This increases the size of the bricks on the shorter wall to match those on the longer wall.

6. Change the U Tile value to 2.5 and the V Tile value to 1.5. This causes the Brick maps to repeat two and a half times horizontally and one and a half times vertically.

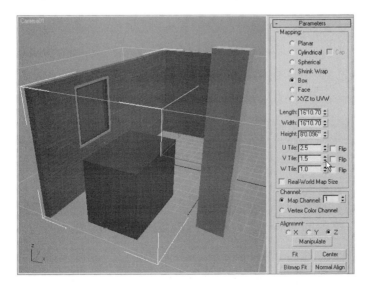

Acquire Mapping Coordinates

In many situations, a material needs to appear the same when applied to several different objects. For example, two different sections of a roof may need to appear with identical mapping even though they are different sizes. The UVW Map modifier includes the Acquire tool for matching one object's mapping gizmo to another's, as shown in the following exercise.

1. Select the BoxShort object.

2. Assign the Brick Wall material and then apply the UVW Map modifier to it. Choose the Box mapping method in the Parameters rollout. The Brick material appears on the box, showing all eight bricks on each side. The bricks are not the same size as those on the wall; this may be more apparent in a rendered view.

3. In the Alignment section of the Parameters rollout, click the Acquire button and then select the wall object.

4. In the Acquire UVW Mapping dialog box, make sure that Acquire Relative is selected and then click OK. Acquire Relative uses the same settings as the target object's gizmo, but it places the gizmo around the current object. Acquire Absolute uses the same settings as the target object's gizmo, and it co-locates the current gizmo with the target object's gizmo.

5. The box's UVW Map modifier's gizmo Size and Tiling values change to match those of the Wall object. Rendering the scene clearly shows the matched mapping between the two objects.

The Fit option, in the Alignment section of the UVW Map modifier's Parameters rollout, shrinks or expands the gizmo to match the extents—or the overall size—of the objects.

Locating the Modifier in the Stack

As with any other modifier in the modifier stack, the UVW Map modifier is applied to the result of the modifier or object below it in the stack. This must be considered when you are locating the modifier or the preferred result may occur. For example, Box mapping has a different result when it is applied to a box before it is bent than when it is applied after it is bent.

1. Select the BoxTall object and clone it to the right. Be sure to make the clone a copy, rather than an instance or a reference.

2. Apply the Checker1 material to both of the objects.

3. Select the original BoxTall and apply the UVW Map modifier. Choose the Box Mapping option.

4. Apply a Bend modifier to the box. Set the Angle to 90 and the Direction to –270. The checker pattern follows the curvature of the newly bent box.

5. Select the second box and apply the Bend modifier with the same settings used in Step 4.

6. Apply the UVW Map modifier and select the Box mapping type. The gizmo in this case fits the extents of the bent box, and not the original box object, resulting in a different layout for the checker pattern.

As you can see, the location of the UVW Map modifier in the stack impacts the final appearance of the objects.

Summary

Creating materials for your objects is the next step after modeling them. Creating materials can give you a sense of accomplishment because it is essentially the last step in making the object look as you envisioned—aside from lighting and rendering, of course.

In this chapter, you learned the basics of materials, what kinds of materials are in 3ds Max, and how to create and edit them in the Material Editors. Then, you learned how choosing the right type of shader will make your surface look right, and then how to apply your knowledge to mapping a pool ball, reflections and all. Next, you learned a few more tricks of the Material Editor and all about the different kinds of maps available in 3ds Max. With that, you created a bump map and an opacity map.

There are several ways to create materials, from simple colors to complex mappings on distinct parameters. Finding the right combination of maps, Shader types, and Material types can make a world of difference in the look of your scenes. It's important to remember, like everything else in CG, texturing takes time, and gaining wisdom with your materials and maps will come with practice.

CHAPTER 8

Introduction to Animation

The best way to learn how to animate is to jump right in and start animating. You will begin this chapter by picking up the Mobile exercise from Chapter 2, "Your First Max Animation," and adding animation to the shapes of the mobile. You'll take a good look at 3ds Max's animation tools so you can start editing animation and training your timing skills.

Topics in this chapter include:

- **Hierarchy in Animation**

- **Using Dummy Objects**

- **Bouncing a Ball Using the Track Editor**

- **Track View**

- **Anticipation and Momentum in Knife Throwing**

Hierarchy in Animation: The Mobile Redux

Do you remember way back when you were reading Chapter 2? Those were good times, weren't they? After setting up the mobile in that exercise, you animated only the bars to rotate, but you left the rotation of the shapes for later. In this chapter, you'll pick up where you left off with the mobile from Chapter 2 and finish the animation using the hierarchies that were set up in that exercise.

> If you skipped the Mobile exercise in Chapter 2, you may want to try it now before you move on with this animation exercise. Understanding hierarchies and how they work in animation is extremely important.

You can begin this exercise by using your own Mobile file from Chapter 2, or you can open `Mobile_v05.max` from the Scenes folder in the Mobile project on the companion CD. This scene file is the same as the file you ended up with in Chapter 2 (`Mobile_v04.max`), with the exception that this version takes the animation of the bars to frame 100 instead of frame 50 as in version 4 of that file.

If you haven't already done so from the previous Chapter 2 exercise, copy the Mobile project from the companion CD to your hard drive. Set your Max project folder by choosing File → Set Project Folder and selecting the Mobile project that you copied from the CD to your hard drive.

Animating the Shapes

With the `Mobile_v05.max` scene open (or your own file), scrub through the animation to become familiar with the scene. The intent here is to create a hierarchy in the mobile and animate the bars. Now you will add rotation to the shapes hanging from the bars. Figure 8.1 shows the mobile in mid-animation.

To add animation to the shapes under the bars, follow these steps:

1. Go to frame 1 of the animation, and click the Auto Key button (Auto Key) at the bottom of the UI.

2. Select the triangle hanging from the bottom bar, and go to frame 50. Rotate the triangle in the Z-axis in either direction at least a full turn of 360 degrees, if not a lot more, as shown here. Don't scrub your animation yet.

3. Still at frame 50, select the square on the bar above, and rotate that shape in the Z-axis several hundred degrees in either direction. Figure 8.2 shows the rotation of the square. The bottom bar goes along with the square's rotation because this is how they were linked in Chapter 2. Don't scrub your animation yet.

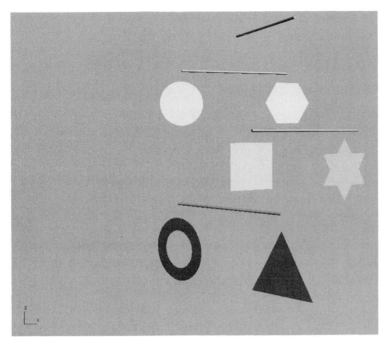

Figure 8.1

The mobile is back!

Figure 8.2

The square is rotated, and its child bar goes along for the ride.

4. Still at frame 50, select the star and rotate it several hundred degrees on the *Z*-axis in either direction, as shown here.

Now scrub your animation and check the results. In theory, all the bars should rotate and so should the shapes hanging on the bars. When you scrub, however, you'll see a big issue crop up that doesn't seem to make sense. The mobile will seem to have lost its mind. The shapes will rotate completely off axis, as if you set rotation keyframes on the *X*- and *Y*-axes as well as the intended *Z*-axis. The same will occur with the lower bar. It will go off its axis and rotate in an unpredictable manner. This behavior is explained in the next section, with easy solutions to fix the issue.

Making a Mistake

Why would we pick an example to show you an incorrect workflow? Learning from *missteps* is as important to learning CG as learning the correct steps. Being able to troubleshoot is essential to becoming good in CG, and the more trouble you get yourself into, the better you will become at digging your way out.

Figure 8.3

The Assign Controller rollout in the Motion panel

This example of strangely rotating hierarchies is an isolated issue that is loosely called *gimbal lock* in many CG circles. Different CG packages have different ways of interpreting exactly how an object rotates when it is rotating along more than one axis. Imagine three cars all staring each other down at a three-way intersection—with the traffic light out. Who goes first in this situation is important to the flow of traffic at the intersection. When a 3d package calculates rotations, it needs to know which axis to rotate first before tending to the rotation of the other axes. In 3ds Max, the *animation controller* is the traffic light, directing the animation. With gimbal lock, you have an incorrect interpretation of the rotations, so the resulting animation seems off axis.

In this exercise, the multiple rotations inherited by the children shapes and bars from their parents caused havoc with their own rotations, so the axes became confused and everything looks just plain wrong. The easiest way to fix this issue is to reassign the animation controllers in charge of the rotations for those objects to one that will not lock up.

Animation Controllers

By default, 3ds Max assigns a Euler XYZ controller to the rotations of objects. This is by far the best controller to use because it gives you the best bang for the buck, as it were. In this example, however, it doesn't quite work. To assign a different controller, follow along here:

1. Select the square; you will start with that object. Switch to the Motion panel (click the Motion Panel tab ( ) in the Command panel, as you see in Figure 8.3. Open the Assign Controller rollout. You'll see that the Rotation controller for the square is set to Euler XZY.

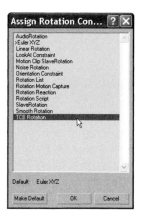

2. Select Euler XYZ from the list in the Motion panel, as shown in Figure 8.3. Click the Assign Controller button ( ) to open the Assign Rotation Controller window shown here. Choose TCB Rotation from the list. If you do not first select the controller from the Controller List, the Assign Controller button will be grayed out and unusable.

3. The square and the bar linked beneath it should snap back into axis. Scrub the animation, and you'll see that the square and the bar beneath it are not behaving as you would expect: they are rotating on the *Z*-axis only, as they should. Figure 8.4 shows the resulting animation. Notice that the star and triangle are still rotating off axis.

4. Select the triangle and repeat Steps 2 and 3 to assign a TCB Rotation controller to the triangle. Do the same for the star. Figure 8.5 shows the proper rotations of the shapes and the bars—but looks are deceiving. We're not done yet!

Figure 8.4

You've fixed the rotation of the square and its children.

Figure 8.5

The mobile seems to rotate properly, but does it really?

If Euler XYZ caused such a ruckus, why isn't TCB Rotation the default for rotating objects? For one thing, the editing options you have with a Euler XYZ controller are head and shoulders above what you get with TCB Rotation. With the Euler XYZ, 3ds Max splits the *X, Y, Z* rotation animation into three separate tracks to give individual control over each axis. This is ideal.

In addition, the TCB Rotation has taken the several hundred degrees of rotation you have animated, and cut it down to within 180 degrees of rotation at most. The square, triangle, and star don't seem to be rotating the several hundred degrees you intended.

It is not a good idea to change the default animation controllers solely based on your experience with this exercise. If you run into a gimbal lock situation in the future, you'll have a good idea what caused it, and you'll be able to troubleshoot it quickly.

Editing the TCB Rotation Keyframes

To fix the fact that the objects do not rotate the several hundred degrees you want, you will have to manually edit the controller to allow a greater degree of rotation:

1. Select the square and open the Key Info rollout, as shown here.

Figure 8.6

Adding more rotation to the square in the Key Info rollout

2. The Key Info rollout shows you the properties of the animation on the selected object on a key-by-key basis. If everything is grayed out, use the arrows at the top of the rollout to move through the keyframes. Go to the first keyframe at frame 0 (shown as Time: 0 in the rollout.) The Angle displays the orientation of the square at the beginning of the animation: 120. Use the arrows again to move to keyframe #2 (Time: 50).

3. The Angle parameter changes to a value of 117.643. The *X* parameter value reads –1.0. The *X, Y, and Z* parameters represent the direction in the respective axes. The value –1 means the square is rotating backward. Don't get confused because this value is now in *X* and not *Z*. Remember, you gave up the individual controls for *X, Y, and Z* when you changed from the Euler XYZ controller. While at this second keyframe, click on Rotation Windup at the bottom of the rollout, and enter the value **500** for Angle. You must first turn on Rotation Windup to enter 500 for the Angle (Figure 8.6).

4. Scrub your animation, and the square will rotate more, as you first intended. Repeat Steps 2 and 3 for the triangle and star to fix their rotations with the TCB Rotation controller.

Any parameter that is animated has a controller. A controller essentially deals with all the animation functions in the scene for 3ds Max, such as storing keyframe values. Interpolating in-betweens is handled by the controllers. By default, the Position XYZ controller is assigned to an animation on an object's position and a Euler XYZ is assigned to its rotation. These controllers are the most useful as they split the *X, Y,* and *Z* into separate tracks to give individual control over each axis. You will have the opportunity to work with and edit individual tracks later in this chapter.

Using Dummy Objects

Another way to circumvent this particular issue of rotation confusion is by using helper objects in 3ds Max called *dummy objects*. Changing the controller for an object is not always the best solution—particularly if the range of movement will be changed. You saw this problem when you changed to TCB Rotation before you had to fix it in Key Info to add more rotation. Using dummy objects, you can insert a helper in the hierarchy that will negate the gimbal lock issue and make it very clear to 3ds Max how the rotations should proceed. As a matter of fact, it's common for animators to make copious use of dummies as controllers for their animation *rigs*. A rig is essentially any setup in the scene that helps you animate objects in the scene.

Dummies are nonrendering objects that are used in several ways for several things. In this case, they are used directly in the hierarchy to straighten out the rotation confusion. In other CG packages, such as Maya, they are called *null nodes*. In our situation, dummies are simply place holders that serve as parents to the mobile shapes that may come down with rotation confusion or gimbal lock.

Placing Dummies in the Mobile

You can begin this exercise by using your own Mobile file from Chapter 2, or by opening Mobile_v05.max from the Scenes folder in the Mobile project on the CD or your hard drive.

To create dummy objects for the animation hierarchy, follow these steps:

1. Go to the Create panel. In the Helpers ( ), click Dummy as shown here.

2. There are no Parameter rollouts or settings for the dummy. Move your cursor to the Front viewport, center it over the circle, and then click and drag to create. Create a dummy that is slightly larger than the shape (Figure 8.7).

Linking the Dummies

If you scrub the animation, you will notice that the circle moves along with the rotation of its parent bar, as it did before. The dummy is not part of the hierarchy yet. You are going to change the structure of the hierarchy in order to break the inheritance of the circle with its parent object, and restructure to add the dummy between the bar and the circle. This is done by relinking the new order.

3. Make sure the Time slider is at frame 0. Go to the main toolbar and click on the Select and Link tool ( ). Use the Select and Link tool to select the circle, and then click and drag to the dummy object. Make sure you don't let go until the cursor changes to the icon to make the proper link, as shown here.

Figure 8.7

Create a dummy object to fit over the circle.

To jump to the beginning of an animation, just press the Home key on your keyboard; this is a shortcut to jump to the start. Likewise, pressing the End key will take you to the end of an animation.

4. You're not done yet. If you scrub the animation, the circle will no longer move with its parent bar. You have to link the dummy to the bar. Select the dummy, and click and drag to the Parent cylinder. This completes the new hierarchy. Now the circle is the child of the dummy, and the dummy is the child of the parent bar above it. Play the animation, and you will see the dummy moving along with the mobile, with the circle in tow, as shown here.

5. Fantastic! Pat yourself on the back. Now it is time to animate the circle shape itself. Move to the end of your timeline (frame 100, press the End key), and click the Auto Key button at the bottom of the interface (you can also press the N key to toggle Auto Key on and off). Select the circle, and rotate a few hundred degrees on the Z-axis in either direction. Do not rotate the dummy, just the circle. Figure 8.8 shows how the circle rotates within the dummy, which then follows with the bar's rotation.

6. Repeat Steps 1 and 2 to create dummies for the other shapes in the mobile. Relink the shapes to their dummies, as you did in Steps 3 and 4. Animate the shapes themselves to your heart's content. If you see funky rotation on the dummies and shapes, either you have made an error in the linking order, or you have animated the dummies rotating and not the shapes themselves.

Play the animation. As you can see, the funky rotation is gone and now you have a perfectly normal rotation. The bar's rotation moves the dummy below it, and the dummy

Figure 8.8
Success! The circle is now rotating properly.

pulls the circle. Because the bar is not directly pulling the circle, the circle is free to rotate without rotation confusion. Feel free to go through this entire exercise another time before moving on. Once you feel confident with how this exercise works, you should have a pretty solid idea of how hierarchies work in animation, and that's a good thing.

Editing Dummies

When you place any of the mobile's dummies, it isn't necessary to have them aligned perfectly with the shape for which the dummy is being used. However, it is a good idea to match them up as best as you can to keep track of which dummy goes with which shape.

Let's say you created a dummy and it is nowhere near the shape, however. The Align tool can move the dummy so it is centered on the shape. To see how the Align tool works, follow along with these steps:

1. Create a dummy any size and anywhere in the mobile scene, as shown here.

2. Make sure the dummy is selected. Go to the main toolbar and select the Align tool ( ). Move your cursor to the shape to which you want to align the dummy and click on it. The Align Selection dialog window will open (Figure 8.9).

3. The Align Selection dialog gives you the choice of aligning an object along any axis, orienting the object (this feature is for rotations), and aligning for the object's scale. Keep the checks in the *X,Y,Z* position, but change the Current and Target Object to Center and then press OK. The dummy will match up with the shape as shown here.

Although it may seem like more work, using dummies is a great workflow for animation. It keeps the scene's animation neater and better defined. As you gain more experience, you will begin to learn when you should use dummies in your hierarchy to make the animation workflow smooth.

Figure 8.9
The Align Selection dialog window

Bouncing Ball

A classic exercise for all animators is creating a bouncing ball. As a matter of fact, you will find bouncing ball tutorials almost everywhere you look. Although you will see it as a straightforward exercise, there is so much you can do with a bouncing ball to denote character that the possibilities are almost limitless. Animating a bouncing ball is a good exercise in physics, as well as cartoon movement. You'll first create a rubber ball, and then you'll add cartoonish movement to accentuate some principles of the animation techniques discussed in Chapter 1, "Basic Concepts." Aspiring animators can come use this exercise for years and always find something new to learn about bouncing a ball.

In preparation, copy the BouncingBall project from the CD to your hard drive. Set your 3ds Max project folder by choosing File → Set Project Folder and selecting the BouncingBall project that you copied from the CD to your hard drive.

Animating the Ball

Your first step is to keyframe the positions of the ball. As introduced in Chapter 1, *keyframing* is the process—borrowed from traditional animation—of setting positions and values at particular frames of the animation. The computer interpolates between these keyframes to fill in the other frames to complete a smooth animation.

Open the `Animation_Ball_00.max` scene file from the BouncingBall folder now on your hard drive.

You'll start with the *gross animation*, or the overall movements. This is also widely known as *blocking*. First, move the ball up and down to begin its choreography.

Follow these steps to animate the ball:

1. The first thing you need to do in this scene is to move the pivot point for the ball. Go to the Hierarchy panel (). Choose Pivot, and under the Adjust Pivot rollout, click the Adjust Pivot Only button. Zoom in on the ball and move the pivot so that it is at the bottom of the ball. Then click on the Affect Pivot Only button again to deactivate—but you already knew that.

2. Turn on the Auto Key button (keyboard shortcut N) and move the timeline to frame 10. Select the ball and move it along the *Z*-axis down to the ground plane. That will be 0 units in *Z* when you release the mouse button in the transform type-ins on the bottom of the interface. You can also just type-in the value and press Enter (Figure 8.10).

This has created two keyframes, one at frame 0 for the original position the ball was in, and one at frame 10 for the new position to which you just moved the ball.

Figure 8.10

At frame 10, move the ball to meet the ground plane.

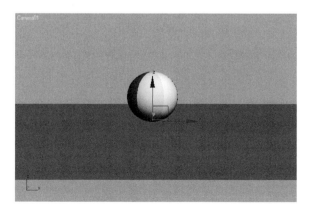

Copying Keyframes

Now you want to move the ball down to the same position in the air as it was at frame 0. Instead of trying to estimate where that was, you can just copy the keyframe at frame 0 to frame 20.

You can see the keyframes you created in the timeline. They are red tick marks in the timeline. Red keys represent Position keyframes, green keys represent Rotation, and Blue keys represent Scale. When a keyframe in the timeline is selected, it turns white. In Figure 8.11, the keyframe at frame 0 is selected and is white.

Figure 8.11

Selected keys in the timeline are white.

3. Select the keyframe at frame 0; it should turn white when it is selected. Hold down the Shift key on the keyboard (this is a shortcut for the Clone tool), and click and drag the selected keyframe to move it to frame 20. This will create a keyframe with the same animation parameters as the keyframe at frame 0.

4. Click and drag on the Time slider to *scrub* through the keyframes.

Using the Track Editor–Curve Editor

Right now the ball is going down, up, and down. To continue the animation for the length of the timeline, you could continue to copy and paste keyframes—but that will be very time-consuming. A better way is to loop or *cycle* through the keyframes you already have. An *animation cycle* is a segment of animation that is repeatable in a loop. The end state of the animation matches up to the beginning state, so there is no hiccup at the loop point.

In 3ds Max, cycling animation is known as *Parameter Curve Out-of-Range Types*. Yeah, that is a mouthful, but it is a fancy way of creating loops and cycles with your animations and specifying how your object will behave outside the range of the keys you have created. This will bring us to the Track View, an animator's best friend—aside from a Golden Labrador and a handful of SweeTarts. You can go through the Track View's UI in the "Track View" section later in this chapter at any time, or you can hang tight and see how you work with Track Editor first using the Bouncing Ball exercise. You will learn the underlying concepts of the Track Editor throughout this exercise as well as its basic UI. Feel free to reference the "Track View" section as you continue.

The Track View is a function of two animation editors, the Curve Editor and the Dope Sheet Editor. The Curve Editor allows you to work with animation depicted as curves on a graph that sets the value of a parameter against time. The Dope Sheet Editor displays keyframes over time on a horizontal graph, without any curves. This graphical display simplifies the process of adjusting animation timing because you can see all the keys at once in a spreadsheet-like format. The Dope Sheet is similar to the traditional animation exposure sheets or X Sheets.

Navigation inside a Track View–Curve Editor is pretty much the same as navigating in a viewport; the same keyboard/mouse combinations work for panning and zooming.

You will use the Track View–Curve Editor (or just Curve Editor for short) to loop your animation in the following riveting steps:

1. With the ball selected, in the main menu, choose Graph Editor → Track View → Curve Editor. In Figure 8.12, the Curve Editor displays the animation curves of the ball so far.

2. A toolbar runs across the top of the Curve Editor under the Menu Bar. In that toolbar, click the Parameter Curve Out-of-Range Types button ( ) shown here.

3. This will open the Param Curve Out-of-Range Types dialog box shown here. Select Loop from this window by clicking its thumbnail. The two little boxes beneath it will turn orange. Click OK. To read up on the other Parameter Curve Out-of-Range Types available, see the "Parameter Curve Out-of-Range Types" sidebar later in this chapter.

4. Once you set the curve to Loop, the Curve Editor displays your animation as shown in Figure 8.13. The out-of-range animation is shown in a dashed line. Scrub your animation in a viewport and see how the ball bounces up and down throughout the timeline range.

Figure 8.12

The Curve Editor shows the animation curves of the ball.

Figure 8.13

The Curve Editor shows the animation loop.

Reading Animation Curves

As you can see, the Track View-Curve Editor gives you control over the animation in a graph setting. Curves allow you to visualize the interpolation of the motion. Understanding what animation curves do in the Curve Editor is critical to getting your animation to look right. Once you are used to reading animation curves, you can judge an object's direction, speed, acceleration, and timing at a mere glance.

The Curve Editor's graph is a representation of an object's parameter, such as position (values shown vertically) over time (time shown horizontally). Every place on the curve represents where the object is; a keyframe does not need to be on the curve. So, the shape of the curve makes a big difference in the motion of the object. Here is a quick primer on how to read a curve in the Curve Editor.

In Figure 8.14, an object's Z Position parameter is being animated. At the beginning, the curve quickly begins to move positively (that is, to the right) in the Z-axis. The object shoots up and comes to an *ease-out*, where it decelerates to a stop, reaching its top height. The ease-out stop is signified by the curving beginning to flatten out at around frame 70.

PARAMETER CURVE OUT-OF-RANGE TYPES

There are several ways to interpret the curves of an animation when they are *out-of-range,* meaning when they extend before your first keyframe and beyond your last keyframe. The Parameter Curve Out-of-Range Types is opened through the Curve Editor with this toolbar button (⌨). The types are the following:

Constant—Used when you do not want any animation out-of-range. This curve type will hold the value of the end and or beginning key of the range for all frames. Constant is the default out-of-range type.

Cycle—Used when you need the animation to loop or cycle by repeating the same animation that is within the range. If the first keyframe does not line up with the last keyframe of the curve range, there will be an abrupt "jump" from the last key to the first with every cycle. If the start and end values do not need to match, and that hiccup in the cycle is desired, use Cycle.

Loop—Used when you need the animation to loop or cycle smoothly despite any differences in the start and end keyframe values. Loop repeats the same animation in the curve range, but it also interpolates between the last and first keyframes in the range to create a smooth loop in the cycle. Loop's ability to create a smooth loop can only go so far before it acts like a Cycle (e.g., when the key values at the start and end are too disparate).

Ping Pong—Used when you want your animation to oscillate back and forth. Ping Pong repeats the same animation in the range, but it plays it front to back and then back to front, and so forth, to alternate the playback, as shown here.

Linear—Used when you need your animation to continue at the same velocity as its beginning or end. The animation curve is projected out from the range in a straight line, picking up the trajectory from the shape of the start or end of the curve, as shown here.

PARAMETER CURVE OUT-OF-RANGE TYPES *(continued)*

Relative Repeat—Used when you need your animation to repeat as in a cycle and to continue building on itself as it cycles. Each repetition is offset by the value at the end of the range, as shown here.

You can select any one of these types for either the *before* or *after* by clicking one of the smaller boxes below the thumbnails. You can set both the before and after out-of-range type by clicking the thumbnail of the type itself.

Figure 8.14

The object quickly accelerates to an ease-out stop.

In Figure 8.15, the object slowly accelerates in an *ease-in* in the positive *Z* direction until it hits frame 75, where it suddenly stops.

Figure 8.15

The object eases in to acceleration and suddenly stops at its fastest velocity.

In Figure 8.16, the object eases in and travels to an ease-out where it decelerates starting at around frame 69 to where it slowly stops at frame 75.

Figure 8.16
Ease-in and ease-out

Finally, in Figure 8.17, the object simply jumps from its Z Position in frame 74, to its new position in frame 75.

Figure 8.17
**Step interpolation
makes the object
"jump" suddenly
from one value to
the next.**

Figure 8.18 shows the Track View–Curve Editor, with notes on its major aspects called out for your information. See the "Track View" section later in this chapter for a more thorough explanation of the UI and toolset for the Track View.

Figure 8.18
The Curve Editor

Refining the Animation

Now that you've played back the gross animation of the bounce, how does it look? Not like a ball bouncing, really, but the framework is getting there. Notice how the speed of the ball is consistent. If this were a real ball, it would be dealing with gravity; the ball would speed up as it gets closer to the ground and there would be "hang time" when the ball is in the air on its way up as gravity takes over to pull it back down.

This means you have to edit the movement that happens in between the keyframes. This is done by adjusting *how* the keyframes shape the curve itself using tangents. When you select a keyframe, a light purple handle will appear, as shown in Figure 8.18 and shown up close here.

This handle adjusts the tangency of the keyframe to change the curvature of the animation curve, which in turn changes the animation. There are different types of tangents, depending on how you want to edit the motion. By default the Smooth tangent is applied to all new keyframes. This is not what you want for the ball; though it is a perfect default tangent type to have.

Editing Animation Curves

Let's edit some tangencies to suit your animation better. The intent is to speed up the curve as it hits the floor and slow it down as it crests its apex. Instead of opening the Curve Editor through the Menu Bar, this time you are going to use the shortcut. At the bottom of the interface, click the Mini Curve Editor button shown here.

Mini Curve Editor

This Mini Curve Editor is almost exactly the same as the one you launch through the main Menu Bar. A few tools are not included in the Mini Curve Editor toolbar, but you can find them in the Menu Bar of the Mini Curve Editor. Figure 8.19 shows the Mini Curve Editor open in the 3ds Max UI.

Figure 8.19

The Mini Curve Editor

To edit the curves, follow these steps:

1. Scroll down the List Controller window on the left of the Mini Curve Editor by dragging the Pan tool (the hand cursor) to find the Ball object/Position XYZ. Click on the Z Position track. This will bring only those curves to the Key window that you want to edit, as shown in Figure 8.19.

2. The Z Position curve is blue, as is almost everything relating to the *Z*-axis. The little gray boxes on the curves are keyframes, as you saw in Figure 8.18. select the keyframe at frame 10. You may need to scrub the Time Ruler out of the way if you are on frame 10. The key will turn white when selected. Remember, if you need to zoom or pan in the Curve Editor's Key Editing window, you can use the same shortcuts you would use navigate in the viewports. You will change this key's tangency to make the ball fall faster as it hits and bounces off the ground.

3. In the Mini Curve Editor toolbar, change the Tangent type for the selected keyframe from the Auto default to Fast by selecting the Fast Tangent icon ( ). When you do this, you will see the Animation Curve change shape as shown here.

4. Select the Perspective view and play the animation. You can easily correlate how the animation works with the curve's shape as you see the timeline travel through the Mini Curve Editor as the animation plays.

Finessing the Animation

Although the animation has improved, the ball has a distinct lack of weight. It still seems too simple and without any character. In situations such as this, an animator can go wild and try several different things as he or she sees fit. This is where creativity helps hone your animation skills, whether you are new to animation or have been doing it for fifty bejillion years.

Animation shows change over time. Good animation conveys the *intent*, the motivation for that change between the frames.

Squash and Stretch

The concept of *squash and stretch* has been an animation staple for as long as there has been animation. It is a way to convey the weight of an object by deforming it to react (usually in an exaggerated way) to gravity, impact, and motion.

You can give the ball a lot of flare by adding squash and stretch to give your object some personality. Follow along with these steps:

1. The Auto Key animation button should still be active. If it isn't, press N to activate. In the Mini Curve Editor, drag the blue double-line Time Bar (called the Track Bar Time slider) to frame 10. (See the following graphic.) Click and hold the Scale tool to access the flyout. Choose the Select and Squash tool ( ). Center the Scale gizmo over the Z-Axis of the Transform gizmo in the Perspective viewport. Click and drag down to Squash down about 20 percent. This will scale down in the Z-axis and scale up in the X- and Y-axes to compensate (Figure 8.20).

2. Move to frame 0. Click and drag up to stretch the ball up about 20 percent (so that the ball's scale in Z is about 120), as shown in Figure 8.21. When you scrub through the animation, you will see that at frame 0 the ball stretched and then the ball squashes and stays squashed for the rest of the time. You'll fix that in the next step.

You need to copy the Scale key from frame 0 to frame 20 first, and then apply a Loop for the Parameter Out-of-Range Type. Because the Mini Curve Editor is open, it obstructs the timeline; therefore, you should copy the keys in the Mini Curve Editor. You can just as easily do it in the regular Curve Editor in the same way:

3. In the Mini Curve Editor, scroll in the Controller window until you find the Scale track for the ball. Highlight it to see the keyframes and animation curve. Click and hold the Move Keys tool in the Curve Editor toolbar ( ) to roll out and access the Move Keys Horizontal tool, as shown here.

Figure 8.20

Use the Squash tool to squash down the ball on impact.

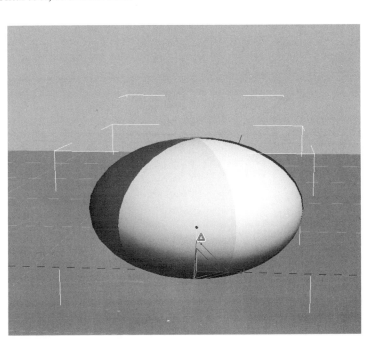

Figure 8.21

Stretch the ball when it is at its apex.

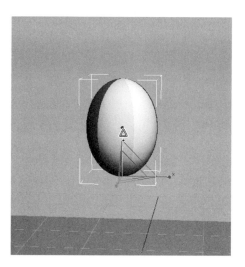

4. Click and drag a selection marquee around the two keyframes at frame 0 in the Scale track to select. Hold the Shift key on the keyboard, and then click and drag the keyframes at frame 0 to frame 20, as shown here.

5. In the Mini Curve Editor's Menu Bar, select Controller → Out-of-Range Types. Choose Loop, and then press OK. Play the animation. The curves are shown here.

Setting the Timing

Well, you squashed and stretched the ball, but it still doesn't look right. That is because the ball should not begin to squash too long *before* it hits the ground. It needs to return to 100 percent scale and stay there for a few frames. *Immediately before* the ball hits the ground, it can squash into the ground plane to heighten the sense of impact. The following steps are easier to perform in the regular Curve Editor rather than in the Mini Curve Editor. Close the Mini Curve Editor by clicking the Close button, as shown here.

Open the Curve Editor to fix the timing, and follow these steps as if they were law:

1. Move the Time slider to frame 8; Auto Key should still be active. In the Curve Editor, in the Controller window, select the ball's Scale track so that only the scale curves appear in the Editing window. In the Curve Editor's toolbar, select the Add Keys button ( ). Your cursor will change to an arrow with a white circle at its lower right. Click on one of the Scale curves to add a keyframe on all the Scale curves (*X, Y,* and *Z*).

2. Because they are selected, the keys will be white. In the Key Status tools, you will find two text type-in boxes. The box on the left is the frame number, and the box on the right is the selected key(s)' value. Because more than one key with a different value is selected, there is no number in that type-in box. Enter **100** (for 100 percent scale) in the right type-in box, and 3ds Max will enter a value of 100 for the scale in *X, Y,* and *Z* for the ball at frame 8, as shown here.

3. Move the Time slider to frame 12, and do the same thing in the Curve Editor. These settings are bracketing the Squash so that the Squash only happens a few frames before and a few frames after the ball hitting the ground, as shown here. Press N to deactivate Auto Key.

Once you play back the animation, the ball will begin to look a lot more like a nice cartoonish one, with a little character. Experiment with changing some of the scale amounts to have the ball squish a little more or less, or stretch it more or less to see how that affects the animation. See if it adds a different personality to the ball. If you can master a bouncing ball, and evoke all sorts of emotion with your audience, you will be a great animator indeed.

Moving the Ball Forward

You can load the `Animation_Ball_01.max` scene file from the BouncingBall project folder on your hard drive (or from the CD) to catch up to this point, or to check your work.

Now that you have worked out the bounce, it's time to add movement to the ball so that it moves across the screen as it bounces. Layering animation in this fashion, where you settle on one movement before moving on to another, is common. That's not to say you won't need to go back and forth and make adjustments through the whole process, but it's generally nicer to work out one layer of the animation before adding another. The following steps will show you how:

1. Move the Time slider to frame 0. Select the ball with the Select and Move tool, and move the ball in the Perspective viewport to the left so it is still within the camera's view. That would be about –30 units in the *X*-axis (Figure 8.22).

2. Move the Time slider to frame 100. Press N to activate the Auto Key again. Move the ball to the right to about 30 units along the *X*-axis.

3. Don't play the animation yet; it isn't going to look right. Go to the Curve Editor, scroll down in the Controller window, and select the X Position track for the ball (Figure 8.23).

Figure 8.22

At frame 0, move the ball to the left of the viewport.

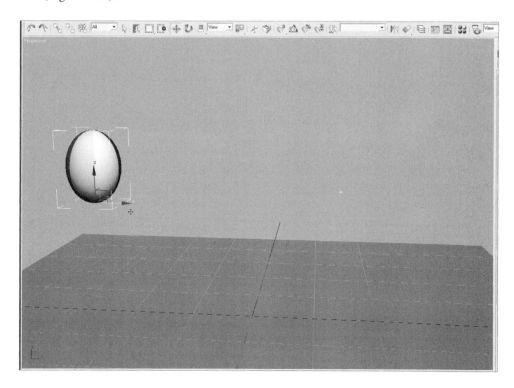

When you created the keyframes for the up and down movement of the ball (which was the Z-axis), 3ds Max automatically created keyframes for the X and Y Position tracks, both with essentially no value. To fix it, keep following with these steps:

4. Select the keyframes on the X Position track at frame 10 and frame 20, and delete them by pressing the Delete key on your keyboard.

5. Select the Parameter Curves Out-of-Range Types button ( ), and select Constant. This will remove the *Loop* from the X Position Track but won't affect the Z Position track for the ball's bounce (Figure 8.24). Press N to deactivate Auto Key. Play the animation.

6. There is still a little problem. Watch the horizontal movement. The ball is slow at the beginning, speeds up in the middle, and then slows again at the end. It eases in and eases out, as you can see in the curve in Figure 8.24. This is caused by the default tangent, which automatically adds a slowdown as the object goes in and out of the keyframe. In the Curve Editor, select both keys for the X Position and click on the Linear Tangent ( ) to create a straight line of movement so there is no speed change in the ball's movement left to right. Press N to deactivate the Auto Key. Figure 8.25 shows the proper curve.

Figure 8.23

The X Position of the ball does not look right.

Figure 8.24

The X Position curve for the ball's movement

Figure 8.25

The X Position curve for the ball's movement now has no ease-in or ease-out.

Adding a Roll

You need to add some rotation, but there are several problems with this. One, you moved the pivot point to the bottom of the ball in the very first step of the exercise. You did that so the squashing would work correctly, that is at the point of contact with the ground. If you were to rotate the ball with the pivot at the bottom, it would look like Figure 8.26.

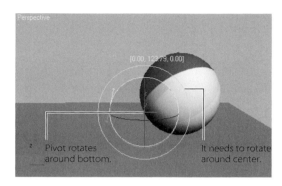

Figure 8.26

The ball will not rotate properly because the pivot is at the bottom.

Using the XForm Modifier

You need a pivot point at the center of the ball, but you can't just move the existing pivot from the bottom to the middle—it would throw off all the squash and stretch animation. Unfortunately, an object can have only one pivot point. To solve the issue, you are going to use a modifier called *XForm*. This modifier has many uses. You're going to use it to add another pivot to the ball in the following steps:

1. Turn off Auto Key if it isn't already. Select the ball. From the main Menu Bar, select Modifiers → Parametric Deformers → XForm. You may also select it from the Modifier List from the Modify panel. XForm will be added to the ball in the Modifier Stack, and an orange bounding box will appear over the ball in the viewport. XForm has no parameters, but it does have sub-objects, as you can see here.

2. Expand the Modifier Stack by clicking on the black box with the plus sign next to Xform. Then click Center. Make sure Auto Key is not active. You will use the Align tool to center the XForm's *center point* on the ball in the next step.

3. Click the Align tool, and then click on the ball. In the dialog box, click Center under Target Object, and then press OK. The XForm's center will move, as shown here.

Now to be clear, this isn't a *pivot point*. This is the *center point* on the XForm modifier. If you go to the Modifier Stack and click on the Sphere, the pivot point will still be at the bottom, as shown here.

Now, the XForm modifier allows the ball to rotate, without Squash and Stretch getting in the way. By separating the rotation animation for the ball's roll into the modifier, the animation on the sphere object is preserved.

Animating the XForm Modifier

To add the ball's roll to the XForm modifier, follow along with these illuminating and incredibly insightful steps:

1. Turn on Auto Key and select the Select and Rotate tool.

2. In the Modifier Stack, click on Gizmo for the sub-object of XForm. This is a very important step because it tells the Modifier to use the XForm's *center* instead of using the pivot point of the ball.

3. Move the Time slider to frame 100 and rotate the Ball 360 degrees on the *Y*-axis (you can use Angle Snap to make it easier to rotate exactly 360 degrees). Click on the XForm to deactivate the Sub-Object mode. Play the animation.

The ball should be a rubbery cartoon ball at this point in the animation. Just for practice, let's say you need to go back and edit the keyframes because you rotated in the wrong direction and the ball's rotation is going backward. Fixing this issue requires you to go back into the Curve Editor as follows:

Open the Curve Editor (Mini or regular). Scroll down in the Controller window until you see the Ball tracks. Below the Ball's Transform track is a new track called *Modified Object*. Expand the track by clicking on the plus sign in the circle next to the name. Go to the gizmo and select Y Rotation Track (Figure 8.27).

You will see the Function curve in the Edit Key work area. You want the keyframe at frame 0 to have the value 0 and the keyframe at frame 100 to be 360 degrees. Select both keyframes and change the Tangent to Linear, as shown in Figure 8.28.

Close the Curve Editor and play the animation. Play the Bounce Ball.mov QuickTime movie file located in the Render-Output folder of the BouncingBall project on your hard drive (or on the CD) to see a render of the animation. You can also load the Animation_Ball_02.max scene file from the Bouncing-Ball project folder on your hard drive (or on the CD) to check your work.

Figure 8.27

The XForm's gizmo selected in the Curve Editor window

Figure 8.28

Setting the rotation of the ball

Bouncing Ball Summary

As you can see, working with the bouncing ball brought gave you quite a bit of experience with the 3ds Max's animation toolset. There are several ways to animate a bouncing ball in 3ds Max. It is definitely a good idea to try this exercise a few times at first, and then to come back to it later—after you have learned other 3ds Max techniques.

Track View

As you have already seen, the Track View → Curve Editor is a powerful tool for creating and editing your animation scenes. In this section, the user interface for the Track View is laid out and explained as a brief reference for you. Figure 8.29 shows the Track View → Curve Editor.

The Curve Editor window can be a bit daunting at first. Now that you've had some experience with it in this chapter, it should seem pretty straightforward. The left side of the window (called the Controller window) displays the objects in the scene in an outline format. These objects have subheadings under them called *tracks* when they are animated. Each track will define animation on one axis of movement or rotation or scale, or one parameter that is keyframed. When you click on a track, its animation information will display in the graph area on the right. In the Curve Editor, you can access the curves and keyframes to edit the animation. In the Dope Sheet version of the Track View, you can access keys in a different manner, as discussed in the next chapter.

You can switch between the Curve Editor and the Dope Sheet by selecting the desired window in the Modes menu in the main Menu Bar. Most of the tools discussed here are also accessible through the Menu Bar and the toolbar. The toolbar is divided into function sets.

Figure 8.29

**The Track View -
Curve Editor**

Key Tools Toolbar

The following table lists the tools used in editing keys in the Curve Editor window.

ICON	NAME	FUNCTION
	Filter	Filter the display in the Curve Editor to make viewing complicated scenes easier.
	Move Keys	Select a keyframe and move it freely in the graph.
	Move Keys Horizontal	Select a keyframe and move it horizontally, to change its timing only.
	Move Keys Vertical	Select a keyframe and move it vertically, to change its value only.
	Slide Keys	Select keyframes and move the group and slide the adjacent keys away as you move the group.
	Scale Keys	Select keys and scale them to expand or compress the amount of time between them.
	Scale Values	Select keys and increase or decrease proportionally the values of the keys without moving them in time.
	Add Keys	Click on a curve to add keys to an existing animation.
	Draw Curves	Draw new curves, or revise existing curves by drawing directly on the animation curve graph.
	Reduce Keys	Reduce keys when you have more keys than necessary on a curve.

You already used a few of these tools when you were getting your bouncing ball animation up to snuff.

Key Tangency Toolbar

As you saw with the bouncing ball, changing the tangency on a few keys can dramatically alter the look of your animation. By default, new keys are set to Auto Tangents, which generally keep the curve smooth. 3ds Max sets an appropriate tangency automatically; however, you can easily change the tangency by manually moving the handles on the keyframes. Once you select an Auto Tangent's handle, 3ds Max will automatically shift the handle to a Custom Handle, allowing you to move it. The following table lists the icons for the tangency tools.

ICON	NAME	FUNCTION
	Set Tangents to Auto	This rollout icon boasts three tools for controlling Auto tangents. The top icon sets both handles to Auto, the middle sets the In tangent, and the bottom icon sets the Out tangent to Auto.
	Set Tangents to Custom	Custom tangents allow you to move the handles to form your own curvature. If you hold the Shift key as you drag a tangent handle, it will break continuity with the other handle, allowing you to have a different In tangency than Out tangency.
	Set Tangents to Fast	Sets the tangent to accelerate in or out of a keyframe quickly, or both.
	Set Tangents to Slow	Sets the tangent to go slowly into or out of the keyframe, or both.
	Set Tangents to Step	Sets the tangent to "jump" from one value to the next in a single frame. The animation will be frozen until the next keyframe when it will jerk to that position or value.
	Set Tangents to Linear	Sets the tangency to a straight linear progression into or out of the keyframe, or both.
	Set Tangents to Smooth	Attempts to keep the curve smooth across all values to achieve a more realistic motion in many cases.

Curves Toolbar

The Curves tools act on the animation curves themselves, allowing you to easily make changes to an animated track. You will run into some of these tools as you become more experienced with Max. Don't worry about memorizing all these functions.

ICON	NAME	FUNCTION
	Lock Selection	Locks the current selection so you don't accidentally select something else.
	Snap Frames	Snaps keys to frames when you move them. When off, you can move keys to sub-frames (i.e., in-between frames).
	Parameter Out-of-Range Curves	Allows you to set the behavior of your animation before and beyond the keyframed range.
	Show Keyable Icons	Toggles an icon to tell you whether a track is keyable or not. Red is keyable, black is not.

continued

continues

ICON	NAME	FUNCTION
	Show Tangents	Toggles the display of tangent handles on individual curves.
	Show All Tangents	Toggles the display of tangent handles on all curves in the graph.
	Lock Tangents	Locks a selection of tangent handles so you can adjust them all at once. When off, however, you only have access to one tangent handle at a time.

Biped Toolbar

These new Curve Editor Biped tools make the process of using the Curve Editor for biped animation much more streamlined than before. Biped tools will be covered in the next chapter. The following table lists the icons and their names for your reference. The Biped toolbar is only visible if you have a biped in your scene.

ICON	NAME
	Show Biped Position Curves
	Show Biped Rotation Curves
	Show Biped X Curves
	Show Biped Y Curves
	Show Biped Z Curves

Navigation Toolbar

These tools are for Track View navigation. Tools such as Pan, Zoom, and Zoom Region work the same as in the Viewport Navigation tools. Some of the tools are designed specifically for the Track View. A few often-used icons are listed in the following table.

ICON	NAME	FUNCTION
	Pan	Use this tool to drag the key window. You can also use the middle mouse button.
	Zoom Horizontal Extents	Adjusts the display such that the entire active time segment is shown.
	Zoom Value Extents	Adjusts the display such that the full height of the curves are visible.
	Zoom	Zooms both time and value proportionally together. This is a rollout with two other Zoom options nested.
	Zoom Region	Drag a region to scale the display to fit.

Anticipation and Momentum in Knife Throwing

This exercise will give you more experience animating in 3ds Max. In it, you'll animate a knife being thrown at a target. You will edit more in the Curve Editor and be introduced to the concept of anticipation in animation, as well as momentum and secondary movement.

In preparation, copy the Knife project from the CD to your hard drive. Set your 3ds Max project folder by choosing File → Set Project Folder and selecting the Knife project that you copied from the CD to your hard drive.

Blocking Out the Animation

To begin this exercise, open the `Animation_Knife_00.max` file in the Knife project and follow along here:

1. Move the Time slider to frame 30 and activate the Auto Key button.

2. Move the knife to the target object, as shown here.

3. Move the Time slider to frame 15, where the knife is halfway between its start and the target, and move the knife slightly up in the Z-axis, so that the knife moves with a slight arc.

4. For now, change the frame range in the Time slider so you're only working between frame 0 and frame 30. Click the Time Configuration button (![ ]) at the bottom of the UI next to the navigation controls. Figure 8.30 shows the Time Configuration window. In the Animation section, change the End Time to **30** from 100. The Time slider will reflect this change immediately.

5. Scrub your animation, and you should see the knife move with a slight ease-in and ease-out toward the target with a slight arc up in the middle. You want the position of the knife to start at frame 10, so open the Curve Editor and scroll down in the Controller window until you see the three X, Y, Z Position tracks for the knife. Hold the Ctrl key and select all three tracks to display their curves (Figure 8.31).

6. Drag a selection marquee around the keyframe at frame 0. In the Curve Editor toolbar, select and hold the Move tool (![ ]) to access the Flyout icons, and select the Horizontal Move tool in the flyout (![ ]). Use this tool to move the keyframes to frame 10.

Figure 8.30

Change the frame range in the Time Configuration window.

7. This will compact the curve, as shown previously, so you will need to move the keys at frame 15 to the new middle, frame 20, as shown here.

That's it for the gross animation or blocking of the shot. Did you have fun?

Figure 8.31

The Initial Curve Editor for the knife

Figure 8.32

Turning on trajectories for the knife

Trajectories

When it comes to animation, it is very helpful to be able to see the path your object is taking over time. This is known as *trajectories* in Max. The easiest way to see the trajectories is to select the knife object, go to the Motion panel, and click Trajectories, as shown in Figure 8.32. Your viewports will display a red curve to show you the path of the knife's motion as it arcs toward the target, as shown in Figure 8.33.

The trajectory will remain displayed until a moving object is selected. The large hollow square points on the trajectory curve represent the keyframes set on the knife so far. Let's adjust the height of the arc using the trajectory curve. Turn on the Sub-Object button at the top of the Motion panel, as shown here.

Keys are your only sub-object choice in the pull-down menu to the right of the button. Select the middle keyframe and move it up or down to suit your tastes, as shown in Figure 8.34. Once you settle on a nice arc for the path of the knife, turn off the Trajectories button.

As you can imagine, the Trajectories panel can be useful in many situations. It not only gives you a view of your object's path, but it also allows you to edit that path easily and in a visual context, which can be so important.

Figure 8.33

The red curve shows the trajectory for the knife's motion.

Figure 8.34

Raise the arc of the knife by altering its trajectory.

Adding Rotation

The next step is to add a bit of rotation to the knife. As an animator, you need to research and gather as much information about your subject matter as you can. I don't mean to suggest that you throw knives at people, but I do suggest that you throw a pen or pencil at something safe to see how it should best be animated. Almost invariably, you'll find that the knife will have to rotate once or twice before it hits its target. To add rotation to the knife, follow allow with these steps:

1. Move to frame 30, and press E for the Select and Rotate tool. Auto Key should still be active. Rotate in the *Y*-axis 443 degrees, as shown here.

2. Open the Curve Editor, scroll down to find the X, Y, and Z Rotation tracks, and select them. Use the Horizontal Move tool to shift the keyframes at 0 to frame 10. Press N to deactivate the Auto Key. Figure 8.35 shows the Curve Editor graph for the knife.

Figure 8.35

Move the first rotation keyframes to frame 10.

3. Play the animation, and you will see that the knife's position and rotation eases in and eases out. A real knife would not ease its rotations or movement. Its speed would be roughly consistent throughout the animation.

4. Go back to the Curve Editor, select the X Position track, and then select all the keyframes and switch the Tangent to Linear. Now select Z Position track; you'll need to finesse this one a bit more than the X Position. You are going to use the handles on the tangents that appear when you select a keyframe. These handles can be adjusted; just center your cursor over the end and click and drag. Figure 8.36 illustrates how you want the Z Position animation curve to look. This will give the trajectory a nice arc and a good speed of travel.

Figure 8.36

Adjust the curve for the knife's arc through the air.

5. Now it is time to edit the Rotation keys. In the Curve Editor scroll to find the X, Y, and Z Rotation tracks. The first thing you can do is add a bit of drama to the knife to make the action more exciting. To this end, you can say that the rotation on the knife is too slow. Select the X Rotation track and select its keyframe at frame 30. In the Key Stats, change the value to –52. The higher the value, the faster the knife will rotate. This will add one full revolution to the animation and some more excitement to the action.

6. Adjust the tangent handles to resemble the curve shown in Figure 8.37. The knife will speed up just a little bit as it leaves the first rotate keyframe. The speed will be even as it goes into the last keyframe.

With just a little bit of fast rotation as the knife leaves frame 10, you give the animation more spice. A little change in the curve can make a big difference in an animation—every little bit counts. The knife should now have a slightly weightier look than before when it rotated with an ease-in and ease-out.

Figure 8.37

Match your curve to this one.

Adding Anticipation

Instead of making the knife just fly through the air toward the target, you should animate it to move back first to create *anticipation*, as if an invisible hand holding the knife pulled back just before throwing it to get more strength in the throw. This anticipation, although small in the greater scheme, can add a nice nuance to the animation and lend a nicer gestalt to the animation. Follow these steps:

1. Move the Time slider to frame 0. Go to the Curve Editor, scroll the Controller window, and select X Rotation track for the knife. In the Curve Editor toolbar, click the Add Keys button ( ), bring your cursor to frame 0 of the curve, and click to create a keyframe. This creates a key at frame 0 with the same parameters as the next keyframe, as shown in Figure 8.38.

Figure 8.38

Adding a key to the beginning to create anticipation for the knife's throw

2. Select the Move tool and select the key at frame 10. In the Key Stats type-in, change the value of that key to **240**. If you play back the animation, it will look weird. The knife will cock back really fast and kind of spin a bit. This is due to the big hump between frames 0 and 10.

3. Keep the tangent at frame 0 the default, but change the tangent on the key at frame 10 to Linear. Play back the animation. You'll have a slight bit of anticipation, but the spice is lost and the knife looks less active and too mechanical.

4. To regain the weight you had in the knife, press Ctrl+Z to undo your change to the tangency on frame 10 and set it back to what you had (just like Figure 8.38). You may have to undo more than once. Now, select the Vertical Move tool and select the In tangent for keyframe 0. This is the tangent handle on the left of the key, as shown here.

It's very common to try something in the course of your work, and rely on Undo to get back to the starting point. You can sometimes expect to Undo several times when you find yourself at a dead end.

5. Press Shift and drag the tangent handle down to create a curve that is similar to the one shown in Figure 8.39. By pressing Shift as you dragged the tangent handle, you *broke* the continuity between the In and Out handles, so that only the In handle was affected. Play back the animation and it should look much better now.

Remember, the smallest tweaks in the Curve Editor can have a huge impact on your animation, for good or for bad.

Follow-Through

The knife needs more weight. A great way to show that in animation is by adding follow-through. This is part of the animation concept of secondary movement that was mentioned in Chapter 1. The follow-through for the knife would be having the knife sink into the target a little bit and push back the target as it transfers momentum to the target. For more on momentum, see the sidebar later in this chapter.

Knife's Follow-Through

To add follow-through to your animation, follow these steps:

1. You want to sink the knife into the target after it impacts. Select the Time Configuration button (shown in the following graphic), and change the End Time to 40 to add 10 frames to your frame range. This will not affect the animation; it will merely append 10 frames to the current frame range.

2. Select the knife and go to frame 30, where it hits the target. In the Curve Editor, select the X Position of the knife. Add a keyframe with the Add Keys tool at frame 35.

3. Note the value of the key in the type-in boxes at the bottom of the Curve Editor window (and *not* the type-in boxes at the bottom of the main UI). In this case, the value in this scene is about −231. You will want to set the value for this key at frame 35 to

Figure 8.39

To create a believable anticipation for the knife throw, set your curve to resemble this one.

about **–224** to sink it farther into the target. If your values are different, adjust accordingly so you don't add too much movement. Also make sure the movement is *into* the target and not back out of the target as if the knife were bouncing out.

4. Keep the tangent for this new key set to Auto. With these relative values, scrub the animation between frames 30 and 35. You should see the knife's *slight* move into the target. The end of your curve should look like the curve seen here.

5. You still need to add a little bit of follow-through to the rotation of the knife to make it sink into the target better. In the Curve Editor, select the X Rotation to display its curve. Add a key to the curve at frame 35. The value of the key at frame 30 should already be about –652. Set the value of the keyframe at frame 35 to be about **–655**, as shown here. Keep the tangent set at Auto.

Be careful about how much the knife sinks into the target. Although it is important to show the weight of the knife, it is also important to show the weight of the target; you do not want the target to look too soft. Make sure your keys at frame 35 for the X Position and X Rotation are not too much.

Transferring Momentum to the Target

To make the momentum work even better for the Knife animation, you will have to push back the target as the knife hits it. The trouble is, if you animate the target moving back, the knife will float in the air. You have to animate the knife *with* the target. However, animating them separately in the hopes they will match up will frustrate you and will more than likely look bad.

If you think that hierarchy has to be involved here, you are absolutely right. Basically, the knife will have to be linked to the target so that when the target is animated, the knife will follow precisely, because it is stuck in the target.

Won't that mess up the animation of the knife? Because the knife will be the child in the hierarchy and can have its own animation separate from the target, you can link it after you are finished with the knife animation and have no issues. Just follow these steps:

1. Go to frame 30, where the knife impacts. Select the Select and Link tool. Select the knife and drag it to the target as shown. Nothing should change until you animate the target object.

2. Move the Time slider to frame 34 and press N to activate the Auto Key tool. With the Select and Rotate tool, select the target object and rotate it back about 5 degrees as shown. The pivot of the target has already been placed properly, at the bottom back edge.

3. Go to the Curve Editor, scroll to find the Y Rotation track for the target object, select the keyframe at frame 0, and move it to frame 30. Then hold the Shift key and click and drag the keyframe (which will make a copy of it) to frame 37. Your curve should resemble the curve in Figure 8.40.

4. Change the Tangent at frame 0 to Fast and leave the other keyframe tangents alone.

Figure 8.40

The target will rock back and forth on impact.

5. Add a little wobble to the target to make the animation even more interesting. This can be done very easily in the Curve Editor. Select the Y Rotation of the target to display just that curve. Use Add Key to add two keyframes at frames 40 and 44. Using the Vertical Move tool, give the key at frame 40 a value of about 1.7. Your curve should resemble the curve shown here.

6. Finally, add a little slide to the target. Get the Select and Move tool, move the Time slider to frame 37, and move the target just a bit along the *X*-axis. Go to the Curve Editor, scroll to the X Position of the target object, select the keyframe at frame 0, and move it to frame 30 so the move starts when the knife hits the target. Change the tangent for frame 30 to Fast and leave the other tangent at Auto.

Done! Play back your animation. Experiment and change some of the final timings of the target's reaction to the impact, as well as some of the values, to see how small changes can make big differences in how the weights of the knife and target look to the viewer.

You can see a sample render of the scene in the `knife_animation.mov` QuickTime file in the RenderOutput folder of the Knife project on the CD (or copied onto your hard drive). You can also load the `Animation_Knife_01.max` scene file from the Scenes folder of the Knife project to check your work.

MOMENTUM

Understanding what momentum is and how it works is pretty important for an animator. When an object is in motion, it has momentum. The amount of momentum is calculated by multiplying the mass of the object by its velocity. The heavier something is, or the faster it is moving, the more momentum it has and the bigger the bruise it will leave if it hits you.

That's why a tiny bullet can cause such a great impact on a piece of wood, for example. Its sheer speed greatly increases its momentum. Likewise, a slow-moving garbage truck can bash your car, relying on its sheer mass for its tremendous momentum.

Basically, when one moving object meets another object that is moving or not, momentum is transferred between them. That means when something hits an object, that target is somehow moved if there is sufficient momentum transferred to it.

It follows that the more weight an object has, the more momentum will transfer to the target. Also, the more velocity an object has, the more momentum will be transferred to the target on collision. You will be able to show the weight of an object in animation by showing how much momentum it transfers when it impacts another object. This could be as simple a as knife hitting a target and moving it back, as you animated in the exercise in this chapter, or as complicated as a heavy-set man walking down the street. In the latter case, because the pavement can't give way underneath the man, the momentum that is transferred is reflected back to the man and absorbed by his body. That makes his body bend and flex and his big belly jiggle up and down with each step.

Impact is a perfect opportunity for an animator to show his subject's weight in motion, and it is always intrinsic in good animation.

Summary

In this, the first of two chapters on animation in this book, you learned the basics of creating and editing animation. You learned how to fix hierarchy problems in animation and how to use dummy objects to help you animate properly. You bounced a ball to learn timing issues and how to edit animation curves through the Curve Editor. You then learned the ins and outs of the Track Editor–Curve Editor before moving on to a thrown knife to learn about trajectories and the concepts behind using secondary movement to help give your animation weight.

Animation can be a lot of fun, but it is also tedious and sometimes aggravating. A lot of time, patience, and practice are required to become good at animation. It all boils down to how the animation makes you think. Is there enough weight to the subjects in the animation? Do the movements make sense? How does nuance enhance the animation? These are all questions you will begin to discover for yourself. This chapter merely introduced you to how to make things move in 3ds Max. It gave you some of the basics of animation techniques to help you develop your eye for motion. Don't stop here. Go back into the chapter and redo some of the exercises. Try different variations on the same themes. Keep working.

CHAPTER 9

Character Studio and IK Animation

At one time or another, almost everyone in the 3D community will want to animate a character, and this chapter examines the 3ds Max toolset that aids the process of character animation. In this chapter, you will learn about the two components that make up Character Studio, the full-featured package for animating bipedal characters, including humans, aliens, robots, and anything else that walks on two feet. Although Character Studio (CS) creates an instant structure for a character, you will also work with Inverse Kinematics (IK), which individually creates structures for animating linked objects.

Character animation is a broad and complex field that everyone would like to experiment with at some point. This chapter introduces you to the basics of using Character Studio and Bones. Further investigation into these tools is a must if you want your character movements to be accurate and realistic.

Topics in this chapter include:

- ▪ **Character Animation**
- ▪ **Character Studio Workflow**
- ▪ **Creating a Biped**
- ▪ **Animating a Biped**
- ▪ **Associating a Biped to a Character**
- ▪ **Using Inverse Kinematics**

Character Animation

The character animation CG specialty is one of the easiest to learn, but one of the toughest to master. It takes a special kind of eye and insight to become an amazing animator. In one word, good character animation comes down to *nuance*. Because humans are animated (i.e., we move around) and surrounded by other people who move, we are innately critical when a character is not animated well. That is because we are so used to seeing detail and nuance in movement that it is a foregone conclusion to us. We never really think twice when we see a real person lean in a special way when they limp. However, we notice when that nuance is missing in an animation of a person limping. As observers, we may not know exactly what is missing, but we instinctively know that something is wrong and it looks funny.

When you character animate, you have to have a keen eye for detail and an understanding of how proportions move on a person's body. Setting up a CG character to walk *exactly* like a human being is amazingly complicated. You must account for muscles, bone structures, and a host of other details that most 3D software does not begin to address.

However, good animation for a character is actually not that difficult right out of the box. Character systems such as Character Studio make it a breeze to set up characters and have them in a walk cycle very quickly. Don't limit your character animation studies to Character Studio. While learning and mastering *how* CS works and how to animate with it, you mustn't lose sight of the fact that you are trying to learn *how to animate* as opposed to learning how to run a piece of software.

In other words, once you gain a solid grasp of how CS and other character tools work, use them to learn how to really animate. Character Studio is just a means to an end. You're here to learn to animate, not to learn how to run CS. Now that we got that out of the way, we can concentrate on getting you comfortable with CS. Have fun!

Character Studio Workflow

Character Studio is a system built into 3ds Max to help automate the creation and animation of a character, although not necessarily just a *biped* (two-footed creature). Character Studio comprises three basic components: the Biped system, the Physique modifier, and the Crowd system. Biped and Physique are used to pose and animate a single character, and the Crowd utility is used to assign similar movements and behaviors to multiple objects in your 3ds Max scene. This chapter covers the Biped and Physique features, but Crowd is beyond the scope of this book.

The first step in the Character Studio workflow is to build or acquire a suitable character model. The model should be *bipedal,* meaning it stands on two feet. In the future, however, you needn't limit yourself to strictly humanoid models; CS is perfectly useful for animating anything from a human to a dinosaur to a bumble bee. If the model's configuration allows it, the model should be in the reference position or "da Vinci pose" with the feet shoulder width apart and the arms extended to the sides with the palms down, as shown in Figure 9.1. This allows the animator to observe all of the model's features, unobstructed by the model itself, in at least two viewports.

Again, the term *bipedal* refers to an animal or character with two feet. In 3ds Max, a *biped* is a predefined, initially humanoid, structure used to define the movements of your character. It is important to understand that you animate the biped that is associated with your model and not the model itself. The biped structure *drives* the model, and using the Physique modifier ensures that your model follows the biped animation. You will work with attaching a model to a biped later in this chapter.

Physique versus Skin

3ds Max has two modifiers that essentially do the same thing. Physique and Skin can both be used to transfer the movement of a skeletal system to a mesh, making the character move with the skeleton rig. Of the two, Physique is the older modifier and Skin is the more current. Historically, Character Studio, which included Physique, was developed by Unreal Pictures and was the first major plug-in for 3ds Max. Character Studio was sold as a separate program in the product's first releases.

Over time, users requested a program similar to Physique be included as part of the base 3ds Max package. Autodesk developed the Skin modifier to satisfy the customers' need for this functionality. When CS was finally included free of charge with 3ds Max, Physique was still bundled with it, and so there were two modifiers to do the same task. Over time, Skin has had numerous improvements that add to its capabilities, while *Physique* has more or less remained the same. You can choose which one you want to learn; they both can accomplish the same work. Some users swear by Physique, others swear at it— and the same goes for Skin. Physique is covered in this chapter.

The default biped, shown in Figure 9.2, consists of legs, feet, toes, arms, hands, fingers, pelvis, spine, neck, and head. After your model is ready, you will create a biped and, using its parameters and the Scale transform, fit the biped closely to the model. The better the biped to model relationship, the easier the animation will be.

BONES AND SKIN

The Bones system and Skin modifier are similar to Character Studio. *Bones* is a series of linked, hierarchical components that are used, in conjunction with the Skin modifier, to control the displacement of a model similar to the Biped and Physique method. Many animators swear by Bones. They appreciate the finer control they are able to achieve over the character's motion and motion restrictions. Others prefer the easily created hierarchies of the Biped system.

Figure 9.1

A bipedal character in the reference position

Figure 9.2

The default biped

After the biped is fit snugly to the model, you will select all of the components of the model, not the biped, and apply the Physique or Skin modifier in a process often referred to as *skinning*. The Physique modifier dictates which object, the pelvis of the biped usually, the model is applied to and it is the node where modifications to the skin are accessed. It may take a while to properly test and refine the relationship between the model and the biped to get it to an acceptable level.

The final step will be to animate your character. You can accomplish this by using a combination of adding walk, run, and jump cycles to the biped, applying freeform animation, and refining the animation keys in the Dope Sheet. Don't expect the default walk, run, and jump cycles to create realistic motion. They are just a starting point and must be tweaked to achieve acceptable movements. Character animation is about nuance and subtlety, and those artistic touches take a significant amount of time and effort to master.

The best way to start is to jump in and examine the tools available. In the next section, you will work with a biped and adjust the parameters and components to modify it.

Creating a Biped

As stated previously, you should create your model first and then create and modify your biped to fit the model. In this section, however, you are going to examine the procedure for creating and modifying a biped first to provide an understanding of its capabilities. Later in this chapter, we will revisit the methods for adjusting your biped specifically to match a model.

Placing a Biped in a Scene

Let's create a Biped system for your scene to get a feel for how CS works. Unlike many of the objects that you've created so far, Biped is located under the Systems category the Create tab of the Command panel rather than the Geometry button.

Follow these steps to create and adjust a biped:

1. From the Command panel, select Create → Systems → Biped.

2. Click and drag in the Perspective viewport to create the biped.

Clicking sets the insertion point, and dragging defines the height of the biped system and defines all of the components. All of the biped's components are sized relative to the biped's Height parameter. Instead of making a single object, you created 30 visible and 5 hidden objects arranged in a linked hierarchy. All of the elements on the left side of the biped's body will be blue, and all of the elements on the right side will be green. This is part of the Character Studio coloring scheme that is carried throughout 3ds Max.

3. Press the H key to see the list of visible objects created with the default biped. All of the objects are indented from the edge of the dialog box, indicating that they are subordinate to, or children of, the objects above them in the list. Close the Select Objects dialog box.

If your Select Objects dialog box does not display a hierarchy in an indented format as shown, check the Display Subtree box near the bottom of the dialog.

4. While the biped is still selected, scroll the Command panel to display the Create Biped rollout.

   This rollout is where changes to the biped's structure are made. You can increase the number of fingers and toes and the number of links in each to match your model. You can even add a tail or ponytails by increasing the number of links for these parameters, or you can discard the arms altogether. Adding neck links will make your biped taller, but adding spine links will only subdivide the torso area for more control in the midsection.

5. Change the parameters as you like. The biped in Figure 9.3 includes additional fingers and toes, as well as a tail and a ponytail.

The root object of the hierarchy is named Bip01, for the first biped that you create in a scene, and all the associated objects will have a Bip01 prefix. Changing the name of the object in the Name and Color rollout changes only the name of the root object and does not cascade throughout the hierarchy. Changing the name in the Root Name section of the Create Biped rollout, however, affects all of the objects in the biped.

Figure 9.3

**A biped with modi-
fied parameters**

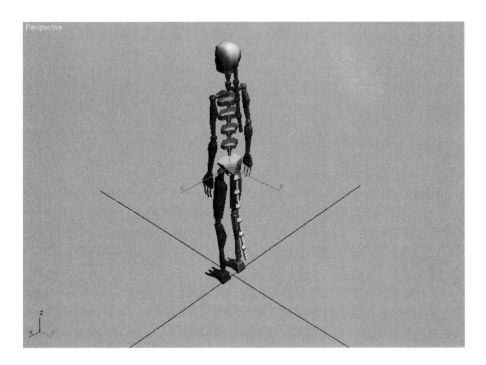

Modifying a Biped

Bipeds are very generic in appearance, and you will rarely, if ever, use the default biped in an actual animation. Biped's have a complete set of tools available for modifying their structure and their behavior to match a model. You will have to select an appropriate editing mode to access the appropriate tools to adjust your biped. This section covers the tools used to adjust the size of a biped's individual elements.

1. Clear your selection set by clicking the Select Object ( ) button in the main toolbar and then clicking on any blank area of a viewport. Nothing in your scene should be selected.

2. Click any part of your biped to select it. Bipeds react differently than other objects: selecting any single component opens the entire object for editing.

3. Click the Modify tab of the Command panel. The purpose of a biped is to create an animation. This is why all of the biped's parameters, including those that control animation and appearance, are consolidated under the Motion tab of the Command panel.

4. Click the Motion tab of the Command panel to display the first level of rollouts to control a biped.

5. In the Biped rollout, click the Figure Mode button to display the rollouts that pertain to the biped's configuration, but not to its animation or footstep control. The Figure Mode button turns blue to indicate the current mode that the system is using.

6. Expand the Structure rollout to access the same parameters that were used when you first created the biped to adjust its basic configuration. Make any additional modifications that you choose.

> In the Body Type area at the bottom of the Structure rollout, you can change the overall appearance of the biped from the default Skeleton to Male, Female, or Classic. The body type has little to do with the biped's capabilities and is more a matter of preference.

7. Select the biped's left upper arm. In the main toolbar, click the Rotate transform button and set the reference coordinate system to Local. Most transforms that are applied to a biped are applied in the Local coordinate system so they are relative to the object, rather than the world or the current viewport.

8. Place your cursor over the green *Y*-axis ring of the Rotate Transform gizmo and drag upward to rotate the upper arm upward, as shown in Figure 9.4. All of the pivot points for the biped elements will be placed at the top of the objects. For example, the upper arm pivots at the shoulder, the lower arm pivots at the elbow, and the hand pivots at the wrist. This is one of Character Studio's great time savers.

9. Click the Scale transform in the main toolbar. The reference coordinate system automatically switches to Local and then grays out to indicate that the parameter cannot be altered. All scale transforms applied to biped components must be applied in the Local reference coordinate system.

10. Click and drag on the *X*-, *Y*-, and *Z*-Axis handles of the Scale Transform gizmo individually. The Y and Z handles make the upper arm large or small, causing your biped to get bulked up or thinned out. Dragging on the X handle changes the length of the upper arm. You should observe the changes in all of the viewports while you're adjusting the scale.

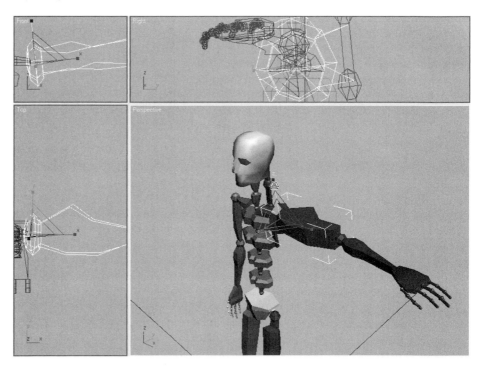

11. Select and adjust the left lower arm, hand, and fingers to suit yourself. Don't worry about the right side yet; it will be covered shortly.

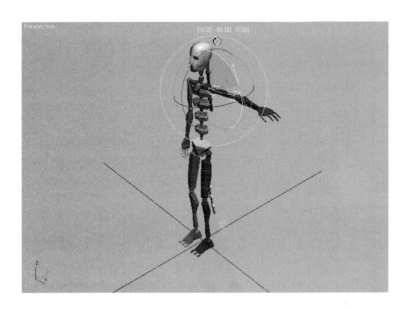

Figure 9.4
Rotating a biped component

12. Select each of the spine links and scale them to give your biped a nice, tapered torso. Dragging the X handle upward will scale the links vertically and push the elements above them upward, increasing the height of the biped. Scaling the top spine link in the positive *Z*-direction will push the clavicles and all other arm components outward, as shown in Figure 9.5. The clavicles are linked to the middle of the top spine link and can be protruded by that link. If necessary, scale the clavicle to extend beyond the top spine link.

Figure 9.5
Scaling the top spine link pushes the arms outward.

13. Select and scale the pelvis to spread the hips out further.

14. Similar to Steps 10 and 11, use the Scale transform to adjust the scale of the bipeds left upper and lower leg and foot.

As you can see, creating a biped is fairly simple. You simply click and drag to place the system and drag to set its height and proportionate size. You then adjust the parameters of the structure in the Motion panel. Finally, you position and adjust the size of each of the biped's components using the transforms.

Copying and Pasting Postures

Most characters are basically symmetrical with some variation in their surface appearance to make them look a bit less than perfect and a bit more natural. Character Studio allows you to set the structure and form—called the *posture*—for elements on one side of a biped's body and then paste those features to the elements on the other side. For instance, when the length, width, and pose of the left arm, hand, and fingers are tweaked as required, the same dimensions and orientations can be pasted to the same components on the right side. You don't need to model the opposite side independently. There is no self-adjusting relationship between the two sides, so any future changes to one side must be pasted again to the other to maintain any symmetry.

1. Continue with the previous exercise or open CSBiped1.max from the companion CD.

2. Select the biped and access Figure mode if necessary.

3. Double-click on the left upper arm. Double-clicking on an object selects that object and all the objects below it in the hierarchy—in this case, the lower arm, hand, and all finger joints.

4. Open the Copy/Paste rollout.

5. Postures must be saved as collections prior to being pasted. Click the Create Collection button and then rename the collection from the default Col01 to **Left Arm**.

6. Just below the blue Posture button, click the Copy Posture button to copy the selected posture to the clipboard. A preview of the copied posture will appear in the Copied Postures area of the Command panel.

7. Click the Paste Posture Opposite button. The size, scale, and orientation of the selected objects will be applied to the reciprocal objects on the opposite side of the biped, as shown in Figure 9.6.

Copied postures are not limited to being pasted within a single biped; they can also be pasted to other bipeds. Simply copy the posture, select any part of another biped, and then click the Paste Posture button.

8. Repeat Steps 3 through 7 to copy the posture of the left leg to the right side of the biped.

Figure 9.6

**Pasting a posture
to the other side
of a biped**

As you've seen in this section, modifying a biped's appearance and posture is simply the process of selecting one of its components and using the Rotate and Scale transforms to change its size and orientation as needed. In the "Associating a Biped to a Character" section, later in this chapter, you will explore the procedures for fitting a biped to a specific model to ensure a smooth animation setup. Now is a good time to save your scene before you proceed to the next section.

Animating a Biped

Bipeds can be animated in several ways, including footstep-driven animation and freeform animation. Just as it sounds, *footstep-driven animation* is the process of adding visible footsteps to your scene and directing the biped to step onto those footsteps at a particular point in time. Footsteps can be added individually or as a set of walk, run, or jump steps; they can be moved or rotated to achieve the desired result. When using footstep-driven animation, the legs and feet of the biped are not the only things animated; the hips, arms, tails, and all other components are animated too. A short animation sequence can generate hundreds, or even thousands, of animation keys.

Footstep-driven animation is often a good starting point, but it is rarely the complete solution to your animation needs. For example, there is no method for turning a biped's head or raising its arms using footsteps. Even when footsteps are used to create the initial movement of a biped, freeform animation is used to augment and tweak it. Freeform animation is created using the procedures discussed in Chapter 8, "Introduction to Animation," which includes using the Auto Key method and the Track View in Curve Editor mode.

The animation keys that are added to the selected objects appear in the Track Bar where they can be moved, modified, or deleted to adjust the animation. Some character animators forgo footstep-driven animation altogether and use freeform animation exclusively for the control it gives by creating keys only where the animator chooses and not throughout the biped. In this section, you will explore both the footstep-driven and freeform methods for animating a biped.

Moving the Biped into Place

As a system, bipeds can't simply be moved using the Move transform in the Main toolbar. To position one correctly, you must select and move the root object using the Body Vertical and Body Horizontal buttons.

1. Continue with the previous exercise or open CSBiped2.max from the companion CD. If you open the CD file, select the biped and enter Figure mode if necessary.

   In the previous exercise, when you scaled either of the leg elements along the *X*-axis, the feet of the biped moved off the construction plane where new objects are created. This plane is where the new footsteps will be placed, so you will want the biped's feet at that same elevation.

2. Maximize the Right viewport and zoom so that you can see the dark, horizontal line indicating the construction plane, the feet, and the pelvis. The pelvis isn't really important at this point, but the root object located inside of it is.

3. In the Track Selection rollout, click the Body Vertical button. This selects the diamond-shaped Bip01 object, which is the root of the hierarchy, and activates the Move transform.

4. Use the Move Transform gizmo to move the biped until the feet rest on the construction plane, as shown in Figure 9.7.

5. Switch back to a four-viewport display.

Adding Footsteps

Adding footsteps is as simple as adding a specified number of steps with a specific gait or clicking the mouse button to place footsteps individually. First, you will place a series of steps, and then you will place steps individually.

1. With the biped selected, click the Footstep Mode button in the Biped rollout. The rollouts change to display the tools for adding and controlling a biped's motion. The Footstep mode and Figure mode are exclusive; you cannot be in both modes at the same time.

2. In the Footstep Creation rollout, make sure that the Walk gait is selected and then click the Create Multiple Footsteps button.

Figure 9.7
Moving the biped to the construction plane

3. In the Create Multiple Footsteps dialog box that appears, assign the Footstep properties including the number of steps, the width and length of each step, and which foot to step with first. Set the Number of Footsteps to 8 and leave the other parameters at their default values, as shown in Figure 9.8. Click the OK button.

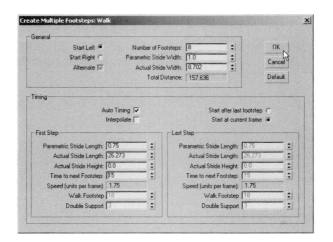

Figure 9.8

Creating multiple footsteps

4. Zoom out in the Perspective viewport to see the footsteps that have been created. Look at the Time slider, and note that the scene now ends at frame 123; that's 23 more frames than the 100 frames the scene had at the beginning of this chapter. 3ds Max recognized that it would take the biped 123 frames, just over 4 seconds, to move through the eight steps that it was given.

5. Click the Play Animation ( ) button in the Playback Controls area. Nothing will happen. The biped must be told explicitly to create animation keys for the steps that have been added to the scene.

6. Drag the Time slider back to frame 0.

In the Footstep Operations rollout, click the Create Keys for Inactive Footsteps button.

The biped will drop its arms and prepare to walk through the footsteps that are now associated with it.

8. Click the Play Animation button again. This time the biped will walk through the footsteps with its arms swinging and its tail and ponytail swaying back and forth.

Controlling the View

Now the problem is that the biped walks off screen so you cannot see the end of the walk cycle. Motion cycles can be very linear and difficult to track, so Character Studio contains the In Place mode to follow a biped's animation. While in the In Place mode, the biped will appear to stay in place while the scene moves around it. The In Place mode cannot be used in a Camera viewport.

1. In the Biped rollout, click the Modes and Display text with the plus sign to the left of it. This is actually a small rollout located inside of another rollout that expands to display additional display-related tools.

2. In the Modes and Displays rollout, click the In Place Mode button.

3. Click the Play Animation button again. This time the biped will appear to be walking in place while the footsteps move underneath it, as shown in Figure 9.9.

4. Stop the animation playback.

Using the In Place mode helps work out the way a character moves without having to navigate throughout 3D space with your viewport. It is important to closely watch the cycle movement and try to finesse parts to suit the character. The In Place mode is great for this because the viewport moves with the character in 3D space and you can concentrate on how its body is moving.

WALK, RUN, OR JUMP?

What is the difference between a walk, run, or jump gait in 3ds Max? The difference is not speed or length of stride; it's the number of feet that the biped places on the ground at any given moment. In a walk gait, the biped has either one foot or both feet on the ground at all times. During a run sequence, the biped has either one foot on the ground or, in mid stride, zero feet on the ground. When the biped is executing a jump sequence, it has either both feet on the ground or zero feet on the ground while it is airborne.

Figure 9.9

The biped does not change position in the viewport when it is in the In Place mode.

Adding a Run and Jump Sequence

Having created a footstep cycle doesn't limit you to just those footsteps. Any extra footstep sequences can be added to a biped. These new footsteps are appended to any existing footsteps. This, in turn, extends the length of the animation, if necessary, to accommodate the additional footsteps. In the next exercise, you will add footsteps to the existing animation cycle.

Continue with the previous exercise or open CSBiped3.max from the companion CD, select any biped component, and access Footstep mode from the Motion panel.

1. Click the Run button ( ) in the Footstep Creation rollout. This will apply a run gait to any footsteps created in the Create Multiple Footsteps dialog box.

2. Click the Create Multiple Footsteps button to open the Create Multiple Footsteps dialog box.

3. Change the Number of Footsteps to 10 and click the OK button.

4. In the Footstep Operations rollout, click the Create Keys for Inactive Footsteps button to associate the new footsteps with the biped.

5. Press the Play Animation button. The biped walks through the first eight steps and then runs through the next ten. As you can see, the run sequence meets the definition of a run, but it is far from realistic. You'll learn later in this chapter how to add to or modify a biped's motion.

6. Click the Jump button in the Footstep Creation rollout, and then click the Create Multiple Footsteps button.

7. In the Create Multiple Footsteps dialog box, set the Number of Footsteps to 4 and click the OK button. Because a jump is defined as a sequence with either two feet or zero feet on the ground at a time, four jump steps will equal two actual jumps.

8. Click the Create Keys for Inactive Footsteps button to associate the new jump footsteps with the biped.

9. Press the Play Animation button. The biped will walk, run, and then end the sequence with two jumps.

> The Actual Stride Height parameter in the Create Multiple Footsteps dialog box determines the height difference from one footstep to the next. For example, to animate your biped walking up a flight of stairs, you would set the Actual Stride Height to the same value as the rise of each stair.

Adding Freeform Animation

Good animation rarely comes from a first try. When you set your keys initially, you will need to edit them to suit good timing and form, as well as fix any issues that may come up. Character animation is relational: when one part of the body is in one movement, another part of the body is in an accompanying or supportive or even opposite form of movement. When you are walking and your right leg swings forward in a step, your right arm swings back and your left arm swings out to compensate. With character work, you have to remain cognizant of the entire body of the character and how it moves.

As with everything that is automated, the walk, run, and jump cycles that CS creates definitely need some work before they will be acceptable as good animation; they definitely lack the human touch, which is the earmark of good animation. For example, based on a standard CS cycle, the biped's head never turns, the torso is very stiff, and the arms swing similarly regardless of the gait type selected. With animating using CS, you will need to add the little nuances of movement that make animation interesting and personable. You will need to add animation to the biped to gain personality. Luckily, you can easily add or modify the biped's existing animation keys with freeform animation using the Auto Key button and the Dope Sheet. The following exercises contain examples of freeform animation.

Moving the Head

Any character's head will move along while the character walks. The following steps will guide you through the process of creating head movement for your biped. Continue with the current project or open the CSBiped4.max file from the companion CD.

1. Select one of the biped's components and, if necessary, exit the Footstep mode by clicking the Footstep Mode button.

2. Drag the Time slider to frame 50, approximately the point when the biped lifts its left foot off of footstep number 2.

Footsteps are numbered, starting with the number 0 and initially alternating from the left to the right side. They are also color-coded, corresponding to the biped, with blue footsteps on the left and green footsteps on the right.

3. Select the biped's head and note the animation keys that appear in the Track Bar, as shown in Figure 9.10.

4. In the Track Bar, select the two keys on either side of the current frame and delete them.

There seems to be an intermittent bug in release 9 of 3ds Max. If the selected keys for the head will not delete, enter and exit the Footstep mode and then try again. They should disappear after the second try.

5. Click the Auto Key button (Auto Key) to turn it on.

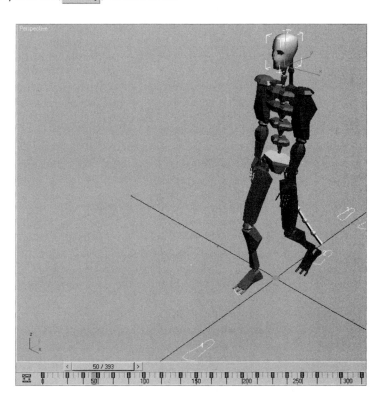

Figure 9.10

Selecting a component of the biped reveals all of that object's animation keys in the Track Bar.

6. Click the Rotate transform button and rotate the head to the left and up, as if it sees somebody in a second floor window off screen. A new key will be created at frame 50, recording the time and value of the head's rotation.

7. Scrub the Time slider back and forth. Watch the head rotate from a neutral position to the orientation that you created and then rotate back to the neutral position.

8. Select all the keys after frame 50 and before frame 100. Delete them by pressing the Delete key. This will make room for the new key that you are about to create. If animation keys are too close together, the animation could appear jerky.

9. Select the key at frame 50, hold the Shift key down, and drag a copy of the key to frame 90. Use the readout at the bottom of the 3ds Max window to drag the key with precision. Copying the key will cause your biped to hold that neck pose for 40 frames or about one and one-third seconds. Scrub the Time slider to review the animation.

10. Select the biped's left upper arm.

11. In the Track Bar, select and delete all keys between frames 50 and 100. The animation keys for the arms define their swing motion and the biped walks. If you scrub the Time slider or play the animation, the biped will hold its arm unnaturally stiff for 60 frames because you deleted the animation keys between two points where it holds its hand forward. That's OK; we're just making room for some new keys.

12. Move the Time slider to frame 60. This is the location for the first new animation key.

Moving the Arms

Now it's time to animate the arms, which are essential components in any walk cycle. To do so, just follow these steps:

1. Rotate the upper arm upward, so that it points to the same location at which the head is looking.

2. Continue adjusting the biped's left arm, hand, and fingers until they appear to be pointing at something, as shown in Figure 9.11.

3. Double-click on the left upper arm to select it and all of the components below it in the hierarchy.

4. In the Track Bar, select the key at frame 60, hold the Shift key down, and drag it to frame 85 to create a copy.

5. Drag the Time slider and watch the Perspective viewport. The biped will walk for bit, notice something off-screen, point at it, and drop its arm while looking forward again before breaking into a run and then a jump.

6. Click the Auto Key button to turn it off.

Figure 9.11

Rotate the biped's arm, hand, and fingers to assume a pointing posture.

Completing the Motion Sequence

The CSBiped5.max file on the companion CD contains the completed scene to this point.

For additional practice, add keys to the animation of the biped's arms when it jogs through the run cycle. For example, when the left foot is fully extended and the heel plants on the ground, the right arm should be bent at the elbow and swung forward and slightly in front of the biped's body. As the right foot swings forward during the next step, the right arm should swing backward and assume a nearly straight posture. Bend each of the spine links and swing both arms backward to prepare the biped for each of the jumps. Use the Body Vertical button in the Track Selection rollout to lower the pelvis into a prelaunch position before the biped launches into its upward motion. Remember to make sure the Auto Key button is turned on to record all the changes that you make as animation keys.

Modifying Animation in the Dope Sheet

What if you need to change the animation that comes with CS? To that end, you will need to edit the keyframes of the biped once you are happy with the base animation cycle. For this, you need to use the Track View Dope Sheet. The Track View Curve Editor is used to edit the function curves between animation keys; however, the Track View Dope Sheet interface is cleaner and is used to edit the specific value and position of the keys. Access to the footstep keys is available only in the Dope Sheet. In this exercise, you will add individual footsteps and modify the footstep timing in the Dope Sheet to make the biped dance and jump.

Control of footstep animation is not available in the Track View Curve Editor. You can, however, convert footstep animation to freeform animation using the Convert button ( ) in the Biped rollout. All existing animation will be retained, but the footstep-driven feature will be replaced by simple function curves that can be edited in the Curve Editor.

Adding Footsteps Manually

With the following steps, you will manually add footsteps to your biped character:

1. Create a new scene with a biped or open CSBiped6.max from the companion CD. This is a biped with no footsteps applied.

2. Enter the Footstep mode.

3. In the Footstep Creation rollout, click the Walk Gait button and then the Create Footsteps (at current frame) button.

4. In the Top viewport, click in several locations to place alternating left and right footsteps.

5. Change the gait to Jump, and then click the Create Footsteps (Append) button to create additional footsteps. Create about 12 footsteps in all.

6. When you are done, use the Move and Rotate transforms to adjust the footstep locations and orientations as desired. Your Top viewport should look similar to Figure 9.12.

7. In the Footstep Operations rollout, click the Create Keys for Inactive Footsteps button and then play the animation.

8. Character Studio doesn't have a collision-detection feature, so it is very possible that limbs will pass through one another. If this happens, the footsteps must be modified to eliminate these conditions.

9. If necessary, move any footsteps that cause collisions or other unwanted conditions during the playback.

Figure 9.12

Manually place the footsteps in the Top viewport.

Using the Dope Sheet

In Chapter 8, you experimented with the Track View Curve Editor and learned how to adjust the values of animation keys while observing the inter-key values displayed as a function curve. When the Track View is in Dope Sheet mode, frames are displayed as individual blocks of time that may or may not contain keys. Although you cannot see the flow from key to key that the Curve Editor displays, the Dope Sheet mode has its advantages, including the ability to add Visibility tracks to control the display of an object and Note tracks for adding text information regarding the keys.

Using the Track View Dope Sheet, you can adjust the point in time when a foot plants on or lifts off the ground, how long the foot is on the ground, and how long the foot is airborne. Rather than appearing as single frame blocks in the Dope Sheet, like other keys do, footstep keys appear as multiframe rectangles that identify each foot's impact time with the footstep.

1. Exit the Footstep mode.

2. In the main toolbar, choose Graph Editors → Track View – Dope Sheet. The Dope Sheet will open.

3. In the Navigation pane on the left, scroll down until you find the Bip01 entry. Expand the Bip01 and Bip01 Footsteps entries. The footstep keys appear as rectangles in the Key pane. As expected, the left keys are colored blue and the right keys are colored green. If necessary, click the Zoom Region button ( ) in the lower-right corner of the Dope Sheet window and drag a zoom window around the footstep keys. The region will expand to fit the key pane.

4. Select a few Footstep keys in the Navigation pane.

The white dot on the left side of a selected key identifies the frame when the heel of the biped's foot first impacts the footstep. Similarly, the white dot on the right side of a selected key identifies when the biped's foot lifts off a footstep. A blue key overlapping a green key indicates that both feet are on the ground. A vertical gray area with no footstep indicates that the biped is airborne and neither foot is on the ground.

5. Select the first key (numbered 0), place the cursor over the right white dot and then drag the dot to the right to extend the length of time that the biped's foot is on the ground.

> You can't move the end of one footstep key beyond the beginning of another one, and you must maintain a one-frame gap between same-side footsteps. You can't move a key to a point in time beyond the active time segment nor can you modify keys for footsteps that have been created, but not yet associated to the biped. In addition, footsteps must be at least two frames long.

6. The double vertical line in the Dope Sheet's key pane is another Time slider that allows you to scrub through the animation. Drag the Dope Sheet's Time slider to a point in time when the biped is airborne, as shown in Figure 9.13. Scrub the Time slider, and the foot will remain planted on the ground and then quickly move to the next footstep. The shorter the gap between footstep keys, the faster the movement between them.

A biped's airborne time is calculated using the standard physics values for acceleration due to gravity: 32 ft/s^2 or 9.8 m/s^2.The biped does not simply hover at a user-defined altitude by moving it in the Z-axis and setting a key, as you would do with most other 3ds Max objects Therefore, increasing the airborne time by increasing the gap between footsteps will boost the height to which the biped rises act against the gravitational force pushing it downward.

7. Select the next-to-last Footstep key and drag it to the right to create a gap approximately 30 frames wide between any frames. This will cause the biped to be airborne for about one second.

It is possible to move a footstep beyond the limits of the active time segment in the Dope Sheet. For example, in a 100-frame animation, you can move the last footstep to start at frame 105 and end at frame 123. When you play the animation, it will begin to loop at frame 100, and you will never see the animation created by the last keys. Use the Alt+R key combination to extend the active time segment to include all existing keys.

Figure 9.13

Drag the Time slider until the biped is airborne.

8. Move the time slider to the frame when both feet are planted before the jump starts. Turn on the Auto Key button.

9. To prepare the biped to leap, select the Bip01 object and move it downward, causing the biped to bend its knees more. Rotate the spine links, neck, and head to bend the torso forward and tuck the chin. Rotate both arms backward into a prejump posture. Be sure to choose Local as the reference coordinate system for the Rotate transform.

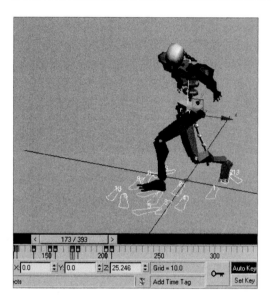

10. Move the Time slider forward until the biped is at the apex of the jump. Rotate the biped's components into positions to your liking. Delete any animation keys that may interfere with your desired motion.

The CSBiped7.max file on the companion CD contains the completed exercise.

As you saw in this section, there are several ways to animate a biped including the footstep-driven method, the freeform method, and a combination of techniques. You can also modify the animation in the Track Bar, with the Auto Key button, and with the Track View Dope Sheet Editor. The next section addresses the methods for associating your biped to a 3D model.

Associating a Biped to a Character

The purpose of a biped is to be the portal through which you add animation to your model, rather than animating the model itself using direct vertex manipulation or deforming modifiers. Any motion assigned to a biped is passed through it to the nearest vertices of the associated model, essentially driving the surfaces of the model. For this reason, it is important that the biped fit as closely as possible to the model.

Creating and Modifying the Biped

In the following steps, you'll create and adjust a biped to fit to a character model:

1. Open the CSAlien.max file from the companion CD. It contains a completed alien model in the reference position.

2. Select all of the model's components, right-click in a viewport and choose Freeze Selection. This will prevent you from inadvertently selecting the alien instead of the biped.

3. Create a biped with a height about the same as the alien's. This will size most of the biped's parts similar to those of the alien.

VIEWING FROZEN OBJECTS

If your background color is similar to the default shade of gray that Max uses to depict frozen objects, the model may seem to disappear against the background. There are several solutions to this situation:

1. You can go to Object Properties, turn off Show Frozen as Gray, turn on See-through, and set all viewports to Smooth + Highlights mode.

2. You can change the shaded color in the Customize User Interface dialog box (Customize → Customize User Interface → Colors).

3. You can change the viewport background color in the Customize User Interface dialog box (Customize → Customize User Interface → Colors).

4. With the biped still selected, click the Motion tab of the Command panel and enter Figure mode. Changes to the biped's features or pose must be made in Figure mode to be retained by the system.

5. Use the Body Vertical and Body Horizontal buttons in the Track Selection rollout and the Move Transform gizmo to position the biped's pelvis in the same location as the model's. With the pelvis located properly, scaling the legs or spine to match the model's proportions will be easier. Check to make sure the location is correct in all of the viewports.

As you did in a previous exercise, you will modify one side of the biped to fit the model and then paste that posture to the other side.

6. In the Front viewport, select the pelvis and scale its width so that the biped's legs fit inside the alien's legs. Scale the pelvis in the Right viewport so that it roughly encompasses the alien's lower region.

7. Select the biped's left upper leg then scale it along the *X*-axis until the knee aligns with the alien's knee. Scale it in the *Y*- and *Z*-axes until it is similar in size to the alien's thigh, as shown in Figure 9.14.

8. Select the biped's left calf. In the Right viewport, rotate the calf to match the model and then scale it in the *X*-axis until the biped's ankle matches the alien's ankle. You may need to select the left foot and use the Move transform, in the Front viewport, to orient the calf to the model. Scale the calf to match the proportions of the alien's calf.

Figure 9.14

Scale the length, width, and depth of the biped's upper leg to match the alien's thigh.

Modifying a biped to match a model can be a time-consuming task that requires continual tweaking and modification. Moving the foot as described in the previous step may require that the upper leg's proportions be readdressed. Don't expect to perform this task quickly without making any revisions to components on which you have previously worked. The better the biped matches the model now, the easier the animation will be later.

9. Continue working down the leg by scaling the biped's foot to match the alien's. Be sure to check the orientation of the foot in the Top viewport. In the Structure rollout, use the Ankle Attach parameter to move the biped's ankle slightly backward, as shown in Figure 9.15.

10. In the Structure rollout, change the number of Toes to 3 and Toe Links to 2.

11. Scale and move the biped's toes to match the model's. Be sure to select the first toe link and use the Local Transform coordinate system to move the toes.

12. Double-click on the left upper leg to select it and all of the objects below it in the hierarchy. Create a collection and then copy/paste the posture of the left leg to the right as you did in the Copy and Paste Postures section in this chapter. The model is not perfectly symmetrical; make any necessary changes to the right side of the biped.

Figure 9.15

Increasing the Ankle Attach parameter to move the ankle

Adjusting the Torso and Arms

Similar to the method used to adjust the legs, you will use the Scale and Rotate transforms to fit the biped to the model. The locations of the arms rely on the scale of the spine links.

1. Continue with the previous exercise or open CSAlien2.max from the companion CD, select the biped, and then access Figure mode.

2. Select each of the spine links in turn, and then rotate and scale them to fit the alien's torso. Only the lowest spine link can be moved, and this will move all of the links above it as well. Each should be scaled down slightly in the X-axis to lower the biped's clavicles to match the model's.

3. Move, rotate, and scale the left clavicle as required to place the biped's shoulder socket in the proper location.

4. Scale and rotate the left upper arm and left forearm using the same techniques you used to adjust the biped's legs.

5. Scale and rotate the left hand as required.

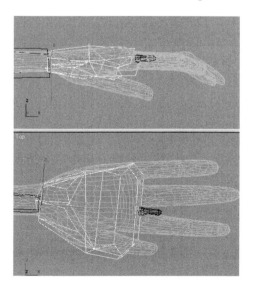

6. In the Structure rollout, increase the number of Fingers to 4 and Finger Links to 2.

Once the fingers have been adjusted, you can not go back and change the number of Fingers or Finger Links. If you do, all modifications to the fingers will be lost.

7. Adjust the biped's fingers to match the models. This can be one of the more tedious tasks in character animation, depending on the complexity and orientation of the model's fingers. Take your time and get it right.

Separate motion tracks, in the Track View, for each finger are new to 3ds Max 9. Previous versions combined all finger animation into a single track, making finger animation difficult to edit or control.

8. When you are done, paste the posture to the right side of the biped and make any required changes.

Adjusting the Neck and Head

The head and neck will seem easy to adjust when compared to the hands. You need to make sure the neck links fill the alien's neck area and scale the head to fit.

1. In the Structure rollout, increase the number of Neck Links to 2.

2. Move, scale, and rotate the neck links to match the proportions of the model's neck.

3. Move and scale the head to the approximate size of the alien's head.

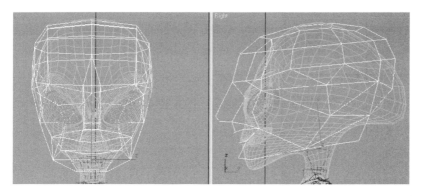

That's it. The biped has been created and adjusted to fit the 3D model, and half the battle is over. In the next section, you will tie the biped to the model and make adjustments to the skinning process. Now would be a good time to save your work.

Applying the Physique Modifier

The Physique modifier is the tool used to associate the 3D model to the biped so that all of the biped's animation is passed through to the model. It's important to remember that the modifier is applied to the model and not to the biped. Continue with the previous exercise or open CSAlien3.max from the companion CD.

1. Right-click in any viewport and select Unfreeze All from the Quad menu to unfreeze the alien model.

2. Select all three of the alien components: the body and both eyes.

3. In the Named Selection Sets field in the main toolbar, enter the name **Alien** to save the alien meshes as a named selection set. By creating named selection sets, you can quickly access all of the desired components by selecting the named selection set from the drop-down list on the main toolbar. For reference, see Chapter 3, "The 3ds Max Interface," for the icons and functions of the named selection sets.

4. Repeat the process with the biped by selecting all of its components and naming the selection set **Alien Biped**.

5. Select the Alien selection set and click the Modify tab of the Command panel.

6. Expand the Modifier List and select the Physique modifier.

7. In the Physique rollout, click the Attach to Node ( ) button. The button will turn yellow and wait for you to identify the root object in the hierarchy that controls the mesh.

8. Press the H key to open the Pick Object dialog box. This method will be easier than trying to click on the object directly in a cluttered scene. Select the Bip01 Pelvis object and click the Pick button, as shown in Figure 9.16.

9. In the Physique Initialization dialog box, accept the defaults and click the Initialize button. The cursor will briefly turn into a coffee cup to indicate that the initialization is in progress. It will return to normal when the process is complete.

Testing the Model

The most time-consuming part of the process is complete. You have created a biped, adjusted all of its component parts to fit your model, and applied the Physique modifier to link the model to the biped. The final step is to test the model by adding animation.

1. Select any element of the biped and click the Motion tab of the Command panel.

2. Enter Footstep mode.

3. Add a footstep sequence as you did in the Animating a Biped section of this chapter. Don't forget to create keys for the inactive footsteps. Exit the Footstep mode when you are done.

4. Activate the In Place mode, and then zoom and pan the Perspective viewport to get a good view of the action.

5. To select the entire biped, select the Alien Biped named-selection set from the drop-down list on the main toolbar.

6. Right-click in any viewport and choose Hide Selection from the Quad menu to hide the biped and obtain an unobstructed view of the model.

7. Click the Play Animation button. Your alien will walk through the scene; it should be similar to the rendered alien shown in Figure 9.17.

Figure 9.16

Use the Pick Object dialog box to select the root object in a cluttered scene.

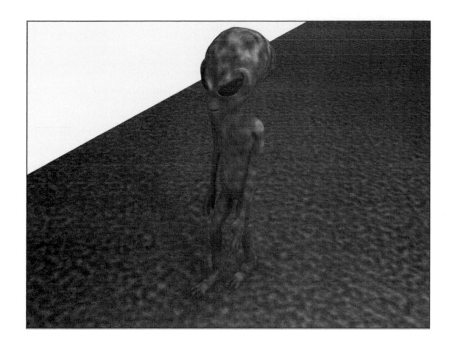

Figure 9.17

The rendered alien during a walk cycle

The completed Character Studio Alien exercise can be found in the CS Alien Complete.max file on the companion CD.

As mentioned at the beginning of the chapter, Character Studio is a very complete character animation package, and we've barely scratched the surface here. There are tools for saving biped configurations and sequences of animation. You can mix animation sequences from different files to create an entirely new motion. When the model does not *skin* properly, you can use envelopes to refine the skinning process, define vertices to be excluded from a specific biped object's influence, or include bulge conditions to define the model's behavior depending on the angle between subsequent biped elements. The list goes on, but the good news is that the CS tutorials and help system that ship with 3ds Max are very thorough and you should find the information in those places to expand your Character Studio skills once you have a solid footing with the basics of CS. It's important to realize that animation requires nuance, and the best animation with the simplest rig and setup will beat a mediocre animation created with the more wonderful, complicated, ingenious setup.

Using Inverse Kinematics

When a hierarchy is set up through linking, the result is a kinematic chain. As you saw in Chapter 2, "Your First Max Animation," transforms are passed from a parent object to all of the children objects down the chain. Imagine your arm is a system of linked 3ds Max objects; when you pivot your forearm (the parent) at the elbow, your hand (the child) and your fingers (the descendants) are also transformed to maintain the relationship between the objects. This is known as Forward Kinematics (FK) and is the default method of passing transforms in a hierarchy.

When Inverse Kinematics (IK) is used, the child object is transformed while the parent and ancestor objects maintain their relationships throughout the chain. Using the same arm analogy, lifting a finger would raise the hand, which would raise the forearm, causing a curl at the elbow. With IK, the end of the chain, the child, is positioned and the rest of the chain upstream rotates and pivots to fit the new layout of the chain to achieve a possible pose. IK setups require the use of an IK solver to determine how the parent objects react to the child transforms and joint constraints to prevent unnecessary twists in the motion.

In the following exercise, we are headed back to the toys of war by linking a machine gun that can be mounted on the tank you built in Chapter 5, "Modeling in 3ds Max: Part II." Here, the goal is to arrange the IK setup so that the gun pivots vertically at the joints only and then pivots at the turret.

Linking the Objects

The machine gun unit consists of the gun itself, two two-component pivot assemblies, two shafts, and the turret ring. The gun is at the top of the hierarchy, and the turret is at the bottom.

1. Open the IKGun1.max file from the companion CD.

2. Begin by linking the Gun object to the Pivot-Top object, the cylindrical object near the gun. The PivotTop object will flash briefly to signify that is has been linked. If you are having difficulty selecting the proper object directly, press the H key to open the Select Parent dialog box.

3. Continue the hierarchy by also linking the PivotTopRing to PivotTop, PivotTop to Shaft1, and Shaft 1 to PivotBottom.

4. Complete the setup by linking PivotBottom-Ring to PivotBottom, PivotBottom to Shaft2, and Shaft2 to Turret. If you open the Select Objects dialog box and make sure the Display Subtree is checked, you hierarchy will look like Figure 9.18.

Figure 9.18

The Select Objects dialog box showing the hierarchy

Creating Joint Constraints

The gun assembly should be able to be rotated only in certain ways. The gun itself should only pivot perpendicular to the PivotTop object, for example. This is accomplished by constraining the Rotate transform for the PivotTop object, the parent of the gun, to a single axis. The transforms are further restricted by limiting the range of motion an object can rotate within an acceptable axis. This method is used to prevent the gun barrel from rotating to the point where it disappears within the tank body. Both of these tasks are accomplished under the Hierarchy tab of the Command panels.

1. In the Command panel, click the Hierarchy tab (![icon]).

2. Click the IK button and then, in the Inverse Kinematics rollout, click the Interactive IK Button. The IK button will turn yellow to signify which family of rollouts is displayed. The Interactive IK button will turn blue to indicate that this feature is active and any transforms applied to objects in the hierarchy are applied in IK mode.

3. In the Perspective viewport, select and move the gun object along the *X*-axis. The gun's orientation changes and all of the hierarchy elements, including the turret, change to maintain the connection, but they all rotate oddly. This is because the orientation at the joints is not constrained to a single axis or limit of degrees.

4. Undo any transforms that were applied.

5. Select the PivotTop object. In the Rotational Joints rollout, uncheck the X Axis and Z Axis Active check boxes.

6. Check the Limited check box in the *Y*-axis section. Increase the From parameter to approximately –65 by dragging the spinners. The Pivot and its children will rotate in the viewport and then snap back to their original orientations when the mouse is released. Drag the To spinner to approximately –40. Limiting the orientation restricts how far the object can rotate in a particular axis, and dragging the spinners gives visual feedback regarding the axis about which the object is rotating.

7. Select Shaft1 and uncheck the Active option the *X*-, *Y*-, and *Z*-axes in the Rotational Joints rollout. Repeat the process for the Shaft2 and gun objects. None of these objects needs to rotate on their own, they just need to follow their parent objects.

8. Select the PivotBottom object. Check the Active and Limited options in the *Y*-axis area. Set the From value to –4 and the To value to 30. Uncheck the X axis and Z Axis Active options.

9. Select the turret object. Only the Z Axis option should be checked so the turret can only rotate laterally and not flip over. Do not check the Limited option; the Turret should be able to rotate freely.

10. In the Object Parameters rollout, check the Terminator option to identify the Turret as the top object in the IK structure.

11. Select the Gun and then click the Link Info button at the top of the Hierarchy panel. In the Rotate section of the Locks rollout, check the X option. The Gun should not rotate in any axis except the local *X*-axis.

12. Select the Turret and check the X, Y, and Z options in the Move section. The Turret should be fixed in place. In a complete 3ds Max scene, the Turret would be linked to a larger structure to define its transforms.

13. Click the IK button at the top of the Hierarchy panel, and then click the Interactive IK button again to turn it on if necessary. Test your IK chain by moving the gun. As it moves, the other objects in the chain will reorient to maintain the proper relationships with their parent objects. Turn off the Interactive IK button when you are done.

Applying the IK Solver

An IK solver calculates the controls required to position and orient the members of an IK chain when one or more members is moved or rotated. The IK solver defines the top of the chain and identifies the goal, or the base of the chain. The IK solver precludes the need to activate the Interactive IK mode in the Hierarchy panel whenever IK is required.

The two appropriate IK solvers for this situation are the HI (History Independent) solver and the HD (History Dependent) solver. The HI solver is better suited for long animation sequences and character animation, and the HD solver is better suited for machine animation. Because the final length of the animation for this setup is unknown, the HD solver will be used here.

Continue with the previous exercise or open the IKGun2.max file from the companion CD.

1. Undo any transforms that were applied during the previous exercise if necessary.

    Right-click the Undo button in the main toolbar to see a list of the recent changes to the scene, with the most recent changes at the top of the list. Click on the entry in the list that defines the last command that you want undone. That command and all of the commands above it will highlight. Press the Enter key to undo all the selected commands.

2. Choose Edit → Hold from the main menu. A few IK operations, including applying an IK solver, are not always undoable. If the result is not correct, choose Edit → Fetch to restore your scene to the point just before the Edit → Hold was executed.

3. Turn off Interactive IK.

4. Select the gun and choose Animation → IK Solvers → HD Solver. A rubber banding line will stretch from the gun's pivot point to the cursor. Place the cursor over the Shaft2 object and click to define it as the end of the IK chain. The IK chain should not be bound to the object that has been designated as the Terminator.

When the cursor is moved over the other viewports while an IK solver is being assigned, the view will update to show the rubber banding line projecting from the object to the cursor in that particular viewport. The viewport does not have to be the active viewport for this viewport change to occur.

5. The End Effector acts as the pivot point of the Terminator object and can be used to straighten out the chain without actually moving the child object. On the Motion panel, in the IK Controller Parameters rollout, click the Link button in the End Effectors area and then click on the Turret. Turret appears in the End Effector Parent field.

6. Select the gun and use the Move Transform to test your IK setup. Moving the gun forward, backward, up, or down will cause the two pivots to rotate within their limits.

The HD solver's IK components are not listed in the Select Objects dialog box because they act on behalf of the objects to which they are assigned. To modify any of its properties, select an object and open the Motion panel of the Command panels. The IK Controller Properties rollout contains the options for modifying the IK chain.

Summary

This chapter introduced you to two powerful tools for reducing the time and effort required to animate objects and characters. Character Studio is a fantastic tool that speeds up the process of character animation. Using the Biped system, you can quickly create and adjust the substructure that controls a 3D model. Once the Physique modifier associates the model to the biped, character animation can be added using footstep-driven or freeform animation.

IK is used throughout mechanical design and character animation, and it is another 3ds Max tool that you may find invaluable once its workflow becomes second nature. The exercises in this chapter examined the basics of an IK setup and the use of an IK solver for a mechanical animation of the tank. The IK setups can include several IK chains controlling the transforms for different components of the same model. Easily selected controls can be placed in the scene for easy selection and manipulation of a complex model's components. IK can also be used for organic character animation, because 3ds Max has different types of IK for character work as well (such as the HI IK or Limb Solver IK). This chapter covered only one type of IK (using the HD solver).

CHAPTER 10

3ds Max Lighting

Light is everything. By light we see, and by light we show. Light shapes the world around us and defines shape, color, and texture. Computer graphics hang on every word light has to whisper. Without faithful lighting, any good computer graphic will fall to its knees and fail. Lighting is the most important aspect of CG, and it just simply cannot be mastered at a snap of the fingers. The trick to correctly lighting a CG is understanding how light works and seeing the visual nuances it has to offer.

In this chapter, you will study the various tools used to light in 3ds Max. This chapter will serve as a primer to this most important aspect of CG. It will *start* you on the path by showing you the tools available and a place *to begin*.

Topics in this chapter include:

- Basic Lighting Concepts
- Three-Point Lighting
- 3ds Max Lights
- Common Light Parameters
- Ambient Light
- Creating Shadows
- Atmospheres and Effects

Basic Lighting Concepts

On a conceptual level, the lighting in 3ds Max mimics the real-world direct-lighting techniques used in photography and filmmaking. Lights of various types are placed around a scene to illuminate the subjects as they would for a still life or a portrait. Your scene and what's in it dictate, to some degree at least, which lights you put where. A number of considerations must be kept in mind when settling on a methodology and light types for CG, but the overall concept of lighting is strikingly similar between a real-world set lighting and CG.

At the basic level, you want your lights to illuminate the scene. Without lights, your cameras have nothing to capture. Although it seems rather easy to throw your lights in, turn them all on, and render the scene, that couldn't be further from the truth.

Lighting is the backbone of CG. Although it is technically easy to insert and configure lights, it is *how* you light that will make or break your scene. That skill really only comes with a good deal of experience and experimentation, and it requires a good eye and some patience.

In this chapter, you will learn the basic procedures for lighting a scene in 3ds Max. No single chapter could explain everything about lighting, and no beginner or intermediate CG student should expect to quickly master the art of lighting CG. In short, lighting touches every single aspect of the CG pipeline. A strong *lighter* understands modeling form and is able to make adjustments to enable efficient lighting. Lighters understand motion and how to light for it. They understand textures and materials, and they frequently are tasked with creating or adjusting materials to work perfectly with their lights. Strong lighters are also rendering experts. When it's time to render, they must know what is and is not doable in a scene. They must diagnose problems and overcome obstacles to make sure every frame is rendered faithfully and with artistic merit.

Develop Your Eye

To be an artist, you must learn to see. This is especially true when CG lighting. There are so many nuances to the real-world lighting around us that we take them for granted. We intuitively understand what we see and how it's lit, and we infer a tremendous amount of visual information without much consideration. With CG lighting, you must re-create these nuances for your scene. That amounts to all the *work* of lighting.

The most valuable thing you can do to improve your lighting technique is to relearn how you see your environment. Simply put, you must refuse to take for granted what you see. If you question why things look the way they do, you'll find that the answers almost always come around to lighting.

Take note of the distinction between light and dark in the room you're in now. Notice the difference in the brightness of highlights and how they dissipate into diffused light and then into shadow.

When you start understanding how real light affects objects, you'll be much better equipped to generate your own light. After all, the key to good lighting starts with the desire to simply create an interesting image.

Your Scene and Its Needs

Your scene needs a careful balance of light and dark. Too much light will flatten your image and lose details in form. This is the first mistake many beginners make; they tend to over-light to make sure everything is lit. Figure 10.1 is a still life rendering that has too many bright lights. The lighting only flattens the image and removes any sense of depth and color.

On the other hand, under-lighting a scene will make it muddy and gray and pretty lifeless. Your details will end up covered in darkness, and everything will flatten out as well. Figure 10.2 shows you the same still life that is under-lit. You hardly notice the details in the mesh.

Your first job as a lighter is to find the balance between over-lighting and under-lighting. It sounds simple, and it is—although it requires lighting a shot several times and test rendering it to check the outcome. Like a photographer, you want your image to have the full range of exposure. You want the richest blacks to the brightest whites in your frame to create a deep sense of detail. Figure 10.3 shows you a fairly well-balanced lighting for the same still life. The light and shadow complement each other, and the lighting works to show off the features of the objects in the scene.

Figure 10.1

An over-lit still life

Figure 10.2

An under-lit still life

Figure 10.3

When the lighting is balanced, the image is more interesting.

Three-Point Lighting

Three-point lighting is a traditional approach to lighting a television shot. After all these years, the concepts still carry over to CG lighting. In this setup, three distinct roles are used to light the subject of a shot. More than one light can be used for each of the three roles, but the scene should in effect seem to have only one primary, or *key*, light, a softer light to fill the scene, and a back light to make the subject pop out from the background.

Figure 10.4

A three-point lighting schematic

This does not mean there are only three lights in the scene. Three-point lighting suggests that there are three primary angles of light for your shot, dependent on where the camera is located.

Three-point lighting ensures that your scene's main subject is well lit and has highlights and a sense of lighting direction using shadow and tone. Figure 10.4 shows you a plan view of the three-point lighting layout. The subject is in the middle of the image.

Key Light

A *key light* is placed in front of the subject for the primary light. The key is placed off to one side to give a sense of direction to the light, because one side will be brighter than the other. Shadows will fall from this light to heighten the sense of direction and increase the depth of the shot.

Although it is possible for several lights to fulfill the role of key light in a scene—for example, three ceiling lights overhead—one light should dominate, creating a definitive direction. Figure 10.5 shows the subject being lit by a single key light.

Here, the key light produces a moody still life. It may be composed of more than one 3ds Max light, although the intent would be that all the lights that comprise the key should come from the same angle, roughly.

Fill Light

A more diffused light than the key light, the *fill light* seems directionless and evenly spread across the subject's dark side. This fills the rest of the subject with light and decreases the dark area caused by the key light.

The fill light shouldn't necessarily cast any shadows onto the subject or the background. In fact, the fill light is actually used to help bring up the darkness and soften the shadows created by the key light. Figure 10.6 shows the same still life with an added fill light in the scene. The fill light clearly softens the shadows and illuminates the dark areas that the key light misses by design.

In most cases, you'll need to place the fill light in front of the subject. The fill, however, is aimed so that it shines from the reverse side of the key light. This angle intentionally targets the dark side of the subject. Even though the still life in Figure 10.6 is still a fairly moody composition, much more is visible than with only the key light in Figure 10.5.

Back Light

The *back,* or *rim, light* is placed behind the subject to create a bit of a halo, which helps makes the subject pop out in the shot. As a result, the subject has more presence against its background. Figure 10.7 shows how helpful a back light can be.

The back light brings the fruit in this still life out from the background and adds some highlights to the edges, giving the composition more focus on the fruit.

Figure 10.5
Key light only

Figure 10.6
A fill light is now included.

Figure 10.7

**A back light makes
the subject pop
right out.**

Don't confuse the back light with the background light, which lights the environment behind the subject.

Three-Point Lighting in Action

The focus of the three-point lighting system is the primary subject of the shot. Of course, this means the lighting is based on the position and angle of the subject to the camera. When a camera is moved for a different shot, even within a scene of the same subject, a new lighting setup is more than likely required. This makes three-point lighting shot-specific and not scene-specific. Of course, once you have a shot set up with the lighting you like, changing it slightly to suit a new camera angle is much easier than starting from scratch.

When the lighting is completed for the subject of a shot, the background will probably need to be lit as well. For the background, you would typically use a directed primary light source that matches the direction of the key light. This becomes your background's main light. Then you would use a softer fill light to light the rest of the background scene and to soften the primary shadows.

Practical Lighting

Practical lighting is a theatrical term describing any lights in a scene that are cast from lighting objects within the scene. For example, a shaded lamp on a night stand in the background of a scene set in a bedroom would need practical lighting when the light is turned on. The practical lighting shouldn't interfere with the main lighting of the scene. Although if the scene's lighting is explicitly coming from such a source, you will have to set up your key light to match the direction and general mood of the practical light in the shot.

Each light-emitting object in your CG scene doesn't automatically call for its own light in 3ds Max. Rendering tricks such as *glow* often simulate the effect of an active scene light. This way, you don't need to actually use a 3ds Max light. Of course, if you need the practical light to illuminate something in the scene, you need to create a light for it.

3ds Max Lights

3ds Max has two *types* of light objects: photometric and standard lights. Photometric lights are lights that possess very specific features to enable a more accurate definition of lighting, as you would see in the real world. Photometric lights have physically based intensity values that more closely mimic the behavior of real light. They are rather advanced and will not be covered in this book.

Standard lights are still extremely powerful and capable of realism, but they are more straightforward to use than photometric lights and less taxing on the system at render time.

A still life arrangement of fruit is included on the companion CD. To practice the lighting techniques as you read through this chapter, load the Still Life_Start.max file in the Lighting Scene Files folder.

Default Light

What happens if you have no lights at all in your 3ds Max scene? In this case, the scene is automatically lit by *default lighting*. When you add light objects, the default lighting is replaced entirely by the new lights. There is very little you can do with the default lighting; it is there for your convenience so you easily can view an object in Shaded mode and test render without creating a light first.

One or Two Default Lights

When you use default lighting, there is only one light. However, you can customize the configuration so that you can have two lights for default lighting.

To change to two default lights, in the main Menu Bar choose Customize → Viewport Configuration. In the Rendering Method tab, you can choose whether you want one light or two lights in your default lights under the Rendering Options heading. Figure 10.8 shows the Viewport Configuration's Rendering Method tab.

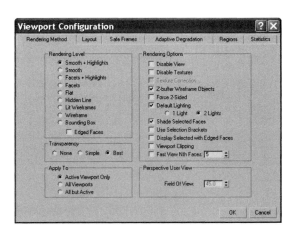

Figure 10.8

You can choose one or two lights for your default lighting.

In a single default light, you have a single key light. This light is linked to the viewport, and it moves with the point of view. Setting up the default lighting to have two lights adds a single fill light that is placed opposite the key light. The key is always placed in front of the scene's object being viewed, on its upper left side. The default fill light, if added, is created behind the object and to the lower right. The link between the default light and the viewport is broken when you have two default lights. In the following images, there is a sphere on the left with a single default light. The same sphere is in the middle with two default lights. In the image on the right, the two default lights are no longer connected to the viewport.

In Figures 10.9 and 10.10, you can see how the second default fill light works in the still life. Figure 10.9 has the single default light, and Figure 10.10 has two default lights. You can see the addition of a second set of highlights on the fruit in Figure 10.10 due to the added fill light.

Converting Default Lights

Remember that the default lights have no parameters and cannot be edited. You can, however, convert the default lighting into light objects that can be edited. You can do this only if the 2 Lights default lighting option is selected in the Viewport Configuration.

Figure 10.9

A single default light provides a key light.

Figure 10.10

Two default lights provide a key light and a fill light.

To add the default lighting to your scene, choose View → Add Default Lights to Scene. If you only have 1 Light default lighting, this menu option will be grayed out. The following dialog box will open, giving you the option to add either one or both default lights to the scene.

3ds Max will bring the default lights in as Omni lights (which you will learn about soon). Once you add the default lights, you can edit them like any other light. However, it's always best to just begin lighting the scene with your own lights created from scratch.

Using Default Lights

Once you add a light, any default lighting (that has not been added to the scene) will be removed. Likewise, if you remove all the lights in a scene, 3ds Max will re-create the default lighting. Figure 10.11 shows the two default lights inserted as Omni lights (the diamond shapes) in the sphere's scene.

Use default lighting as a temporary solution. It gives you an easy way to have a constant light that travels with the viewport's point of view—provided it's the single default light. This helps you see the detail in your modeling, animation, and texturing without having to worry about creating and placing lights, especially lights that would follow the viewport.

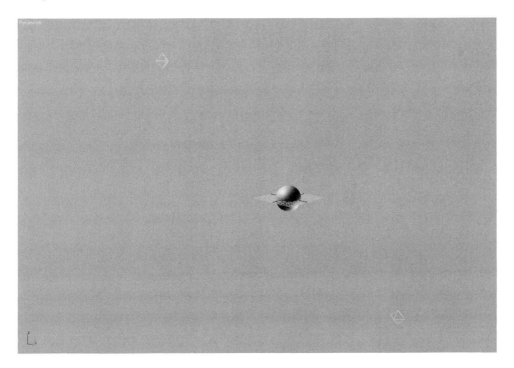

Figure 10.11

Default lights are created in the scene as Omni lights.

Standard Lights

Standard lights will be the staple of your lighting diet for some time to come. They are the only lights covered in this book. The lights in 3ds Max try to mimic the way real lights work. For example, a light bulb that emits light all around itself would be an Omni light in 3ds Max. A desk lamp that shines light in a specific direction in a cone shape would be a spotlight. Each of the different Standard lights cast light differently. We will look at the most commonly used lights.

3ds Max has a total of eight light types in its Standard Light collection. The following lights are in the collection:

Target Spotlight

Free Spotlight

Target Direct Light

Free Direct Light

Omni Light

Skylight

mr Area Omni Light

mr Area Spotlight

The last two on this list have the prefix "mr" to signify that they are mental ray–specific lights. Mental ray is an advanced renderer that is commonly used in production today. It offers many sophisticated and frequently complex methods of lighting that enhance the realism of a rendered scene. Because mental ray is fairly complex, it will not be covered in this book, so its lights will not be covered in this chapter. After you read this chapter, you should be familiar enough with lighting to get started and try new things without using any advanced lighting and rendering methodologies. You will, however, get the chance to light a radiosity effect in the next chapter.

Target Spotlight

A *Target spotlight*, as seen in Figure 10.12, is one of the most commonly used lights because it is extremely versatile. A spotlight casts light in a focused beam, similar to a flashlight. This type of lighting allows you to light specific areas of a scene without casting any unwanted light on areas that may not need that light. You can control the size of the *hotspot*. This is the size of the cast beam.

The light is created with two nodes, the light itself (*light source*) and the Target node at which the light points at all times. This way you are able to animate the light following the subject of the scene easily, as a spotlight would follow a singer on stage. Simply select the target and move it as you would any other object in 3ds Max. The Target Spot will rotate to follow the target. Similarly, you can animate the light source, and it will orient itself accordingly to aim at the stationary target. You could of course animate both as well.

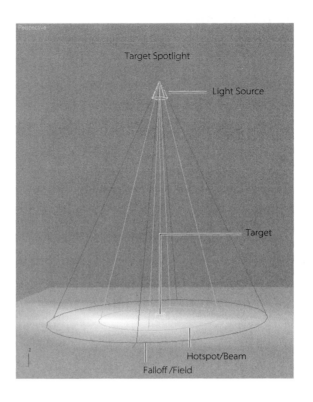

Figure 10.12
A Target spotlight

CREATING A TARGET SPOT

Create a Target Spot by going to the Create panel and clicking the Lights button ( ) to access the light creation tools seen here.

Click the Target Spot button, and in the Top viewport, click and drag to create a Target spotlight, as shown here.

FALLOFF/FIELD

Select the light source of the Target Spot. Go to the Modify panel, and open the Spotlight Parameters rollout as shown in the following graphic. The *falloff* is the area in which the intensity of the beam falls off, or dissipates, creating a soft area around the Hotspot circle, as seen in Figure 10.13. The falloff is represented in the viewport by the area between the inner light-blue cone and the dark-blue outer cone. The light diminishes to 0 by the outer region.

SPOTLIGHT SHAPE

You can also change the shape of a spotlight from circular to rectangular by selecting either Circle or Rectangle in the Spotlight Parameters rollout. In addition, using the Aspect value, you can set the height-to-width ratio for the hotspot for either Circle or Rectangle spots. Figure 10.14 shows a rectangular spot with an Aspect of 4.0.

Figure 10.13

The falloff of a hotspot

Figure 10.14

A spotlight can also be rectangular.

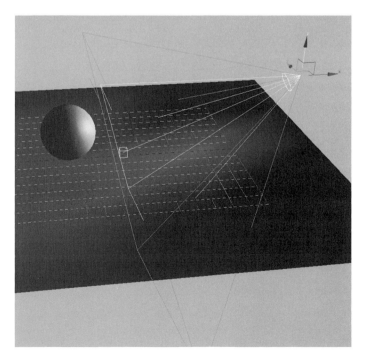

When rendered, the rectangular spot looks like the image here.

SELECTING THE LIGHT

You can move (and animate) the entire light, including the light and the target, by selecting the light object in the viewport in the middle of its display, as shown in the following graphic on the left. To access the parameters of the light, you have to select the light, as shown on the right. The target does not list any parameters for the light.

INTERACTIVE CONE SETTINGS

3ds Max has the ability to control the Hotspot/Beam and the Falloff/Field parameters in the viewport. Follow these simple steps to interactively change a spotlight's hotspot and falloff:

1. Select the spotlight's source.

2. Click the Select and Manipulate tool in the main toolbar (🔧).

3. Click and drag the green circles at the end of the spotlight cone to set the hotspot and falloff ranges, as shown here.

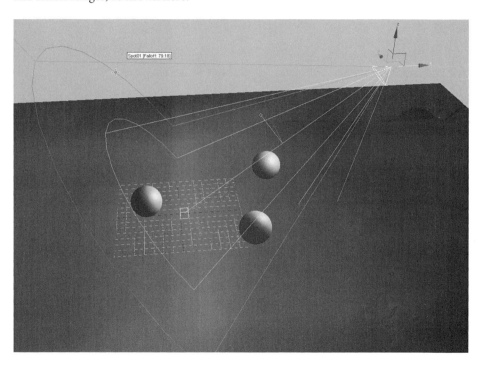

Target Direct Light

A *Target Direct light* has Target and Light nodes to help you control the direction and animation of the light. It also has a hotspot and beam, as well as a falloff much like the Target Spot. However, where the Target Spot emits light rays from a single point (the light source) outward in a cone shape, the Target Direct light casts parallel rays of light within its beam area. This helps simulate the lighting effect of the Sun, because its light rays (for all practical purposes on Earth) are parallel. Figure 10.15 shows a Target Direct light in a viewport.

Figure 10.15
A Target Direct light

Because the directional rays are parallel, the Target Direct lights have a beam in a straight cylindrical or rectangular box shape instead of a cone.

You create a Target Direct light much the same way as a Target Spot. Select Target Direct from the Create panel and click in an Orthographic window to set the light and define the Target direction and length of the light by dragging.

Select the light for the Target Direct and open the Modify panel. In the Directional Parameters rollout, you'll find the same parameters for the Target Direct light that you had for the Target Spot. The procedure to select the light is the same as for the Target Spot as well. You can select the middle of the light for the whole object, or you can select either the target or light. You have to select the light to bring up the parameters for the light object.

Although the spotlight and the directional light don't seem to be very different, the way they light is strikingly different, as you can see in the following graphics. The image on the left is a Target Spot casting light and a shadow on a sphere and ground plane. The image on the right is a Target Direct from the same angle, distance, and falloff casting a light on the same sphere and ground plane.

The spotlight rays cast an entirely different hotspot and shadow than the directional light, despite having the same values for those parameters.

It's preferable to create lights in the Orthographic viewports because they give you a better idea of size and direction than a Perspective or Camera viewport.

Free Spotlight

A *Free Spot* is virtually identical to a Target Spot, except that this light has no target object. You can move and rotate the free spot however you want, relying on rotation instead of the target to aim it in any direction. A Free spotlight is shown in Figure 10.16.

Figure 10.16

A Free spotlight does not have a target.

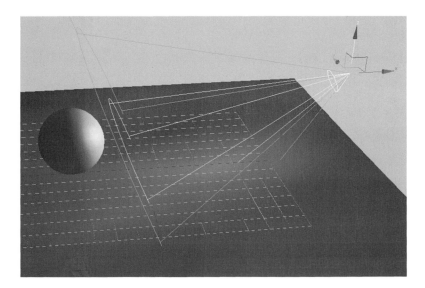

To create a Free spotlight, simple choose Free Spot in the Create panel and click in a viewport and drag to set its initial direction and length. The one other difference with a Free Spot is that whereas the length of the Target spotlight is controlled by its target, a Free Spot has a parameter in the General Parameters rollout of the Modify panel, as shown here. You set the length by adjusting this unmarked value next to the Targeted check box. You will study the General Parameters rollout in the next section.

Adjusting the length of a spotlight will not matter when the light is rendered; however, seeing a longer light in the viewports can help you line up the light with objects in the scene. Likewise, you can shorten the length of the light to clear some wireframe clutter from your viewports.

Spotlights (including Target Spots) are great for key lighting because they are very easy to control.

Free Direct Light

The *Free Direct light* is identical to the Target Direct light, but it doesn't have the Target node. Its parameters are the same as the Free Spot's, and it is selected and moved in the same way. Figure 10.17 shows a Free Directional light.

Directional lights (including Target Directs) are also great lights to use as key lights. You can also use them for fill lights, although the beam size must be large to avoid seeing the edges of the hotspot.

Directional lights are also used frequently to simulate sunlight, although their beams must be quite wide to avoid any chance of seeing the hotspot or falloff area.

Figure 10.17

A Free Directional light

Omni Light

The *Omni light* in 3ds Max is a point light that emanates light from a single point in all directions around it. Figure 10.18 shows an Omni light.

Unlike the Spot and Directional lights, the Omni light does not have a special rollout, and its General Parameters rollout is much simpler, as shown here.

An Omni light is shown rendered in Figure 10.19. Notice how the ground plane is brighter directly below where the light sits.

Omni lights are not very good for simulating sunlight, as Directional lights are. The Omni light's rays spread from a single point source, so by the time they reach their subjects, the light direction and shadows will be too disparate across a scene. In the following graphic, an Omni light in the image on the left creates different shadow and lighting directions for all the objects in the scene, and the Directional light in the image on the right creates a uniform direction for the light and shadow, as would the Sun here on Earth.

Figure 10.18

An Omni light is a single-point source light.

Figure 10.19

An Omni light lights the sphere and floor.

Try to avoid casting shadows with Omni lights because they will use a lot more memory than a spotlight casting shadows.

Omni lights are good for fill lights as well as for simulating certain practical light sources that have a brighter center and falloff evenly around that bright spot in all three axes. You could even use Omni lights for all three points in your three-point lighting system, as seen here on the fruit still life scene. The scene has a nice soft feel.

Skylight

Skylight is a special 3ds Max light used with a special rendering method to quickly generate a scene rendered in a soft outdoor light. We will not be covering this more advanced lighting and rendering methodology; however, here is a quick introduction to the light itself.

Figure 10.20 shows a skylight high above the scene with the three spheres. It is created by simply selecting the Skylight button in the Create panel and clicking to place it in a viewport. The skylight's Skylight Parameters rollout is shown here.

The skylight is used to create a soft, global lighting to simulate light from the sky. This look is often seen with renders using Global Illumination or Radiosity. In these lighting/rendering solutions, the skylight creates a sky dome that sits around the objects in the scene. Light is emitted, essentially, from the entire surface area of the dome to cast an even light throughout the scene, much as a sky lights an outdoor area.

The rendering of a Skylight scene, as shown in Figure 10.21, is flat and bright. There is no definition because shadows are not enabled. Turning on shadows gives you a beautiful render, as seen in Figure 10.22, with soft shadows and contact shadows that really make the spheres look as if they are sitting outside on an afternoon day.

Figure 10.20

A skylight placed over the spheres and ground plane

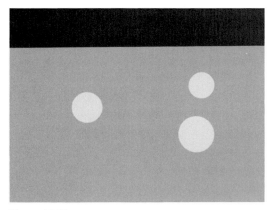

Figure 10.21

The skylight flattens out the spheres and blows them out.

Figure 10.22

Turning shadows on for the skylight dramatically increases render times, but it gives a nice effect with soft shadows mimicking a radiosity effect.

The render time for this frame, however, is significantly longer than any of the other renders so far in this chapter. Calculating soft light such as this is quite intensive, unless a lighting plug-in such as Light Tracer is enabled in the render setup.

> The Skylight light is not intended to be used without some other light source(s) in the scene. It is designed to be used only with Radiosity, Light Tracer, or mental ray rendering techniques. As these techniques are more advanced, they will not be covered in this book. It is important to learn traditional lighting and rendering methods before moving into advanced techniques.

Common Light Parameters

Most of the parameters for the Standard lights are the same for all the lights and will be described in this section. You may want to create a spot or directional light so you can follow along with the information about light parameters given here.

General Parameters Rollout

The General Parameters rollout for all the Standard lights (except for skylight) is shown in Figure 10.23. In the Light Type section, you can change the type of light that is currently selected. Simply choose the type (Spot, Directional, Omni) from the drop-down menu. 3ds Max will replace the light with the new light type; it won't change its position or orientation. This can be immensely helpful when you are deciding which light will work best for a scene. Otherwise, you would have to delete and re-create lights to find the solution that best suited your scene best.

You can turn a Free Spot or Free Directional to a target of the same kind by simply checking the Targeted check box. Of course, the On check box controls whether the light is on or off in the scene.

In the Shadows section of the General Parameters rollout for these lights, you will find the controls for the shadow casting properties of the selected light. Use the drop-down menu to select the *type* of shadows to cast. The two most frequently used shadow types, Shadow Map and Ray Traced, are discussed later in the chapter.

The Use Global Settings toggle can be very useful. When it is turned on, all of the lights in your scene will be set to use the same Shadow Parameters of the light you have selected and for which you have enabled Use Global Settings. This is useful in the event you need the same type of shadows cast from all the lights in the scene. It can save you the hassle of specifying the settings for all the lights. It does, however, limit you to the same shadow settings for all the lights. While you are learning, you should leave Use Global Settings off and set each light manually as needed. Again, shadows are covered a little later in this chapter.

Figure 10.23

The General Parameters rollout for all the Standard lights is the same.

Intensity/Color/Attenuation Rollout

Figure 10.24

The Intensity/
Color/Attenuation
rollout

The Intensity/Color/Attenuation rollout, shown in Figure 10.24, is used to adjust your light's brightness and color settings.

Light Intensity

The Multiplier parameter works like a dimmer switch for a light. The higher the value is, the brighter the light will be. The Multiplier can go into negative values. A negative amount will subtract light from your scene, allowing you to create dark areas within lit areas or to remove excess light from a surface that has unwanted spill light.

Light Color

The Color Swatch next to the Multiplier is used to add color to your light. Simply click on the color swatch to open the Color Selector. The darker the color, the darker the light.

Light Decay

Under the Decay section, you can set the way your light fades out across distance. This is not the same as falloff with spots and directional lights, though. Falloff occurs on the sides of a hotspot, whereas *decay* happens along the path of the light as it travels away from the light. Figure 10.25 shows a light with no decay type set. Figure 10.26 shows the same light with its decay Type set to Inverse Decay. Figure 10.27 shows the same light with decay Type set to Inverse Square Decay. Notice the decay rate increases with each successive figure.

If no decay is set for a light, its intensity remains at full strength from the light to infinity. An Inverse Decay diminishes the intensity of the illumination over distance traveled according to some brainy formula. An Inverse Square Decay more closely resembles the

Figure 10.25

A light with no decay illuminates all the numbers evenly.

Figure 10.26

A light with Inverse Decay illuminates the back numbers less.

decay of real world light, and it is a stronger rate of decay than Inverse Decay. Use this decay rate to drop off the effect of a light quickly before it reaches too far into the scene; however, you will need a stronger Multiplier value to increase your light's intensity to compensate for the much faster decay.

In Figure 10.28, you can quickly see and set the start of a decay in spot and directional lights by changing the Start value in the Decay section of the rollout. In the following images, you can see a decay start that is closer to the light and its effect on the render in the top-left corner, while the start of the decay is moved closer to the spheres in the image on the right.

Light Attenuation

Light attenuation is another way to diminish the intensity of a light over distance. With attenuation, however, you have more implicit control on the start and end of the fade, and you can specify an area where the light fades in and then fades out. You simply set the Attenuation distances to the desired effect.

Figure 10.27

A light with Inverse Square Decay illuminates the first two numbers and begins to lose the remaining three.

Figure 10.28

Seeing the start of a light's decay helps you see how it will illuminate your scene.

NEAR ATTENUATION GROUP

The following values set the distances where the light fades into existence:

Start—The distance at which the light starts to fade in.

End—The distance at which the light reaches its full intensity.

Use—Toggles on/off the use of near attenuation for the light.

Figure 10.29 shows a render of near attenuation at work. The first numbers are darker, the back number are brighter. Figure 10.30 shows a spotlight and the Attenuation display in the viewport.

FAR ATTENUATION GROUP

The following values set the distances where the illumination fades out of existence:

Start—The distance at which the illumination starts to fade away.

End—The distance at which the illumination has faded to nothing.

Use—Toggles on/off the use of far attenuation for the illumination.

Figure 10.31 shows a render of the far attenuation on the same set of numbers, using the same light as before. Now the lights fade into darkness the farther back they are in the scene, which is similar to decay. Figure 10.32 shows the far attenuation display for the spotlight. Figure 10.33 shows the attenuation display for an Omni light in a viewport.

You can always use both near and far attenuation to set a sliver of light in your scene, as shown in Figure 10.34. As you can see, attenuation is a more precise way to set a diminishing light intensity over the Decay Type.

Figure 10.29

Near attenuation fades in the light.

Figure 10.30

The spotlight displays the attenuation distances.

Figure 10.31
Far attenuation fades out the light.

Figure 10.32
The spotlight displays the attenuation distances.

Figure 10.33
The attenuation display for an Omni light

Figure 10.34

Using both near and far attenuation gives you a slice of light where you need it.

Both decay and attenuation are important to use when the light needs to be realistic. Light decays in real life; your renders will assume a higher fidelity when the lights in them decay. The effect may be subtle, but it can make a large difference.

Advanced Effects Rollout

The Advanced Effects rollout (shown in the following graphic) enables you to control how a light affects the surfaces it illuminates. You can increase or decrease the contrast and softness of a light's effect on a surface. You can also dictate which lighting component of the light is rendered on the surface.

Contrast and Soften

By adjusting the Contrast and Soften Diffuse Edges values, you can alter the way the light hits your surface. The following image on the left was rendered with default Contrast and Soften Diffuse Edges values, and the image on the right was rendered with a Contrast of 25 and a Soften Diffuse Edges value of 50. The image on the right has deeper contrast, but with slightly softer values leading from the diffuse color.

Contrast—Changes the contrast level between the diffuse and ambient areas of the surface when lit.

Soften Diffuse Edge—Controls the softness of the edge between the diffuse and ambient areas of the lit surface.

Light Components

Light in a CG program is differentiated into an *ambient*, a *diffuse*, and a *specular* component. You may recall these components covered in Chapter 7, "Materials and Mapping." The ambient component of light is the general ambient light in a scene. There is no direction to ambient light, and the light itself is cast evenly across the extent of the scene. The diffuse component of light is the way it illuminates an object by spreading across its surface. The specular component of light is how the light creates highlights on a surface, especially when that surface is glossy.

In the Affect Surfaces section of the Advanced Effects rollout, you can toggle the check boxes that will render *only* those components of the light on the surfaces they illuminate. This is a good way to separate your renders into lighting components that you can later control in compositing, although it leads to a longer workflow.

Figure 10.35 is rendered with the diffuse component of the lights in the scene. Figure 10.36 shows only the specular highlights rendered. Figure 10.37 shows only the ambient light rendered on the objects.

Figure 10.35
Only the diffuse component of the lights are rendered.

Figure 10.36
Only the specular component of the lights are rendered.

Figure 10.37
Only the ambient light in the scene is rendered.

Ambient Light

Ambient light in 3ds Max is not a light per se, but rather it is a global setting in the render environment. Ambient light, in short, is an even light with no direction or source. It is a way to globally brighten the entire scene to add an even light to all objects. Using too much ambient light will wash out your objects and give you flat renders.

To set an ambient light level in your scene, in the main Menu select Rendering → Environment to open the Environment and Effects window shown in Figure 10.38.

To set an ambient light, click on the Ambient color swatch under the Global Lighting section and pick an appropriate color. The brighter the color value, the brighter the ambient light will be throughout the scene.

> You can also create an ambient light in your scene by creating an Omni light and toggling on the Ambient Only check box under the light's Advanced Effects Parameters rollout.

Creating Shadows

Don't be too quick to smother your scene with light or too eager to show off your careful modeling work and textures. Leaving objects in shadow and darkness is as important as revealing them in light. You can say a lot visually by not showing parts of a whole and leaving some interpretation to the audience.

A careful balance of light and dark is important for a composition. The realism of a scene is greatly increased with the simple addition of well-placed shadows. Don't be afraid of the dark. Use it liberally, but in balance.

You can create the following types of shadows in 3ds Max:

Advanced Raytraced

mental ray Shadow Map

Area Shadow

Shadow Map

Raytraced Shadows

Each type of shadow has its benefits and its drawbacks. The two most common types used are Shadow Maps and Raytraced Shadows.

When you use shadows, controls in the Shadow Parameters rollout and the shadow type-specific rollouts are available when you select the shadow type.

Figure 10.38

The Environment and Effects window

Shadow Parameters Rollout

The settings in the Shadow Parameters rollout govern the common parameters for all shadow types discussed here. In this rollout, you can adjust the color of your shadow as well as its density (i.e., how dark it appears).

You should always check your light's Multiplier values first to make sure your fill light does not wash out your shadows before you adjust the shadow parameters themselves. For instance, the fill light(s) generally have a lower intensity than the key light(s).

Click on the Color swatch to pick a color for your shadows. More often than not, you will have your shadow colors at black, if not close to black. You can also control the density of the shadows by adjusting the Density value. As you can see in Figure 10.39, adjusting the density changes how much of the shadow is rendered. A Density of 0 will turn off your shadows in essence.

Interestingly enough, you can also apply a map to your shadow by checking the Map box and clicking on the button bar currently labeled None. From there, you can choose a map. In Figure 10.40, a checker map was mapped to the shadow.

Figure 10.39
Shadow Density

Figure 10.40
You can map a texture to the shadow.

Selecting a Shadow Type

For the most part, you will be more than happy with the results from a Shadow Map shadow in your scenes. However, to get shadows to respond to transparencies, you will need to use Ray Traced Shadows. Additionally, if you need to soften your shadows the farther they are cast from the object, you will need to use Area Shadows. These shadow types are discussed next.

Shadow Maps

Seeming to be the fastest way to cast a shadow, the Shadow Map shadow generates a bitmap file during a pre-rendering pass of the scene. This map is used to place the shadows in the final render. However, Shadow Map shadows do not show the color cast through transparent or translucent objects. Once you select Shadow Maps in the General Parameters rollout for a light, the rollout appears. It is shown here.

Because this shadow type relies on maps, it is important to be able to control the resolution of the generated maps. When you are close to a shadow, the resolution needs to be higher for the cast shadow than if it were farther from the camera in order to avoid jagged edges around the shadow.

The following parameters are useful for Shadow Map creation:

Bias—The shadow is moved, according to the value set, closer or farther away from the object casting the shadow. Figure 10.41 shows how the bias moves the shadow away the higher the value is set.

Size—Detailed shadows will need detailed Shadow Maps. Increase the Size value, and 3ds Max will increase the number of subdivisions for the map which in turn increases the detail of the shadow cast. Figure 10.42 compares Shadow Map sizes of 64 and 1024. Notice how the shadows on the left (Size = 64) are mushy and barely

Figure 10.41

The Bias offsets the shadow from the casting object.

noticeable and the shadows on the right (Size = 1024) are crisp and clean. You don't want to set your Shadow Map Size too high, though. It will increase render time for little to no effect. A range between 512 and 1024 is usually good for most cases.

In some scenes, you may discover that no shadow map size will give you good results (for instance in large outdoor scenes). In these cases, you will have to revert to a different shadow method, such as Ray Traced Shadows.

Sample Range—This creates and controls the softness of the edge of shadow-mapped shadows. The higher the value, the softer the edges of the shadow. Figure 10.43 shows you how a soft edge (on the left) can make the lighting seem less strong or farther away from the subject than crisp shadows (on the right).

Figure 10.42
The Shadow Map size affects the shadow detail.

Figure 10.43
Soft edge shadows

Ray Traced Shadows

Raytracing involves tracing a ray of light from every light source in all directions and tracing the reflection to the camera lens. You can create more accurate shadows with raytracing. However, the render takes significantly longer to calculate. Additionally, Ray Traced shadows are always hard edged, yet they are realistic for transparent and translucent objects. Figure 10.44 shows the still life render with a plane casting a shadow over the fruit. The plane has a checker mapped to its opacity, so it has alternating transparent and opaque squares defining the checkerboard.

On the left side of the image, the light is casting Shadow Map shadows, while on the right the light is casting Ray Traced Shadows.

Use Ray Traced shadows when you need highly accurate shadows or when Shadow Map resolutions are just not high enough to get you the crisp edges you need. You can also use Ray Traced Shadows to cast shadows from wireframe rendered objects.

The Ray Traced Shadow rollout, shown here, controls the shadow. The Ray Bias parameter is the same as the Shadow Map Bias in that it controls how far from the casting object the shadow is cast.

Creating Soft Shadows Due to Distance

The only way you will be able to create a natural shadow that softens the farther it gets from the casting object is to use Area Shadows. These types of shadows are natural. If you notice a telephone pole's shadow, the farther the shadow is from the pole, the softer the shadow becomes. Adding such a shadow to a render can greatly increase the realism of the scene.

To enable a soft shadow such as this, select Area Shadows as your shadow type. By default, the Area Shadow will work for you. Figure 10.45 shows a regular Ray Traced shadow. Figure 10.46 shows an Area shadow at the default settings.

Figure 10.44

Ray Traced shadows react to transparencies, and Shadow Maps do not

Figure 10.45

A Ray Traced shadow is too hard-edged.

Figure 10.46

An Area shadow begins to soften at the ends.

Go to the Area Shadows rollout shown here. To adjust the softness of the shadows, you will *not* want to increase the Sample Spread because that parameter, just like the Sample Range of the Shadow Map shadow, softens the *entire* shadow. A true shadow is crisp where it meets the casting object and softens as it casts away.

To further soften the ends of the shadows, in the Area Light rollout, set the Length to 80 and the Width to 60. This will increase the softness of the shadow in a realistic way, while keeping the contact shadow crisp. However, the render, shown here, does not look very good. The soft ends are very grainy.

You will need to increase the quality of the shadow, so set the Shadow Integrity to 6 and the Shadow Quality to 10. The render will take longer, but you will get a beautiful shadow, as shown in Figure 10.47.

Figure 10.47

**Increase the shadow
quality to obtain a
very realistic
shadow.**

Atmospheres and Effects

Creating atmospheric effects with lights, such as fog or volume lights, is accomplished
through the Atmospheres and Effects rollout, as shown here.

Using this rollout, you can assign and manage atmosphere effects and other rendering
effects that are associated with lights. In the following exercise, you will learn how to
create a volumetric light (similar to a flashlight shining through fog). You will also learn
how to exclude objects from a light, so that the light does not illuminate them. This is an
important trick to know.

Creating a Volumetric Light

Let's create a fog light using the following steps:

1. Open the Still Life Volume.max scene file in the Lighting Scenes folder on the companion CD. Go to Create Panel → Lights and click on the Target Direct Light. Move
   your cursor to the Top viewport, click and drag from the top of the viewport down
   toward the still life. As seen here.

2. Now move to the Front viewport and move the light up along the *Y*-axis, and then move the target so it is centered to point the light directly at the fruit, as shown here.

3. If you do a Quick Render, you will see that the scene is being lit from the direction of the light (Figure 10.48). Now you need some shadows in the scene.

Adding Shadows

4. In the General Parameters rollout for the light, go to the Shadows section and check the box to enable shadows. Select Shadow Map from the drop-down menu. This will turn on Shadow Maps shadows for this light.

5. Go to the Shadow Map Parameters rollout and set the size to 1024; this will add some sharpness to the shadow's edge and make it more like a daylight shadow. If you do a Quick Render, you won't see any shadows (as shown in the following graphic). This is because the window is blocking the light. The window glass object has a Material that has the Opacity turned down to 0; however, Shadow Map shadows don't recognize transparency in materials. To solve this problem, you need to Exclude the Window Glass object from the Light.

Figure 10.48

A test render of the fruit

Excluding Object from a Light

6. The Exclude button is in the General Parameters rollout for the light, just below the Shadows. Click the Exclude button to bring up the Exclude/Include window shown in Figure 10.49.

7. Click on the Glass object and press the right arrows in the middle of the window (Figure 10.49) to add the Glass to the other side, excluding the object from receiving light and casting light. Click OK.

8. Quick Render your scene to take a look. Now you can see shadows. We didn't exclude the whole window with its frame because the inside frame is a nice detail to cast shadows. Figure 10.50 shows the render with the shadows.

Figure 10.49

The Exclude/Include window allows you to exclude certain objects from being lit by the light in the scene.

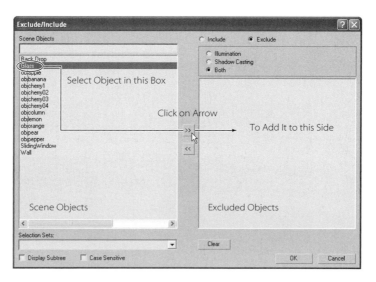

Adding a Volumetric Effect

9. The whole point of this exercise is to add volume to the light. This will give this scene some much needed atmosphere. Go to the Atmosphere and Effects rollout for the light. Select Add from the rollout to open the Add Atmosphere or Effect window, which is shown here.

10. In the window, select Volume Light and click OK to add the effect to the light.

11. Volume Light will be added to the rollout, as shown here. Render the scene. You should see a render similar to Figure 10.51.

To adjust the volume light, select the Volume Light entry in the rollout and click the Setup button. This will bring up the Environment and Effects dialog window. Scroll down to *Volume Light Parameters* section to access the settings for the volume light, seen in Figure 10.52. Experiment with different settings to see how the volume light renders. The settings are described next.

Figure 10.50
Shadows!

Figure 10.51
Volume light!

Volume Light Parameters

The default parameters for a Volume light will give you some nice volume in the light for most scenes, right off the bat. However, to tweak or change the volume settings to your liking, you will be editing these following parameters:

Exponential—The density of the volume light will increase exponentially with distance. By default (Exponential is off), density will increase linearly with distance. You will want to enable Exponential only when you need to render transparent objects in volume fog.

Density—This value sets the fog's density. The denser the fog is, the more light will reflect off the fog inside the volume. The most realistic fogs can be rendered with about 2 to 6 percent Density value.

Figure 10.52

The Environment and Effects window displays the Volume Light parameters.

Most of the parameters are for troubleshooting volume problems in your scene if it is not rendering very well. Sometimes you just don't know what that problem is and you have to experiment with switches and buttons. The Noise settings are another cool feature to add some randomness to your volume:

Noise On—This toggles the noise on and off. Render times will increase slightly with **Noise** enabled for the volume.

Amount—This is the amount of noise that is applied to the fog. Of course a value of 0 creates no noise. If the Amount is set to 1, the fog renders with pure noise.

Size, Uniformity, Phase—These settings determine the look of the noise, along with setting a Noise Type (Regular, Fractal, or Turbulence).

Adding atmosphere to a scene can heighten the sense of realism and mood. Creating a little bit of a volume for some lights can go a long way to improving the look of your renders. However, adding volume to lights can slow your renders, so use it with care. Also be aware that adding too much volume to a scene may look peculiar, so use volumetric light sparingly and with good reason—that is, if it is called for in the scene and adds ambience to the image.

Light Lister

If several lights are in your scene and you need to adjust all of them, selecting each light and making one adjustment at a time can become tedious. This is where 3ds Max's Light Lister comes in way handy. Accessed through the main Menu Bar by choosing Tools → Light Lister, this floating palette gives you control over all of your scene lights, as seen in Figure 10.53.

Figure 10.53
**The Light Lister
window**

You can choose to view/edit all the lights in your scene or just ones that are selected. Using this easy dialog window gives you instant access to pretty much all the important light parameters in one place. When you adjust the values for any parameter in the Light Lister window, the changes are reflected in the appropriate place in the Modify panel for that changed light. This is the perfect tool to edit your lights once you have them set up initially.

Summary

Lighting is no laughing matter. It is the aspect of CG that is arguably the most difficult to master (alongside character animation perhaps), and it is the most easily criticized. People in the CG industry can tell very quickly when lighting is done poorly.

In this chapter, you began by reviewing some key concepts in CG lighting, including Three-Point lighting. Then you learned the different types of lights that 3ds Max has to offer, from default lights to Target Spots, and how to use them. You dove into the common light parameters to gauge how best to control the lights in your scene before you moved on to creating all different types of shadows. The chapter finished with a quick exercise on creating a volumetric light for a fog effect and a tour of the Light Lister window.

Several books are devoted to CG lighting. It is a craft that takes getting used to, and this chapter serves to introduce you to the concepts and tools you need to begin. The onus is on you to take the models you have created—and the ones you will create in the future—texture them, and light scenes with them to develop an eye for the ins and outs of lighting. There really is no quick way to learn how to light. It would be quite a disservice to pretend that a chapter, or even an entire book, will give you everything you need to know. Take the information and references in this chapter and apply them on your own. Working on your own may not sound like fun, and it may not seem as easy as being guided step by step, but it is honestly the best education you will get.

CHAPTER 11

3ds Max Rendering

Rendering is the last step in creating your CG work, but it is the first step to consider when you start to build a scene. During rendering, the computer calculates the scene's surface properties, lighting, shadows, and object movement and then it saves a sequence of images. To get to the point where the computer takes over, you'll need to set up your camera and render settings so that you'll get exactly what you need from your scene.

This chapter will show you how to render your scene using 3ds Max's scanline renderer and how to create reflections and refractions using raytracing.

Topics in this chapter include:

- **Rendering Setup**
- **Motion Blur**
- **Cameras**
- **Previewing with Active Shade**
- **Render Elements**
- **Raytraced Reflections and Refractions**

Rendering Setup

In a manner of speaking, everything you do in CG can be considered setup for rendering. More specifically, how you set up your render settings and what final decisions you make about your 3ds Max scene ultimately determine how your work will look. In many ways, you should be thinking about rendering all along—especially if you are creating 3d assets for a game, where the 3d scenes are rendered in real time by the game engine. If you create models and textures with the final image in mind and gear the lighting toward elegantly showing off the scene, the final touches will be relatively easy to set up.

To set the proper settings, you begin with the Render Scene dialog box.

Render Scene Dialog Box

The Render Scene dialog box is where you define your render output for 3ds Max. You can open this dialog box by clicking the Render Scene icon ( ) in the main toolbar, by selecting Rendering → Render, or by pressing F10. You've already seen how to Quick Render ( ) a frame in your scene to check your work. The settings in the Render Scene dialog box are used even when the Quick Render button is invoked, so it's important to understand how this dialog box works. Figure 11.1 shows the Common tab in the Render Scene dialog box.

Common Tab

The Render Scene dialog box is divided into five tabs; each tab has settings grouped by function. The Common tab stores the settings for the overall needs of the render—for example, image size, frame range to render, and the type of renderer to use.

In the Common Parameters rollout, you will find the most necessary render settings. They are described in the following sections.

TIME OUTPUT

In this section, you can set the frame range of your render output by selecting one of the following options (shown here):

Single This option renders the current frame only. It is set to single by default.

Active Time Segment This option renders the frame range in the timeline.

Range This option renders the frame range specified in the text boxes.

Frames This option renders the frames typed in the text box. You can enter frame numbers separated by commas or specified as ranges, such as **3-13**, to render only the specified frames.

Every Nth Frame This option is enabled when you are rendering more than one frame. It allows you to render every *n*th frame, where *n* is a whole number, so you can specify how many frames to skip.

Typically, you will be rendering single frames as you model, texture, and light the scene. The closer you are to final rendering, especially for scenes with moving cameras or lights, the more you will need to render a sequence of images to check the animation of the scene and how the lighting works. This is where the Every Nth Frame function comes in very handy. Using it, you can render every five frames, for example, to quickly see a render test range of your scene without having to render the entire frame range.

You should always test render at least a few frames of an animation before you render the entire frame range, because the smallest omission or error can cost you hours of rendering and effectively bottleneck production flow and get several people annoyed at you. This practice is a good habit to start. Whenever you want to launch a render of the entire scene, render at least one frame to check the output. If you have animated lights or cameras, use the Every Nth Frame option to test a few frames.

OUTPUT SIZE

The image size of your render, which is set in the Output Size section (shown here), will depend on your output format—that is, how you want to show your render. Chapter 1, "Basic Concepts," explains the popular resolutions used in production.

By default, the dialog box is set to render images at a resolution of 640 × 480 pixels, defined by the Width and Height parameters respectively. This resolution has an image aspect of 1.333, meaning the ratio of the frame's width to its height. Changing the Image Aspect value will adjust the size of your image along the Height to correspond with the existing Width to accommodate the newly requested aspect ratio. Different displays have different aspect ratios. For example, regular television is 1.33:1 (simply called 1.33) and a high definition television is a widescreen with a ratio of 1.78:1 (simply called 1.78). The resolution of your output will define the screen ratio.

Figure 11.01

The Common tab in the Render Scene dialog box

Pixel aspect affects the image because it actually changes the shape of the pixel from a square to a rectangle. This is due to how TV screens are built (standard definition, not HD). When output is displayed on a TV screen, the image will be squeezed slightly horizontally. Therefore, renders are created a bit wider so that when they are displayed on a TV screen, they will appear normal. This is especially visible when you render a round object as shown in the following graphic. On the left, the sphere is rendered with a pixel aspect of 1.0 (i.e. 1:1 ratio). On the right, the sphere is rendered with a pixel aspect of 0.9 (i.e. 0.9:1 ratio). However, when the sphere on the right is displayed on a standard TV, it will appear round and not stretched in this manner.

 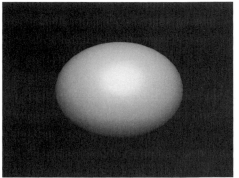

You hardly ever have to worry about Pixel Aspect ratios. They are mentioned only for those who may be outputting directly to DV tape or DVD. Luckily, grouping the Output Size section of the Render Scene window is a drop-down menu for choosing presets from different film and video resolutions. Custom is the default, and it allows you to set your own resolution. You can also select one of the Preset Resolution buttons. For DVD or TV output, you should select the NTSC D-1 (video) preset. For output to a DV tape, you should select the NTSC DV (video) preset. They both have a pixel aspect ratio of 0.9 to account for the TV "squeeze." Of course, if you are in Europe, you will need to select the PAL equivalents of the aforementioned presets, because TV resolutions and frame rates differ internationally. For more on aspect ratios and frame rates, see Chapter 1.

The higher the resolution, the longer the scene will take to render. Doubling the resolution might quadruple the render time. To save time when you're working with large frame sequences, you can render tests at half the resolution of the final output and render every fifth frame or so.

The image quality of a render also affects how long a render will take. In addition to turning down the resolution for a test, you can also use a lower-quality render and you can turn off certain effects, such as Atmospherics (light fog). Quality settings are explained in the following section.

OPTIONS

The Options section (shown in the following graphic), lets you access several global toggles. Three boxes are checked by default. You can toggle the rendering of specific elements in

your scene. For example, if you are using Atmospherics (Volume light) or Effects (Lens Flare) and don't want them to render, you can uncheck the appropriate box(es). This is a shortcut to turn off the Effect or Atmosphere.

RENDER OUTPUT

What's good does it do to render a scene if you don't save the files? When you are done setting up the dialog for your image output, you need to tell 3ds Max where to render the images and what file format to use. Use the Render Output section shown here to indicate that the file should be saved.

The Image Format can be selected to be a single image file or sequence of image files that form a sequence or it can be a movie file such as a QuickTime. In fact, 3ds Max supports many image file formats. The most common movie format is arguably QuickTime. A sequence of frames is typically rendered to Targa or TIFF files.

Choosing a Filename

To specify a location and file type to render to, click the Files button to open the Render Output File dialog box shown in Figure 11.2. Simply select the folder to which you want to render, and set the filename. You can set the file type using the Save As Type pull-down menu.

Figure 11.2

The Render Output File dialog box defines how the render saves to disk.

Proper file naming is very important when you render a scene, particularly when you are rendering a sequence of images and have hundreds of frames. Saved images are usually identified by a filename, a frame number, and an extension in the form `filename_####.ext`— for example, `stillife_0234.tif`. This format is used in production facilities and accepted by most compositing programs, such as Combustion or After Effects.

When you enter the filename for an image sequence, as shown here, you can include an underscore (the _ character) *after* the filename and before the frame number to help differentiate the two. This is especially useful if you use version numbers in your scene names. If you don't use an underscore (or similar character) between the filename and frame number, your rendered image files can be confusing, as shown in the file list in Figure 11.3.

> It's a good idea to name your rendered images according to the scene's filename. This way you can always know from which scene file a rendered image was produced without rooting through several files and/or guessing.

The extension portion of the image filename is a three-letter abbreviation that corresponds to the type of file you are rendering. By specifying a file format in the Save As Type drop-down menu, you automatically set the extension for the file in its filename. This way you ensure that you can identify the file type.

Figure 11.3

Image filenames without a separator between the filename and frame number are confusing to look at and might play out of sequence.

Name	Size	Type
testrange_v010000.tif	1,013 KB	TIF Image
testrange_v010002.tif	1,013 KB	TIF Image
testrange_v010004.tif	1,013 KB	TIF Image
testrange_v010006.tif	1,013 KB	TIF Image
testrange_v010008.tif	1,013 KB	TIF Image
testrange_v010010.tif	1,013 KB	TIF Image
testrange_v010012.tif	1,013 KB	TIF Image
testrange_v010014.tif	1,013 KB	TIF Image
testrange_v010016.tif	1,013 KB	TIF Image
testrange_v010018.tif	1,013 KB	TIF Image
testrange_v010020.tif	1,013 KB	TIF Image
testrange_v010022.tif	1,013 KB	TIF Image
testrange_v010024.tif	1,013 KB	TIF Image
testrange_v010026.tif	1,013 KB	TIF Image
testrange_v010028.tif	1,013 KB	TIF Image
testrange_v010030.tif	1,013 KB	TIF Image
testrange_v010032.tif	1,013 KB	TIF Image
testrange_v010034.tif	1,013 KB	TIF Image
testrange_v010036.tif	1,013 KB	TIF Image
testrange_v010038.tif	1,013 KB	TIF Image
testrange_v010040.tif	1,013 KB	TIF Image
testrange_v010042.tif	1,013 KB	TIF Image
testrange_v010044.tif	1,013 KB	TIF Image
testrange_v010046.tif	1,013 KB	TIF Image
testrange_v010048.tif	1,013 KB	TIF Image
testrange_v010050.tif	1,013 KB	TIF Image
testrange_v010052.tif	1,013 KB	TIF Image
testrange_v010054.tif	1,013 KB	TIF Image
testrange_v010056.tif	1,013 KB	TIF Image
testrange_v010058.tif	1,013 KB	TIF Image
testrange_v010060.tif	1,013 KB	TIF Image
testrange_v010062.tif	1,013 KB	TIF Image
testrange_v010064.tif	1,013 KB	TIF Image

Image File Type

You can save your images in a wide range of formats when you render with 3ds Max. The format you choose depends on your own preference and your output needs. For example, JPEG (Joint Photographic Experts Group) files may be great for the small file sizes preferred on the Internet, but their color compression and lack of alpha channel (a feature discussed later in this chapter in the "Image Channels and the Rendered Frame Window" sidebar) make them undesirable for professional film or television production work beyond test renders and *dailies*, a meeting where the day's (or week's) work on a production is looked at and discussed for direction.

Furthermore, it's best to render a sequence of images rather than a movie file for two reasons. First, you would want your renders to be their best quality with little to no image compression. Second, if a render fails during a movie render, you must rerender the entire sequence. With an image sequence, however, you can pick up where the last frame left off. The best file type format to render to is Targa or TIFF (Tagged Image File Format). These file formats enjoy universal support, have little to no image quality loss due to compression, and support an alpha channel. Almost all image-editing and compositing packages can read Targa and TIFF formatted files, so either is a safe choice most of the time. For more on image formats, see Chapter 1.

IMAGE CHANNELS AND THE RENDERED FRAME WINDOW

Image files are composed of red, green, and blue channels. Each channel specifies the amount of that primary additive color in the image. (See Chapter 1 for more on how computers define color.) In addition, some file formats can also save a fourth channel, called the alpha channel. This channel defines the transparency level of the image. Just as the red channel defines how much red is in an area of the image, the *alpha channel* defines how transparent the image is when layered or composited on another image. If the alpha channel is black, the image is perfectly see-through. If the alpha channel is white, the image is opaque. The alpha channel is also known as the *matte*. An object that has a transparency in its material will render with a gray alpha channel, as shown here.

The alpha channel is displayed in the Rendered Frame window. You have seen this window display your test renders several times throughout this book. It is shown here.

To view an image's alpha channel in the Rendered Frame window, click the Display Alpha Channel icon. To reset the view to RGB (full-color view), click the Display Alpha Channel icon again. You can also see how much red, green, or blue is present in the frame by clicking any one of the red, green, and blue disc icons that are the Enable RGB Channel icons.

To save an image you like in the Rendered Frame window, click the Save Bitmap button. The Clone Rendered Frame button is quite useful in that it creates a copy of this window for you so you can compare a newer render to an older render without needing to save the images.

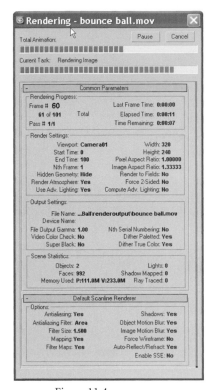

Figure 11.4

**The Render Process-
ing dialog box
shows you every-
thing you want to
know about your
current render.**

Render Processing

When you click the Render button in the Render Scene dialog box, the Render Processing dialog box pops up (Figure 11.4). This dialog box shows the parameters being used and it displays a process bar indicating the render's progress. You can pause or cancel the render by clicking the appropriate button. Rendering can consume most, if not all, of your system's resources. Pausing a render will not let you access your scene in 3ds Max, but it will stop the process on your system momentarily so that you can tend to another PC task.

Assign Renderer

The Assign Renderer rollout displays which renderers are assigned to your scene. Two types of renderers are available in 3ds Max by default (without any additional plugins installed):

Default Scanline Renderer The scanline renderer renders the scene as a series of horizontal lines.

mental ray Renderer A general-purpose renderer that can generate physically correct simulations of lighting effects.

mental ray is not covered in this book because it is an advanced renderer. All of the renders in this book are accomplished using the default Scanline renderer.

Rendering the Bouncing Ball

Seeing is believing, but doing is understanding. In this exercise, you will render the bouncing ball animation from Chapter 8, "Introduction to Animation," to get the feel for rendering an animation in 3ds Max. Just follow these steps:

1. Set your Project folder to the BouncingBall project that you copied to your hard drive from the CD. Open the `Animation_Ball_02.max` file in the Scenes folder. Let's render a movie to see the animation.

2. Open the Render Scene dialog box. In the Time Output section, select Active Time Segment: 0 to 100.

3. In the Output Size section, select the 320 × 240 preset button and leave Image/Pixel Aspect as is.

4. Leave the Options group at the default, and skip down to the Render Output section. Click the Files button to open an Explorer window. Navigate to where you want to save the output file. Name the file **Bounce Ball**, and click the drop-down menu next to Save As Type to choose MOV Quick Time File (`*.mov`) for your render file type.

By default, 3ds Max will render your file(s) to the RenderOutput folder in the current project.

Apple's QuickTime movie file format gives you a multitude of options for compression and quality. The quality settings for the QuickTime file are not the same as the render quality settings.

5. After you select MOV Quick Time File and click the Save button, the Compression Settings window, shown in Figure 11.5, opens. Set the parameters for the QuickTime as indicated:

Compression Type: Photo-JPEG

Frames per second: 30

Compressor Depth: Color

Quality: Best

Click OK.

If you are concerned about the file size of your renders, you can slide the Quality to a lower quality setting for the compressor. The Photo-JPEG compressor makes fairly good images with small file sizes. However, you'll want to deliver your renders at the highest quality you can muster. To improve quality, use a different Compressor Type. For example, Animation is lossless and makes big files, but those big files look much better!

6. Skip down to the bottom of the Render Scene dialog box, and verify that Production is selected. Select the viewport you want to render in the Viewport drop-down menu. You need to render Camera01.

7. Click Render. The Rendered Frame window will show you a preview of the render as it goes through the frames, and the Rendering Process dialog box will appear.

After the render is complete, use a file browser to navigate to your render location (by default it is set to the RenderOutput folder for the Bouncing-Ball project). Double-click the QuickTime file to see your movie, and enjoy a latte.

Figure 11.5

QuickTime compression settings affect the quality of the rendered QuickTime video file.

Renderer Tab Basics

The Renderer tab, found in the Render Scene dialog box, has options that determine the look and quality of the render. The options that are displayed in this tab depend on which renderer you assigned to render your scene. We are going to cover the Default Scanline only. This rollout sets the parameters for the Default Scanline renderer.

Most of the features in Options (shown here) are used to make rendering a scene more efficient. If you want to do a quick render of an animation, for example, turn off Mapping and Shadows. You will still see the movement, but the processing will go faster.

Antialiasing

Aliasing is the staircase effect you see in an image just at the edge of a line or area of color, particularly when that edge is at an angle, as shown in Figure 11.6. *Antialiasing* can smooth this stepped effect on diagonal or curved lines. It blurs and mixes the color values of pixels adjacent to the jagged line or curve, as shown in Figure 11.7. Turning this feature off will speed up your renders, but the quality loss will be noticeable.

Figure 11.6

Aliasing is the stepped effect on diagonal and curved lines. Notice the top ridges of the fruit and its stem.

Figure 11.7

Antialiasing helps smooth jagged diagonal and curved lines.

Filters

Filters are the last step in antialiasing. You can use them to access different methods of calculating the antialiasing at the subpixel level in order to sharpen or soften your final output. You don't need to worry about which filter to use until you have much more rendering experience under your belt. The Area filter, the default filter, will work great.

If you are curious about the different filter types, select a filter. A short description of it will appear in the box below the Filter Maps check box.

Motion Blur

With *motion blur,* a renderer can simulate how the eye or a camera sees an object in motion. When an object moves relatively fast, your eye (or a camera) perceives a blur on the object. Using motion blur for an animation can greatly enhance the fidelity of your render, although it adds more processing time. Use motion blur sparingly in most scenes. It takes a careful eye to choose the right blur amount for an object.

The Renderer tab in the Render Scene dialog box has two sections used for setting the type of motion blur you need.

Object Motion Blur

The Object Motion Blur section (shown here) lets you access the motion blur settings.

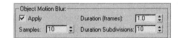

The Object Motion Blur settings are as follows:

Duration (Frames) The higher the Duration number, the more blur you get. You can see the difference in the motion blur for the ball in Figure 11.8.

Samples This setting determines how many duration subdivision copies are sampled. The higher the Samples number, the better the motion blur quality.

Duration Subdivisions This setting determines how many copies of each object are rendered within the duration. The higher the Subdivisions number, the smoother the motion blur will look.

Figure 11.8
Different durations give different motion blur lengths.

Duration Set to 0.5   Duration Set to 1.0   Duration Set to 2.0

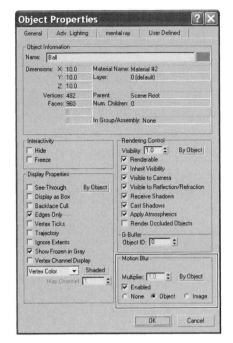

Figure 11.9

Choose the type of motion blur for an object using its Object Properties window.

Setting the Duration very high and the Samples and Duration Subdivisions low will give you a ghosting effect that will kill the look of the motion blur. You will need to find the right balance to achieve a believable blur. Remember that more is less. Just a touch of motion blur may be all a scene needs.

Image Motion Blur

As you'll notice in the Render Scene dialog box, Object Motion Blur is turned on by default. However, you still need to enable motion blur on a *per object* basis; this means you have to toggle motion blur on for any object that you want to render with blur.

To turn on motion blur, select the object and right-click on it in a viewport. From the context menu, choose Object Properties. Select the type of Motion Blur (shown in Figure 11.9) you want, and then adjust the parameters in the Renderer tab.

The difference between Object and Image motion blur types can be seen in Figure 11.10. The bouncing ball on the left is rendered with *Object* motion blur, and the one on the right is rendered with *Image* motion blur. Both are rendered with the same Duration. The Image motion blur renders smoother, although it may not be as accurate because it is a smearing effect created *after* the object is rendered into the image. The Object blur renders the blur during the scanline rendering process itself.

For now, you only need to be concerned with the Duration parameter for an Image motion blur. This setting, as with the Object motion blur, sets the amount (and therefore the length) of the blur. Remember not to go overboard with motion blur. A little goes a long way.

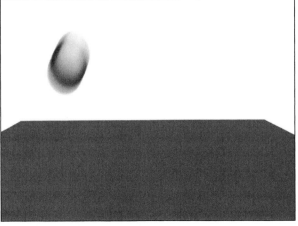

Figure 11.10

Different motion blur types give you different results. The one on the left is Object motion blur, and the one on the right is Image motion blur.

Previewing with ActiveShade

ActiveShade is a fantastic 3ds Max feature that lets you interactively preview a render as you make changes in the scene. This is particularly helpful for texturing and lighting because the floating ActiveShade window updates whenever you make a light or material change in the scene.

To enable ActiveShade, open the Render Scene dialog box ( ). At the bottom of the window, click to toggle on the ActiveShade rendering, as shown in the following graphic. Pick your viewport, and either click the ActiveShade button in the Render Scene dialog box or click the Quick Render button in the main toolbar. The icon in the main toolbar changes ( ) as you switch from Production rendering to ActiveShade rendering. ActiveShade doesn't render Atmospheric effects.

> You can have only one ActiveShade window open at a time. If you try to open another window, an alert will ask whether you want to close the other window.

You can also turn a viewport into an ActiveShade window. Select the view where you want to enable ActiveShade, and right-click the viewport's name. Select Views → ActiveShade from the context menu as shown here.

That viewport will then become an ActiveShade window and will update a render every time you make changes to the scene. This helps keep the clutter of open windows to a minimum.

Cameras

Cameras in 3ds Max, as shown in a viewport in Figure 11.11, capture and output all the fun in your scene. In theory, the cameras in 3ds Max work as much like real cameras as possible. Hence, the more you know about photography, the easier these concepts are to understand.

The *camera*, in essence, creates a perspective through which you can see and render your scene. You can have as many cameras in the scene as you want. However, it's a good idea to place and keep the camera you're planning to use to render positioned in the shot as you wish for your final framing. You can use the Perspective viewport to move around your scene as you work, leaving the render camera alone.

Creating a Camera

There are two types of cameras in 3ds Max: Target and Free. A *Target camera*, much like a Target spotlight, has a Target node that allows it to look at a spot defined by where the target is placed (or animated). A Target camera is easier to aim than a Free camera because you simply position the target object at the center of interest, and the camera will always aim there.

Figure 11.11

A camera as seen in a viewport

Figure 11.11

A camera as seen in a viewport

On the other hand, *Free cameras* have only one node, so they must be rotated to aim at the subject, much as a Free spotlight. When your scene requires the camera to follow an action, you will be better off with a Target camera.

You can create a camera by clicking on the Cameras icon ( ) in the Create panel and selecting either of the two camera types, as shown here.

To create a Target camera, click in a viewport to lay down the Camera node, and then drag to pull out and place the Target node. To create a Free camera, simply click in a viewport to place it.

Using Cameras

A camera's main feature is the *lens,* which sets the *focal length* in millimeters and the *FOV (Field of View)*, which determines how wide an area the camera sees. By default, a 3ds Max camera lens is 43.456mm with an FOV of 45 degrees. This default lens will most likely meet all your camera needs, but in case you need to change the lens, you can use the Lens or FOV parameters to create a new lens using the spinner or by entering a value. The 3ds Max Lens and FOV are tied together. One drives the other because the focal length of a real lens sets the field of view. To change a lens, you can also pick from the stock lenses available for a camera in its Modify panel parameters, as shown in Figure 11.12.

Figure 11.12

Stock lenses make it easy to pick the right lens for a scene.

The most interactive way to adjust a camera is to use the Viewport Navigation tools. You can then place the camera while you see its field of view in that viewport. The Camera viewport must be selected for the viewport camera tools to be available to you in the lower-right corner of the UI. You can move the camera or change the Lens or FOV. Chapter 3, "The 3ds Max Interface," has a complete list of the tools in the "Viewport Navigation Controls" subsection. You can also change a camera by just selecting the camera object and moving and rotating it just as you would any other object.

Talk Is Cheap!

The best way to explain how to use a camera is to create one, as in the following steps:

1. Open the Camera Create.max scene file in the Rendering Scene Files folder on the CD. This is the fruit still life from the lighting chapter, but without a camera. Creating a camera is the same as creating a light. It's easier to create a camera in the Top viewport, so you can easily orient it in reference to your scene objects. Figure 11.13 shows the intended position of a camera for this scene.

2. In the Create panel, click the Cameras icon ( ). Select the Target camera and go to the Top viewport. Click from the bottom of the viewport and drag to the still life as shown in Figure 11.14. The first click creates the camera object. The mouse drag and release sets the location of the target.

3. The camera was created along the ground plane. You need to move the entire camera up using the Front viewport. The easiest way to do this is to select the camera and target using the line that connects the camera and target. That will select both the target and camera so you can move them as a unit. Use the Move tool to relocate the camera higher in the scene to place it at the level of the fruits.

4. To see the Camera viewport, select a viewport and press the C key. This changes the viewport to whatever camera is currently selected. If there are multiple cameras in your scene and none are selected, when you press C, you will get a dialog that gives a list of the cameras in the scene from which you can choose, as shown here.

5. Now Quick Render the scene through the camera you just created and positioned. Find a good framing for the still life and set your camera.

Figure 11.13

The camera would go here.

Figure 11.14

Create a camera to look at the still life

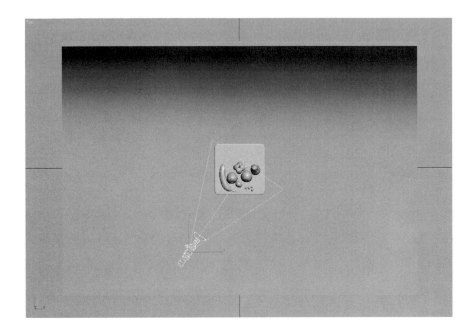

When the camera is set up, take some time to move it around and see the changes in the viewport. Moving a camera from side to side is known as a *truck*. Moving a camera in and out is called a *dolly*. Rotating a camera is called a *roll*. Also change the Lens and FOV settings to see the results.

> Zooming a lens (changing the Lens parameter) is not the same as a dolly in or dolly out. The field of view changes when you zoom, and it stays constant when you dolly. They will both yield different framings.

Animating a Camera

Now that the camera is in the scene, let's add some animation to the camera. Camera animation is done in the same way you would animate any object. You can animate the camera or the target or both. You can also animate the camera parameters such as the lens or FOV.

In the previous scene, select the camera, move the Time slider to frame 30. Press N to activate Auto Key, or click its icon. Use the Move tool to move the camera farther away from the still life. The idea is to create a dolly out of the still life.

Now scrub through the animation and make any edit you desire.

> If you are comfortable using the Perspective viewport, you can convert it to a Camera view by pressing Ctrl+C. Cool trick!

Clipping Planes

You can limit what your camera sees in a scene. For example, in a huge scene, you can exclude or *clip* the geometry that is beyond a certain distance by using *clipping planes*. This helps keep the amount of geometry that needs to be calculated at a minimum. Each camera has a clipping plane for distance (*far*) and foreground (*near*), as shown in Figures 11.15 and 11.16 respectively. The near clipping plane will clip geometry *within* the distance designated from the camera lens.

You can also use clipping planes to create a cutaway look for a model. Simply set your near clipping plane to a distance *into* the object, and the object will render as if it were sliced, giving you a perfect cutaway look.

Figure 11.15

A far clipping plane cuts off the distant extents of a scene.

Figure 11.16

A near clipping plane cuts off the extents directly in front of a camera.

Likewise, if you find a model or scene you have imported looks odd or is cut off, check to make sure your clipping planes are adjusted to fit the extents of the scene, especially with imported models.

To enable clipping planes, click the Clip Manually check box and set the distances needed, as shown here.

Once you turn on manual clipping planes, the camera will display the near and far extents in the viewports with a red plane marker, as shown in Figure 11.17.

Figure 11.17

A camera will display its manual clipping planes in a viewport when Clip Manually is enabled.

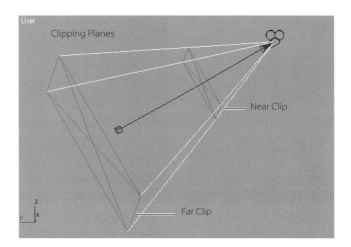

Safe Frame

Because every TV is different, what you see on one screen may look somewhat different on a different screen. To help make sure the action of your scene is contained within a safe area on all TV screens, you can enable the Safe Frame view in any viewport. This will, as shown in Figure 11.18, show you a set of three boundaries in your viewport.

Figure 11.18

Safe Frame gives you a suggested boundary for the action of your framing.

The Live area is the extent of what will be rendered. The Action Safe area is the boundary where you should be assured that the action in the scene will display on most if not all TV screens. Most TVs will display somewhere between the Action Safe and the Live areas. Finally, the Title Safe boundary is where you can feel comfortable rendering text in your frame. Because some TVs distort the image slightly at the edges, any text that falls outside the Title Safe area may not be readable. Although they are based on TV technology from years ago, these conventions hold true in professional production to this day. The Safe Frame areas are still good guidelines to use when framing your shot.

To view Show Safe Frame in the chosen viewport, right-click on the name in the viewport to access the context menu, and then choose Safe Frame from the list.

Render Elements

The Render Elements tab is another tab in the Rendering Scene dialog box. You might not need this feature as a beginner, but you will be surprised at the control you get when you render your scene into separate passes to composite later. As a beginner, you should concentrate on becoming familiar with rendering and lighting. As the months pass and you feel more comfortable rendering, you should discover that most CG is layered.

This means that separate passes are rendered outside of 3ds Max and layered or composited together with finer control in a program such as Photoshop for still images, and Combustion, After Effects, or Shake for image sequences. The ability to layer is another reason why rendering to image files is preferred over rendering to movie files.

However, you will need to understand compositing to be able to control and layer the elements back together.

Shadows and reflections are the main elements that you might consider rendering separately, especially when you are first learning. When these elements are separate, you gain a greater degree of control in compositing because you can affect the shadows or reflections any way you want (soften, color, transparency, etc.) as you composite them back on top of the image. For example, if you render a scene of a tree casting a shadow across a lawn, you will have to render the entire scene again if you decide to lighten the shadow color. If you have the shadow as a separate pass, you can very easily and interactively change the darkness of the shadow as you composite it in Shake, for instance.

Follow along with these steps:

1. Select the Render Elements tab in the Rendering Scene window, click the Add button, and select the element you want to render. The following list describes common elements to render:

    Alpha Renders a black and white matte to be used in compositing. This is especially helpful when you need different mattes for different objects in your scene. The fruit still life is shown rendered Alpha only in Figure 11.19.

Figure 11.19
The Alpha element

Reflection Renders only the reflections so you can composite them separately. Figure 11.20 shows the fruit still life's reflections in the pedestal rendered as an element.

Figure 11.20
**The Reflection
element**

Refraction Renders only refracting elements in transparent or translucent objects so they may be layered in the composite at a later time.

Self-Illumination Renders the incandescence of an object's material separately so its intensity may be controlled in composite.

Shadow Renders only the shadows cast in the scene into the Alpha channel of the image. Figure 11.21 shows the fruit still life's shadow element. Keep in mind that you will have to render to an image format that has an Alpha channel, such as TIFF.

Figure 11.21
The Shadows element as shown in the Alpha channel of the image

Specular Renders only the highlights on an object's glossy material. Figure 11.22 shows the specular highlights on the fruit.

Figure 11.22
The Specular element

Z-Depth Renders a grayscale image that responds to the depth of a scene. The closer an object or a part of an object is, the whiter it renders. The farther from the camera an object or its parts are, the darker the render. This pass is then used in a compositing program, such as After Effects, to create a sense of haze or blur to add a depth of field to the image. Figure 11.23 shows a Z-Depth pass generated for the still life scene.

Figure 11.23

The Z-Depth element

2. Once you select a render element, it will be added to the Element Rendering List. Then you'll need to go down to the Selected Element parameters to input where you will save the bitmap elements, as shown here. The dialog box will name the element automatically. However, when you go into the Explorer window to save it, you should name it again.

3. If you want each element to be rendered in its own Rendered Frame window, check the Display Elements box. If it is unchecked, the program will render the elements to a file and the Render Frame window will not show you the progress of each element.

4. Click the Render button to begin a render. 3ds Max will render the entire scene, and then output the elements as needed.

Rendering Effects

Rendering Effects offers a variety of special effects such as lens effects, film grain, and blur to add to your render. Rendering Effects allows you to create effects without having to render to see the results. They are rendered after your scene is rendered, and they are added to the rendered image automatically.

Lens Effects: Glow

You will add a glow effect to a light bulb hanging over the fruit still life in a scene. For this scene, you can *glow* the light or the light bulb object. You will glow the light bulb object in the following steps:

1. Load the `Still Life_Glow.max` scene file from the Rendering Scene Files folder on the companion CD.

2. Right-click on the light bulb object. From the context menu, select Object Properties, as shown here.

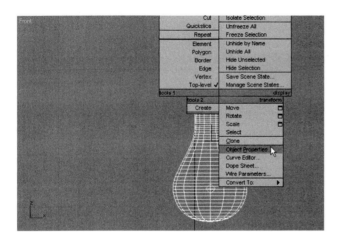

3. In the dialog box, go to the G-Buffer section and assign 2 as the Object ID number for the glow effect, as shown in Figure 11.24. This tells 3ds Max which object gets the glow. The number you assign doesn't matter unless you want different glows on different objects. In that case, each glow object would receive its own Object ID number.

   Another way you can assign glow is through the object's material. Go to the Material Editor, and in the toolbar, click and hold on the Material ID channel. The benefit of using the material for the glow is that you can glow any object that has the material applied.

   You can also glow a light; this property can only be set through Object Properties.

4. In the Menu Bar, choose Rendering → Effects to open the Environment and Effects window. Click the Add button. Then pick Lens Effects from the Add Effect dialog box. Figure 11.25 shows that the Lens Effects have been added.

Using the Preview in the Environment and Effects window (in the Effects tab) provides a much easier way to view the Effects than rendering a frame does. You can select whether you want to preview all of the effects (All) in the scene or just the one you are working on (Current). Toggling Interactive updates the preview when you change the Effects parameters by opening a Render window and updating it as you make changes. Enabling Interactive may cause your computer to slow down, so leave it unchecked and use the Update Effect button when you want to see an update.

5. Scroll down to Lens Effects Parameters and select Glow to add to the box on the right, as shown here.

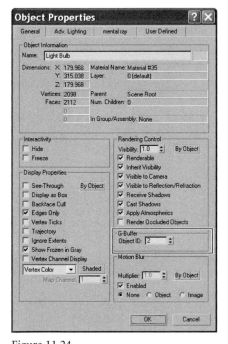

Figure 11.24

Set a unique number for the Object ID.

Figure 11.25

Adding the Lens Effects to the Environment and Effects window

6. While still in the Environment and Effects window, scroll down to Glow Element. This is where you create the settings for the Glow Effect. There are two tabs:

   Parameters This tab is where you set the size and color of the glow, as shown here.

   Options This tab is where you can assign the glow to the object desired. Under Image Sources, you have to choose how the glow will be applied to the object, through the material or object properties.

7. Click the Options tab. Because you are creating the light bulb's glow through the light bulb object's Object ID, set the Object ID parameter to 2, as shown here. Leave the other parameters at their default values.

8. Click over to the Parameters tab to set the glow's size. Setting the size for the glow can be a bit tricky because the size of the glow depends on the size of your object. Set the Size value to 5. Leave the Intensity set at the default; once you render the effect, you can adjust the Intensity.

9. To add color to the glow, you can use two methods: You can set the Use Source Color parameter to set the glow color to a percentage of the object's material color. You also can use the Radial Color parameter to set the colors for the inside of the glow (color swatch on the left) and the outside of the glow (color swatch on the right). In this case, set the Use Source Color to 65 because the light bulb has a yellow material applied. If you have Interactive Preview enabled (see the note earlier), you can see how the glow looks. Otherwise, run a Quick Render to check the look.

10. The default intensity looks okay, but it could be brighter. Change the Intensity to 165. Render. Okay, it looks good. See Figure 11.26.

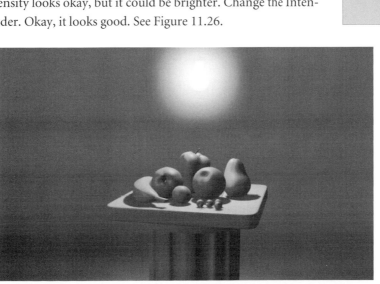

Figure 11.26

Glow!

Raytraced Reflections and Refractions

In this section, you will learn how to create realistic reflections and refractions in your renders. As you saw in Chapter 7, "Materials and Mapping," you can apply an image map to an object material's Reflection parameter to add a fake reflection to the object. To get a true reflection of the other objects in the scene, you will need to use raytracing methodology. There are essentially two ways to create raytraced reflections in a scene: by using a Raytrace map or by using a Raytrace material.

The Raytrace material is a more detailed solution; however, it can take twice as much time as using a Raytrace map, because the Raytrace material requires more calculation.

As you learned in Chapter 4, "Modeling in 3ds Max: Part I," determining the level of detail you need for a reflective surface is important. There is no reason to use the Raytrace material for a reflection unless your camera is right up on the object. In many cases, the Raytrace map looks great and saves tons of rendering time. Keep in mind though, the amount of control you will have with a Raytrace map is significantly less than with the Raytrace material.

First, you will try using the Raytrace material.

Raytrace Material

In the following steps, you will learn how to use the Raytrace material to create reflections in a scene.

Creating the Raytrace Material

1. Open the `Still Life_Raytrace.max` file found in the Render Scene Files folder on the companion CD. Change the Camera view to Camera01 in one of the viewports.

2. Open the Material Editor and select a sample slot. Click the Get Material button (shown here) and select the Raytrace material (materials have a blue sphere icon on the left) from the Material selections, as shown in Figure 11.27.

3. The parameters to create reflections are available through the Raytrace Basic Parameters rollout, as shown here. Leave most of these parameters at their default values, but

    change the Reflect color swatch to white from black. This will set the reflection of the material all the way to the maximum reflectivity.

4. Change the Diffuse Color swatch to black to turn the column black. This will make the column appear as a reflective black glass material in the render.

5. Apply the Raytrace material to the Column in the scene. Render. Figure 11.28 shows the result.

Tweaking the Render

The render will show the Raytrace material on the column reflecting like a flat mirror. It looks very convincing, but you may notice the jagged edges or artifacts around the reflected objects. This is aliasing in the reflections. The antialiasing filters set by default may not be enough. When the defaults aren't enough, it is time for the big guns: *SuperSampling*. SuperSampling is an extra pass of antialiasing. By default, 3ds Max applies a single Super-Sample over all the materials in the scene.

However, if a specific material needs more antialiasing, you can apply a separate SuperSample method to that material.

In the current Still Life scene, select the material slot for the column's Raytrace material. Go to the Super-Sampling rollout and uncheck Use Global Settings. Check Enable Local Supersampler. In the pull-down menu, choose Adaptive Halton, as shown here.

The Adaptive Halton method performs well in this case. However, always try the regular patterns first; they tend to render faster. Quick Render the scene, and you will notice a marked improvement in the quality of the reflections (Figure 11.29).

Figure 11.27

Select the Raytrace material.

Figure 11.28

The Raytrace material renders reflections.

Figure 11.29

Reflections with the Raytrace material with SuperSampling enabled

Raytrace Mapping

You can apply raytracing *only* to a specific map, as opposed to the entire material. Because raytracing typically takes longer to render, this can save time. In this case, you will assign a Raytrace map to the Reflection map of a material to get true reflections in the scene, at a faster render time than using the material as you just did. Follow these steps:

1. In the same scene, open the Material Editor and select an unassigned sample slot. Keep the Material set to Standard Material.

2. In the Maps rollout, click the mapping bar labeled *None* next to Reflections. Choose from the Raytrace map in the Material/Map browser, as shown here. Leave the Raytrace Map parameters at the default, as shown in Figure 11.30.

3. Click the Go to Parent button ( ) in the Raytrace Map Parameters view to return to the material's parameters.

4. Go to the Blinn Basic parameters and change the diffuse color to black to match the black column from the previous render.

5. In the Specular Highlights section, change the Specular Level to 98, and Glossiness to 90, as shown here.

6. Apply the material to the column object in the scene and Quick Render.

7. You will notice the same aliasing in the reflections as in the previous example. Set the SuperSampling as you did with the prior example, and render again.

Take a look at both the images created with reflections created using the Raytrace material and the Standard material with Raytrace map applied to Reflections. They look almost the same. This is good to know because it takes about half the time to render the Raytrace map. However, you will notice slightly better detail in the reflections created with the Raytrace material. You and the requirements of your scene will determine which reflection method works best in a particular situation. However, it's good always start with the Raytrace map to see if it creates enough detail without too much bother.

Refractions Using the Raytrace Material

Creating raytraced refractions in glass can be accomplished using the same two workflows as raytraced reflections. The same conditions apply here. The Raytrace material renders nicer, but it takes longer than using a Raytrace map for the Refraction map in a material.

Figure 11.30

The Raytrace Map parameters

Keep in mind that render times are much slower with refractions, especially if you add SuperSample to the mix—so don't freak out. Next you will create refractions using the Raytrace material:

1. In the same scene, change the Camera01 viewport to Camera02. This gives you a better view of the wine glass through which we will refract, as shown here.

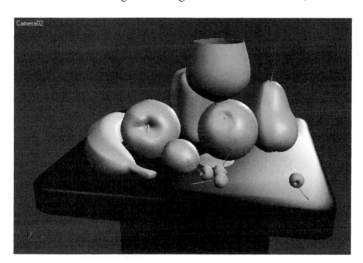

2. In the Material Editor, select an unassigned sample slot and click the Get Material button. This material will be for the wine glass.

3. Choose the Raytrace material from the Material/Map browser.

4. Go to the Raytrace Basic Parameters rollout, and change the color swatch for Transparency to white from black. Black is opaque and white is fully transparent.

Figure 11.31

The Extended Parameters rollout for the Raytrace material

5. Uncheck the box next to Reflect and change that spinner to 20. This sets a slight reflection for the material.

6. Take a look at the Index of Refr parameter. This value sets the *Index of Refraction* (IOR) value that determines how much the material should refract its background. For more on IOR, see the Refraction sidebar in this chapter. The value is already set to 1.55. Leave it at that value.

7. Go to the Extended Parameters rollout (Figure 11.31). The Reflections section of the parameters is at the bottom. Select Additive and change Gain to 0.7. This gives a bit of reflection brightness for the clear wine glass.

8. Go to the SuperSampling rollout and uncheck Use Global Setting. Enable Local SuperSampler and keep it set to Max 2.5 Star.

9. In the Specular Highlights group, change the Specular Level to 98, and Glossiness to 90 as shown here.

10. Apply the material to the wine glass. The glass will turn transparent in the viewport. Quick Render. Figure 11.32 shows the result.

You will notice a very nice wine glass render, with the bell pepper refracting through it slightly. Change the Index of Refr parameter on the material to 8.0 and you will see a much greater refraction, as shown in Figure 11.33. That may work better for a nice heavy bottle, but it is too much for the glass. An Index of Refr parameter between 1.5 and 2.5 works pretty well for the wine glass, particularly at the bottom of the glass where it rounds down to meet the stem.

Figure 11.32

The wine glass refraction is rendered with the Raytrace material.

Figure 11.33

A much more pro-nounced refraction is rendered with an IOR of 8.0.

Refractions Using Raytrace Mapping

Just as you did with the reflections, you will now use a Raytrace map on the Refraction parameter for the wine glass material. In the following steps, you will create another refraction render for the wine glass:

1. While still in the same scene, open the Material Editor and select an unassigned sample slot. You are going to keep the material asset to Standard.

2. Go to the Maps rollout and click the bar labeled *None,* which is next to Refraction. Choose the Raytrace map from the Material/Map Browser. The material in the sample slot will turn transparent.

3. Click the Go to Parent button to return to the material's parameters.

4. Go to the Maps rollout and click the bar labeled *None* next to Reflection. Choose the *Raytrace* map from the Material/Map Browser. Be warned that this setting will take a long time to render the image. If you have a slower computer or perhaps are in a rush, uncheck the Reflection map box to turn off the reflection entirely.

5. Click the Go to Parent button to return to the material's parameters.

6. Go to the Maps rollout and change the amount of the Reflection to 6. This will reduce the amount of reflection.

7. Go to the Blinn Basic Parameters rollout and change the Opacity value to 0.

8. Go to the SuperSampling rollout and uncheck Use Global Setting. Enable Local SuperSampler and keep it as Max 2.5 Star.

9. In the Specular Highlights group, change the Specular Level to 98, and Glossiness to 90.

10. Apply the material to the column object in the scene and render (Figure 11.34).

Figure 11.34

Use Raytrace map on the Refraction parameter to create a refraction in the wine glass.

You can control the IOR through the material's parameters in the Extended Parameters rollout, in the Advanced Transparency section, shown here. Set the IOR to different numbers to see how the render compares to the Raytrace Material renders.

The render will take quite some time to finish. The raytracing reflections and refractions slow down the render quite a bit. You can leave out the reflections if you'd like, but that will reduce the believability of the wine glass. You can also map a reflection as you did with the pool ball in Chapter 7; however, having true reflections will make the wine glass look much more realistic. When you raytrace both the reflection and the refraction, using the Raytrace material seems to be the better way to go.

REFRACTIONS

Refraction is the bending of light that creates a distortion of an image seen through a transparent or translucent object, such as glass. How light passes through from one medium, such as air, and into another medium, such as glass, determines how much light is bent and therefore how much refraction is seen. This phenomenon is simulated in a material using the Index of Refraction parameter (IOR). When there is no refraction, the IOR is set to 1; that is, there is no difference in the medium into and out of which the light is traveling. With an IOR higher than 1, the background distorts inside the object, such as when viewing a table through a crystal ball. With an IOR lower than 1, the refraction occurs at the edge of the transparent object, such as an air bubble in water.

The typical IOR value for glass is about 1.5. Because IOR relates to an object's density, you may need to adjust the IOR to get the best possible result for different types of glass, for instance. The denser the object, the higher the IOR needs to be set. Of course, refractions require that an object be semitransparent so that you can see through it to the object(s) behind it that are being refracted.

Summary

Rendering is the way you get to show your finished result to the world. It enables the vector scene to be displayed in bitmap images or movie files. Getting to this point in your scene takes quite a bit of work, but once you see the results playing back on your screen, it all seems worth it. Nothing is more fulfilling than seeing your creation come to life, and that's what rendering is all about. However, don't consider the rendering process merely the last thing to do. Rendering may be the last step of the process, but you should travel the entire journey with rendering in mind, from design to models to animation to lighting. Always allow enough time to ensure that your animations render properly and at their best quality. Most beginners seriously underestimate the time needed to properly complete this step in CG production.

In this chapter, you learned the basics of rendering with Autodesk 3ds Max 9. You first began by learning about render output and the types of files to which you can render. You rendered the Bouncing Ball exercise from Chapter 8 and then enabled motion blur. Then you learned about cameras and rendering separate passes with Render Elements. Finally, you learned how to render glows and how to use raytracing to render true reflections and refractions in a scene.

After you have rendered many scenes, you'll have a much better understanding of how to set up your scene from the very beginning to efficiently achieve a great result. It won't hurt to go over the examples in this chapter more than once and try to render your own scenes in different ways.

CHAPTER 12

Particles and Dynamics

Animating large numbers of similar objects frequently can be a time-consuming and arduous task. With hundreds, if not thousands, of individual objects and their animated parameters and transforms to consider, this is a task that, one object at a time, could quickly become overwhelming. 3ds Max has several tools for animating large numbers of objects in a scene including instanced objects, externally referencing objects, instanced modifiers, the Crowd utility for characters, and particle systems for controlling any number of particles. Particles are usually small objects, often in large numbers, that can represent rain, snow, a swarm of insects, a barrage of bullets, or anything else that requires a large quantity of objects that follow a similar path.

Another method of creating animations for several objects simultaneously is through the use of reactor, the physics engine contained within 3ds Max. Using reactor, you can calculate the interactions between many rigid and soft body objects or simulate fluids or rope dynamics.

Topics in this chapter include:

- **Understanding Particle Systems**
- **Setting Up a Particle System**
- **Particle Systems and Space Warps**
- **Using Rigid Body Dynamics**
- **Using Soft Body Dynamics**

Understanding Particle Systems

Particle systems are a means to manage the infinite possibilities that can be encountered when controlling thousands of seemingly random objects in a scene. The particles can follow a tight stream or emanate in all directions from the surface of an object. The particles themselves can be pixel-sized elements on the screen or instanced geometry from an object in the scene. Particles can react to *space warps,* such as wind and gravity, and bounce off objects called *deflectors* to give them a natural flow through a scene. Particles can even spawn new particles upon collision.

All particle systems have two common components: the emitter and the particles. The *emitter,* as you would guess, is the object from which the particles originate. The location and, to a lesser extent, the orientation of the emitter are vital to the particles' origination point in the scene. Emitters are nonrendering objects, making their size and color unimportant. The particles themselves are the elements that spew from the emitter. The number of particles can range from a few (to simulate a burst from a gun) to thousands (to simulate smoke from a burning building). The number of particles visible in a viewport can adversely affect the viewport refresh speed and your ability to quickly navigate within the viewports. By default, far fewer particles are shown in the viewports than actually render in the scene. This helps maintain a reasonable system performance level.

Particle System Types

Two types of particle systems are available in 3ds Max: event-driven and non-event-driven particle systems.

Event-Driven Particle Systems

Event-driven particle systems use a series of tests and operators grouped into components called *events.* An operator affects the appearance and action of the individual particles and can, among many other abilities, change the shape or rotation of the particles, add a material or external force, or even delete the particles on a per-particle basis. Tests check for conditions such as a particle's age, its speed, and whether it has collided with a deflector. Particles move down the list of operators and tests in an event and, if the particles pass the requirements of a test they encounter, they can leave the current event and move to the next. If they do not pass the test, the particles continue down the list in the current event. Particles that do not pass any test in an event commonly are deleted or recycled through the event until they do pass a test. Events are wired together in a flowchart style to clearly display the path, from event to event, that the particles follow.

Particle Flow is the event-driven particle system in 3ds Max, and it is a very comprehensive solution to most particle system requirements. The upper-left pane in the Particle View window in Figure 12.1 shows a partial layout of the events in a Particle Flow setup.

Figure 12.1
The Particle View window and a Particle Flow emitter

Events are the named boxes, operators are the gray boxes, and tests appear as yellow diamonds. To the right of the Particle View window is a common example of one of the several emitter types that a Particle Flow can utilize. Using Particle Flow, you can create almost any particle-based effect, including rain, snow, mist, a flurry of arrows and spears, and objects assembling and disassembling in a blast of particles. Unfortunately, an in-depth examination of Particle Flow is beyond the scope of this book.

Non-Event-Driven Particle Systems

Non-event-driven particle systems rely on the parameters set in the Modify panel to control the appearance and content of the particles. All particles are treated identically by the system's parameters, and there are no tests to modify the behavior for certain particles. Non-event-driven particle systems have been around for a long time; they are stable, easy to learn, and an acceptable solution for many particle requirements. Non-event-driven particle systems are the focus of this chapter. These particles can be bound to space warps to control their apparent reactions to scene events, and they can be instructed to follow a path.

Six different non-event-driven particle systems are available in 3ds Max; each has its own strengths. They all have similar setups and, after you understand one type, the others are easy to master.

The Super Spray particle system is the most commonly used non-event-driven particle system in Max. It features a spherical emitter with a directional arrow to indicate the initial direction of the particles. It has eight rollouts containing the parameters that control the appearance and performance of the particles. The particles can emerge over a specified range of time or throughout the length of the scene's duration. When rendered, they can appear as one of several 2D or 3D shapes, instanced scene geometry, or as interconnecting blobs that ebb and flow as they near each other. The particles can even spawn additional particles when they collide and load a predesigned series of parameters called a *preset*. The Super Spray particle system essentially replaced the older, less-comprehensive Spray particle system, and it will be the main focus of this chapter.

Rather than being the emitter, the Particle Array particle system that is created in a viewport is only a visual link to the particle system emitter itself. The PArray uses a scene object as the emitter for the particles. While the parameters are adjusted with the PArray selected, the particles are emitted from the vertices, edges, or faces of the designated object. When used in conjunction with the PBomb space warp and the Object Fragments setting, acceptable object explosions can be created.

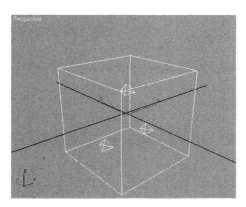

The Particle Cloud particle system contains particles within a volume defined by the emitter or by selecting a 3D object in the scene to act as the constraining volume. When instanced geometry is used as the particle type, an array of space cruisers or a school of fish can be represented by the PCloud system. The PCloud object does not render, and any object used to constrain the particles can be hidden to give the illusion that the particles are not held in place by an external force.

Instanced geometry takes instanced copies of an object and assigns one instance to the particles in a scene. You can animate a school of fish, for example, by assigning an instanced fish model to particle locations, and then animating the particles to school together and swim along.

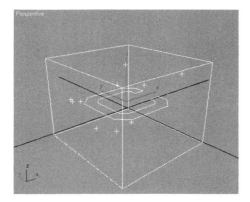

The Blizzard particle system is similar to the Super Spray particle system in its toolset and capabilities. The presets that ship with Blizzard are designed to simulate the particle motion of rain, snow, or mist. The Blizzard particle system has replaced the less-capable Snow particle system.

The Spray and Snow particle systems are the original particle systems that shipped with the initial release of 3D Studio Max, the first Windows release after four DOS-based versions of 3D Studio. At the time, they were cutting edge and beneficial, but they have not been improved significantly since their implementation. Spray and Snow do not offer primitive or instanced geometry as particles, presets, or particle spawning. The concepts used with these two systems are similar to the other more-advanced systems, but they are seldom used anymore.

Setting Up a Particle System

Particles are renderable objects in Max, so a particle system is created in the Geometry tab of the Command panel. Like most other objects in 3ds Max, the particle system's parameters can be changed immediately in the Create panel, but they must be changed in the Modify panel after the object is selected at a later point in time. To set up a particle system, follow these steps.

1. Click Create → Geometry → Particle Systems from the Command panel and then click on the Super Spray button in the Object Type rollout. The particle system's parameters appear in the Command panel.

2. Click and drag in the Perspective viewport to create the Super Spray emitter. The emitters do not render, so the size does not matter; the arrow will point in the positive Z direction, as shown in Figure 12.2.

3. Drag the time slider to the right until the particles extend beyond the limits of the viewport. Frame number 10 should be sufficient.

   The Basic Parameters rollout controls how the particles spread as they exit the emitter, the size of the emitter, and how they display in the viewports.

4. In the Basic Parameters rollout, set both Spread values to 30 to spread the particles out 30 degrees in both the local *X*- and local *Y*-axes of the emitter. The Off Axis parameter rocks the emission direction along the *X* axis and the Off Plane parameter rotates the angle of emission around the *Z*-axis. Both of these should remain at zero.

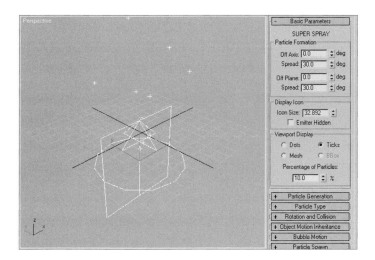

5. In the Viewport Display area, make sure Ticks is selected and the Percentage of Particles is set to 10. This ensures that the particles appear as small crosses in the viewports, regardless of the type of particle used, and that only 10 percent of the particles that are actually emitted are displayed in the viewport. Both of these parameters are used to ensure a minimal loss of performance in the viewport when using particles.

6. Click the Quick Render button ( ) in the main toolbar. The particles appear as small dots in the Rendered Frame window. If you cannot see them, try changing the object color in the Name and Color rollout. In the next section, you will increase the size of the particles in the Rendered Frame Window by increasing the particle's Size parameter. More particles are visible in the rendering than in the viewport because the Percentage of Particles value affects only the viewports and not the renderings.

Figure 12.2

The Super Spray emitter created in the Perspective viewport

The Particle Generation Parameters

The parameters in the Particle Generation rollout control the emission of the particles including the quantity, speed, size, and life span. If you can't see any particles in your scene, the first place to look should be the Particle Generation rollout.

1. Expand the Particle Generation rollout. In the Particle Quantity area, the Use Rate value determines the number of particles emitted at each frame and the Use Total value determines how many particles are emitted over the active life of the system. Only one of these options can be active at a time. Increase the Use Rate value to 12.

2. Increase the Speed value to 15 to increase the velocity of the particles.

3. In the Playback Controls area, click the Play Animation button ( ). The particles spew from the emitter briefly and then stop. The particles have a distinct beginning and ending time that controls when the emitter can eject any particles.

4. In the Particle Timing section of the Particle Generation rollout, change the Emit Start value to 10 and the Emit Stop value to 100 and then click the Play Animation button again. The particle system will pause for 10 frames at the beginning of the active time segment and then emit 12 particles every frame for the remaining 90 frames.

5. Drag the Time slider to frame 50 or so and then zoom out in the Perspective viewport until the limits of the particles extents are visible. Play the animation again. The particles increase their distance from the emitter until frame 45 and then travel no farther.

There are several parameters that determine when a particle is visible. The Emit Start and Emit Stop parameters mentioned earlier bracket the frames when the particles are emitted. The Display Until parameter in the Particle Timing area defines the last frame when any particle is visible. Regardless of whether this frame falls within the Start and Stop values, when the Display Until frame is reached, no further particles appear in the viewports or in any renderings. Another parameter that controls the display of particles is the Life value. The Life value determines how long each particle exists in a scene from when it is emitted until it disappears. Currently, the Life value is set to 30 so that at frame 45, which is 30 frames after the emission begins at frame 15, the particles disappear. Particles that are emitted after frame 10 also live for 30 frames, moving the same distance from the emitter before dying.

6. Change the Life value to 40, allowing the particles to travel one-third farther from the emitter, and change the Variation to 20, adding randomness to the particle's lifespan.

7. Play the animation. The particles now travel farther from the emitter and die between 32 and 48 frames after being emitted.

8. In the Particle Size area, change the Size value to 10 and then render one frame of the scene at some point after frame 30. The result should look similar to Figure 12.3.

Figure 12.3

The Super Spray particle system rendered in the Perspective viewport

Notice that the particles are smaller very near the emitter and also very far away from the emitter. By default, the Grow For value causes the particles to grow from a size of zero to full size over the first 10 frames of their lives. The Fade For parameter causes those same particles to shrink from full size to zero size during the last 10 frames of their lives.

9. Change the Fade For value to 0, so the particles retain their size at the end of their lives, and leave Grow For at its default.

10. Render the Perspective viewport again and notice how the particles grow, but never shrink.

VARIATION

In many situations utilizing particle systems, the particles are intended to appear as many similar but random objects. When the particles all have identical parameters (such as speed, life span, or rotation), the illusion of randomness disappears, which can greatly detract from its sense of reality. To alleviate this situation, in many of the parameter areas of the Super Spray particle system's rollouts, you will find a Variation parameter. The Variation settings modify their related parameters on a per-particle basis to add seeming randomness to the system. For example, changing the Variation parameter (below the Speed parameter) to 20 assigned a velocity to each particle within 20 percent of the Speed value. When the Speed parameter is set to 10 and Variation is set to 20, each particle is assigned to a random speed between 8 and 12—20 percent on either side of 10.

Putting It Together

Now that you have a basic understanding of particle systems, you will continue to work with them by creating a system that represents the bullets fired from a gun and the brass expelled from the ejection port. This will require two particle systems, one for each type of object leaving the gun. We will also examine the different particle types that can be emitted.

Creating the Particle Systems

The basic process of creating a particle system is fairly simple; you place the emitter in the scene, fine tune its location and orientation, and then adjust the system's parameters. The third item mentioned is the one that will take the most experimentation to perfect.

1. Open the Particle Gun.max file from the companion CD. This file is similar to the completed IK gun file created in Chapter 9, "Character Studio and IK Animation," with a target, floor, materials, lights, and a camera added. The lights and camera have been hidden for clarity.

2. In the Top viewport, create a Super Spray particle system. Move and rotate it so that the emitter is recessed slightly into the barrel of the gun, similar to Figure 12.4. Turn on the Angle Snap Toggle (⚠) to rotate the system precisely 90 degrees.

Figure 12.4

The Top and Right viewports showing the proper placement of the Super Spray particle emitter

3. Click the Select and Link button ( ) in the main toolbar.

4. Click on the particle system; a rubber banding line stretches from the emitter to the cursor. Place the cursor over the gun barrel and then click again. The gun flashes white to indicate that the linking is complete. Any changes in the gun's orientation or position are now passed down to the particle system, keeping it colocated and oriented with the gun.

5. Rename this particle system to **Super Spray Bullets**.

6. Create a second Super Spray particle system and place it on the right side of the gun body. Orient the emitter so that the particles are ejected upward and away from the gun, as shown in Figure 12.5. In the figure, the target and its supports have been hidden for clarity.

> You may see a random particle or two already emitted by the particle systems. These are caused by the Emit Start time being set to the initial frame of the scene. This anomaly is corrected in the next section.

7. Link this particle system to the gun, just as you did with the other in Steps 3 and 4.

8. Rename this system to **Super Spray Brass**.

Configuring the Particle System Timing

The amount of particles emitted over time defines the density of the particles in the scene. The speed of the particles also factors into the proximity of the particles.

1. In the Time Controls area, click the Time Configuration button ( )

Figure 12.5

The Top and Front viewports showing the proper placement of the second Super Spray particle emitter

2. In the Time Configuration dialog box, change the Length value to 300 and then click the OK button. At 30 frames per second (fps), the scene is now 10 seconds long.

3. Select Super Spray Bullets and then click the Modify tab of the Command panel.

4. In the Particle Generation rollout, set the Use Rate to 10, the Speed to 10.0, the Emit Start value to 45, and the Emit Stop value to 255. After a one-and-a-half second pause, the gun will fire 10 rounds per frame continuously for seven seconds.

5. Change the Display Until value to 300 so that the particles appear in the scene for the entire active time segment. Set the Life value to 255 (the scene length minus the frames prior to the first particle emission) so the particles do not die out in the scene.

6. In the Particle Size section, change the Size value to 4. Drag the Time slider to approximately frame 80 and then render the Camera viewport. The scene should look similar to Figure 12.6.

The particles appear as triangles that grow as they travel away from the emitter. This is not the look that you want for the particles when you are creating a traditional gun; the rounds should all appear the same size for the life of the particles. The particle type is covered in the next section and in the "Particle Systems and Space Warps" section later in this chapter. The conditions that allow the particles to pass through the target object are also addressed.

Figure 12.6
The rendered camera viewport showing the particles

Selecting the Particle Type

There are several types of particles that can be emitted by a particle system. Standard particles consist of eight different 2D and 3D particles including cubes, spheres, and six-pointed stars. The Facing Standard particle type is a square, 2D particle that maintains a continuous orientation perpendicular to the viewport. Using opacity mapped materials in conjunction with Facing particles can give the illusion of smoke or steam without using a massive number of particles.

MetaParticles use what is known as metaball technology where each particle appears as a blob with a sphere of influence surrounding it. Whenever the two spheres of influence from two particles in close proximity overlap, the particles meld together in an organic manner similar to mercury or the wax in a lava lamp. Using MetaParticles can be computationally intensive, so caution should be a priority when that is the selected particle type. Start with a quantity of particles fewer than you would expect to use and then increase the amount, as required, after test rendering the scene.

Geometry that exists in the scene can also be substituted for the particles at render time. Using instanced geometry, a particle system can emit any objects from jet fighters to fire fighters, or nearly any other geometry in the scene, using the material from the object that is instanced. The original scene object can be hidden so as not to appear in the render of the scene, while still being instanced by the particle system.

1. With the Super Spray Bullets particle system selected, expand the Particle Type rollout.

2. In the Particle Types section, select MetaParticles.

3. From the Menu Bar, choose Edit → Hold to temporarily save the scene. If rendering the scene causes a system crash, it can be restored to this point using Edit → Fetch. 3ds Max is a stable program, but rendering MetaParticles can significantly task a computer system.

4. Render the scene. The particles that are near to each other combine to form blobs of meshes.

5. In the MetaParticle Parameters section, decrease the Tension to 0.1. Tension controls a particle's effort to maintain a spherical shape while in proximity to another particle. Lowering the Tension increases the amount of inter-particle combining.

6. Render the scene again to see the effect of the lower Tension value.

7. MetaParticles would be the solution if this were a plasma rifle, rather than a conventional machine gun. In this case, instanced geometry is the appropriate particle choice.

8. Right-click on a blank area of the Active viewport and choose Unhide by Name from the Quad menu. Select the bullet and brass objects from the list in the Unhide Objects dialog box and then click the Unhide button. Two small objects, a bullet and a brass casing, appear below the gun.

9. At the top of the Particle Type rollout, select Instanced Geometry as the particle type. In the Instancing Parameters section, click the Pick Object button.

10. Select the Bullet object in the scene. If necessary, press the H key to open the Pick Object dialog box to select the object by name. The bullet flashes white briefly to indicate that the selection is successful and the object name is now identified in the Instancing Parameters section as the instanced geometry object.

11. Render the Camera viewport. There are still a few problems that need to be corrected. The particles are growing as they leave the emitter, the particles grow to be too large for the gun barrel, and the bullets rotate in several axes, rather than maintaining a forward orientation. The bullets also display their object color, the color used by the particles system, rather than the material applied to the Bullet object.

12. In the Particle Size section of the Particle Generation rollout, set the Grow For and Fade For parameters to 0. This will cause the particles to maintain a constant size throughout their life spans.

13. When using standard or metaparticles, the Size parameter defines the size of the particle. When using instanced geometry, it becomes a multiplier of the object's actual size. With the current Size value set to 4, the bullets are scaled to four times their modeled size. Set the Size value to 1.

14. Expand the Rotation and Collision rollout. In the Spin Axis Controls section, select Direction of Travel/Mblur to make each bullet's orientation follow its direction of travel.

15. At the bottom of the Particle Type rollout, make sure that the Instanced Geometry radio button is selected and then click the Get Material From button.

16. Render the camera viewport again. All of the particles are now oriented properly.

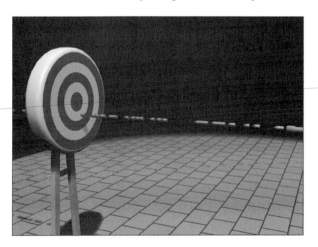

Setting Up the Other Particle System

We have a particle system set up to emit the bullets, and now we need one that ejects the brass casings. In many cases, the same parameters must be maintained among the two systems so these parameters will be wired together, ensuring a common value between them.

1. Continue with the previous exercise or open the `Particle Gun1.max` file from the companion CD.

2. Select the Super Spray Brass particle system.

3. In the Particle Generation rollout, set the Size to 1 and set both the Grow For and Fade For values to 0. Set Emit Start to 45, Emit Stop to 255, and Life to 300.

4. In the Particle Motion section, reduce the Speed value to 5. The rate of particles emitted is still set to 10; the Speed value just determines the velocity of the particles as they leave the emitter.

5. In the Particle Type rollout, choose Instanced Geometry in the Particle Types section and then click the Pick Object button. Select the brass object as the geometry to be instanced.

6. Select the Instanced Geometry option in the Mat'l Mapping and Source section at the bottom of the Particle Type rollout, and then click the Get Material From button to define the material applied to the particles.

7. In the Rotation and Collision rollout, select the Direction of Travel/Mblur option.

8. Select the bullet and brass objects and hide them.

9. Drag the time slider. The Super Spray Brass particle system emits particles for 30 frames and then stops before the Super Spray Bullets particle system begins. This disconnect is addressed in the next section.

Wiring the Parameters Together

The values that define the parameters unique to each particle system in the scene have been set properly. Several values, such as the Use Rate, must maintain the same value for both particle systems so that, for example, the amount of brass ejected matches the number of bullets fired. These parameters can always be adjusted manually; however, the Parameter Wiring tool forces one object's parameters to drive another's. In the following exercise, the parameter values of the Super Spray Bullets particle system are used to define the parameter values of the Super Spray Brass particle system.

1. Continue with the previous exercise or load the `Particle Gun2.max` file from the companion CD.

2. Select the Super Spray Bullets particle system. Right-click in the viewport and choose Wire Parameters from the Quad menu.

3. From the small pop-up menu that appears, choose Object (SuperSpray) and then Birth Rate from the cascading menu. A rubber banding line connects the particle system to the cursor. At this point, the object to be wired to the Super Spray Bullet's Birth Rate parameter must be selected.

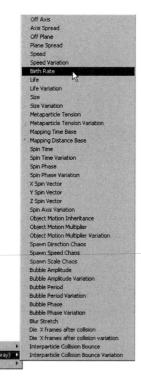

4. Press the H key to open the Pick Object dialog box, select Super Spray Brass, and then click the Pick button.

5. From the small pop-up menu that appears, choose Object (SuperSpray) and then Birth Rate from the cascading menu.

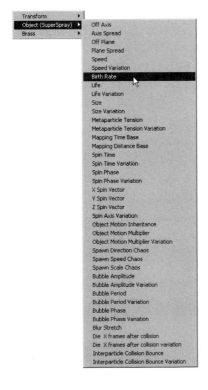

6. The Parameter Wiring dialog box opens, as shown in Figure 12.7. The Birth Rate parameters are highlighted in both the left and right windows. The left side of the dialog box displays the Super Spray Bullets particle system's parameter, and the right side displays the parameters for the Super Spray Brass particle system.

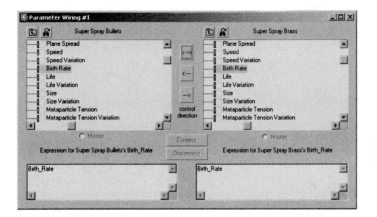

Figure 12.7

The Parameter Wiring dialog box with the Birth Rate parameters highlighted

7. The control direction, defining which parameter controls the other, can be set so that either one of the parameters controls the other, or bidirectional control can be set so that either parameter can change the other. In this case, the bullet rate is used to control the brass rate. Click the right arrow between the two parameter windows.

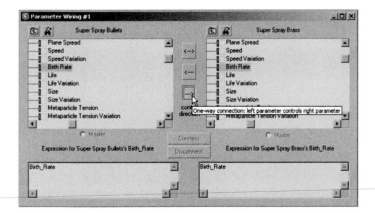

8. Complete the wiring process by clicking the Connect button. The parameters in each window will turn red to indicate that they are wired.

9. Select the Super Spray Bullets particle system and change the Use Rate to 12.

10. Select the Super Spray Brass particle system and examine its Use Rate. It is now set to 12 as well.

> You can try to change the Use Rate for the Super Spray Brass particle system, but it won't work. The related spinners simply do not work, and they shouldn't because the particle system's Use Rate is defined by the Use Rate of the Super Spray Brass particle system. You can highlight and change the value manually; however, nothing will really happen. When you deselect the system and then select it again, the Use Rate reverts to the value set by the other system.

11. Select the Life parameter in both windows; click the right arrow and then the Connect button. The Life parameters are now wired together as well.

> Unfortunately, the Emit Start, Emit Stop, and Display Until parameters are not exposed to the Parameter Wiring dialog box. These values must be changed for each particle system individually.

12. Close the Parameter Wiring dialog box.

13. Drag the time Slider. The two particle systems emit equal numbers of particles at the same time. The brass ejects in a straight line from the gun body; this is corrected in the next section.

The particle systems have been created and linked to the gun so that they maintain the proper position and orientation when the gun moves or rotates. The systems have been adjusted to fire bullets from the barrel and eject brass from the side at an equal and wired rate. In the next section, the processes of adding space warps to interject gravity into the scene and to cause the particles to collide with scene objects are covered.

Particle Systems and Space Warps

Space warps are nonrendering objects that can modify or manipulate the objects in a scene. Modifier-based space warps, for example, deform objects based on the object's proximity to the space warp. In this section, the focus is on the Forces and Deflectors categories of space warps; the space warps that affect particle systems.

The Forces space warps affect particle systems by altering the trajectory of the particles as they move through the scene. Each space warp displays as an icon in the viewports that must be bound to each object that it is designated to affect. The bindings appear as wide gray lines at the top of the Modifier Stack.

The Forces space warps are listed here:

Motor Applies a directional spin to the particles, creating a circular movement. The orientation of the Space Warp icon defines the direction of the rotation.

Vortex Similar to the Motor space warp, Vortex causes the particles to move in a circular motion but also decreases the radius of the motion over distance, creating a funnel-shaped motion.

Path Follow Requires the particles to follow a spline path. The particle timing is controlled by the Path Follow's parameters.

Displace Changes the particle trajectory by pushing them based on the space warp's Strength and Decay values. Image maps can also be used to define the amount of displacement.

Wind Adds a directional force to the particles based on the space warp's orientation. Randomness can be added to increase the realism of the simulation.

Push Applies a constant, directional force to the particles.

Drag Rather than changing the direction of the particles, Drag slows the speed of the particles as they pass through its influence.

PBomb Disperses particles with a linear or spherical force. This can be effective when used with the Particle Array particle system.

Gravity Applies a constant acceleration used to simulate the affect of gravity on the particles. Gravity can be applied in a linear fashion

Adding Gravity to a Scene

When looking at the particle systems in the previous exercises, especially the Super Spray Brass system, it's evident that the motion of the particles is not realistic. The particles are emitted at approximately a 45-degree angle up and away from the gun body. The particles maintain a perfectly straight trajectory and never fall to the earth as they should. In this exercise, gravity is added to both particle systems to cause the bullets and brass to drop.

1. Continue with the previous exercise or load the `Particle Gun3.max` file from the companion CD.

2. Drag the Time slider to frame 100.

3. Click Create → Space Warps. Choose Forces from the drop-down menu if necessary, and then click the Gravity button.

4. Click and drag in the Top viewport to place and size the Gravity Space Warp icon. The size and the location are unimportant, but the orientation of the icon defines the direction of the gravitational force.

5. Select the Super Spray Brass particle system. Click the Bind to Space Warp button (⌗) in the main toolbar.

Figure 12.8

After the Gravity is bound to the particle system, the particles drop through the floor.

6. Click on the Particle System emitter or the particles themselves and drag the cursor toward the Gravity. A rubber banding line connects the particle system to the cursor.

7. Place the cursor over the Gravity space warp, the cursor's appearance changes to identify it as a valid object for binding, and then release the mouse button. The space warp flashes briefly to indicate a successful binding and the particles now drop through the floor as shown in Figure 12.8.

8. Select the Super Spray Bullets space warp and bind it to the Gravity space warp as well.

9. Play the animation. The particles from both systems are affected by the gravity, but the bullets drop too far for their distance from the gun to the target. Reducing the amount of gravity isn't appropriate because the brass would fall too slowly and the gravitational force should be consistent throughout the scene. This situation is fixed by increasing the velocity of the bullets as they leave the barrel.

10. The Bind to Space Warp button is still active. Click the Select Object button, and then select the Super Spray Bullets particle system.

11. Make sure the Time slider is at a frame well into the animation so that changes to the system are reflected in the viewports.

12. In the Modify panel, click the SuperSpray entry in the Modifier Stack to expose the particle system's parameters.

13. In the Particle Generation rollout, increase the Speed value to 50. The visible trajectories of the particles will flatten out.

At the bottom of the Rotation and Collision rollout, you will find the Interparticle Collisions section. Enabling this parameter causes Max to calculate and determine the result of any situation where two particles impact each other. This can add a measure of realism to the way the particles react, but it can also consume a significant amount of system resources. Use this feature with caution and always Hold the scene prior to enabling or testing the feature.

Controlling the Particles with Deflectors

As you can see in the previous exercises, particles travel through a scene, guided by space warps but unaffected by geometry. *Deflectors* are a type of space warp that causes the particles that impact it to bounce as if they have collided with an unmovable surface. The amount of Bounce assigned to a deflector is a multiplier that defines the velocity of a particle after it impacts the space warp. A Bounce value of 0.5 results in the particle's speed being reduced to 50 percent of the speed it was when it hit the deflector. Most deflectors have Time On and Time Off parameters that control when the deflector is active.

Deflecting the Brass at the Floor

To get the spent casings to collide with the ground, follow these steps:

1. Continue with the previous exercise or load the `Particle Gun4.max` file from the companion CD.

2. Drag the Time slider to frame 100.

3. Click Create → Space Warps. Choose Deflectors from the drop-down menu and then click the POmniFlect button.

4. In the Top viewport, click and drag to define the two opposite corners of the deflector. The deflector should be similar in size to the floor object in the scene. Unlike the Forces space warps, deflectors must be positioned in the stream of the particles.

UNDERSTANDING DEFLECTOR NAMES

The names assigned to the different deflectors distinguish the shapes and properties of those deflectors. Understanding the deflector naming convention is key to selecting the correct deflector for the task at hand.

- If the deflector name begins with a *P* or an *S*, the deflector is Planar or Spherical in shape.
- If the deflector name begins with a *U*, this is a universal deflector and any scene geometry can be assigned as a deflector, instead of the Deflector icon itself.
- If the deflector name ends with "OmniFlect," this deflector affects all particles that impact it. The OmniFlect deflectors are more advanced than the simpler space warps that end with "Deflector."
- If the deflector name ends with "DynaFlect," this deflector affects all particles that impact it and, when used with dynamic simulations, can affect other objects in the scene.

5. Move the deflector 0.3 units in the positive *Z* direction. The impact point is based on the particle location. When using instanced geometry, the particle location is defined by the center point of the geometry. The bullets and brass are about 0.3 units in radius, so moving the deflector up 0.3 units prevents the particles from sinking into the floor.

6. Select the Super Spray Brass particle system and then click the Bind to Space Warp button in the Main toolbar. Click on the particle system, or particles, drag to the perimeter of the deflector, and then release to bind the deflector to the particle system.

7. Activate the camera viewport and then play the animation. The particles initially bounce equal in height to their highest point after being ejected, but they discontinue shortly afterward.

8. Select the deflector object in the viewport, not the deflector binding in the Modifier Stack.

9. In the Timing section of the Parameters rollout, set the Time Off value to 300 to leave the deflector on during the entire active time segment.

10. In the Reflection section, set the Bounce value to 0.25 and the Variation to 10 percent. Increase Chaos to 50 percent so the particles' directions are not constrained to a straight line.

11. In the Common section, increase the Friction value to 4.0 to prevent the particles from spreading too far along the deflector's surface.

12. Play the animation. The brass is ejected from the side of the gun, falls to the floor, and spreads a bit from the point of impact.

Deflecting the Bullets at the Target

The brass is handled, and now the bullet collisions need to be addressed equally as well.

1. Click Create → Space Warps and then click the UOmniFlect button.

2. In the Top viewport, click and drag to place and size the universal deflector. The size and position do not matter. This is just a visible icon. A scene object will be selected to act as the deflector.

3. Select the Super Spray Bullets particle system, and bind it to the UOmniflect icon, not the Target object. Bind the particle system to the POmniFlect deflector as well.

4. Click the Select Object button and then select the UOmniFlect icon.

5. Click the Pick Object button and then select the target object in the scene.

6. In the Timing section, set the Time Off value to 300.

7. In the reflection section, set Bounce to 0.01, Variation to 10, and Chaos to 4.

8. Play the animation. The particles hit the target, fall to the floor, and then spread out a bit.

As you can see, the proper use of Force and Deflector space warps, in conjunction with particle systems, can successfully animate thousands of small objects within the constraints of a scene. The completed scene can be examined using the `Particle Gun Complete.max` and `Particle Gun.avi` files on the companion CD. In the remaining sections in this chapter, we will look at the implementation of rigid and soft body dynamics in physics simulations.

Using Rigid Body Dynamics

Part of the core package of 3ds Max is the physics engine known as reactor. With reactor, complex physical conditions are accurately animated showing the interaction of the scene objects with each other and with external forces such as wind or gravity. Objects are assigned mass, elasticity, and friction properties and designated as movable or immovable objects. Rigid body dynamics, soft body dynamics, rope, and cloth simulations are all within the limits of reactor's toolset. The Real Time Preview window displays a lower resolution, unrendered example of the animation to be created. Reactor calculates the animation, but the standard practice of creating keyframes is the final output of the simulations. These keyframes can be edited and manipulated; however, the integrity of the simulation could be compromised.

Creating the Simulation Objects

In this exercise, a series of primitive objects are dropped onto a complex inclined object to examine the interaction of the scene objects. Although this is a simple example of the use of the physics simulator, reactor can be used to simulate the interactions of very complex scenes with many colliding objects and external forces.

1. Open the `Rigid.max file` from the companion CD. This consists of an inclined box with additional boxes, cylinders, and a hemisphere placed on its surface to make the simulation more complex.

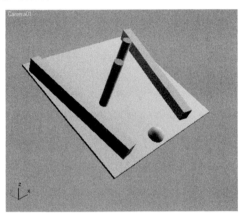

2. Create two rows of spheres above the objects. Make sure they are all over the top edge of the large box and fit between the two angled boxes.

3. Create a row of small boxes between the rows of spheres, and rotate them each about all three axes.

4. From the Extended Primitives category of geometry objects, create a Star2 hedra and position it near the other objects. The scene should look similar to Figure 12.9.

5. Open the Material Editor and then apply the Checker material to all of the objects you created. The Checker Diffuse Color map helps discern the rotation of each object in the simulation.

Figure 12.9

**The scene after cre-
ating additional
objects for the
simulation**

Assigning the Physical Properties

Each object in the scene must be assigned the correct properties to define their reactions during the simulation. Objects that are to be stable and immovable are assigned a Mass value of 0.

1. Select all of the objects that existed in the scene when the file was first opened.

2. From the reactor toolbar, click the Open Property Editor button (▣) to open the Rigid Body Properties dialog box. If the reactor toolbar is not visible, right-click on a blank area of any toolbar and then choose reactor from the pop-up menu.

3. Make sure Mass is set to 0 in the Physical Properties rollout and Mesh Convex Hull is selected in the Simulation Geometry rollout.

THE SIMULATION GEOMETRY ROLLOUT

- The Simulation Geometry rollout defines how reactor defines the surfaces of an object during the simulation. The Bounding Box and Bounding Sphere options place the extents of the objects, as far as the simulation is concerned, at the limits of the smallest possible box or sphere that could encompass them.

- Mesh Convex Hull closely follows the extents of the object, with all vertices included within the simulation volume, while spanning any concave areas. Complicated meshes can increase the calculation time when using Mesh Convex Hull, so the Proxy Convex Hull options allow a less dense substitution object to be used to define the simulation parameters.

- When Concave Mesh is used, the actual surface of the geometry is used. This can drastically increase the calculation time and should only be used when necessary. Using the Proxy Concave Mesh option can reduce the simulation time when using a complicated object.

- 3ds Max assigns the Not Shared option to the selected geometry when multiple objects are selected that do not utilize the same Simulation Geometry setting.

4. Select all of the spheres that you created. Set their Mass value to 1.0 and choose Bounding Sphere in the Simulation Geometry rollout. When using a spherical object, Bounding Sphere is more accurate and calculates faster than Mesh Convex Hull.

Most 3D geometry works as expected during a reactor simulation. Reactor, however, contains its own plane object for use whenever flat, 2D surfaces are required. When a 3ds Max plane is used instead of a reactor plane, Concave Mesh must be chosen as the Simulation Geometry type.

5. Select all of the boxes that you created, assign a Mass value of 1.0, and choose the Bounding Box option.

6. Select the hedra. Increase its Mass to 1.0 and select Mesh Convex Hull for the simulation.

Creating the Collection

Scene objects must be members of a collection to be included in any simulations. The collections appear as simple icons in the viewports that are selected to access the simulation's parameters, including editing the list of included objects.

1. Continue with the previous exercise or open the `Rigid1.max` file from the companion CD.

2. Click the Create Rigid Body Collection button ( ) in the reactor toolbar.

3. Click in any viewport to place the Rigid Body Collection icon. The location does not matter.

4. In the Command panel, click the Add button at the bottom of the RB Collection Properties rollout.

5. In the Select Rigid Bodies dialog box that opens, select all of the objects in the scene except for the collection itself and then click the Select button. The object names will appear in the Rigid Bodies field in the Command panel.

In most cases, no objects in a scene are required to be in a simulation. They should be omitted if their impact to the simulation is not required. For example, in a scene where marbles spill across a table and onto a floor, the marbles, table, and floor must be included, but the nearby lamp or the ceiling should be omitted.

Testing the Simulation

Reactor provides the Real-Time Preview window where you can view the simulation. Materials and lighting are not considered for this preview; therefore it is much faster, but less accurate, than rendering the animation.

1. Click the Preview Animation button ( ) in the reactor toolbar. Reactor analyzes the simulation and then opens the reactor Real-Time Preview window shown in Figure 12.10.

Figure 12.10

The reactor Real-Time Preview window showing the scene

2. Press the P key to begin the preview, and then press P again to stop it.

3. After the preview runs its course, choose Simulation → Reset to place the objects at their starting points and review the animation.

> You can click and drag in the Preview window to arc-rotate around the simulation objects.

4. The hedra is large for the scene and may cause a bottleneck. Close the Preview window.

5. Select the hedra and reduce its Radius value.

6. Select all of the objects that existed when the scene was first opened, and then open the Rigid Body Properties dialog box.

7. Set the Friction property to 0.1.

8. Select the remaining objects in the scene, and set the friction to 0.1 as well.

9. Rearrange the objects to change the simulation.

10. Continue to preview the animation and rearrange the objects until the simulation meets your liking.

Creating the Animation

The Preview window showed what the animation will be like, but the animation keys have not been created. The next exercise creates keys for all the objects in the collection. Creating the keys is not undoable, so it is recommended that an Edit ➔ Hold be performed prior to creating the animation.

1. In the Time Configuration dialog box, increase the length of the scene's animation to 200 frames.

2. Click Edit ➔ Hold from the Main menu.

3. Click the Create Animation button (▦) from the reactor toolbar.

4. Click OK in the reactor dialog box that opens and warns you that the action cannot be undone.

5. Max creates keys at every frame for every object in the simulation.

> The process of creating keys with reactor cannot be undone, but the objects can be selected and their keys can be deleted in the Track Bar, the Dope Sheet, or the Function Curve dialog boxes.

6. Play the animation. The scene animates through frame 100 and then stops. The default value for all simulations is 100 frames.

7. To restore the scene to its state before Max created the animation, click Edit → Fetch from the main menu and then click the Yes button in the dialog box that opens.

8. Click the Utilities tab (T) of the Command panel.

9. Click the reactor button in the Utilities rollout.

> In reactor, *solvers* provide the algorithms that determine each object's reactions in the simulation. The two available solver options in 3ds Max 9 are Havok 1 and Havok 3. The Havok 1 solver has more functionality and can handle all types of simulation objects. Havok 3 is faster and more accurate, but it can solve only for rigid body objects. If only rigid body objects are used in a simulation, Havok 3 is usually the better choice.

10. In the About rollout, select Havok 3 from the Choose Solver drop-down menu. Havok 3 is the better choice when using only rigid body objects.

11. Expand the Preview & Animation rollout and change the End Frame value to 200.

12. Click Edit → Hold again, and then click the Create Animation button.

13. 3ds Max creates the simulation. You can fetch the scene and rearrange the objects as you want to change the simulation parameters. Remember to hold the scene before creating the animation each time.

The completed exercise is available as the `Rigid Complete.max` file in the Dynamics Scene Files folder on the companion CD and the final rendering as `Rigid Complete.avi`.

Using Soft Body Dynamics

Soft body objects differ from rigid body objects in that they can deform upon impact with other objects in the scene. To be included in a simulation as soft body objects, scene objects must have the Soft Body modifier applied and be members of a soft body collection. Soft body objects can interact with rigid body objects in the same simulation. Physical properties are assigned to soft body objects in the same manner that they are assigned to their rigid counterparts.

Creating the Collections

Before you can simulate the reactions between soft body objects, all objects considered in the simulation must be contained in a collection.

1. Open the Soft.max file from the Dynamics Scene Files folder on the companion CD. This is a simpler version of the project used in the previous exercises with the Mass and Simulation Geometry options already selected.

2. Select all of the base objects, and then click the Create Rigid Body Collection button in the reactor toolbar. The icon is placed at the center of the selection, and the selected objects are added to the collection.

3. Select the spheres and boxes with the Checker material applied.

4. Click the Apply Soft Body Modifier button ( ) in the reactor toolbar.

> In 3ds Max 9, the Soft Body modifier is applied incorrectly when it is applied to instanced objects. It is applied to each instance for the total number of instances selected. For example, if you have eight instanced objects and apply the Soft Body modifier to them, each object will have the modifier applied to it eight times. For this exercise, the objects used are not instances.

5. With the objects still selected, click the Create Soft Body Collection button ( ) in the reactor toolbar. The dropping objects are automatically added to the soft body collection.

6. Move the Collection icons away from the scene geometry. Your Perspective viewport should look similar to Figure 12.11.

Creating the Animation

In the previous exercise, the Havok 3 solver was selected because of its capabilities when using rigid body objects exclusively. With the combination of both soft and rigid objects in this exercise, the Havok 1 solver is the better choice.

1. In the Utilities panel, click the reactor button and then choose Havok 1 from the drop-down menu in the About rollout.

2. Click the Preview Animation button in the reactor toolbar. Play the animation in the reactor Real-Time Preview window. The animation plays slower than the rigid body preview due to the more complex animation required by the deforming meshes.

Figure 12.11

The Perspective viewport with the rigid and soft body collections

In a complex scene, or on a slower computer, the reactor Real-Time Preview may display the scene at a rate that is too slow to easily determine the effectiveness of the simulation. In these cases, you need to create the animation and then, if revisions are required, delete all of the simulation objects' animation keys before making any changes and re-creating the animation.

3. Close the Preview window.

4. Select one of the spheres and then, in the Modify panel, change its Mass to 2, Stiffness to 4, and Friction to 0.1. Repeat this step with one more sphere and one of the boxes. The parameters of individual objects can be set in the reactor SoftBody Modifiers settings. The larger mass value will cause the object to impact with a greater force.

5. Test the animation again. Continue to make changes and then, when you are satisfied, Hold the scene.

6. Click the Create Animation button in the reactor toolbar to create the animation using the properties assigned to the objects.

The completed exercise can be found on the companion CD as Soft Complete.max and Soft Compete.avi.

Summary

This chapter introduced you to both Max's non-event-driven particle systems and the reactor physics simulation engine. Using particles, thousands of seemingly random or purposeful objects can be animated by effectively manipulating the particle system's parameters. Particles can appear as primitive shapes, interconnecting blobs, or any instanced geometry object from the scene. Particle systems can be affected by external forces, such as gravity, wind, or vortex, and they can bounce off many types of deflectors positioned within the flow of particles.

The reactor component of Max is a powerful tool for creating accurate animations based on the interactions of scene objects. Rigid or soft body objects in collections can impact each other and deform, bounce, or slide away based on the objects' physical properties. Animations can be previewed and then thousands of animation keys can be created quickly to fulfill a scene's physics-based animation requirements.

Index